YCHOLOGY

The Study of People

HARVEY MINDESS / PAUL R. MUNFORD

PSYCHOLOGY

The

Study of

People

P S Y C

HARVEY MINDESS
Antioch University West

PAUL R. MUNFORD
Department of Psychiatry
and Biobehavioral Sciences,

University of California,
Los Angeles

The HOLOGY Study of People

GOODYEAR PUBLISHING COMPANY, INC.

Santa Monica, California

This book is dedicated to
VERONICA, ANNA, ARNA, and ALISON

BF121
.M5775

Library of Congress Cataloging in Publication Data

MINDESS, HARVEY, 1928—
  Psychology.

  Includes bibliographies and index.
  1. Psychology.   I. Munford, Paul, joint author.
II. Title.
BF121.M5775   150   79–22763
ISBN   0–87620–675–5

Y–6755–6

Current Printing (last digit):

10   9   8   7   6   5   4   3   2   1

Designer: Bruce Kortebein, Design Office
Production Editors: Sue Adkins and Laurie Greenstein

Printed in the United States of America

Contents

Section Five Frontiers of Investigation

Preface

Psychology is the study of people. The ways in which we grow from infancy to old age; the ways in which we think, feel, and behave; the ways in which we learn and fail to learn; the ways in which we influence and interact with each other; the ways in which we acquire problems and overcome our problems: all these topics are psychology's domain.

The field contains few absolute answers. Everything from the meaning of dreams to the value of IQ tests is debated by psychologists of different persuasions. In their investigations and debates, however, they have produced a lot of valuable information. It is our intention to convey some of this information to you. We do not wish to convert you to any particular point of view. We simply hope we can help you see how fascinating it can be to study people.

We have tried to compose a clear, candid picture of psychology as it is today. In order to create a text that could be covered in a one-semester course, however, we have had to overlook certain areas of the field. Because we are more interested in getting you to think carefully than in giving you facts and figures to memorize, we have emphasized standpoints and controversies and deemphasized the results of specific studies.

On the whole, we believe this book will tell you what psychologists do, how they reason and investigate their subject matter, what they agree on, and what they argue about. We hope it will also tell you something useful about yourself.

Acknowledgments

We would like to thank Melanie Allen for her contribution to "The History and Future of Psychology," Charles Bell for his contribution to "Learning About Learning," Laurel Brodsley for her contribution to "Psychology in the Classroom," Anna Mindess for her contribution to

"Social Patterns and Pressures," Alice Scully for her contribution to "The Nervous System, the Brain, and the Endocrine Glands," and Joy Turek for her contribution to "Numbers Count" and her dedication, perceptiveness, and invaluable assistance with many other parts of this book.

We would also like to thank the following authors and publishers for permission to quote selected passages from their works:

FRANK BARRON, MURRAY JARVICK, and STERLING BUNNELL, "The Hallucinogenic Drugs," *Scientific American*;

EVA and RICHARD BLUM, *Alcoholism*, Jossey-Bass;

ROBERT CRICHTON, "On the Secret of Santa Vittoria," in *Afterwords: Novelists on Their Novels*, Harper and Row;

JOHN CUSTANCE, *Wisdom, Madness, or Folly*, Rosica Colin Ltd. and Farrar, Strauss, and Giroux;

KENNETH KOCH, *I Never Told Anybody*, Random House;

ARTHUR KOESTLER, *The Roots of Coincidence*, Random House;

JEREMY LARNER and RALPH TEFFERTELLER, *The Addict in the Streets*, Grove Press;

CARL ROGERS, *On Becoming a Person*, Houghton Mifflin Co.;

J. B. RHINE, *New World of the Mind*, Wm. Morrow Co.

Our special thanks to Judith Kampen for permission to quote from her student paper on creativity and to Kabriel Kreiswirth, Ed Wexler, and Rob LeDuca for the use of their cartoons. The illustrations at the head of each chapter were drawn by Jan Cook. The pictures for the Projective Biography Technique were drawn by Betty Levin and that technique was conceived in collaboration with Dorothy Loeb.

Photo Acknowledgements

Section One

Personal Development

OVERVIEW

sychology's observations on the normal person in our society are presented in the initial section of this text. Chapters 1, 2, and 3 describe the person at various stages of development: as an infant, a child, an adolescent, a young adult, a middle-aged adult, and an elderly man or woman. Chapter 4 compares leading theories of personality. Chapter 5 brings together the views of various psychologists on the characteristics of the healthy individual.

As a whole, then, this section should help you see yourself, your family, and your friends from the psychological perspective. It will also acquaint you with issues that have occupied the field for decades. *To what extent are our personal characteristics inborn? To what extent are they learned from our environment? How do parents mold their children's attitudes and habits? Is behavior controlled by unconscious impulses, shaped by social rewards, or determined by choice and free will? In what ways do people differ from one another? In what ways are we all alike? What does it take to become a mature, fully functioning adult?*

These are issues on which every intelligent person may have an opinion. Psychologists do not pretend to know the final answers, but they can lay claim to membership in a field that has tried systematically, unceasingly, and sometimes ingeniously, to penetrate their core.

Infancy and Childhood

ow do we grow from infancy to old age? How does our behavior change? How do our minds and personalities mature? What common problems do we face at different stages of our lives and how do we attempt to solve them? These are some of the questions psychology sets out to answer.

We intend to survey the entire human lifespan in the opening section of this book. Chapter 1 will discuss the growth that occurs in infancy and childhood. Chapter 2 will deal with adolescence. Chapter 3 will explore the development and dilemmas of adulthood and old age. What we hope to get across is a sense of the remarkable journey we make from the time we are born to the time we die—a journey filled with difficulties and achievements, suffering and joy, but always marked by definite stages which psychologists have begun to chart.

Psychology cannot sum up the pattern of a human life, or of life in general, in any simple formula. It engages, however, in a continual attempt to see clearer, dig deeper, and put facts together in ways that will help us understand ourselves better.

We invite you to join us in reviewing some of the main discoveries psychologists have made about human development. When you know what they are, you may be impressed. On the other hand, you may find them insignificant. Or perhaps you will come away intrigued, confused, excited, discouraged, and wishing that someone could explain it all really clearly. If you get that far, you may be on your way to becoming a psychologist yourself. In that case, welcome to the club!

4

Mother Love

A series of studies by Rene Spitz and his associates has made it clear that, in the absence of mother love, infants suffer terribly.[1] Spitz studied a group of children raised in a foundling home. The babies had been breast-fed by their own or substitute mothers for the first three months of their lives. During this period they had developed normally. Then they were put in the home, where they received adequate food, medical attention, and physical care. Most of the time, however, they were left in cribs without affectionate handling or personal attention. Very soon the babies began to show a noticeable degree of retardation. Their faces became expressionless; their movements appeared uncoordinated. Some seemed to be wasting away from malnutrition. About thirty percent died before they reached one year of age. Of the infants who survived, many were unable to walk or talk by the age of four.

To develop normally, a baby needs a parent who can provide not only its physical comfort but also the security of tender, loving care. Most parents, of course, are capable of furnishing these essentials. Others, however, do not give their children the emotional support they need. In these unfortunate cases, the youngsters will have to struggle to develop their potentials and some, sad to say, will be hampered or scarred for life.

The Family Climate

The infant, we must recognize, is born to two people who already have their own psychological strengths and weaknesses. The parents' strengths will be of benefit to the child. They will help him or her grow up happy, industrious, and loving. The parents' weaknesses, however, will also play a part, interfering with their ability to properly **nurture** their offspring.

nurture
to nourish or raise in a caring, protective fashion

Some children are unwanted and some are conceived for the wrong reasons: to patch up an unhappy marriage or to give a neglected wife something to occupy her attention. Even in more normal circumstances, the presence of the child may trigger hidden conflicts that the parents have within them. An insecure woman, for instance, may see her tiny daughter as a rival for her husband's affection, while a childish man may resent the fact that, with a real baby in the home, his wife doesn't baby him as much as she used to.

From the very beginning, each human being is part of a family atmosphere that affects him or her in both beneficial and harmful ways. Beneath the surface of what parents do for their children lies a complex set of expectations, resentments, hopes, and fears. These factors influence the kinds of people the children grow up to be. The family's emotional climate, in other words, is as important to the child's development as weather and soil conditions are to the development of trees, shrubs, and flowers.

A happy family.

The Heredity-Environment Dispute

The parents' attitudes and handling of the child are not, of course, the only factors that shape psychological growth. Later in life other people will influence the child's emerging character and, before anyone has a chance to have any effect, **inherited traits** lay the groundwork for his or her characteristics.

inherited traits
qualities or characteristics with which we are born

The question of what we inherit has long been debated. Many years ago, it was widely believed that intelligence, special talents, insanity, and criminality were all more or less inborn. Then a shift of opinion took place and many psychologists began to assert that almost everything we become is learned from our environment. Those who continued to believe in the importance of heredity would point to cases in which insanity, mental retardation, or musical genius appeared to run in families. Those who were beginning to believe in the greater importance of the environment would point to other evidence. They cited cases of identical twins reared in different homes who developed very different characteristics despite identical heredity.

The argument was bitter, heated, and prolonged, but it was never resolved. Perhaps too few of the people involved in it were willing to admit that heredity and environment are both important in determining human behavior.

6

In the early 1900s an eminent psychologist, Boris Sidis, made a highly publicized attempt to raise his son to be a genius. Sidis believed that we all have much more potential than we realize. He declared that if we could teach children to "observe accurately and think correctly" in the first few years of life, we could regularly produce brilliant people. In his own words,

> You must begin a child's education as soon as he displays any power to think. . . . Keep alive within him the quickening power of curiosity. Do not repress him. Answer his questions; give him the information he craves, seeing to it always that he understands your explanations. You need not be afraid of overstraining his mind. On the contrary, you will be developing it as it should be developed.

On the basis of this theory, Sidis exposed his own child, from the time he was an infant, to a program of intensive education.

What were the results?

At the age of two, William James Sidis already could read and at four he could use the typewriter, writing in English and French. Upon entering the first grade, he passed through seven grades in six months. At the age of eight, already an accomplished mathematician, he was able to devise a new logarithmic table based on the number 12 instead of 10, and at the age of nine he passed the entrance examination at Harvard.

It should be noted, however, that after graduating from law school, William James Sidis rejected the intellectualism that had been instilled in him. He spent the rest of his life as a manual laborer.[2]

This case has been used by some psychologists to demonstrate the far-reaching effects of the environment on a person's development. Opponents of this view, on the other hand, maintain that Sidis' son must have been gifted at birth or he would never have been able to accomplish what he did. Furthermore, they use the fact that the boy became a laborer as an argument against the manipulation of children even by well-meaning parents.

The heredity-environment dispute has become less heated in recent years. A consensus of opinion appears to be spreading which states that certain characteristics (the acuteness of our sense organs, the functioning of our endocrine glands, the structure of our brains) are mainly determined by heredity, that other characteristics (knowledge, goals, values, habits, feelings about ourselves and others) are mainly instilled by our environment, and that still other characteristics (intelligence, muscular coordination, basic temperament) are produced by an intricate interplay of both heredity and environment.

To complicate the matter further, many psychologists today—and the authors of this text are among them—take the position that some of our characteristics are self-determined. Our abilities and disabilities are not simply forced upon us. Knowingly or not, we often choose to develop them ourselves. In addition to the traits we are born with and those that are fostered by our environment, we must consider those we create ourselves.

The famous Jewish humorist Sholom Aleichem, for example, tells in his autobiography how he decided to become a humorous writer.[3] He was barely nine years old when his mother died and his father—poor, overworked, and burdened with thirteen children—took a new wife. She turned out to be a mean, hot-tempered stepmother who frequently beat the children and even more frequently cursed them. In his despair, the little boy began to amuse himself by compiling what he called "a dictionary of a stepmother's curses." In this notebook, he put down in alphabetical order all the terrible things she called them. Reading it over, he would sadly laugh himself to sleep. One night, however, his father caught him in the act, took the notebook out of his hands, and showed it to his wife. To the child's great relief, they found it funny too, and from that time on, he says, he knew he would try to write humor as a profession.

This case seems to us a fine example of a person choosing one of his own most important characteristics, although it was also clearly encouraged by his environment, both in the unhappy conditions that led him to seek relief through humor and in the fortunate reward of his parents' appreciation of his efforts.

Basic Trust

All psychologists agree on the importance of early experiences on the development of the individual. Perhaps the most crucial are those that result in what Erik Erikson has called basic trust.[4] While dependent upon the care of others, infants who learn that those they rely on are in fact reliable—who find that their parents fulfill their needs in an atmosphere of warmth, love, and happiness—acquire a core of trust in other people that eventually enables them to trust themselves as well. In contrast, children who learn that those they depend on are unreliable, inconsistent, or unhappy in fulfilling their needs are likely to acquire distrust of other people which will make it very difficult for them to maintain close relationships in later life.

The emotional wounds of infancy are not, of course, incurable. The effects of poor mothering, for instance, can be undone by a great deal of healthy mothering in later childhood and trust in people may be established by favorable experiences in later life. To counter these early **trauma** traumas, however, sometimes takes an enormous amount of time and a psychologically energy. Many years of psychological treatment may be required to repair damaging experience the damage done by poor parents in the first few months of life.

trauma
a psychologically
damaging experience

The Preschool Years

Between one and two years of age, most normal children learn to walk and talk. While making life more interesting for the child, these new abilities can cause problems in the home. Since parents rarely wish to live in a jumble of discarded toys and broken knickknacks, the words "No!" and "Don't touch!" now begin to be heard very frequently.

Between the ages of two and three, most children are toilet trained. This added restraint on their freedom increases their awareness that certain kinds of self-control are expected of them. Teaching the toddler to use the potty is not just an effort to make parents' tasks less unpleasant. It is one of the first ways in which the child is taught to behave in a

8

socialized manner. As such, it can be a happy time in which he or she learns that self-control is rewarded with praise and admiration—not to mention dry pants.

Unfortunately, in many cases the period comes to resemble a minor nightmare. If the parents are irritable, screaming and spanking become daily events, and the child may learn to cope with their harsh demands by defying or deceiving them.

Impatience and rigidity make many adults intolerant of their children's so-called negative behavior. What they fail to appreciate is the fact that it is perfectly natural for the two- or three-year-old to want his or her way all the time. At birth, every infant is a totally self-centered creature. Consideration for others must be acquired, of course, if the individual is to become an adjusted member of society, but intolerance of the child's natural selfishness is not the best way of winning his or her cooperation.

A blend of strength and kindness seems to be the ideal formula for raising children. Easy as it is to prescribe, however, many parents find it difficult to practice. Because of their own personality problems, a large percentage of mothers and fathers fail either to express the warmth their children need to feel close to them or to display the firmness they need to respect and obey them.

Consider the case of Norman K. The only child of a couple who had married in their thirties, he was his mother's pride and joy. Since she had feared she would have no children, she poured attention on her baby, who repaid her by being cute and clever. By the time he was three years old, he and she had formed a "mutual admiration society." When he began to explore his environment and grabbed, pulled, and broke things, she did not have the heart to slap his little hands or raise her voice in anger. As he grew older and demanded more sweets than she thought were good for him, she found it hard to deny him lest he throw a tantrum. When he objected to her carrying on a conversation with her husband, she soon cut the conversation short. Norman, therefore, became convinced that, by behaving in a cute yet demanding way, he could always get his mother to do what he wanted. His father, on the other hand, found the child a serious rival for his wife's affection. Ashamed of his jealousy, he withdrew from the contest by involving himself more and more in his business. His resentment, however, showed through in the rough way he handled the child when he dressed him and in the irritability the boy's antics produced in him. Is it any wonder that, in later years, Norman related to women in a seductive, controlling fashion and avoided close contact with men as much as he possibly could?

Cooperation or Competition?

peers
one's social equals

Once the child begins to play in the neighborhood or attend a nursery school, competition with **peers** becomes a part of the daily routine. The desire to dominate others or at least to control them enough to get them to satisfy our needs is part of every person's makeup. The desire to please others so they will like us, however, is equally basic. Every child, from the age of three or four, is faced with the problem of working out a compromise between the desire to control and the desire to please.

Those who are successful acquire a pattern of behavior that takes both needs into account. Those who are unsuccessful either feel compelled to dominate so ruthlessly that they find themselves disliked or else feel compelled to comply so totally with everyone else's wishes that they end up unsatisfied.

What determines one's success in resolving this basic conflict? The manner in which the child's demands and needs have been handled at home have already set him or her on a certain path. Not only mother and father but also brothers and sisters may, by their reactions, convince a child that he or she can be bossy and get away with it or that he or she had better be responsive to other people's wishes. What often happens is that a child develops a behavior pattern that works in the family and then continues it in the outside world. A boy, for example, may find that by acting the bully at home—terrorizing his **siblings,** snarling at his parents—he succeeds in getting his way. They are anxious to keep him happy, so they give in to his demands. Other children, however, and adults who do not care about his happiness may refuse to give in to him. Nevertheless, early habits are so hard to lose that he continues acting tough; from time to time he comes across people who do give in to him, thus encouraging his original behavior. His failure to work out a compromise between his desire to control and his desire to please, then, may be traced to his family's inability to resist his bullying.

siblings
brothers and sisters

Magical Thinking

While the growing child must endure frustration in his or her contacts with the world, the desire to remain in charge lives on in the form of magical thinking. Daydreams and fantasies provide every young person, and many older ones as well, with an outlet for the wishes that reality denies. The normal adolescent and adult who engage in wishful daydreams know, of course, that what they dream up is fantasy. To the preschool child, however, the distinction is not so clear. For him or her, fantastic wishes may very well come true—and so, unfortunately, may fantastic fears.

The young child lives in a mental state that is open to the terrors of witches and monsters as well as to the glory of becoming a hero or a movie star. Nightmares are common and, when their secret hopes or anxieties force them to do so, little children may invent stories that, by adult standards, are obvious lies.

A three-year-old boy is terrified of the dark because he believes a huge green octopus with long slimy tentacles is crouched in the corner of his room waiting for a chance to devour him. His parents patiently explain that octopi live only in the sea. They try to prove the nonexistence of the octopus in his room by switching on the light. The fearful child, however, stubbornly maintains that he can see it crouching in the corner when his parents are asleep. He begs them to let him keep the light on or, better yet, sleep in their bed.

10   What we see here is not a case of lying but a common example of the young child's fantasy and fear overcoming his ability to reason.

That this kind of thinking is characteristic of the preschool child was demonstrated almost 100 years ago by the eminent psychologist G. Stanley Hall. In a classic study, he had schoolteachers question five- and six-year-old children about the stars, the sky, God, death, and other such cosmic matters. He reports their conception of death as follows: "When people die they just go, or are put in a hole, or a box or a black wagon that goes to heaven, or they fly up or are drawn or slung up into the sky where God catches them. They never can get out of the hole, and yet all good people somehow get where God is. He lifts them up, they go up on a ladder or rope, or they carry them up, but keep their eyes shut so they do not know the way, or they are shoved up through a hole. When children get there they have candy, rocking-horses, guns, and everything in the toy shop or picture book, play marbles, top, ball, cards, hookey, hear brass bands, have nice clothes, gold watches, pets, ice cream and soda-water, and no school."[5]

The children's conception of death, as reported by Hall, seems to be a blend of factual information, stories they were probably told by their parents, and their own wishful fantasy.

Curiosity

Free-floating curiosity about the world is also characteristic of the preschool child. He or she may pepper mother and father with endless questions. "What's that?", "How come?", and "Why?" may be repeated so often that it begins to seem that the child is not so much interested in information as in engaging his parents in something resembling conversation. Whatever the actual reasons, however—learning something new, getting parents' attention, or trying to hold a conversation—the curiosity game is a sign of the maturation that is occurring. It should be taken as an indication of mental growth in a child who may lapse back at night to the infantile habits of thumbsucking or clutching a baby blanket as a source of security.

The amount of curiosity a child displays and the interest he or she maintains in learning new things is dependent, in part, on the exposure he or she has had to interesting stimuli in infancy. The baby who was shown many colorful sights and sounds, whose parents took time to read stories to him or her, who was introduced at an early age to games and pets, picture books and toys, has a headstart in learning over the baby who was neglected and restrained.

Studies done by research psychologists provide support for the view that stimulation in infancy promotes curiosity and learning ability. Sayegh and Dennis, for instance, found institutionalized infants who suffered from neglect to be retarded in their development. They therefore gave a group of these infants an hour a day of enrichment experience. The babies were placed in upright positions, their interest in objects was encouraged, and they were helped to acquire skill in handling objects. After fifteen days, this group showed significant gains in development.[6] Leitch and Escalona, on the other hand, produced *over*stimulation in infants by presenting them with more toys than they could possibly handle. When they kept this up for a period of time, the babies' behavior deteriorated. Although they were highly alert and aroused, they behaved in a more infantile manner than they normally would have.[7] The conclusion most psychologists have drawn from studies such as these is that there is an optimal amount of stimulation that helps childrens' curiosity and learning ability progress. Too little and too much can both interfere with the child's development. The art of parenting, therefore, would seem to involve a sense of how much stimulation is best for a given child at a given time and, of course, a willingness to provide it.

Jean Piaget and the Development of Logical Thinking

A Swiss psychologist by the name of Jean Piaget established a worldwide reputation in the 1950s by his investigations of children's mental growth. Observing and questioning his own and other children as they grew from year to year, he discovered that children have ideas about the world that are neither inherited or learned, but that reveal their level of mental development.[8] In their early years, in other words, most girls and boys entertain ideas that they later outgrow.

Most four-year-olds, for example, believe the moon follows them when they go for a walk at night. They also believe that anything that moves, including the ocean and wind, is alive. We cannot say that these ideas are inborn, for they appear at a certain stage of development and are replaced by more logical ideas at a later stage. Nor can we say that they are taught, for adults do not believe them, so they would hardly teach them to their youngsters.

To take another example, the child of three or four, confronted with two identical glasses filled with water, will say that they both have "the same to drink." If the water from one of the glasses is poured into a tall, narrow beaker in front of the child's eyes, however, he or she will say that the taller container has "more to drink" than the shorter one. Not until the age of six or seven do most children understand that changing the shape of a quantity does not change its amount.

Piaget calls this kind of development *mental growth by integration,* in that a higher level idea (amount is determined by height and width) is formed by the integration of two lower level ideas (amount is determined by height; amount is determined by width). In his attempts to explain the nature of children's thinking, he contrasts this process with *mental growth by substitution.* In the area of moral judgment, for instance, young children judge a person according to how much damage he or she does rather than according to his or her intentions. If a child helping mother set the table trips and breaks twelve cups, while another child who has been forbidden to climb a cupboard does so and breaks one cup, young children say the first one deserves more punishment while older children say the second one does. According to Piaget, objective morality based on the amount of damage done has been replaced, or substituted, by subjective morality based on the person's intentions.

Without going further into the complications of his theories, we may conclude that his findings force us to recognize that young children comprehend the world in radically different ways than adults comprehend it—not because children are stubborn or selfish or lazy or rebellious, but because their minds interpret their experiences according to different formulas.

The Juvenile Period

The juvenile period begins at age five with the start of formal schooling. Now the child must learn to conform to a fairly rigid scheduling of his or her activities. A certain time to wake up, a certain time to be at school, sitting quietly in class, getting homework done: these requirements and many others make the life of a school-aged child much more orderly and dutiful than it had been before.

What this demands of the youngster, psychologically, is an acceptance of responsibilities and routines. Those who make the adjustment readily are rewarded with adult approval; those who rebel and refuse to become self-disciplined use up a great deal of energy in fighting the "system."

In the long run, unquestioning conformity or stubborn nonconformity can each lead to serious problems. Easily disciplined, highly responsible individuals often suffer from a lack of spontaneity. They may find it impossible to express their feelings fully. Irresponsible, undisciplined individuals, on the other hand, often suffer the frustration of never completing any undertaking. Their selfishness may also make them unpopular. Healthy adjustment clearly requires a blend of conformity and nonconformity. In the early years, however, the emphasis is on conformity.

Peer-group activities also undergo significant changes during this period. From free play to games with rules to competitive sports and social encounters, the process is again one of accepting routines and more goal-directed activity. On the playground, as in the classroom, the juvenile is initiated into our striving, hard-working society.

According to Erik Erikson, the growing boy or girl must develop *a sense of industry* or suffer lifelong feelings of inferiority. All civilizations demand productive labor from their members. Whether it be physical or mental, domestic or professional, every adult is expected to perform some service to his or her community. The child who acquires the habits that serve as a basis for industrious behavior is, therefore, well-prepared for the future. The child who fails to acquire them will soon come to feel deficient in comparison with other people.[9]

Gender Identity

Meanwhile, another important process is going on. Both boys and girls are developing what we may call their gender identity—their sense of themselves as a boy or girl, rather than merely a child. In the preschool years, the importance of feeling boyish or girlish is minor; in adolescence, relating to the opposite sex becomes extremely important; in the juvenile period, the formation of gender identity takes center stage.

Our society is presently transforming its old definitions of masculinity and femininity. Long hair and colorful attire for men; new kinds of careers for women; the sharing of domestic duties; the elimination of the double standard of sexual behavior: these are some of the changes that

A girl baseball player on a traditionally all-boy team.

are taking place. What was formerly regarded as "man's nature" in contrast to "woman's nature" is being revised.

Beyond that, the feminist movement is making great strides in convincing us that we have done ourselves harm by treating females as though they were inferior to males. We have been made to realize that, in many ways, girls have been brought up to feel that they are less competent, less rational, less reliable, less objective, and less intelligent than boys. As a result, they have been led to see themselves as dependent creatures who must have a man to feel complete. Feminists dispute this point of view, arguing that it not only harms women's ability to live with themselves but also distorts men's values.

14

Regardless of how we conceive of man's and woman's nature, however, it is increasingly important, in the preteen years, for both boys and girls to feel content with their identities as boys or girls. The achievement of such contentment is aided by close relationships with same-sex peers. When nine- or ten-year-olds band together into tightknit groups of their own sex and reject the opposite sex as stupid, annoying, or just plain "yecch!", they are consolidating their gender identity or, in other words, priding themselves on being whatever they are.

The formation of gender identity is also aided by a positive relationship with one's parent of the same sex. In a study by Sears, it was found that sons of fathers who were warm, permissive, and easygoing tended to behave in a manner appropriate to their sex.[10] Boys, in other words, do not need a "macho" male for a father in order to be comfortable with their developing masculinity. What they need is a father who is comfortable with himself and with whom they can form a close relationship. It stands to reason that the same is true of girls and their mothers. Exaggerated demonstrations of femininity are hardly necessary, but a close relationship with a mother who enjoys being a woman is very important.

In the first few years of life, both boys and girls have traditionally been closer to their mothers than their fathers. Because of mother's role in feeding, dressing, and caring for baby, the infant's security has been vested in her. During the juvenile period, however, boys have been expected to identify with their fathers and to begin to act like little men. It has always been more shameful for a boy to seem effeminate than for a girl to act tomboyish. These standards appear to be changing. Many mothers and fathers now share equally in infant care and the notion that a normal boy must subdue his sensitive, aesthetic, or sentimental feelings is becoming outmoded.

Moral Development

A final process that takes place in the juvenile period is the change from morality based on fear of punishment to morality based on compassion for other people. In the preschool years, most children learn to respect other people's rights simply because their parents demand it. The very young child refrains from hitting, stealing, cheating, and lying because he or she fears the consequences of getting caught. A slap, a scream, a dirty look from mother or father, and the threat of losing their affection are essentially what keep the two- to five-year-old on the straight and narrow. In the juvenile period, however, many youngsters begin to put themselves in the other person's place, to image how it would feel to be hit or cheated, and to care enough to stop even when there is no chance of getting caught.

internalized

taken to heart or made a part of one's own way of thinking

According to some psychologists, they have **internalized** their parents' standards. Now, if they feel like doing something of which their parents would disapprove, they punish themselves by making them-

antisocial personalities

criminals and those who ignore other people's rights

selves feel guilty. At this stage, an effective conscience is being formed **15** and, difficult as it may be to observe from the outside, the inner change is momentous. It marks the difference between a barbaric and a civilized human being. Those children who fail to make the transition, who continue to behave themselves simply out of fear of punishment, remain potential **antisocial personalities,** while those who develop a conscience based on compassion become the true contributors to a more humane society.

Ruth W. was a model child. Polite and mannerly, she addressed her male teachers as "sir," and her female teachers as "ma'am." She always dressed neatly and cleanly, and in the presence of adults she behaved demurely and wore a fixed smile on her face. Other girls, however, shunned her company, complaining privately that she was a gossip and had something bad to say about everyone behind their backs.

At the age of twelve, Ruth told her parents that one of her female teachers had been drinking vodka in the teachers' lounge and coming into the classroom drunk. An investigation revealed that this teacher had been going through a crisis in her personal life and had occasionally taken a drink during some of the more hectic days at school. Since there was no evidence of drunkenness and her work had always been satisfactory, no official action was taken against her. Ruth, however, maintained that she had done her duty by spying on the teacher and reporting her, and she could never understand why, after this event, her peers liked her even less than before.

Since the early 1960s, Lawrence Kohlberg, a professor at Harvard, has been studying the development of moral thought in children. After interviewing 170 children of various ages from six to sixteen and having them respond to what he calls *moral dilemmas,* Kohlberg came to the conclusion that we can differentiate six stages in the development of moral reasoning. Before discussing his stages, let us consider one of the dilemmas he asked his subjects to solve.

"Joe's father promised he could go to camp if he earned the fifty dollars for it, and then changed his mind and asked Joe to give him the money he had earned. Joe lied and said he had only earned ten dollars and went to camp using the other forty dollars he had made. Before he went, he told his younger brother Alex about the money and about lying to their father. Should Alex tell their father?[11]

One ten-year-old boy replied, "In one way it would be right to tell on his brother or his father might get mad at him and spank him. In another way it would be right to keep quiet or his brother might beat him up." Kohlberg says this boy "does not appear to have a conception of moral obligation." His judgment is based entirely on the possibility of being punished and he does not even consider the question of what is morally right or wrong.

There are no "correct" answers to Kohlberg's moral dilemmas, but the way in which one arrives at a position on them indicates the stage of moral development at which one tends to think. The six stages he describes are grouped by pairs into three moral levels. The first level, which Kohlberg calls *pre-moral* is illustrated by the boy we quoted above. The second, which he calls *morality of conventional role-conformity* is attained

16

when one thinks less in terms of punishment than in terms of what our society, or those in authority, define as right and wrong. (A person responding to the camp-money dilemma at this level might say, "Since the father is the head of the household and a child should not lie to his parent, I guess Alex should tell on his brother.") The third and highest level is the *morality of self-accepted moral principles.* (A person responding to the camp-money dilemma at this level might say, "Both Joe and his father are in the wrong, Joe for lying and his father for breaking his promise. If Alex tells on his brother, he will also be in the wrong for squealing. If he doesn't tell, he is holding back some information that his father has a right to know, so whatever he does he's in a spot. Since I think that squealing on your friends is worse than keeping your mouth shut, however, I would say he shouldn't tell.")

The value of Kohlberg's work is that it sheds light on the sequence of moral development and encourages psychologists to study this crucial aspect of human behavior more carefully than they have done so far.

Summary

In this chapter we have described important milestones in the development of the infant and child. We have discussed the interplay of heredity and environment and have stressed the role of the family in determining a child's characteristics. Competitive versus cooperative drives, magical thinking, the development of logical thinking, the formation of gender identity, and the stages of moral development have occupied our attention. We have tried to give you an overview of the momentous changes that take place in a human being in the first ten or twelve years of life. Whether one remembers these events from one's own early years or observes them in a growing child, one cannot help but be impressed by the subtle yet striking ways in which a young person grows.

Class Projects

1. Arrange a visit to a nursery school or preschool day-care center. Ask the people in charge to explain their goals in dealing with children at this age level. Observe the children yourself to see if you can detect any differences between boys and girls, three- and four-year-olds, or any other groups. If you were running a center for children like these, would you do it differently from what you have seen? If so, explain why.

2. List several traits of your own that you think you inherited. List several traits that you think you learned from your environment. Now see if you can locate some traits that you developed of your own free will. Discuss them in class.

3. Administer the following moral dilemma to children of different ages. Try to figure out what their stage of moral development is.

   A poor woman finds a purse containing $500 in cash. Since she does not know to whom it belongs, she looks in the newspaper the next day to see if someone has announced such a loss. Sure enough there is an ad reading, 'If anyone reading this ad has found my purse containing $500, please call me **17** at the following number . . .' She calls to report the find, and asks what reward is being offered. The owner of the purse says there is no reward, and demands that she return it immediately. What do you think she should do?

References

1. RENE SPITZ, *The First Year of Life* (New York: International University Press, 1965).

2. BARBARA HAUCK and MAURICE FREEHILL, *The Gifted—Case Studies* (Dubuque, IA: Brown, 1972).

3. SHOLOM ALEICHEM, *The Great Fair* (New York: Noonday Press, 1965).

4. ERIK ERIKSON, *Childhood and Society*, 2nd ed. (New York: Norton, 1963).

5. G. STANLEY HALL, "The Contents of Children's Minds," *Princeton Review*, 1883, *11*, pp. 249-253.

6. W. DENNIS and Y. SAYEGH, "The Effect of Supplementary Experiences Upon the Behavioral Development of Infants in Institutions," *Child Development*, 1965, *36*, pp. 81-90.

7. M. LEITCH and S. ESCALONA, "Reactions of Infants to Stress," *Psychoanalytic Study of the Child*, 1949, *5*, pp. 121-140.

8. JEAN PIAGET, *Language and Thought of the Child* (New York: Humanities Press, 1965).

9. R. R. SEARS, E. E. MACCOBY and H. LEVIN. *Patterns of Child Rearing.* (Evanston, IL: Row, Peterson, 1957).

10. LAWRENCE KOHLBERG, "The Development of Children's Orientation Toward a Moral Order: 1. Sequence in the Development of Moral Thought," *Vita Humana*, 1963, *6*, pp.11-33.

Suggested Readings

1. AMBRON, S. *Child Development.* San Francisco: Rinehart Press, 1975.

2. McCLINTON, BARBARA S. and MEIER, BLANCHE G. *Beginnings: Psychology of Early Childhood.* St. Louis: Mosby, 1978.

3. BRUNNER, J.S. *Studies in Cognitive Growth.* New York: Wiley, 1967.

4. DENNENBERG, V. H. "Stimulation in Infancy, Emotional Reactivity and Exploration," in *Neurophysiology and Emotion*, ed. D. C. Glass. New York: Russell Sage Foundation and Rockefellow Press, 1967.

5. ERICKSON, ERIK. *Childhood and Society.* New York: Norton, 1963.

6. JONHSON, ROLAND and MEDINNUS, GENE. *Child Psychology.* New York: Wiley, 1975.

7. KAGAN, J. *Change and Continuity in Infancy.* New York: Wiley, 1971.

8. LIDZ, THEODORE. *The Person.* New York: Basic Books, 1968.

9. MILLER, SUSANNA. *Psychology of Play.* New York: Penguin Books, 1968.

10. STAATS, A. W. *Children's Learning, Intelligence and Personality: Principles of a Behavioral Interactional Approach.* New York: Harper and Row, 1971.

11. WINNICOTT, DONALD WOODS. *The Child and the Family: First Relationships.* London: Tavistock Publications, 1962.

12. Ibid. *The Child and the Outside World: Studies in Developing Relationships.* London: Tavistock Publications, 1957.

Adolescence

2

**A**re the teenage years an especially important part of life? Are people between the ages of thirteen and nineteen very different than people in other age groups? Some psychologists think so. They call adolescence a "period of storm and stress," and claim that teenagers are much more unstable than people in any other stage of life. Other psychologists disagree, claiming that this period can be as calm and pleasant as any other.

In this chapter, we will present these divergent opinions and see what they are based on. We will also discuss the common problems most adolescents in our culture encounter.

Since we will be talking about a period of life that you have recently lived through, we expect you to be very critical of everything we have to say. Some of you will probably feel that we have given too much emphasis to topics like sex and love, while others will feel we haven't given them enough. Some will object to our comments on adolescent aggression, while others will say we have treated the matter too lightly. Some will disagree with our discussion of rebellion against the family, some will object to our observations on conformity to the peer group, and—if that weren't enough—some of you will probably claim that the entire chapter is beside the point!

All of which goes to prove what we have been suspecting for some time: you have to be crazy to write a psychology text.

20

Adolescence: A Period of Storm and Stress?

Adolescence has been called "the period of storm and stress." Because the teens are a time of transition from childhood to adulthood, because of the rapid physiological changes that take place during **puberty,** and because the upsurge of sexual impulses creates embarrassment and tension in our society, the years between thirteen and nineteen have been portrayed as filled with conflict.

puberty

the stage of maturation in which the person becomes capable of sexual reproduction

J. C. Gustin promotes this view in his essay "The Revolt of Youth."[1] "One of the most poignant moments in the psychology of man," he writes,

> is the scene between the adolescent and the parent, glaring at each other with hopeless despair. They yearn for each other with aching desperation; they long for the familiar signs of understanding. Instead they find that they no longer speak the same language . . . at the precise moment when each needs the reassuring warmth of the other, there is a breakdown of communication as though a bolt of lightning had cut the lines that had bound them together. Picture our adolescent now poised at the brink of adulthood. Racked by sexual desire, frustrated by outer prohibitions and inner inhibitions; desperately longing for independence yet fearful of isolation; eager for responsibilities yet fraught with anxieties about inferiority; flooded by irrational impulses yet committed to rules of propriety, he is hopelessly and helplessly confused and an enigma to everyone and himself.

Other leading psychologists take a far different view. Albert Bandura, for example, believes that the "storm and stress" view of adolescence is an exaggeration. In his article, "The Stormy Decade: Fact or Fiction?"[2], Bandura says,

> The adolescent presumably is engaged in a struggle to emancipate himself from his parents. He therefore resists any dependence upon them for their guidance, approval, or company and rebels against any restrictions and controls that they impose upon his behavior . . . he begins to adopt idiosyncratic clothing, mannerisms, lingo, and other forms of peer-group behavior . . . he is ambivalent, frightened, unpredictable, and often irresponsible. . . . Moreover, since the adolescent is neither child nor adult, he is highly confused even about his own identity. The foregoing storm and stress picture of adolescence receives little support from detailed information that I obtained in a study of middle-class families.

Bandura goes on to argue that the average adolescent in our society is no more confused or unstable than his elders and that the adolescent period is no more troublesome than any other stage in life.

Whatever position we take between these extremes, there can be no **21** doubt that the years from thirteen to nineteen present a number of challenges to the developing individual. The rapid spurt in physical maturation, the growing desire for sexual experience, the shift of allegiance from family to peer group, the need to prove one's masculinity or femininity, the increasing awareness of the importance of vocational choice, and the awakening to the harsh realities of life all demand new forms of adaptation.

Sex and Love

While changes in height, weight, strength, and bodily proportions affect the adolescent's self-concept, sexual maturation is the most dramatic shift of all. In the early years the child was primarily a child and only secondarily a boy or girl. Puberty, however, focuses everyone's attention on his boyness or her girlness. In the juvenile period each person's popularity within his or her own sex group was of foremost importance. With the development of sexual interests one's attractiveness to the opposite sex becomes more important. **Heterosexual goals** take precedence over the goals of achieving good grades, pleasing parents, or being successful in athletics. Formerly an excellent student or a well-behaved member of the family, an adolescent boy or girl may become unruly and moody. The happy-go-lucky preteener may become a self-conscious loner or a loud showoff or some strange combination of the two.

heterosexual goals
attraction to the opposite sex

Yet the individual's childhood character lasts. Barring radical shifts in the family environment, the angry child is likely to remain an angry adolescent. Also, many teenagers develop their sexual awareness gradually, so that it affects their behavior over a period of years. They give up their childish interests and attachments little by little. It is not uncommon to find a fifteen-year-old girl wearing makeup and sexy clothing, flirting with older boys at school, yet cuddling her Raggedy Ann doll when she goes home. A boy of the same age may brag about his conquests while he enjoys a game of softball with his pals.

Regardless of how rapidly or slowly sexual interests develop, however, they almost always result in inner and outer conflicts. Although our society's morality is changing, total freedom of sexual expression for adolescent children is not allowed. To some extent, therefore, the natural impulses of adolescents are repressed, diverted, or privately indulged.

masturbation
sexual stimulation of oneself

According to reliable estimates, at least ninety percent of all boys and sixty percent of all girls practice **masturbation** as a form of sexual release. Most psychologists agree that it is a normal, nonharmful activity for persons who do not have heterosexual contact. Yet many young people suffer feelings of guilt and anxiety over masturbation because they have either been told that it is unhealthy or they have sensed their parents' embarrassment and discomfort regarding the topic.

Sexual curiosity, too, is a source of shame and guilt to many teenagers. The normal desire to know about reproduction and sexual plea-

22

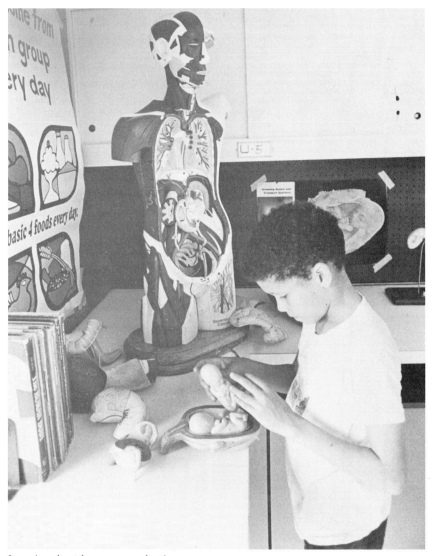

Learning about human reproduction.

sure leaves many young people embarrassed and confused. Adults, who are informative about other issues, are often reluctant to discuss sexual matters. As a result, the adolescent is likely to acquire his or her sexual knowledge in exchanges with equally embarrassed, confused, or misinformed friends.

Fortunately, more and more school systems are introducing frank discussions of sex as part of their curriculum. Also, more and more parents are finding it possible to relate sexual information to their children in a comfortable manner. It will probably be many years, however, before the facts of life are communicated as casually in our society as they have always been in many other cultures.

When it comes to actual sexual experience, adolescents in America are bound to suffer conflict. Having passed through puberty, they naturally desire it but, being inexperienced and both financially and emotionally dependent on their parents, they are rarely equipped to handle its possible consequences. Not only unwanted pregnancies but, more subtly, the emotional commitment that one of the partners may require is often too demanding for the insecure young person to cope with.

When feelings of first love are aroused, on the other hand, they may produce the most intense bliss and heartache the adolescent has ever known. All of his or her hiden longings for a soulmate, all of his or her secret dreams of fulfillment in the arms of a cherished lover are awakened. As long as it appears that the one on whom these hopes have been placed returns them in equal measure, the relationship is filled with joy and contentment. The moment it appears that one's partner is cooling off, however, loneliness and sadness descend like a cloud of doom.

The task of learning, through sweet and bitter experiences, how to create and maintain romantic relationships is one of the most important challenges of adolescence. Throughout the better part of adult life, the individual who loves and is loved by others enjoys a sense of fulfillment second to none. Not one of the other goals we strive for—fame, money, security, knowledge, competence, power—assures our happiness as well as love.

Most of us, however, misunderstand the nature of love and seek for it in ways that are destined to fail. We believe, for instance, that love occurs as if by magic when we meet the right person. Psychologists, however, have shown that love, like every other human emotion, occurs as the result of certain inner conditions being acted upon by certain external conditions. Young people are apt to fall in love, for example, when previous emotional ties, like dependent attachments on mother and father, are being broken. At such times, the young person's readiness for love is very great.

In *The Art of Loving*[3] Erich Fromm describes three common misconceptions which prevent us from having fulfilling love experiences. He writes,

> Most people see the problem of love primarily as that of being loved rather than that of loving. Hence the problem to them is how to be lovable. In pursuit of this aim they follow several paths. One, which is especially used by men, is to be successful, to be as powerful and rich as the social margin of one's position permits. Another, used especially by women, is to make oneself attractive by cultivating one's body, dress, etc. . . .
>
> A second [misconception] is the assumption that the problem of love is the problem of an object, not the problem of a faculty. People think that to love is simple, but that to find the right object to love—or to be loved by—is difficult. [Nothing, says Fromm, could be farther from the truth.]
>
> The third [misconception] lies in the confusion between the

initial experience of falling in love and the permanent state of being in love. If two people who have been strangers, as all of us are, suddenly let the wall between them break down, and feel close, feel one, this moment of oneness is one of the most exhilirating, most exciting experiences in life. However, this type of love is, by its very nature, not lasting. The two persons become well-acquainted, their intimacy loses more and more its miraculous character, until their antagonism, their disappointments, their mutual boredom kill whatever is left of the initial excitement. Yet, in the beginning they do not know all this: in fact, they take the intensity of the infatuation, this being crazy about each other, for proof of the intensity of their love, while it may only prove the degree of their preceding loneliness.

According to Fromm, our numerous failures in love would be lessened if we could recognize that it is more important to allow ourselves to love than to seek to be loved, that it is more difficult to cultivate the faculty of loving than to find a person on whom to practice it, and that the experience of falling in love is very different from the state of being in love.

Although many psychologists believe that love operates like other human emotions, few studies have been done on how or why a romantic attachment develops. It has been suggested that perhaps we are afraid that objectifying the experience of love will lessen its meaning, that perhaps it seems too contradictory to quantify and analyze something as unscientific as adoration. In any case, it is an area relatively untouched by research psychologists. One notable exception is the work of Zick Rubin.

In 1973, Rubin conducted an experiment on love. First, he developed a "love scale" including such items as:

"I would do anything for _ _ _ _ _ _ _ _ _ _ _ _ _ _ _ _ _ ."
"It would be hard for me to get along without

_ ."
The scale was given to 182 dating college students. They had to rate each item, in terms of their current romantic partner, from 1–not at all true to 9–definitely true.

Among other things, Rubin wanted to see if responses to the questionnaire matched actual behavior. He unobtrusively observed the couples as they waited for the experiment to begin. He discovered that those who received high scores on the scale also spent more time gazing into each other's eyes than those who had low scores.

From this experiment we may conclude that the age-old idea that love means absorption and fascination with the other person is indeed true.[4]

Shifts of Allegiance

While enjoying the thrills and suffering the misery of early love, adolescents go through other meaningful experiences as well. Among the most significant is the shift of loyalty from family to peer group. Whereas in childhood the opinions held by mother and father played a major role in shaping those of the youngster, in the teenage years the opinions of friends take priority. Most children of liberal parents automatically consider themselves liberals; most children of conservative parents automatically consider themselves conservatives. If the family places great value on material possessions, the child is apt to believe that money is all important; if the family makes religious observance a matter of central concern, the child is led to feel that religion must be taken seriously. By adolescence, on the other hand, the young person has learned that values vastly different from those of his or her family are held by other respectable people. In addition, he or she has acquired a need to separate from the family in order to assert his or her individuality. In flying free of the family nest, the teenager desperately needs the support of friends to bolster his or her fledgling venture into independence.

The need to be accepted and respected by one's contemporaries, to have friends with whom to share experiences and emotions—these are some of the ingredients that create peer-group affiliation. It is widely agreed (by adults) that peer-group identification is a crucial factor in adolescent development. Unfortunately, many people view it as only a negative force. For parents it may serve as an alibi or explanation of a child's poor behavior: "My son would never have tried drugs but his so-called friends pressured him into it." A group of bearded psychologists (not the authors of this text, of course) may decry adolescent conformity in clothing and speech. To our minds, however, it may be positive, negative, or benign, depending on the character of the adolescent and who he or she needs to be identified with. Consider the following brief case studies.

"Thirteen-year-old Joy listened to modern rock-and-roll music like other girls her age. A senior-high-school combo called "The Lions Roar" became quite popular with the older high-school boys and girls. Joy's older sister and her friends said that "The Lions Roar" was even better than some of the nationally known rock bands.

Joy had never heard "The Lions Roar" play. Nevertheless, she would frequently say that they were far better than the records she listened to."[5]

Dan, a seventeen-year-old high-school senior, had always been a quiet, lonely student. He did reasonably well in most of his subjects but always pulled straight-As in art. As long as he could remember he had spent some time each day sketching. His parents, however, refused to take his drawing and painting seriously. They believed he should focus his attention on other studies that would lead to college, to better jobs, and, eventually, to more money.

When the class yearbook committee was being formed, some of the students sought Dan out to design the pages and do the illustrations for the yearbook. At first he was reluctant but the students voted to give him his own room to work in and an unlimited supply of materials. Also, they gave him support—they liked his drawings and told him so. By the time the yearbook was done, Dan was well-known and well-liked by many of his peers.

This experience gave him the strength he needed. He ignored his parents' wishes, applied to an art school, and became a successful painter.

As you can see, Joy's desire to be associated with older teens proved not very harmful to her development and, in Dan's case, the support he received from his peers had a beneficial effect on his future life.

Many adolescents, engaged in making the break from their families' value systems, veer sharply to the opposite extreme and adopt positions designed to anger mother and father. Raised in homes where cleanliness and neatness were considered virtues, they take to dressing in an unkempt manner; brought up to consider marriage acceptable only within their particular racial or religious group, they fall in love with people from other groups. They become scornful of everything their parents stand for, and their contribution to family discussions ranges from silent disapproval to sneering sarcasm.

26

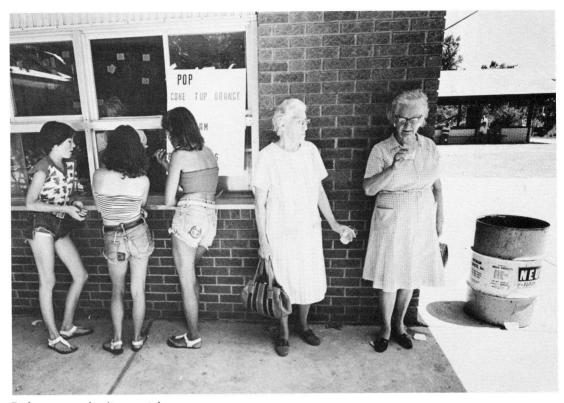

Each peer group has its own style.

Family harmony is strained, sometimes to the breaking point, in these years of change. Contributing to the tension is the fact that the children go through adolescence at about the time their parents are going through the crisis of middle age. In their mid-forties, most men and women are forced to come to terms with the realization that many of their youthful dreams will never be fulfilled. They see, too, that they are aging, that they are losing some of their former vigor and attractiveness. Then, to top it off, they find the children they have loved and protected turning against them or, at the very least, going off to pursue their own lives with little regard for the parents' feelings. It is not uncommon, in this context, for tempers to flare, wounds to fester, and a mood of resentment to prevail.

As though this were not enough, adolescents also face the task of proving their masculinity and femininity. By exhibiting their skill on the athletic field, dressing in the peer-group's current fashion, displaying courage, "coolness," or whatever are considered manly qualities, boys attempt to convince themselves and their acquaintances that they are admirable young men. By dressing in a sexually attractive manner and displaying sensitivity, deep feeling, or whatever are considered womanly virtues, girls attempt to prove that they are admirable young **27** women.

These attempts are essential steps on the road to maturity. Adolescents who lack the basics of healthy sex-role identity, however, may be driven to exaggerated maneuvers in their desperation to prove their masculinity or femininity. Boys who have never formed an attachment to a strong, kind father-figure sometimes engage in malicious, violent behavior in the mistaken belief that they are demonstrating manliness. Girls who have never felt close to a warm, understanding mother-figure sometimes engage in many casual sexual encounters in the mistaken belief that they are demonstrating womanliness. The motivation for these kinds of acts may also come from hostility against the parents who never provided the affection they needed, but the malicious boy and the promiscuous adolescent girl frequently interpret their own behavior as proof of their masculine strength and feminine attractiveness.

Adolescent Aggression

It is widely believed that adolescents are more apt than other age groups to engage in aggressive activity. In the form of competitive sports, such activity is socially approved. We think it not only normal but character building for boys and girls to strive for victory on the playing fields of our schools. When teenage aggression occurs on the streets, however, in the form of gang violence or crime, we take a much different view. We are understandably concerned about the robberies, beatings, rapes, and murders committed by adolescents.

Psychologists have explored the sources of this type of antisocial activity. One of the contributing factors, some studies show, is the prevalence of violence on television. A study reported by Eron, Huesmann, Lefkowitz, and Walder in 1972 measured the amount of violence seen by children on television with the amount of aggression exhibited by these same subjects ten years later. They discovered that those who had seen more violence consistently demonstrated more aggressiveness.

Other psychologists have done similar research and come to different conclusions. In fact, some have proved the opposite point-of-view. In 1971, Feshbach and Singer conducted a study of ten- to seventeen-year-old boys who were either in private school or a detention home. The boys aggressiveness was measured before the experiment and then again after six weeks of controlled television viewing (some subjects were restricted to watching violent programs on TV, while others could only watch nonviolent ones). The boys in the private school appeared to be unaffected by the type of program they were allowed to watch. The boys in the detention homes who watched violent TV programs, however, exhibited *less* verbal and physical aggression than those who observed nonviolent programs. Indeed, according to Feshbach and Singer, the more initially violent the subject, the more viewing violence on TV seemed to reduce aggressive behavior.[6]

To complicate matters further, this precise experiment was redone by a researcher named Wells, later in 1971, and he arrived at the opposite conclusion. A recent survey of the literature also strongly supports the belief that viewing violence on TV encourages aggression.[7]

There are many forms of adolescent aggression and many targets—parents, other authority figures, institutions, peers, and even the adolescent himself. One of the most dismal statistics to consider is the number of teenage suicides and suicide attempts. We are not, unfortunately, able to offer a definitive answer on why such things occur. One possible explanation, as we have pointed out, is that observing violence may create violence. It is possible that watching wars, murders, and death may simply harden our response to these acts—they may lose their meaning. It may be that some adolescents live in a more violent world than ever before. Living in a ghetto where crime is an accepted part of everyday life and where there is little chance for appropriate expressions of discontent may inevitably lead the adolescent to antisocial activities. Perhaps the explanation is different; as some psychologists believe, violence may be biologically determined, either genetically or hormonally. Hyperactivity, epilepsy, and other organic conditions have been found to be associated with aggressive behavior. In all likelihood, organic and social factors are both involved. The way in which they reinforce each other, however, still remains to be clarified.

The following case study is an illustration of adolescent antisocial behavior and its possible causes.

Paul, a fifteen-year-old boy, was referred for treatment by the juvenile authorities. He had committed a series of destructive acts: shooting out store windows with a B-B gun, setting fires in trash cans, and slashing automobile tires. On examination, he was found to have a history of hyperactivity as a young child. It had been controlled, however, by careful attention from his parents. Then he was sent to a boarding school where he was both unpopular and unsuccessful. His vandalism began after two months at this school—an indication that under the stress of the situation he had regressed to an earlier pattern of behavior.

Vocational Decisions

From ages seventeen or eighteen on, both boys and girls become increasingly aware of the importance of making a vocational decision. What am I going to do when I get out of high school? Go to college? Get a job? Get married? Bum around? What am I going to do with my life? What do I want to be? Sooner or later, questions like these demand a response from every young person approaching adulthood.

Many adolescents find their careers mapped out for them by their parents. Through a hundred subtle hints over the years, mother and father may have made it clear that they expect their children to go to college, their sons to adopt a profession, their daughters to marry well. Or they may have let them know that, in their opinion, people who don't make a lot of money can never be happy. The adolescent may accept these opinions uncritically and choose the vocation that his or her parents think best or reject their advice and pursue a career guaranteed to shock them. The majority seem to accept certain elements of their parents' views, ignore other elements, and end up with choices partly influenced by friends, teachers, opportunities, and their own assessment of their abilities and needs.

The influence of the parents, however, is sometimes subtly damaging. Studies conducted by Matina Horner, for instance, have shown that fear of success, or the motive to avoid success, is common in women of high intelligence coming from homes where high achievement is valued.[8] In these cases, it seems, the parents pay lip service to their daughters' career goals, but really want them to be securely married to a good provider. The daughters get the message and, without knowing exactly why, develop an uneasiness about achieving anything outstanding. They tend to believe that successful women are unattractive. Therefore, they avoid becoming what they think will turn suitors away and end up frustrating their own legitimate drives.

The importance of the decisions made at this time can hardly be overemphasized, yet most people make them gropingly, ambivalently, unsure of the wisdom of their choices and unaware of the motives prompting them to move in the directions they eventually select. Vocational counselors can help the young person choose a career on a realistic basis, but only a small proportion of teenagers consult them.

Awareness of World Affairs

While all this is happening, the more mature adolescents are also becoming conscious of the widespread problems of our society and the entire world. Crime, poverty, warfare, and racial strife, environmental pollution, population control, women's rights, and drug abuse—these issues hit the headlines of newspapers and magazines every week. By the age of eighteen or nineteen many people have come to realize that such issues are not theoretical, impersonal problems but practical, significant matters that affect their own lives, possibly in drastic ways.

Both because of the recognition that they themselves may be vitally affected by these social conditions and because of a growing ability to empathize with the sufferings of others, many teenagers become preoccupied with the misery and injustice that prevails in the world at large. While this preoccupation may lead, at times, to a sense of futility and an attitude of cynicism, it can also become the springboard for involvement with organizations committed to social change.

The adolescent's views on world affairs and suggestions for curing society's ills are often put down as naive and impossibly idealistic. As people get older, in fact, they tend to view their own youthful beliefs in this light. Not appreciating the complexity of social problems and the resistance most adults feel toward any disruption of the status quo, adolescents, it is said, support unrealistic programs that cannot succeed

30

in the world as it is. Unfortunately, there is some truth in this charge; yet, without idealistic dreamers and people who are willing, perhaps foolishly, to disrupt the status quo, social progress would be a very slow business at best. The history of dramatic social change, in this country as well as all others, inevitably shows the involvement, at least in the early stages, of men and women whose enthusiasm is often labelled "adolescent."

Summary

Adolescence is believed by many psychologists and most parents to be the most difficult stage of maturation. We have considered why this may be true. The adolescent—no longer a child, not yet an adult—is beset by conflicts. Allegiance to the peer group challenges one's former ties to the family. The possibility of engaging in aggressive behavior or becoming the victim of other's violent acts becomes real. Romantic love and sexual attraction are being experienced for the first time. Scholastic decisions and career choices have to be made. Yet, in the opinion of other psychologists, adolescence is not necessarily a time of turmoil. Having read and discussed this chapter and having (we hope) compared it with your own recent adolescence, you should have a keener sense of the psychological ingredients of this stage of life.

Class Projects

1. Interview someone who grew up in a culture very different from your own. Get the person to describe teenage behavior and attitudes in his or her homeland. Compare his or her concerns and expectations with your own as a teenager. In this way you will probably begin to see how arbitrary many of our beliefs are.
2. On the basis of your own experience and observation of people close to you, discuss the following questions. (1) What factors determine readiness or reluctance to fall in love? (2) What factors determine choice of love object (i.e., the particular person with whom one falls in love)?
3. List several items of importance to you (for example, vocational choice, political beliefs, attitudes toward marriage and family) and answer these questions about them: (1) How did these values change as you grew from childhood to adolescence to adulthood? (2) From whom did you acquire your values at each stage of development—parents, siblings, peers, teachers?

References

1. J. C. Gustin, "The Revolt of Youth," in *Issues of Adolescent Psychology*, ed. Dorothy Rogers (New York: Appleton-Century-Crofts, 1969).
2. Albert Bandura, "The Stormy Decade: Fact or Fiction," in *Issues in Adolescent Psychology*, ed. Dorothy Rogers. (New York: Appleton-Century-Crofts, 1969).
3. Erich Fromm, *The Art of Loving* (New York: Harper & Brothers, 1956).

4. Zick Rubin, "Measurement of Romantic Love," *Journal of Personality and Social Research*, 1979, *16*, pp. 265-273.

5. J. D. Krumboltz and H.B. Krumboltz, *Changing Children's Behavior* (Englewood Cliffs, NJ: Prentice-Hall, 1972).

6. S. Fesbach and R. D. Singer, *Television and Aggression: An Experimental Field Study* (San Francisco: Jossey-Bass, 1971).

7. H. J. Eysenck and D. K. B. Nias, *Sex, Violence and the Media* (New York: St. Martins, 1978).

8. Matina Horner, "The Motive to Avoid Success," *Psychology Today,* 1969, *6*, pp. 36-38.

Suggested Readings

1. Baldwin, James. *Go Tell It On the Mountain.* New York: Knopf, 1953.

2. Bandura, A. and Walters, R. *Adolescent Aggression.* New York: Ronald, 1959.

3. Blos, Peter. *On Adolescence.* New York: Free Press of Glencoe, 1962.

4. Conger, J. J. *Adolescence and Youth: Psychological Development in a Changing World.* New York: Harper and Row, 1972.

5. Newman, Barbara M. and Newman, Philip R. *An Introduction to the Psychology of the Adolescent.* Homewood, IL: The Dorsey Press, 1979.

6. Salinger, J. D. *Catcher in the Rye.* Boston: Little, Brown & Company, 1945.

Adulthood and Old Age

3

A chievements and responsibilities both increase as life advances. Our twenties and thirties are often thought of as our prime, our forties and fifties as the time to enjoy the fruits of our labors, our sixties and seventies as our declining years.

The facts, however, do not always fit this simple formula. Some people make their greatest achievements in their teens and early twenties, some fail to do much until their forties or fifties, some never enjoy the fruits of their labors, and some seem to keep going strong into their eighties.

Each person's life is unique, and yet there are common experiences that most of us share. Establishing a marriage or some form of lasting relationship, raising a family, and developing a career are enterprises that engage most people for much of their adult lives.

While we will dwell, in this chapter, on the problems adults have to handle, we do not consider adulthood mainly a time of hardship and struggle. From our personal experience as well as our observation of relatives, friends, and clients, we believe that the years of maturity can be quite as enjoyable as the days of youth.

In any case, enjoyment is not the only criterion of the quality of life. Personal accomplishment, contribution to the welfare of others, and the meaningfulness of one's experiences and efforts are certainly important too. In assessing adulthood and old age, we should try to keep all of these factors in mind.

Early Adulthood

Without any doubt, the most important decisions made by most young adults are their choices of a career and of a marriage partner. In many cases, these choices shape the adult's entire life.

The work one chooses to do and the person one chooses to marry or live with are determined in large part by one's personal abilities and needs. In turn, the work and the partner one has chosen play a large part in determining the kind of person one is to become.

Careers and life styles

A career represents much more than the learning of certain skills and the performance of certain duties. It represents an entire way of living. The physician, the attorney, the plumber, the teacher: each associates with others in the same line of work and shares the habits, values, and viewpoints that are customary in that field. Salespeople, for example, learn the art of persuasion—they learn to convince people to buy what they have to sell. This trait tends to carry over into their personal relationships. Artists, in contrast, learn to struggle with the problems of communicating subtle feelings and inspiring esthetic pleasure. They learn to value creativity more than competence, originality more than conventionality. These traits may be carried over into their social lives as well.

It is often the case that people take up an occupation because they feel attracted to its lifestyle. In the practice of that occupation, the lifestyle is reinforced until it becomes part and parcel of the person's being. It is not without reason that, allowing for wide variations, we expect a schoolteacher to exhibit certain traits, a mechanic to exhibit different traits, an actor, a politician, and a psychologist each to exhibit traits related to his or her profession. There are many individual differences, of course, within any given field of work. Every single individual, in fact, is in some important respects unique. Yet it cannot be denied that the work one does shapes one's outlook and behavior in various ways.

An amusing observation along this line was made a few years ago at a meeting of the American Psychological Association. It was in 1970, when beards were becoming popular among intellectuals, liberals, and those who fancied themselves part of the vanguard of social change. An informal tally at the meeting, which was attended by thousands of psychologists, indicated that close to eighty percent of the males were sporting some kind of facial hair.

More meaningful, perhaps, is the fact that psychologists by and large tend to share certain political views, as do the members of other professions. Physicians, for instance, are notably conservative, while psychologists and other social scientists are notably liberal.

Marriage and its consequences

The young adult's choice of a marriage partner may be even more significant than the choice of a career. In previous historical eras, marriages were arranged by families and men chose wives who seemed capable of fulfilling certain domestic duties. In contrast, most people today believe that love should be the thing that brings husband and wife together. There is no evidence, however, that marriages based on love are any happier or more successful in the long run than were marriages made for less romantic reasons. It is difficult for most of us to accept this fact. Brought up, as we were, in the unquestioned belief that "love makes the world go round," we find it hard to credit other reasons for people choosing to live together. Of course, in those old-fashioned marriages that did survive and prosper, the marriage partners came to care deeply for one another. We may conclude, therefore, that love is not by any means unimportant in marriage, but that being "in love" or **infatuated** is not a necessary precondition to making a successful union.

infatuation
the state of being carried away by unreasoning passion or attraction

The experience of "falling in love" is a highly unpredictable phenomenon. It seems to be directed by unconscious needs and the people involved are frequently blind to the drives that drew them together. Though the principals may hate to admit it, many cases of infatuation are based on one or both partners' need to get away from home, to defy parental values, to replace mother or father with someone very similar or distinctly different, or to balance out a one-sided personality by relating closely to someone with opposite traits.

It is common, for instance, for a shy young man to fall in love with a self-assured young woman or for a prudish girl to be fascinated by a loose-living swinger. A single trait rarely causes people to fall in love. However, in combination with other traits—a certain set of physical characteristics, a relative age range, and possibly some racial or religious qualifications—psychological factors such as those we have mentioned are frequently the deciding items in bringing about a marriage.

Jane W., a quiet-spoken girl from a rural community, went away from home to a large Midwestern university. She had often felt bored and restless in her home town, yet she had formed no conscious intention to move away for good. While at college, however, she fell in love with a boy from the big city. His personality and way of living were tremendously exciting to her. They seemed to offer everything that she had wanted for years. Despite her parents' objections, she married him and tried to adopt his style of life.

The fact that a marriage has been made on the basis of unconscious needs does not mean that it is necessarily unsound. To the contrary, the union may prove to be precisely the thing that can help both husband and wife resolve their problems. In fortunate cases, at least, the experiences of sharing a life together and of being vitally concerned about one another's welfare may foster emotional maturity in both of the partners.

Many times, unfortunately, this happy state of affairs does not materialize. Infatuated lovers become disillusioned by the experience of living together day in and day out. They discover irritating traits in each other of which they were unaware. Her admirable self-assurance begins to look like self-centered conceit; his attractive humility begins to resemble dependent weakness. As natural differences become more pronounced, a power struggle begins. Each partner attempts to convince or manipulate the other to conduct their mutual affairs according to his or her preferences. If husband and wife do not learn to compromise their conflicting desires, if they cannot tolerate each other's differences, the marriage which began so joyously deteriorates into resentment and bickering or ends in divorce.

Many people consult psychologists, psychiatrists, or marriage counselors in their attempts to straighten out marital relationships that seem to be going wrong. These professionals report that, in almost every case, a communication problem has arisen between husband and wife. The marriage partners do not speak openly to one another, do not reveal their true feelings, or, if they do, are not received in the manner intended. Each partner misinterprets what he or she hears, for each has an interest in maintaining a self-protective view of the relationship. Accordingly, one of the primary tasks of the counselor is to help reestablish clearer lines of communication between the partners.

That, in itself, is rarely a complete solution. Deeper problems may exist which need to be aired and clarified. It is notable that in many (though not all) cases of marital discord, sexual difficulties are involved. This does not mean that sex is necessarily the cause of all the trouble. Yet the husband's and wife's ability to find mutual satisfaction in their intimacy is a sensitive indicator of their ability to find happiness with one another.

The raising of children, too, is frequently a source of discord between marriage partners. No event is more likely to evoke deep feelings of bliss than the birth of a child, yet no challenge is more likely to produce anxiety and provoke heated conflict than the raising of that child. In becoming parents, men and women commonly feel that they have fulfilled a crucial part of their role in life. Nothing, in addition, is more gratifying than the opportunity to guide and protect one's children while they are growing up. At the same time, mothers and fathers are likely to project their own problems onto their youngsters. A son may remind a father of his own father's indifference. A daughter may revive a mother's jealousy toward her own younger sister. The child may be used by either parent as a substitute provider of the love they are not getting from each other. In other words, the arrival of children becomes a mixed blessing: an agent of both joy and dissension in the marriage.

What sometimes happens when marriages go wrong is that one of the members of the family becomes the *identified patient*. In these cases, everyone in the family, including the identified patient, agrees that he or she is the cause of all the unhappiness in the home. While it well may be that this person has, or takes on, patterns of behavior that are disruptive to the family harmony, there is also a tendency to use the person as a scapegoat, blaming him or her for more than is his or her share.

scapegoat
a person who is made to bear the blame for others' mistakes

A new approach to these problems has come to be known as *family therapy*. In contrast to more traditional forms of therapy which generally focus on a single individual, family therapy takes the rela-

tionships within the home as its main object of study. The family is considered as a system and interviewed as a group. All members are invited—parents, children, and even grandparents if they are living in the home. The therapist does not attempt to expose any single individual's personality problems but concentrates on what is wrong in the way the members of the family interact. Here is an excerpt from an actual session. (The therapist is interviewing a psychiatric patient, his wife, and his son:

MR. S: I think it is my problem. I'm the one that has the problem.
THERAPIST: Don't be so sure.
MR. S: Well, it seems to be.
THERAPIST: Okay.
MR. S: I'm the one that was in the hospital and everything.
THERAPIST: Yeah, that doesn't still tell me it's your problem. OK, go ahead. What is your problem?
MR. S: Just nervous, upset all the time. . . .
THERAPIST: Do you think that you are the problem?
MR. S: Oh, I kind of think so. I don't know if it's caused by anybody but I'm the one that has the problem.
THERAPIST: Mm. If. Let's follow your line of thinking. If it would be caused by somebody or something outside of yourself, what would you say your problem is?
MR. S: You know, I'd be very surprised.

THERAPIST: Let's think in the family. Who makes you upset?
MR. S: I don't think anybody makes me upset.
THERAPIST: Let me ask your wife.

(At this point he turns to the wife and tries to get her to say what she thinks are the causes of her husband's problems. Then he turns to the son and continues the discussion as follows.)

THERAPIST: Your father said he is the problem and your mother agrees . . . but what are the things that make your father, that irritate him, that make him upset, so he gets pissed off?
SON: I don't know. I don't think it's like anybody puts it on him. It's just that, I don't know.
THERAPIST: I just can't believe that, you know. People are always part of—when people live together, then they irritate each other, you know. I am sure your father irritates you sometimes. And I am sure that your grandfather irritates you sometimes. And you in turn irritate your grandfather and your mother and father. I am sure of that. Am I right?

In this interview, it should be clear, the therapist is attempting to get other members of the family to see how they contribute to the patient's problems.[1]

For the vast majority of people in our culture, advancement in their chosen career, solidification of their marital relationship, and the care and raising of their family are the primary undertakings of the years between twenty and forty. Each of these tasks is full of problems, some basic to the situation and some created by the individual's own personality. Nevertheless, each may also bring satisfaction to the young adult. A challenging job, a secure, loving marriage, and the pleasure of helping one's children grow up happily are the factors that make most people feel that their lives are worthwhile.

Middle Age

If we define middle age as the years between forty and sixty, its most significant psychological event is the realization that one's life has assumed its final form. From the age of forty, both men and women begin to become aware of the fact that opportunities for new experiences are lessening. They will have to come to terms, therefore, with whatever they have managed to make of their lives.

It is rather unlikely (though not impossible) that talents which have not been exercised before middle age will then blossom forth to any meaningful extent. People in their forties and fifties may, of course, acquire new and exciting interests, but they are not apt to enter a brand new profession. In all probability, they must decide to make do with whatever line of work they have been engaged in heretofore. Their degree of success, too, may increase in a gradual way, but it is not likely to make amazing leaps.

Mature men and women must also recognize that the possibility of radical improvement in their love lives lessens with every passing year. With good fortune, the quality of their marriage may, like wine, improve with age; as often as not, however, it tends to deteriorate. Small resentments, disappointments, missed opportunities that everyone accumulates over the years wear one's patience thin. The middle-aged husband and wife are quicker to snap at each other or to turn away in defeat than they were ten years earlier.

In an attempt to stem the tide, many people at this time of life decide to get divorced or turn to extramarital affairs. Middle-aged persons are apt to seek relationships with younger partners. A man, in particular, might seek thereby to renew the virility he feels he is losing. In finding new partners to love, middle-aged people may feel they will exercise better judgment than they did when they were inexperienced. The renewal of self-esteem in the discovery that they are still attractive is the primary reason for such behavior.

The search, unfortunately, is not always successful. Life as a divorced person may turn out to be no happier than married life. Extramarital affairs may bring disappointment in their wake. Opportunities, in any case, are not unlimited, so sooner or later we all must accept the fact that we have had our chances and have made more or less what we could of them.

While this seems a dismal prospect, it is not entirely so. Easing up on the restless quest for more and more success, giving up the ambition to become somehow better than we are, can bring a great sense of relief and relaxation. A significant accomplishment of middle age can be a clear-eyed acceptance of oneself without unrealistic dreams of glory.

An equally significant achievement can be the self-esteem one gets from the fact that one has met life's challenges and done as well as possible. Having completed his or her education, married, raised a family, made a living, acquired specific skills and knowledge, and contributed to the community, the middle-aged person can legitimately feel the satisfaction of a job well done.

In addition, there is the possibility of achieving what Erik Erikson calls "the sense of integrity." A contented awareness of one's own particular style of being, combined with the philosophical detachment that allows one to respect other styles, is another reward of the middle years.

The man or woman who determines to make the most of what he or she already is and to quit grieving over what he or she has never managed to become may begin to enjoy life more fully than ever before. The excitement and vigor of youth may be gone, but the peaceful self-assurance that comes with experience can take over.

Besides, life offers many pleasures to young and old alike: the ever-present joys of an evening stroll or a morning run, of flowers and trees and the change of seasons, of tasty food and pleasant companionship, of laughter and music and movies and art. So, despite its difficulties, middle age can be a time of enjoyment too.

The problematical aspects of this time must still be contended with, however. Among them is the increasing awareness of physical deterioration. Both men and women tend to lose their youthful figures, wrinkles appear, hair begins to turn gray, and—much more frightening—the incidence of heart attacks, cancer, diabetes, and other serious illnesses mounts. In their forties and fifties, almost all human beings must learn to live with the knowledge that their days of perfect health are on the wane.

During the same period, most parents must come to grips with the fact that their children are growing up and leaving them. While in some ways the lessening of responsibility for the children's welfare can come as welcome relief, it is extremely difficult for many people to give up the role they have been playing for the last two decades. Allowing one's children to lead their own lives and to make their own mistakes and learning that, in their years of establishing themselves, they may show little consideration for their parents' feelings are tasks for which many parents are unprepared.

Letting go of the children without bitterness or regret means reestablishing an old way of life between the husband and wife or finding new involvements to replace the gratifications of parenthood. If mother and father still love each other deeply and if they share common interests and activities, this stage in their lives can become, not a time of loss, but a time of rebirth. If their caring for each other has worn thin, however, it can force them to face the bleakness of a marriage that has been held together by the children.

In view of these changes and challenges, it is not surprising that many people in their middle years suffer periods of depression and anxiety. The shifts that are demanded in one's basic pattern of living and in one's concept of oneself seem, at times, too much to accept. Compounded, as they often are, by menopause in women, by the loneliness which occurs when the children have left, by the awareness in the man who has worked all his life that his productive years are numbered, they can give rise to thoughts of suicide. It is all the more remarkable, therefore, that most people have the strength to weather these storms and learn to enjoy their altered circumstances.

Most psychologists and psychiatrists would be unwilling to explain the illnesses of middle age simply as physical deterioration. They correctly point out that both environmental and psychological factors play a part in the quality of an individual's health: if one's life is unsettled and traumatic, rather than calm and fulfilled, the likelihood of illness increases. The following two studies appear to verify this point of view.

In the first, Thomas Holmes assigned quantitative values to stressful occurrences of adulthood. The greater the amount of stress, the larger the number. He called these measures Life Change Units (LCU) and predicted that individuals who received scores of more than 300 LCUs would, very possibly, develop a major illness in the next two years.[2] This is a portion of his scale.

40

Events	Scale of Impact	Events	Scale of Impact
Death of spouse	100	Sex difficulties	39
Divorce	73	Gain of new family member	39
Marital separation	65	Business readjustment	39
Jail term	63	Change in financial state	38
Death of a close family member	63	Death of close friend	37
Personal injury or illness	53	Change to different line of work	36
Marriage	50	Change in number of	
Fired at work	47	arguments with spouse	35
Marital reconciliation	45	Mortgage over $10,000	31
Retirement	45	Foreclosure of mortgage or loan	30
Change in health of family member	44	Change in responsibilities	29
Pregnancy	40		

In the second study, a similar scale was constructed at the University of Washington School of Medicine and administered to nearly 400 subjects. Holmes' predictions were borne out, for thirty-seven percent of those subjects with moderate crisis scale scores suffered a major health change and seventy percent of those with high crisis scores suffered a major health change.[3]

Old Age

If the physical deterioration that began, in subtle ways, in their forties and fifties was a cause of concern to most people, its progressive worsening throughout their sixties and seventies can become a daily preoccupation. Not only do the elderly man and woman have to accept a loss of attractiveness, not only do they have to accept a loss of vitality—they must accept, as well, the increasing probability of death.

True, they may survive in relative health into their eighties, but most old people find that more and more of their time is spent consulting doctors. If we add to this the fact that, with every passing year, acquaintances, friends, and relatives take ill and die, the prospects begin to seem grim indeed.

In our society, unfortunately, death has been treated as a "no-no." Although we all know it is the inevitable end to everyone's life, we avoid talking about it, especially in the presence of sick and elderly people. We act as though the mere mention of the event might make it more likely to happen. We think it appropriate to reassure people that they are going to go on living even when we know they have a fatal disease. As a result, many stricken persons endure long periods of confusion and anxiety while those who are closest to them feed them on false hopes in the belief that they are thereby easing their burden.

We also tend to draw away from close contact with dying persons, preferring to surround them with medical apparatus and treat them as physical bodies rather than as people whose feelings need to be considered. This attitude has been called into question by physicians and psychologists who claim that dying people, when told the truth and offered warmth and understanding by relatives, friends, and doctors, often attain an attitude of acceptance that allows them to die in peace and dignity.

Elisabeth Kübler-Ross, a psychiatrist who has devoted many years to the study and treatment of dying patients, has described five psychological stages they go through after they learn they cannot be cured:

1) denial of the seriousness of their condition;

2) anger at God, fate, or whomever they deem responsible;

3) bargaining about what they will do if they are allowed to live;

4) depression and loss of interest in things around them;

5) acceptance of their approaching death.

As Kübler-Ross has pointed out, "those [who get close to dying persons] will discover that it can be a mutually gratifying experience; they will learn much about the human mind . . . and will emerge enriched and perhaps with fewer anxieties about their own finality."[4]

What we have presented in this chapter is the common, long-standing view of adulthood and old age. There has never been much debate or even much interest in these stages of life. Developmental psychologists, almost unanimously, have focused on the very early years of growth. All this, however, is beginning to change. Major universities are studying the psychology and sociology of aging. *Gerontology,* as it is called, has become an area of specialization. It has shed light

The Ethel Percy Andrus Center for the Study of Gerontology at the University of Southern California.

on the heretofore overlooked fact that we tend to program the quality of our later years without realizing we are doing so. By alienating friends and family, neglecting to broaden their interests, and centering their lives around their occupation, some people stack the cards in favor of a lonely old age. Those who plan for their retirement, however—not just financially but also socially and emotionally—are more likely to enjoy their declining years. Consequently, more and more businesses are employing preretirement counselors to help individuals deal with this time of life.

A few generations ago, it was common for aging grandparents to be contained within the bosom of the family. They enjoyed the feeling that they belonged, that they still had a place in the environment with which they were familiar. It has become common practice today for the old to live in retirement communities, convalescent hospitals, and other sorts of residences. As a consequence, gerontologists have attempted to educate the people who run these places to help the residents find meaningful activities.

A poet, Kenneth Koch, has taught very old people in nursing homes to write poetry. In many cases, these people were uneducated and unsophisticated. Koch gave them simple objects—a seashell or a flower—and asked them to write down their feelings and memories. The results were astonishing. With little training or prodding, they created beautiful and moving poems.[5]

> Writing poems reminds me of my grandmother
> She used to tell me things but I've forgotten what she told me
> She told me about the bumblebees
> She said they wouldn't sting me

Writing poems reminds me of the bumblebees playing around and making perfume.
Nadya Catalfano (age 94)

Motherless, fatherless, sisterless,
All gone and no more
I felt so lonely
Yet within me I felt a joy of joyfulness
When I read poems relating to things around me
Like the sun in the skies
It gives me hope for the future.
Mary Zahorjko (age 94)

Adult Developmental Stages

Finally, now that both ends of the life cycle have been studied, attention is being focused on the middle years. In a book called *The Seasons of a Man's Life*, Daniel J. Levinson suggests that we can define adult stages of development as clearly as we can those of childhood. After conducting long-term studies of forty men (ten executives, ten biologists, ten factory workers, ten novelists), he defines the developmental stages of adulthood as follows.

Early Adult Transition (ages 17–22): a time to terminate preadulthood and begin early adulthood, to end or modify relationships and form an initial adult identity.

Entering the Adult World (ages 22–28): the novice adult stage, including **43** choices in occupation and marriage. The two essential tasks of this stage are exploration of options for adult living and creating a stable life structure.

Age Thirty Transition (28–33): the years in which to correct any errors in the initial structure of adulthood. In many cases, this is a time of stress and crisis.

Settling Down (33–40): this is the culmination of early adulthood. It includes one's establishment of a place in society within the realms of occupation and family and one's striving for advancement.

Mid-Life Transition (40–45): a time to reexamine one's life and answer basic questions such as, What have I done with my life? What is it I truly want?

Early Middle Adulthood (45–50): during this period the individual acts on the decisions made during the reappraisal period.

Age Fifty Transition (50–55): essentially a repeat of the age thirty transition, involving a correcting of errors in the way one has so far structured one's life.[6]

Whether these stages are really as clearcut as Levinson suggests may be open to question. To the authors of this text, at least, he seems to be making finer distinctions than one can readily observe. Nevertheless, his work represents an attempt to view adulthood as a time of development, too. It suggests the interesting possibility that there is more regularity in the stages of life we all pass through than had formerly been recognized.

Summary

This chapter has surveyed adulthood and old age, highlighting such issues as one's choice of occupation and marriage partner, the problems that may arise in the course of a marriage and the raising of a family, accepting the limitations that come with advancing years, enjoying the fruits of one's labors, coping with illness, infirmity, and approaching death, and achieving a sense of meaningfulness in one's life as a whole.

Class Projects
1. Compare two or three people who practice the same occupation. Try to define the characteristics they share in common and the characteristics that are unique to each person. Make the same sort of comparison with people who practice dissimilar occupations. Do you find that those in the same occupation are more alike? If so, how would you explain it?

44

2. Have a group of students portray three generations of one family. Let there be a grandmother, a grandfather, a mother, a father, and several children. Improvise a scene built around a crisis situation, such as one of the children having been arrested for vandalism or one of the grandparents being sent away to a home for the elderly. Let each person play his or her role as realistically as possible and see if the scene throws light on the needs, perceptions, and values of people at different stages of life.

3. Can you visualize a situation in today's world in which the presence of elderly grandparents would be an enrichment rather than a burden on a family's way of life? What do you think you could learn from people forty to fifty years older than you? What do you think they could learn from you?

References

1. SALVADOR MINUCHIN, *Families and Family Therapy* (Cambridge, Mass.: Harvard University Press, 1974).
2. T. S. HOLMES and T. H. HOLMES, "Short-term Intrusions into the Life-Style Routine," *Journal of Psychosomatic Research*, 1970, *14*, pp. 121-132.
3. R. H. RAHE, J. D. McKEAN and R. J. ARTHUR, "A Longitudinal Study of Life Change and Illness Patterns," *Journal of Psychosomatic Research*, 1967, *10*, pp. 355-366.
4. ELISABETH KÜBLER-ROSS, *On Death and Dying* (New York: Macmillan, 1969).
5. KENNETH KOCH, *I Never Told Anybody* (New York: Random House, 1977).
6. DANIEL LEVINSON, *The Seasons of a Man's Life* (New York: Knopf, 1978).

Suggested Readings

1. BALTES, P. B. and SCHAIE, K. W. "Aging and I. Q.: Myth of the Twilight Years," *Psychology Today*, 1974, *7*, pp. 35-50.
2. COMFORT, A. *Aging: The Biology of Senescence.* New York: Holt, Rinehart & Winston, 1964.
3. Ibid. *A Good Age.* New York: Crown, 1976.
4. LIDZ, THEODORE. *The Person.* New York: Basic Books, 1968.
5. SHEEHY, GAIL. *Passages.* New York: Dutton, 1976.
6. TURNER, JEFFREY S. and HELMS, DONALD B. *Life Span Development.* Philadelphia: Saunders, 1979.

Theories of Personality

4

**P**ersonality means something like charm to the average man or woman. To "have personality" is to have an attractive style, to be lively and interesting. To psychologists, however, personality refers to all the attitudes, emotions, interests, thoughts, and behavior that typify a person's way of being. It may be attractive, unusual, or commonplace. It simply means the kind of person one is.

The kind of person one is, however, is far from a simple matter. Although we are apt to sum each other up, at times, as "wonderful," "horrible," "kind," "mean," "generous," "tight," "brilliant," "stupid," and so on, it should be obvious that no one's personality can be defined in a word or two. Every individual possesses a complex combination of qualities, and even that combination may vary from time to time.

What makes us become the kinds of people we are? What are the best ways to describe and explain a single person's personality or personality in general? Sigmund Freud, C. G. Jung, Gordon Allport, B. F. Skinner, Carl Rogers, and Eric Berne are only a few of the notable psychologists who have attempted to answer these questions. Even we, the authors of this text, have tried our hands at it. Despite these varied efforts, no system explains personality completely, so there is plenty of room for future psychologists to contribute new ideas.

In this chapter, we will survey the major theories put forth by the people mentioned above. We will also provide exercises through which you can apply these theories to your own personality. If the students in your class should have divided opinions on which of the theories makes the most sense, or on whether they make any sense at all, don't be surprised. That's the way it is among psychologists, too.

The Basic Questions

How can we best describe a person's personality? How much of it is inborn, how much is learned? Is personality affected by one's sex? How important are the first few years of life in determining one's personality? Can an adult's personality be changed and, if so, how?

These are the basic questions for which psychologists are still seeking answers. There is one more question; it is perhaps the most important, certainly the most difficult question of all. It is hinted at in Gordon Allport's statement, "Personality is what a man *really* is." This statement raises the issue, "Of what does our *true self* consist?"

Many theories attempt to describe personality clearly and take a stand on how much of it is inborn, how much learned. Some claim it is affected by one's sex, while others disagree. Some emphasize the importance of the first few years of life, while others downplay it. Some theories address themselves to the problem of changing personality traits, while others ignore it. A few of them even take on the difficult question of our "true self." Let us review the major theories to see what they tell us.

Freud's Psychoanalytic Theory

Sigmund Freud, a Viennese psychiatrist who revolutionized the treatment of emotional and mental disorders at the beginning of this century, believed that our personalities are shaped by our early childhood experiences. By the age of five, he said, our basic characteristics have been formed. Whatever we become from that time on is rooted in the soil of those early years of life.

motivation

the drives or feelings that make us do what we do

In addition, Freud was convinced that much of our **motivation** is unconscious. We do not know what makes us act and feel in some of the ways we do, he argued, for we cannot admit what we are really like. Consider a boy who has a lot of resentment against his father. The boy may claim that his feelings are due to the fact that his father never paid much attention to him or to the fact that they always had different outlooks on life. Freud would have objected that these are superficial reasons and that the real source of the boy's resentment may be his rivalry with his father for his mother's love.

These views are clearly controversial. In Freud's time, many people were horrified at what he had to say. Even today, some psychologists disagree with him and some accept only part of his teachings. Many, however, believe his ideas were brilliant.

Id, ego, superego

According to Freud, personality may be best described as an interaction of three systems of feeling and thought. The *id* is the system with which

Sigmund Freud.

we are born; it consists entirely of pleasure-seeking drives. Corresponding to what we commonly call instincts, the id part of our nature simply wants to feel good. It cares nothing for other people's needs or for long-range goals. What it desires is immediate gratification. Sexual drives, aggressive impulses, laziness, greediness, and gluttony all spring from the id. A person who was entirely under the control of his or her id would do nothing but eat, sleep, have sex, and take advantage of other people.

In opposition to the id stands the *superego*. Corresponding to what we call conscience, the superego is a system of dos and don'ts. It is entirely concerned with duties and obligations, with doing right and avoiding wrong. We acquire our superego from the teaching and example of our parents and other authority figures. Once it becomes a part of us, it tries to force us to be considerate, moral, and future oriented. A person who was entirely under the control of his or her superego would do nothing but good deeds from morning to night.

Since the id and the superego are in conflict with each other, there develops in each of us an *ego* whose job it is to make peace between them. Corresponding to what we call reason, the ego represents our ability to harmonize demands from the other parts of our personality and bring them in line with our reality situation. When you wake on a schoolday morning, for instance, your id may entice you to sink back into sweet sleep. Your superego may prompt you to leap out of bed and get right to work. Your ego attempts to take stock of the situation, decides what has to be done and what can be put off for awhile, and eases you awake in a comfortable but responsible manner.

The cultivation of a strong ego, according to Freud, is the goal of personality development. This does not mean that the ego must completely dominate the id and superego. All parts of the personality are necessary to a mature, well-rounded individual. The ego, however, must become the main system, for Freud believed that most personality problems arise from the domination of either the id or the superego.[1]

Three roommates, Carol, Barbara, and Jan, were invited to a party on a Sunday night. Each of them had an early class the next morning, but they agreed to go to the party for a little while. They arrived around 8:00 PM.

Carol, the most social of the three, immediately began drinking and dancing and flirting with several of the fellows. Barbara had a glass of wine and sat down to talk to an old friend. Jan refused to drink anything but water because she was on a diet, worried about the drive home, and sat in a corner thinking about what she would have to do at school the next day.

By 9:30, Carol was rather high. Jan, on the other hand, was ready to leave. She was disgusted with Carol's behavior, saying it was "immature." Carol, in turn, thought Jan was "a pain." The two of them began to argue, then turned to Barbara to see what she wanted to do. Barbara suggested they stay a little longer, pointing out that even with the drive home they could still be in bed before 11:00. She suggested to Carol that she not have any more to drink if she wanted to feel fresh for class the next morning and tried to get Jan interested in talking to some of her friends.

Each of these women appears to be controlled by a different part of her personality: Carol by her id, Jan by her superego, and Barbara by her ego. While the differences between people are not usually so clear-cut, if you observe yourself and your friends very closely you may be able to discern the dominance of the id, the ego, or the superego in certain individuals.

Defense mechanisms

In an attempt to ward off anxiety, said Freud, our egos resort to a number of defense mechanisms. They range from relatively childish to relatively mature operations of the mind, but they all share the function of protecting us from discomfort.

Repression is the most common defense of all. By repression, Freud meant our tendency to forget unpleasant events and unacceptable impulses. When we think, feel, or experience something that upsets us, we automatically try to block it out of our minds. We cannot always do this successfully, and the more mature we are the less we try to do it, but all of us do it from time to time.

Most people deny that they repress very much. Yet many of us have only a hazy memory of our childhood and some of us cannot remember what we did, thought, and felt a few weeks ago. This suggests that repression is common. The fond memories with which we recall the past, the popular idea of "the good old days," also results from repression. The irritations, frustrations, and disappointments that were part of the past have been conveniently forgotten, leaving only a misty memory of the pleasant things we enjoyed.

Repression is also in evidence when we forget the name of a person we know or fail to remember an important appointment (say a visit to the dentist). It can frequently be shown that, deep down, we really wished to forget that person or that appointment because we associated them with something unpleasant.

When repression fails, our egos make use of other defenses. Outright *denial* is commonly used by very young children. In the face of evidence that they did or said something unacceptable, they simply deny it. "I didn't start the fight, he did" and "I didn't break the vase. It fell by itself" are examples of denial. It differs from lying only in that people who use it as a defense believe that what they are saying is true.

A slightly more sophisticated form of evasion is known as *avoidance*. Here the person neither represses nor denies the upsetting topic, but simply avoids thinking about it. People who constantly change the subject when a conversation touches on tender feelings and people who divert themselves by running around or watching television when they have important things to do are practicing avoidance.

Another common defense is called *regression*. When we are faced with worries and responsibilities, we may regress (that is, go back) to an earlier state of mind in which we felt more secure and carefree. School-age children sometimes regress to thumb-sucking. Adults may regress to adolescent behavior when they feel the demands of their lives are too much to accept. We all know the comfort of cuddling up to a warm, protective mother-figure, someone whose soothing attitude encourages us to believe that everything will be all right no matter how troubled we may be. Our attraction to such a person is a regressive tendency, for it represents an attempt to recapture the bliss of infancy.

A more complicated move is the defense known as *reaction formation*. When people engage in this maneuver, they make themselves believe they feel the very opposite of what they really feel. "I don't love him; I hate him"—the protest of someone who is too embarrassed to confess their affection—is a reaction formation. So, too, is the reverse—"I don't hate him; I love him"—when the person who says it really feels a lot of resentment but cannot admit it. Another kind of reaction formation may be expressed when a friend of ours enjoys some exceptional good fortune. If we find it unacceptable to envy their success, we may go overboard in gushing about how happy we are for them. In yet another instance, when we feel intimidated or defeated by events in our lives, we may turn our fear into courage, our despair into determination. Strange as it seems, human beings are very capable of these stark reversals. While at times they seem to accomplish nothing but the avoidance of unpleasantness, at other times they help us achieve worthwhile goals.

Rationalization is an excellent example of a defense that ranges from detrimental to helpful. The term refers to our tendency to claim that our feelings are always reasonable. Rather than confess that we love or hate certain people or activities for reasons we do not understand or would rather not admit, we make up explanations to prove to ourselves that our emotions are justified. "I resent her because she's such a selfish person" is a rationalization if the truth would be "I resent her because I am not as pretty as she is." On the other hand, consider a statement such as "I plan to study psychology because I want to understand human nature." This may be a rationalization of a need to understand oneself, yet it may lead to a productive career.

Projection is another defense that has both beneficial and harmful effects. It refers to our tendency to see in other people feelings and thoughts that are really in ourselves. When we are unable to admit a certain attitude as part of our own mental makeup, we may make ourselves believe that it belongs to those around us. A simple example is the feeling on the part of self-conscious people that everyone is looking at them when the truth is that they themselves are too self-absorbed. Another example is the complaint made by racists that those they don't like are all lazy, lustful, and dishonest. Very often it is the racist himself who is, or would like to be, lazy, lustful, and dishonest.

Creative artists generally project the contents of their minds more richly than other people. Rather than being a problem for them, however, it is an asset in their profession. The Russian writer Dostoevsky, for example, created powerful works of fiction by investing his characters with the conflicting feelings and thoughts that raged within himself. Dostoevsky was both a fervent believer in the teachings of the church and a brilliant skeptic who doubted that God could have created a world so full of injustice and suffering. By having the heroes and heroines of his novels struggle with this conflict, he created books of deep significance.[2]

The act of transforming personal feelings into socially valuable behavior is called *sublimation*. Artists, scientists, politicians, entertainers, and other prominent groups, according to Freud, are driven to pursue their careers by a need to sublimate their unconscious impulses. Entertainers, for instance, want even more than most of us to be the center of attention. In order to satisfy this desire in a socially acceptable way, they are drawn to the stage. Diplomats and politicians, similarly, have an intense desire for power. They wish more than anything to control the world and to make others live according to their ideas. In its naked form such a wish is unacceptable, so they sublimate it into the pursuit of **53** public office.

The defense mechanisms we have been discussing play important parts in our personalities. In their most negative form, they allow us to deceive ourselves about our true feelings and thoughts. Less negatively, they enable us to accept ourselves by hiding our raw impulses. Finally, in their most positive form, they help us to transform purely selfish, immature emotions into more mature, humanitarian interests.

The next time you feel threatened by an upsetting event, try to detect the defenses you resort to in order to make yourself feel better. They may be difficult to recognize because they normally occur unconsciously. You can become more aware of them, however, in the following way. Make a list of the defenses described above—repression, de- nial, avoidance, regression, reaction formation, rationalization, projection, and sublimation—with an explanation in your own words of what each one is. Then check this list when you know you have been coping with some unpleasant event and see if you can recall using one or more of them to reduce your discomfort.

Jung's Personality Types

Carl Gustav Jung was a follower of Freud who broke away in 1911 to form his own school of analysis. A brilliant thinker, he produced a deep and unusual theory of personality. Some of his ideas are so widely accepted that they have become part of our everyday language. Others are little understood, even by psychologists.

Introversion and extraversion

Perhaps the most popular terms Jung ever invented were *introvert* and *extravert.* You may already know that an introvert is a person who prefers to be alone while an extravert is a person who prefers to be sociable. Jung believed that these were natural, inborn types of personality organization, although he made it clear that no one is entirely one way or the other. The differences among us are a matter of degree, yet all human beings tend to move more or less in one of these two directions. Either we seek opportunities to mingle with other people or we shun social contacts in favor of meditation and solitary activities.

The labels introvert and extravert are widely accepted in this country. Americans' evaluation of them is different from Jung's, however. We seem to believe that extraversion is the healthier form of personality organization, whereas Jung took pains to show that both extraversion and introversion have their good and bad points. Extraverts may cultivate more human relationships, but their manner of relating is more superficial. Introverts may cultivate a more intimate knowledge of themselves, but their ability to sustain interest in other people is limited.

One of the goals of personality development, according to Jung, is to cultivate those characteristics that are submerged in us. The natural introvert needs to learn how to relate to a wide variety of people and to be comfortable in social gatherings; the natural extravert needs to learn to enjoy solitude and contemplation. These goals are easy to formulate but difficult to pursue. Our inclination is to do what comes easiest to us. If we wish to become mature, however, we need to practice what comes hardest.[3]

The four functions

A less well-known aspect of Jung's personality theory holds that there are four psychological functions we all can rely upon to orient ourselves in the world. *Thinking, feeling, sensation,* and *intuition* are the terms Jung used to describe these functions. By thinking, he meant reliance on our intellect, the use of our logic or reason to figure things out. By feeling, he meant reliance on our emotions, the experience and expression of love, anger, fear, envy, joy, despair, and all the other sentiments that life evokes. By sensation, he meant reliance on the data that is fed to us by our senses, all the things we see, hear, smell, touch, and taste. By intuition, he meant reliance on our capacity to grasp hidden implications, our ability to dig out the meaning and significance of events. According to Jung, all four of these functions are available to every one of us, but each of us tends to rely mainly on only one or two.

Each of us, therefore, is either a thinking type, a feeling type, a sensation type, or an intuitive type, depending on which function dominates our personality. Carrying the analysis a step further, we may be an intuitive-thinking type, an intuitive-feeling type, a thinking-sensation type, and so on, depending on which two functions we use most of all. Few people, says Jung, cultivate three of their functions to any great extent, and fewer still cultivate all four. The latter, however, is one of the goals of personality development. A mature individual, from the Jungian point of view, would be fully capable of thinking clearly, feeling deeply, responding to all the stimuli in his or her environment, and grasping the implicit meaning of events.

In a common situation—say, reporting on a highway accident—the thinking type of personality would focus on the sequence of events. He or she would sketch it out logically, perhaps draw a plan of the way the cars were headed, and figure out the objective causes of the accident. The feeling type would dwell on the shock and pain the victims must have suffered and would respond with sympathy to those who were hurt and anger to those responsible. The sensation type would describe in great detail the makes and colors of the cars, the ages and appearances of the people involved, possibly even the conditions of the highway and the prevailing weather. The intuitive type, finally, would be most intrigued by the significance and implications of the event. He or she would speculate on why these particular cars were destined to smash up at just this particular time and what such an accident means about the quality of life in our society.

Can you tell which of the above reactions would most likely be your main one? If so, you may get an inkling of your personality type according to Jung. You may also try to analyze yourself in this context by asking which of the four functions you usually rely on. Is your first reaction to events generally cool and logical or excited and emotional? Are you more interested in all the details of something or in its deeper meaning? If you can answer these questions, you can deduce that, to become more mature, one of the things you will need to do will be to cultivate the functions you normally underplay.

There are many deeper aspects to both Freud's and Jung's personality theories, but it would take too much space to go into them here. If you wish to learn more about them, please refer to the readings suggested at the end of this chapter.

Allport's Psychology of the Individual

A distinguished American psychologist, Gordon Allport, wrote several books on personality. He emphasized the uniqueness of the individual and argued that theories of personality types, however clever, fail to do justice to our individuality. We must study each person's distinctiveness, he taught, if we wish to understand what he or she is really like.

neurotic

people who suffer from emotional problems that interfere with their ability to lead productive, happy lives

Allport believed that normal personalities are very different from **neurotic** and **psychotic** personalities. Neurotics and psychotics, he said, are still highly influenced by their childhood, while the normal man or woman has outgrown the past and is firmly rooted in the present. We understand normal people better by learning what they think and feel today and what they hope to achieve tomorrow than we do by delving back into their past.

psychotic

people who suffer severe mental disorders involving strange, bizarre ideas and morbid symptoms

At the same time, Allport taught, we must recognize that in the process of growing up each person develops a set of *traits* that characterizes his or her personality. He distinguished three different classes of traits whose interaction makes us the kinds of people we are. A *cardinal trait* is an all-encompassing tendency to behave in a certain way. Not everybody develops one, but those who do guide all their activities in accordance with it. Hitler and other dictators were ruled by the cardinal trait of powerseeking, while Freud's cardinal trait was acquiring insight. *Central traits* are less overwhelming than cardinal traits, but in clusters of five to ten they determine most people's personalities. The pursuit of fame and money combined with a high regard for physical beauty and being the center of attention, plus some insensitivity toward other people's feelings constitute the central traits of certain movie stars. Kindness, generosity, and self-denial, in combination with religiousness, seriousness, and a high regard for hard work might be the central traits of some priests and nuns. *Secondary traits* like fear of the dark, enjoyment of classical music, and so on are less important, but they fill out the details of our individuality. When we have defined all the central and secondary traits a person possesses, said Allport, we have described his or her personality.

56

Here is a list of the central and secondary traits of one of the authors of this book. See if they give you a clear idea of the kind of person he is.

Central traits: intellectual; mild mannered; hard working; humorous; caring; idealistic; anxious to please; somewhat creative; pretends to be modest but really has a high opinion of himself.

Secondary traits: enjoys writing, teaching, reading, and competitive sports; more sociable than solitary; domestic, a family man; dislikes being tough with others, refusing their requests or ordering them to do things they don't want to do; cannot tolerate fanaticism of any sort.

A final item in Allport's theory is what he called *functional autonomy.* A given form of behavior, he insisted, can become functionally autonomous—that is, an end in itself—in spite of the fact that it was originally begun for another reason. A good example is cigarette smoking. People often begin to smoke as a defiant gesture against their parents or in order to fit in with their peer group, but in time smoking may become a pleasure in itself. The same is true of healthier habits. A person may begin to read a lot in order to get good grades, but in time he or she may become fond of reading for the enjoyment and knowledge it gives.

This idea has important implications. On the one hand, it suggests that we do not have to look for hidden motives in adult behavior. The reason we engage in an activity may be part of the activity itself. On the other hand, it indicates that, rather than being controlled by a small number of drives like hunger, sex, aggression, and status seeking, we develop a great variety of appetites and interests, each of which is important in its own right.

The mature person, according to Allport, is not primarily self-centered or mainly interested in immediate gratification. He or she is involved in planning for the future and doing things for other people. Besides that, he or she has a great deal of insight, a rich sense of humor, and a unifying philosophy of life. The fully developed personality, from his point of view, is the very opposite of a narrow-minded, ignorant, and instinct-dominated creature.[4]

The Behaviorist Position

At least one group of psychologists feels that all this speculation about the structure and development of personality is a waste of time. The behaviorists contend that personality is simply a name for patterns of behavior and, since most behavior follows the principles of learning, psychologists should focus their attention on learning and let it go at that.

B. F. Skinner, the movement's leading spokesman, argues that all behavior is affected by its consequences (that is, reward and punishment or pleasant and unpleasant results). People act as they do because they have been rewarded or punished for acting that way. These reinforcements may be subtle and difficult to locate, but they are always present. A preference for certain foods is due to their having tasted good in the past, a dislike for certain people is due to their having made us feel badly. Even so-called neurotic behavior like a fanatical insistence on cleanliness and orderliness is due to its reinforcing effects: praise for being neat and clean, perhaps, or the pleasure of living in immaculate surroundings. It is unnecessary, says Skinner, to argue internal events like Freud's "unconscious" or Allport's "traits." Human behavior can be adequately explained without resorting to these cloudy, confusing concepts.

Not all behaviorists, however, are as strict as Skinner. John Dollard and Neal Miller, for instance, find it necessary to argue the existence of primary drives (i.e., internal stimuli of great strength and persistence) impelling us to act. Such drives, they admit, are the original sources of behavior, though they agree with Skinner that the specific ways in which we express them are the result of learning. Thus, hunger is a primary drive impelling us to eat, but exactly what we choose to eat depends on what we have learned tastes good. Our need for attention is also a primary drive, but our choice of people from whom we seek attention depends on the experiences we have had with various kinds of people. Some adolescents, for example, seek attention mainly from adults, while others seek it mainly from their peers. The behaviorist explanation of this difference would base it on past experience; those who have learned that they can get the kind of response they are seeking more readily from adults will tend to move in that direction, while those who have found that they receive more favorable attention from their peers will concentrate their efforts on that source. The emphasis, it should be clear, is still on learning as the main cause of behavior, though Dollard and Miller admit that we have drives with which we were born.

Albert Bandura and Richard Walters also view personality as a set of learned responses, but they expand Skinner's outlook in another way. They focus on the importance of imitation or *modelling* in the development of our personalities. In one experiment, for instance, they had one group of children watch an adult commit aggressive acts on a large doll, while another group watched another adult sit quietly in a room, ignoring the doll. Later, when all the children were mildly frustrated and left alone with the doll, those who had witnessed the aggressive adult were themselves more aggressive, leading the experimenters to believe that the adults had served as models for the children's behavior.[5] Bandura and Walters maintain that much of our behavior can be explained on the basis of our having modelled ourselves after people in our environment.

Fred L. was brought up by very religious parents. The family went to church every Sunday, said a prayer before each meal, and tried in all ways to lead morally upright lives. When Fred went away to college, he came in contact with non-religious people for the first time in his life. Many of his teachers and classmates did not practice any of the religious customs he had grown up with. Still, he had a lot of respect for these people's intelligence, and they in turn respected him. In behavioral

58 terms, Fred received much reinforcement from both his family and his college associates.

After some years of uncertainty, Fred decided to major in religious studies and eventually became a well-known professor of theology. His choice of career, it seems, was based on a compromise between the models of his parents and his teachers.

Rogers' Self Theory

Despite the objections of the behaviorists, many prominent psychologists continue to believe it useful to theorize about the components of personality. Carl Rogers divides our inner self into two main systems: our *organismic self* (the totality of our being) and our *self-concept* (awareness of our being).

In the very young infant, according to Rogers, there is no self-concept. As we develop, however, we begin to form ideas about ourselves, and these ideas include value judgments. We think or feel, "I am good" or "I am bad," "I am a clever boy . . . a pretty girl . . . a stupid child . . . shy . . . funny . . . strong . . . and so on." As soon as we do this, unfortunately, we put ourselves in a state of conflict. Our organismic self enjoys or produces experiences that our self-concept has learned to label undesirable. We are therefore forced to struggle with a universal human dilemma: how to reconcile our self-concept and our organismic self or, in simpler terms, how to accept ourselves as we really are.

actualize
to bring something to fulfillment, as a rose bush does when it produces leaves and flowers

Our organism's motivation, says Rogers, is simply to maintain and **actualize** itself. Like a plant or an animal, it strives to survive, grow, prosper, and fulfill its life cycle. Our self-concept can operate in harmony with it by accepting its needs as justified or oppose it by thinking, "That's not nice, not right, I shouldn't want it or feel it or do it." In Rogers' words, "Psychological adjustment exists when the concept of the self is such that all sensory and visceral experiences of the organism are, or may be, assimilated into a consistent relationship with the concept of the self." To put it more briefly, people are most well-adjusted when they accept themselves most fully.[6]

Eric Berne and T. A. Theory

Since the late 1960s, a branch of psychology known as transactional analysis (T. A. for short) has become very influential both as a form of therapy and as a theory of personality. Created by Eric Berne, its central ideas have spread across the nation and have been adopted not only by psychologists but also by businesspeople and other professionals.

Briefly stated, T. A. theory holds that our personalities are made up of three interacting parts: our *Parent*, our *Child*, and our *Adult*. These parts are known as *ego states*. Our Parent ego state feels and causes us to behave as our mother or father, or whoever raised us, did in the past. Our Child ego state has the same feelings and habits we had when we were very young. Our Adult ego state figures things out realistically and acts in a rational manner. Furthermore, the Parent in us can be a critical voice or a helpful one, while the Child in us can be a set of natural, spontaneous impulses or a conforming, parent-pleasing set of responses. If we were to go to a football game on a night before an important exam, scold ourselves on the way home for whooping it up instead of studying, and wake up early the next morning and manage to prepare ourselves adequately for the test, we would have been behaving first as our Natural Child, second as our Critical Parent, and finally as our Adult.

According to Berne and his followers, our ego states frequently disagree with each other. We often feel that one part of us wants to do one thing while another part of us resists it. The task of developing a healthy personality, they say, is largely the task of getting our Parent, our Child, and our Adult to cooperate, generally under the leadership of our Adult.

Transactional theory includes some other interesting observations as well. It points out, for example, that we often engage in *game-playing* behavior in which our real motives are different from what we pretend they are. Let us say that a group of people are watching television, but one of them doesn't seem to be enjoying it. His neighbor may say to him, apparently with sympathy, "Don't you like the show?" And then, if he admits he doesn't, that person may put him down by adding, "Well, there must be something wrong with you. Everybody else seems to like it." Under the pretense of caring, this person has managed to get in a dig at his or her friend. Berne calls this kind of game, "Now I've Got You." In his popular book, *Games People Play,* he describes and analyzes many interactions of this sort.[7]

Perhaps most important, T. A. theory holds that we all conduct our lives according to a *script* or life plan that our Child adopted when we were very young. As adolescents or adults, we are no longer aware of this plan, but it directs our activities nevertheless. Our script, says Berne, is either a healthy one or an unhealthy one, depending on whether or not we were led to feel as children that we were basically lovable and that other people were essentially trustworthy.

Children who did not acquire these positive feelings often create a script whose basic message is, "It never pays to get close to people." They may then go through life avoiding intimate relationships and always managing to keep others at arm's length. If people become aware of their scripts, however, and determine to change them, they can improve the whole course of their lives.

The teachings of Berne and his followers are among the most popular of all current theories of personality. Psychologists belonging to other schools of thought sometimes criticize T. A. as superficial, but the public appears to find it attractive.

The Mindess–Munford Position

We have observed that many people, when they begin to think about personality, tend to conclude that there is one "best" personality pattern, or perhaps one best pattern for men and another for women. We disagree with this notion, for our experience has convinced us that there are many different ways for both men and women to achieve effective adaptations to their environment and to express their individuality.

Here, for example, are four types of personality organization common to both sexes.

compulsive—neat, prompt, efficient, orderly, controlled, upset by disorganization and emotional eruptions

impulsive—spontaneous, natural, self-indulgent, unpredictable, resists following orders

inhibited—shy, sensitive, withdraws from social contacts, fears rejection, and suffers a lack of self-esteem

aggressive—competitive, outspoken, demanding, fears passivity, compliance, and weakness

While no actual person fits any of these descriptions perfectly, we all know people to whom they apply to a recognizable extent. The point is, however, that one can be either well-adjusted or maladjusted within the framework of any of these types. Carried to extremes, any type would become a personality problem. Within limits, though, there is no evidence that either compulsiveness, impulsiveness, inhibitedness, or aggressiveness is better or more normal than the other patterns.

This being the case, it is startling to see how locked in we are to our own particular personality type and how difficult it is for us to acknowledge the appropriateness of a personality very different from our own. Once we have grown out of childhood, we each identify with a set of characteristics. Even if they prove ineffective in dealing with other people or handling the problems life brings our way, we are very resistant to giving them up. More unfortunate still, we tend to be very critical of characteristics opposite to our own. The bold, aggressive individual looks down on his or her quiet, soft-hearted acquaintances; the neat, compulsive person is shocked by those who keep their belongings in a mess; the intellectual finds athletes crude; the conventional citizen thinks hippies are less than human.

The motivation behind our judgments is basically self-serving: we disparage those whose ways of life stand in opposition to our own because, if we gave them credit, we would have to question the value of our own life style. Since we hate to admit that the way we have chosen to live may not be so great after all, we uphold ourselves by putting down other ways.

If, as the authors of this textbook claim, there are many kinds of **61** healthy personality organization, how can each of us determine if our own personality is sound? In the absence of clearcut sickness, such as we will describe in later chapters, the best indicators of the soundness of personality are:

a) our attitude toward ourselves

b) our ability to handle the problems that are part of our lives

c) our contentment or dissatisfaction with life in general

d) the reactions we elicit from people who know us well.

If we genuinely accept ourselves, are willing and able to tackle our problems, enjoy the greater part of our activities, and elicit favorable reactions from those who know us best, our personality is undoubtedly sound. If we dislike ourselves, are unwilling or unable to take care of our problems, feel unhappy most of the time, and evoke unfavorable reactions from the people closest to us, we must conclude that we are psychologically in bad shape.

What can we suggest, however, when the evidence is mixed? Suppose a woman has a high opinion of herself but finds that nobody who gets to know her likes her very much, or consider a man whom everyone adores but who secretly feels inferior and unworthy: Can we assume that these people have personality problems? Our opinion is that, if the situation persists for months or years, they do. Whether their problems demand professional help, however, is another question. Our personalities, like our bodies, are subject to minor and temporary, as well as major and permanent, disturbances. The individual, perhaps in consultation with those whose opinion he or she trusts, must decide if the problem is serious enough to require professional attention.

Summary

In this chapter, we have given you a sampling of different theories of personality. The views of Freud, Jung, Allport, Rogers, Skinner, Bandura and Walters, and Berne were all surveyed. We also added some observations of our own. In no case were we able to present the theorist's views completely, but we tried to convey the essence of each person's standpoint.

Psychology, you should know by now, is a field with plenty of room for debate. An issue like this one—how to define personality, how to describe a person's inner being, or whether to try to describe it at all—is bound to be controversial. And so it is. No one has yet proposed a theory that everyone else agrees is best. With the information we have provided, however, we hope you will now be able to consider this problem in terms of your own experience.

62   **Class Projects**

1. Now that you have read a little about various psychologists' theories of personality, can you contribute any observations of your own on the question, "Of what does our true self consist?" Do you think a person's personality is revealed in outward behavior? Do you think that most of us know ourselves very well? Do you think our personalities can be improved and, if so, how? A class discussion or debate on these issues may be illuminating because, as you dig into them, you should find that they are much more complicated than they appear at first glance.

2. Imagine yourself in the following situation. You have been shopping at the supermarket and, on the way home, discover that the checker gave you ten dollars too much in change. You are in a hurry to get home, however, as you have an important date tonight. What would your id want you to do? What would your superego recommend? What kind of solution might your ego come up with? What do you think you would actually do?

   By engaging in an imaginary game like this, you can dramatize the workings of your personality as Freud describes it. You can also come to see the relative strengths of your own id, superego, and ego.

3. Do you agree or disagree with Allport's views on personality? Can you define your own central traits? Your secondary traits? Can you find an activity you engage in that is functionally autonomous (i.e., which you started doing for some other reason but which you now do simply because you enjoy it)? Can you distinguish more and less mature personalities in terms of Allport's signs of maturity? Try to do these things in order to see how Allport's teachings relate to actual people.

4. Imagine your personality in terms of Rogers' theory. How closely do you think your self-concept harmonizes with your organismic self? Here is a simple exercise that may give you some insight into their relationship. First check the adjectives that best describe the kind of person you usually try to be. Then check the adjectives that describe the kind of person you usually are. Try to react as truthfully as possible. The agreement or disagreement between your two columns of check marks will be a rough indication of the harmony or disharmony between what Rogers calls your self and your organism. (It can only be rough because, even when we are totally candid, we do not recognize all our organism's components.)

Adjective	I try to be	I usually am
imaginative		
moody		
childish		
spiritual		
messy		
aggressive		
warm		
weak		
sociable		
sensitive		
emotional		
conscientious		
talkative		
dull		

devious		
straightforward		
serious		
strong		
cold		
generous		
withdrawn		
unemotional		
simple		
sensual		
neat		
stingy		
cowardly		
bright		
passive		
friendly		
shy		
foolish		
humorous		
playful		
realistic		
studious		

References

1. CALVIN HALL, *A Primer of Freudian Psychology* (New York: World, 1954).
2. ERNEST J. SIMMONS, *Dostoevsky: An Intimate Portrait* (New York: Vintage Books, 1940).
3. C. G. JUNG, *Psychological Types* (New York: Harcourt, 1933).
4. GORDON ALLPORT, *Pattern and Growth in Personality* (New York: Holt, Rinehart & Winston, 1961).
5. ALBERT BANDURA and RICHARD WALTERS, *Social Learning and Personality Development* (New York: Holt, Rinehart & Winston, 1963).
6. CARL ROGERS, *On Becoming a Person* (Boston: Houghton Mifflin, 1961).
7. ERIC BERNE, *Games People Play* (New York: Grove Press, 1964).

Suggested Readings

1. CATTELL, R. B. "Personality Pinned Down," *Psychology Today*, 1973, 7, pp. 40-46.
2. ENGLER, BARBARA. *Personality Theories: An Introduction.* Dallas, TX: Houghton Mifflin, 1979.
3. HALL, CALVIN S. and LINDZEY, GARDNER. *Theories of Personality,* 2nd ed. New York: John Wiley, 1970.
4. LUNDIN, R. W. *Personality: a Behavioral Analysis.* New York: Macmillan, 1969.
5. MADDI, S. R. *Personality Theories: a Comparative Analysis.* Homewood, IL: The Dorsey Press, 1968.
6. SCHULTZ, DUANE. *Theories of Personality.* Monterey, CA: Brooks/Cole, 1976.

The Healthy Personality

5

**M**ost psychologists avoid making declarations on the healthy personality. Few objective studies have been done and opinions are influenced by personal biases. Low-keyed, moderate people are apt to believe that moderation is indicative of mental health; high-strung, emotional types are apt to believe that access to emotions is more important.

Despite this lack of agreement on what constitutes soundness or healthiness of personality, several eminent psychologists have given serious thought to the matter. In this chapter, we will present their ideas as well as our own.

We will also relate some startling facts that show how easily most of us can be led into unhealthy forms of behavior. These facts, as you will see, suggest that a healthy personality is not something solid that we either have or don't have. It is a state of being that we approach at times and drift away from at other times.

The central issue is how to cultivate a healthy personality. We will make some suggestions at the end of the chapter, but one thing we can say right now: Lecturing people on how to be healthy is about as likely to produce results as telling a flower to bloom. It is much more practical to provide the proper conditions—the human equivalents of sun, rain, and fertile soil.

Some experts contend that most children grow up healthier in a permissive, accepting atmosphere than in a structured, demanding one. Others say the reverse is true. It is our belief that both positions are oversimplified, for people are even more varied than plants. Some do best in one kind of environment, some in another.

Please do not be discouraged by our refusal to give you neat answers to complex issues. There are plenty of authors who will tell you how to live right and anything else you might want to know. Our purpose, in contrast, is to get you to think things through. We want to encourage you to learn what the experts have to say, but only as a prelude to developing your own point of view.

The Invasion from Mars

On October 30, 1938, on his weekly radio program, Orson Welles presented a brilliant dramatization of a flying saucer landing on a farm in New Jersey. In the play, strange creatures were reported emerging from the craft, killing hundreds of people with heat rays, withstanding the assault of police and army units, and causing widespread fire and destruction throughout the states of New Jersey and New York.

Although four announcements were made during the one-hour program that it was only a fictional play, hundreds of thousands of listeners were frightened enough to break down in tears, pray for the protection of God, resign themselves to death, or jump into their cars and race madly up and down highways in a desperate attempt to escape. It would have been a simple matter for these people to switch to another station to check the truth of what they had heard, but very few did so. They were much more inclined to give way to their fears and rush around in mass confusion.

These reactions, as reported by Hadley Cantril in *The Invasion from Mars: A Study in the Psychology of Panic,*[1] provide a sad commentary on the stability and thoughtfulness of the American public. True, it happened many years ago and under world conditions that made many people jittery (the rise of Nazi Germany), but there is no evidence that most of us have grown more relaxed or reasonable since then.

Luckily, the reactions to Orson Welles' broadcast were more embarrassing than harmful. They dramatically reveal, however, how easy it is for many adults to abandon their common sense and give in to irrational fears.

What Then Is Mental Health?

We will all agree that running amok is no sign of mental health. But what is? What can we name with some conviction as the main ingredients of the healthy personality?

Before attempting to answer, we would like to make the point that a healthy personality is not an unchangeable thing. It is different at different stages of life, under different cultural conditions, and in relation to different events. It may be quite healthy for a child of six to have absolute faith in his or her parents' ability to provide protection and guidance; the same attitude, however, would not be so healthy in a person of eighteen. It may be quite healthy for a person growing up in a small religious community to accept traditional beliefs with little question; it would not be so healthy for a person growing up in a fast-moving urban center to be so unquestioning of what he or she is taught. It may be quite healthy for a person in the midst of a civil war to be continually alert, suspicious, and ready to become belligerent at a moment's notice; for a **67** person living in a pleasant, secure state of peace, on the other hand, such a cluster of characteristics would seem inappropriate.

Having established the relativity of mental health, let us list some standard ingredients that most psychologists would include. They refer to the healthy adult in modern American society, no claim being made for their importance in other cultures or in other historical eras. With this in mind, we may say that he or she should:

1) have a fair amount of self-esteem

2) have a clear perception of reality

3) be aware of his or her feelings

4) be responsive to the feelings of other people

5) be capable of handling problems in a calm and objective manner

6) be assertive without being hostile

7) have fun out of life yet enjoy productive work

8) be able to relate to others with trust and affection

9) have an ethical set of values

10) have a good sense of humor, a certain amount of creativity, and a philosophical or religious outlook on life

Lists are easy to make, but this is a tall order and, in the actual doing, it may be more problematical than it appears at first glance.

Where, for instance, does self-esteem stop short of conceit? How can we tell if a man who thinks well of himself is mature and self-confident or smug and arrogant? In extreme cases, the difference may be obvious, but many times it is difficult to determine.

How, to take another example, do we distinguish assertiveness from hostility? If you and your friend have a misunderstanding and you raise your voice and call him or her unkind names, you may consider it a justifiable assertion of your feelings, yet your friend may accuse you of being unduly hostile.

In the same vein, when we talk about relating to others with trust and affection, whom do we mean? All others, including thieves and rapists and murderers? Or only some others; if so, whom?

The point we are trying to make is that the characteristics of the healthy personality need closer, more careful definition.

Obedience to Authority

Even more dramatic, in certain respects, than the reactions of listeners to Welles' *Invasion from Mars* were the reactions of subjects to a series of experiments carried out at Yale University from 1960 to 1963. Devised and conducted by Stanley Milgram and reported in his book, *Obedience to Authority*,[2] these experiments caused a furor when they were published. They proved that most normal adults—people who consider themselves kind-hearted and reasonable—can be led to inflict severe pain on other human beings simply by having an authority tell them to do so.

The experimental setup and results may be described as follows.

Two people are asked to take part in a study of memory and learning. One of them is called a "teacher" and the other a "learner." The experimenter explains that the study is concerned with the effects of punishment on learning. The learner is taken into a room, seated in a chair, his arms strapped down, and an electrode attached to his wrist. He is told that he must learn a list of word pairs; whenever he makes an error, he will receive electric shocks of increasing intensity.

The target of the experiment [however] is the "teacher." After watching the learner being strapped into place, he is taken into an adjoining room and seated before an impressive shock generator. Its main feature is a line of thirty switches, ranging from 15 volts to 450 volts. . . . There are also verbal designations which range from SLIGHT SHOCK to DANGER–SEVERE SHOCK. The teacher is told to administer the learning test to the man in the other room. When the learner responds correctly, the teacher moves on to the next item; when the other man gives an incorrect answer, the teacher is to give him an electric shock. He is to start at the lowest shock level and increase the level each time the man makes an error. . . .

The "teacher," says Milgram, is a genuinely naive subject who has come to the laboratory to participate in an experiment. The learner, or victim, is an actor who actually receives no shock at all [but the teacher has no way of knowing this]. The point of the experiment is to see how far a person will proceed in a situation in which he is ordered to inflict increasing pain on a protesting victim. At what point will the subject refuse to obey the experimenter?

The "learner," Milgram goes on, realistically pretends that he is suffering more and more as the experiment continues. At first he grunts in discomfort; then he groans; then he asks to be released; and eventually he cries and screams in agony. And what does the "teacher" do? "The results of the experiment are both surprising and dismaying. Despite the fact that many subjects experience stress, despite the fact that many protest to the experimenter, *a substantial proportion continue to the last shock on the generator.*"

As we all agreed that the healthy adult would not behave like the people who panicked over Orson Welles' broadcast, we can now agree that those who inflicted pain in Stanley Milgram's experiment were not **69** particularly healthy. Or were they? The point has been made that healthiness of personality, like healthiness of body, is not something we either have or don't have, but something that comes and goes at different times and under different circumstances. At least some of the people who panicked or pressed the last switch may have been, at other times in their lives, more or less healthy individuals.

Do you see how debatable these issues can become?

Sigmund Freud on Mental Health

While Freud never wrote a book on the topic of mental health, he made it clear that he saw us all as more prone to irrationality than we care to admit. In his view, our reasoning powers and general goodwill are often controlled by our unconscious drives. It is the aim of healthy development, he taught, to outgrow our childishness, but most of us never do so completely.

In a letter to Albert Einstein, Freud expressed the opinion that most people have little compassion for each other. Einstein had been wondering why his efforts to get the public to support a plan for world peace had been a failure. Freud informed him that, hard as it is to believe, most people do not hate violence and bloodshed unless they or their loved ones are threatened. In other words, he felt that we are often more savage, or at least less concerned about human suffering, than we openly confess.[3]

Do you think Freud's view was too cynical? If so, how do you explain the results of Milgram's experiment? What do you say to the fact that city dwellers will watch a mugging or a murder on the street and refuse to call the police because they "don't want to get involved"? And now be honest with yourself and ask how much you really care about the victims of war in far off places. Enough to do anything about it? If so, you are in the minority.

In our opinion, Freud was on the mark in describing most of us as less than reasonable, less than compassionate, less than mature and healthy at many times in our lives. The important question, then, is how to improve.

C. G. Jung and Individuation

C. G. Jung believed that we all have an instinctive drive toward maturity. He called it "the process of individuation" and expressed the opinion

70

that, if it is not blocked, it will occur as naturally as an oak tree grows from an acorn.

What are the characteristics of the "individuated" or mature person, from Jung's point of view? Here are a few of his remarks on the subject.[4]

"The development of personality means fidelity to the law of one's own being." The mature individual, we may say, is true to him or her self.

"The development of personality is at once a charisma and a curse, because its first fruit is the conscious and unavoidable segregation of the single individual from the herd." The mature person must suffer a certain amount of isolation, because true independence means that we cannot totally belong to any group.

"To round itself out, life calls not for perfection but for completeness." The fully developed person is not without flaws. What we must strive for is wholeness, not purity.

There is a wealth of inference in these three points. The last one alone highlights the difference between psychology's view of personal development and the view held by most religions. Religion teaches us to be good but psychology teaches us to be whole. Neither Freud nor Jung nor any other psychologist would deny the ideal of goodness, but they would insist that we never really overcome our "bad" traits and must therefore learn to live with them.

credo
a statement of beliefs or
principles

Jung's other two points have to do with independence, and independence is one of psychology's most fundamental **credos.** Ralph Waldo Emerson said, "Whoso would be a man, must be a nonconformist." And, "Trust thyself: every heart vibrates to that iron string."[5] Most psychologists endorse these sentiments. In infancy, we are totally dependent creatures and must conform, more or less, to our parents' expectations in order to survive. Later, we must conform to our peers in order to have friends, to our schools in order to receive an education, and to our communities in order to be allowed to walk the streets. These are not bad learning experiences, for society could not exist without certain rules of conduct. The more we wish to become our own true selves, however, the more we must transcend what everyone else expects of us and learn to operate out of our own convictions.

There is yet another aspect to Jung's view of personal development. "If you sum up what people [who have followed the path of individuation] tell you about their experience, you can formulate it in about this way. They came to themselves, they could accept themselves, they were able to become reconciled to adverse circumstances and events. This is much like what was formerly expressed by saying: he has made his peace with God, he has sacrificed his own will, he has submitted himself to the will of God." As these words suggest, Jung saw maturity not as something we achieve but as something we allow to happen. It is an outlook that has much in common with the teachings of Zen Buddhism, as well as with the Christian concept of receiving the grace of God.

Erikson's Stages of Emotional Development

Erik Erikson, an eminent psychologist whose ideas we have already referred to, has proposed the notion that, in order to develop a healthy adult personality, every person must achieve eight stages of emotional development. We may describe these stages, or ingredients of maturity, as follows.

1) *The Sense of Trust.* This is the component of the healthy personality that is the first to emerge. The crucial time for its development is in the first year of life, and it is fostered by parents who respond to the infant's needs in a sensitive, loving, and reliable fashion.

2) *The Sense of Autonomy.* In the second and third years of life, the child must develop a sense of self-reliance based on the repeated experience that he or she is a person who is permitted to make choices and express his or her impulses.

3) *The Sense of Initiative.* Closely related to the sense of autonomy is the ability to express one's will without too great a feeling of guilt. The child of four or five must be permitted to use his or her initiative in relating to other people and exploring the environment.

4) *The Sense of Industry.* From ages six to twelve, the child must consolidate a feeling of competence based on his or her demonstrated ability to accomplish goals and handle tasks successfully. He or she must learn that diligent work brings the satisfaction of achievement and that he or she has what it takes to acquire useful knowledge and skills by persistent effort.

5) *The Sense of Identity.* The central problem of adolescence is the establishment of a sense of oneself as distinct from other people. What are my abilities, my needs, my values, my limitations? What kind of a person am I and what do I have it within me to become? These are the questions that demand to be answered, not theoretically but in the development of a feeling of identity or selfhood.

6) *The Sense of Intimacy.* Also during the adolescent years, the healthy individual must acquire the ability to be emotionally open to other people, not in the infantile way of being so dependent on others that one clings to them and unthinkingly adopts their views but in the more adult way of knowing one's

differentness and yet striving to bridge the gap in order to experience the joy of close communion.

7) *The Parental Sense.* In early adulthood, both men and women must develop the desire to produce and nourish the next generation. If not in the raising of one's own children, this drive may be satisfied in relation to children in general or, in a somewhat displaced fashion, in the production of ideas and objects that further the ongoing life of the community.

8) *The Sense of Integrity.* The final component of the healthy personality is the sense of oneself as a meaningful person existing in relation to other people, past and present, and deserving of respect and comradeship. In Erikson's words,

Integrity means a new and different love of one's parents, free of the wish that they should have been different, and an acceptance of the fact that one's life is one's own responsibility. It is a sense of comradeship with men and women of distant times and of different pursuits, who have created orders and objects and sayings conveying human dignity and love. Although aware of the relativity of all the various life styles that have given meaning to human striving, the possessor of integrity is ready to defend the dignity of his own life style against all physical and economic threats.[6]

Although a full explanation of Erikson's theory would require a much more detailed description, we feel that some consideration of his trend of thought can be enlightening.

Abraham Maslow on Self-Actualization

Abraham Maslow was one of the first American psychologists to study the healthy personality in adulthood. After examining the characteristics of people functioning at very high levels of efficiency and self-fulfillment, he concluded that they had these attributes in common:

1) They are realistic.

2) They accept themselves, other people, and the world at large.

3) They are spontaneous.

4) They are more problem-centered than self-centered.

5) They are independent.

6) They are often detached and need privacy.

7) They may have mystical or spiritual experiences.

8) They identify with the human race rather than with national, racial, religious, or socioeconomic subgroups.

9) Their intimate relationships, while few, are deeply emotional.

10) Their values are democratic.

11) Their sense of humor is philosophical rather than hostile.

12) They resist conformity.

13) They are creative.

14) They transcend their environment rather than merely coping with it. [7]

While there is no solid evidence that these traits are essential to a healthy personality, and while some of the items he lists seem limited to this place and time, it is encouraging to know that a renowned psychologist took the time to study highly functioning individuals and discover what they had in common.

Maslow called the process of achieving maturity "self-actualization." Like Jung's "individuation," the term implies a coming to oneself, becoming who one really is, as well as a fulfillment of one's potentials. Others have called it "self-realization" or "the acquisition of identity," but whatever name they use, they are all talking about the same thing. Unfortunately, as we have said before, it is difficult to describe it distinctly, and even more difficult to learn how to achieve it. If naming our destination, however, and describing it in general terms is a first step in taking a trip, we can say that psychology is on its way.

Carl Rogers on the Fully Functioning Person

Another distinguished psychologist who has expressed his views on the matter is Carl Rogers, one of the foremost figures in the humanist movement. In his book *On Becoming a Person*, he says:

> The best way I can state the aim of life is to use the words of Kierkegaard, 'To be that self which one truly is.' The person who is attempting to achieve this goal, he goes on, first shows a tendency to move away from a self that he is not. He also moves

away from the image of what he ought to be. He moves away from what his culture expects him to be. He moves away from the imperative to please others, and he moves toward being independent. He also moves toward being a process: an evolving rather than a settled creature. He shows a desire to be all of himself in each moment of his life. He becomes more open and accepting of other people as he becomes more accepting of himself. Yet his life is not one of total contentment or unclouded happiness. It is a movement, not a state of being; it is a direction, not a destination.[8]

Rogers' views, like those of other psychologists in the humanist school, appear to pivot on the notion of *authenticity:* becoming one's true self rather than putting on a fake front or engaging in "game playing" behavior. It is surely an unarguable ideal, but whether it can be achieved with any finality is another question. Rogers and his colleagues believe it can, but other psychologists have suggested that what some people call authentic is just another kind of put-on.

Emotional outbursts, for example, are often taken as truly authentic behavior, because the person who is crying or shouting or carrying on is not in control of himself or herself. It is equally possible, however, that this person has learned that it is precisely this kind of behavior that gets him or her what he or she wants, so it can also be a technique of getting one's way. It seems, then, that only the person involved knows if he or she is being authentic or simply playing the authenticity bit—and even that is not certain, since we are all prone to self-deception.

Rogers' emphasis on change, on the other hand, is less open to this kind of criticism. We can easily tell if a person's behavior has changed, so the humanists' contention that we should welcome change as part of development is founded on firmer ground. They do not, however, tell us how to do it, nor do they clearly distinguish change for the better from change for the worse.

Rogers voices the faith that we will change, we will grow, we will become more authentic if we are accepted as we are and simply allowed to evolve. His experience as a therapist appears to bear it out, but there are many psychologists who doubt that it happens as spontaneously as he seems to believe.

Self-Directed Behavior

Those who belong to the behaviorist school speak in very different terms about making desired changes in ourselves. They advocate the systematic application of "techniques of self-modification."[9] What we must do, according to them, is begin with a self-contract: a clear cut agreement with ourselves about what we want to change and how we intend to do it. It is also important, they insist, that we keep careful records of our progress, divide our attempts at self-improvement into very small steps that can be accomplished in a regular sequence, and reward ourselves in a prearranged way each time we make a step forward.

If you wished to develop more physical stamina, a psychologist of the behaviorist school might instruct you to take the following steps. 1) Express your goal in terms of a self-contract like, "I want to become able to walk four miles a day (or do a hundred pushups). First I will determine how far I can now walk (or how many pushups I can do). Then I will gradually add more yards each day (or pushups). The increase in distance or number of pushups will be determined by adding just enough to keep making progress without becoming exhausted;" 2) Keep a written record of what you did to fulfill this contract each and every day 3) Reward yourself by giving yourself a hot shower or a piece of fruit or something else you enjoy immediately after each day's accomplishment of the desired goal.

It is this kind of clear cut approach, the behaviorists say, that produces observable results. Whether personal development can always be broken down into such definable units, however, is open to question. When it can, the behaviorist approach is probably effective, but when our goals involve such things as being able to love other people more sincerely or being able to accept the certainty of our own eventual death calmly, it may be less appropriate.

A Confession

The authors of this text have their personal preferences among the views we have been discussing. One of us (never mind who) inclines very strongly toward the behaviorist position, while the other prefers a mixture of Freudian, Jungian, and humanist outlooks. As it has been possible for us to write this book together and still remain friends (more or less), we are convinced that it is possible for the proponents of different views to cooperate in helping people further their personal development.

Theoretical bias aside, we are both of the opinion that maturity is a many-branched tree with innumerable variations in the forms it may take. We can be childish, neurotic, or maladjusted in a lot of different ways and we can be sound or healthy in just as many ways. Even more intriguing is the fact that the most effective people the human race has produced have had their odd or neurotic characteristics. Some totally healthy people may exist, but we are much more likely to find the qualities psychologists call healthy mixed in with those we would have to call immature.

Mohandas K. Gandhi was one of the most remarkable men who ever lived.[10, 11] Political and spiritual leader of India, revered by millions, he invented the technique of militant nonviolence, laid his life on the line, and single-handedly changed the policies of the British Empire.

Was Gandhi what psychologists would call a completely healthy personality? Probably not. He

Gandhi with some of his followers.

possessed many of the qualities that Maslow and others have listed—he was realistic, independent, self-accepting, and so on—but he also displayed characteristics that might be labelled unhealthy. He was overbearing in his treatment of his wife, he became estranged from his eldest son, and his lengthy fasts, used to force the British authorities to see things his way, may have been an outgrowth

of guilt feelings he had about eating forbidden food.   **77**

Similarly, other great benefactors of humanity—Marie Curie, Vincent van Gogh, Ludwig van Beethoven, Albert Einstein—all had characteristics that would be considered unhealthy.

Our point in mentioning these examples is that, desirable as a healthy personality may be, it is not essential to being an effective person.

Primary Prevention: A Way to Begin

How to assure the development of healthy personalities remains a cloudy issue. Freud, Jung, Erikson, Maslow, Rogers, and the behaviorists all have some suggestions to make, but none of them has the answer neatly packaged and ready to go. The authors of this text haven't got it either. We believe the examples set by our parents, teachers, and other adults are influential to us as children, but we also believe we can, by using our intelligence and will power, make some headway on our own.

primary prevention
the prevention of mental and behavioral disorders before they begin

An exciting new trend in the field of mental health that may in time prove fruitful is the growing interest in **primary prevention.** More and more psychologists, psychiatrists, and social workers are of the opinion that prevention is better than cure. They believe that we stand a stronger chance of helping people develop healthy personalities if we do something about their lives in infancy and childhood, rather than waiting until adolescence or adulthood and trying to correct what has gone wrong.

Since 1975, the University of Vermont has sponsored an Annual Conference on the Primary Prevention of Psychopathology. Papers have been given on a wide range of topics, all relating to the notion that mental health can be fostered by giving appropriate assistance to the families of young children. Exactly what kind of assistance to provide, how to deliver it, and how to assess its impact, is still unclear, but a beginning is being made in meetings such as this.[12]

Many mental health workers, as you can see, are searching for practical, effective ways to promote the healthy personality. On their behalf, we invite you to join in the quest.

Summary

In this chapter we have sketched the characteristics of the healthy personality as described by Erik Erikson, Abraham Maslow, and other contemporary psychologists. We have also summarized the views of Freud, Jung, and Rogers. Suggestions for how to achieve maturity and mental health have been discussed, and the promising field of "primary prevention" has been introduced. We have tried to make it clear that healthy personality traits often coexist with immature, neurotic, or otherwise unhealthy ones, and we have shown that the most effective leaders of civilization are not necessarily completely healthy personalities. On the whole, what we tried to convey was a sense of the complexity, excitement, and promise of this particular area of psychological inquiry.

References

1. HADLEY CANTRIL, *The Invasion From Mars: A Study in the Psychology of Panic* (Princeton, NJ: Princeton University Press, 1940).
2. STANLEY MILGRAM, *Obedience to Authority: An Experimental View* (New York: Harper and Row, 1974).
3. PETER MICHELMORE, *Einstein: Profile of the Man* (New York: Dodd, Mead, 1962).
4. C. G. JUNG, *Psychological Reflections,* ed. Jolandi Jacobi (New York: Harper and Brothers, 1961).
5. RALPH WALDO EMERSON, *The Complete Essays and Other Writings of Ralph Waldo Emerson,* ed. Brooks Atkinson (New York: Modern Library, 1940).
6. ERIK ERIKSON, *Childhood and Society,* 2nd ed. (New York: Norton, 1963).

Suggested Readings

1. GANDHI, MOHANDAS K. *An Autobiography.* Boston: Beacon, 1957.
2. MASLOW, ABRAHAM. *Toward a Psychology of Being.* New York: Van Nostrand, 1962.
3. DYER, WAYNE W. *Your Erroneous Zones.* New York: Avon Books, 1977.
4. KILEY, JOHN C. *Self Rescue.* New York: McGraw-Hill, 1977.
5. MAHONEY, M. and THORESEN, C. *Self-Control: Power to the Person.* Monterey, Ca.: Brooks/Cole, 1974.
6. ROGERS, CARL. *On Becoming a Person.* Boston: Houghton Mifflin, 1961.

Class Projects

1. Choose any one of the personal qualities we named as elements of maturity (e.g. self-esteem; handling problems in a calm and objective manner; responsiveness to the feelings of other people; assertiveness without hostility; a good sense of humor). For the next week, keep a daily log of the instances in which you practiced this trait and those in which you could have but neglected or failed to do so. If, on the basis of this evidence, you decide to improve, set yourself a goal of gradual improvement and continue to keep the daily log to see how well you are doing.

2. Plan a "primary prevention" project for parents of young children in your community. What do you think they would need to know to raise their children in a psychologically healthy atmosphere? Is knowledge alone enough? What might they need in the way of practical assistance? marital counseling? financial aid? What group of parents would you focus on? Newly married? Unmarried? Parents of firstborn children? People who have been in mental institutions? On what basis would you make your decisions? Addressing these issues, we believe, will help you appreciate the complexities and possiblities of this problem.

SOME THOUGHTS OF OUR OWN

In chapters 4 and 5, we presented some personal observations on personality organization and the characteristics of the healthy individual. As we mentioned in chapter five, we are ourselves divided only on the question of whether a behaviorist view of human functioning makes more sense than a psychoanalytic or humanistic view. Otherwise, we agree with all the findings and theories outlined in this section—agree, that is, that they are useful to a psychological understanding of the normal person.

We would like to make a point of our personal differences, however. Since, as we told you in chapter five, we have managed to collaborate on the writing of this book and remain good friends, we believe it possible for psychologists to resolve their differences and work together toward the common goal of understanding human behavior and helping human beings in distress. In this respect, we hope our example will stand as a model for those of you who plan to enter the field.

Section Two

People and Their Problems

OVERVIEW

sychological disturbances—what causes them, how they are recognized, and how we attempt to treat them—these are the topics we delve into in the second section of this text.

Chapter 6, dealing with intelligence and personality tests, is a bridge between sections one and two, since tests are given to normal, well-adjusted people as well as to people suffering from serious disturbances. Chapters 7 and 8 describe the major neuroses and psychoses that occur in our society, chapter 9 explains the systems of treatment that are currently in use, and chapter 10 rounds out this section by discussing the harmful effects of alcohol and drugs and the potential benefits of good nutrition on our mental well-being.

Is it an invasion of privacy to give people tests that may reveal hidden problems? What kinds of behavior or experience do we consider "sick"? Is instability inborn, created in early childhood, or determined by events throughout one's life? Why do people hang on to their problems even when they understand them and realize how they are harming themselves? What is the best form of treatment to use in specific cases? What can be done to reduce the incidence of mental disorder in our society? These are a few of the issues underlying this area of psychology. After reading the following chapters, you should be able to express an informed opinion on them.

IQs and Inkblots

6

ne of the things psychologists learn is how to use psychological tests. Intelligence tests, personality tests, academic achievement tests, and vocational aptitude tests—many psychologists consider these the tools of their trade. Others, however, cast doubt on the merit of such devices and even suggest they be done away with. Nevertheless, they continue to play an important part in the field as a whole. Test results often influence both psychiatric treatment and the decisions of schools and industrial organizations.

Some people fear that our society is becoming too test oriented. In science-fiction fashion, they believe a time will come when everything—from the people we will be allowed to marry to the age to which we will be allowed to live—will be determined by our test scores. To most psychologists, such fears are laughable. No tests provide that kind of information and few psychologists are secretly plotting to take over the world.

In this chapter, you will learn about the main tests used today. We will explain their scope and limitations and describe situations in which their use is indicated. We will also summarize the major arguments for and against tests in general.

Intelligence Tests

mental age

a figure expressed in years and months indicating how well a child has done in comparison to the average child of any given age. If your mental age is thirteen years, six months, you do about as well as the average thirteen-and-a-half-year-old.

chronological age

one's actual age, also expressed in years and months

Verbal IQ

a score indicating how well one can do in answering questions on a variety of subjects involving reasoning and memory

Performance IQ

a score indicating how well one can do in solving problems based on visual and motor skills

Full Scale IQ

a combination score based on the above

Intelligence testing began around the turn of this century. Alfred Binet, a French psychologist, was asked to devise a system for identifying "feeble-minded" children. He put together a number of questions that tapped the child's ability to reason, as well as a number of tasks using pictures, puzzles, and little toys which the child had to figure out, identify, or remember. On the basis of these items, he developed a test from which he could calculate a child's **mental age** and compare it to his or her **chronological age.**

The test Binet created was later brought to this country. It was further refined at Stanford University and became known as the Stanford-Binet Intelligence Scale.

The Stanford-Binet is still widely used today. Its popularity has been overtaken only by the Wechsler Intelligence Scale for Children (WISC-R) and the Wechsler Adult Intelligence Scale (WAIS), both of which were invented by an American psychologist, David Wechsler.

These tests consist of questions and tasks designed to measure the major areas of intellectual functioning. They result in a **Verbal IQ,** a **Performance IQ,** and a **Full Scale IQ,** as well as a pattern of scores on the individual subtests. It is possible for a trained psychologist, using the Stanford-Binet, WISC-R, or WAIS, to tell how bright a person is, what kind of mental problems he or she can solve unusually well and what kinds he or she finds difficult. It is also possible, from the test results, to predict how well a person will do in school or college. Such predictions are not always correct, but when carefully done—taking into account other important things like the child's motivation to learn academic subjects, his or her home environment, and the presence or absence of emotional problems—they can be fairly accurate.

The WISC-R and WAIS are designed so that IQ scores from 90 to 109 represent the average or normal range of intelligence. A person who earns less than 70 can be considered mentally retarded while a person who earns more than 140 is bordering on genius. To break it down further, the chart in Figure 6.1 lists IQ scores, their classification, and the percentage of people in the United States who fall into each category.

IQ	Classification	Percent of U.S. Population
130 and above	Very Superior	2.2
120–129	Superior	6.7
110–119	Bright Normal	16.1
90–109	Average	50.0
80–89	Dull Normal	16.1
70–79	Borderline	6.7
69 and below	Mental Defective	2.2

Figure 6.1: IQ scores.

The verbal subtests on the WISC-R and WAIS cover the following areas. We give an example of a typical question in each area.

Information—what month comes before September?

Comprehension—what should you do if you witness a hit-and-run accident?

Arithmetic—if oranges cost ten cents each, how much would a dozen cost?

The performance subtests include: finding what is missing in a picture; putting colored blocks together to form designs; arranging pictures to tell a story; putting together jigsaw puzzles; and copying little signs as quickly as possible. An example is the following question. What is missing from this picture?

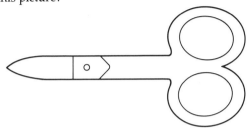

What is intelligence?

Like beauty, humor, and courage, intelligence is a quality we recognize and admire, but one which is very difficult to define. We may think of it as a combination of things like understanding, the ability to see relationships, the ability to reason, and the ability to learn. We must admit, however, that there is no hard and fast way to pin it down.

Carol S. was in a quandary. She was about to finish college and had a good job offer at an advertising agency. Her dream, however, was to go on to law school. She wondered if she had the intellectual ability to succeed. After some consideration, Carol decided to go to a psychologist and take a series of tests.

The results on the WAIS indicated that Carol's Full Scale IQ was 128 (or in the superior range), her Verbal IQ was 129 and her Performance IQ was 126. She did exceptionally well on the vocabulary and comprehension subtests. These scores, as well as the information gathered from the other tests, led the psychologist to conclude, "Carol has the ability to do well in law school if she is motivated. Her IQ is high enough for success if she applies herself to her studies. It is particularly encouraging to note the pattern of subtest scores: Carol's highest scores are in areas relevant to her ambitions. If she is serious about graduate school, I would recommend that she go ahead."

It is important to understand that there are many areas in which intelligence can operate. A person may be brilliant in one field and only average in other fields; he or she may be brilliant in many fields; he or she may be below average in many. Geniuses like Einstein and Beethoven were not exceptional in everything and there are ordinary people who do some things masterfully.

86

Heredity versus environment

The extent to which intelligence is inherited or learned remains an issue of heated debate. All psychologists agree that both heredity and environment are factors in intelligence; however, which one is more important is a major controversy in the field. Some psychologists claim that intelligence is primarily determined by the genes we receive from our parents. In its extreme, this theory says that certain family or racial groups are naturally more intelligent than others. Arthur Jensen, a professor at the University of California, has voiced this point of view. He believes there is an inborn difference in the intelligence of whites and blacks. Most psychologists disagree with this viewpoint. The way children are raised, they say, and the opportunities they are given for learning play a far more important role in determining their intelligence.[1] As an example, consider two children who have naturally superior mathematical aptitude. One is reared in a family that enjoys number games, brain-twisting puzzles, and arithmetical cleverness. The other is reared in a home where these kinds of activities do not occur. The first child is much more likely than the second to develop keen mathematical abilities.

Pros and cons of intelligence testing

Some critics feel that IQ tests are too academically oriented. They argue that these tests may measure the ability to do well in school but do not measure natural cleverness or creative thinking. Others charge that the tests were devised for a white, middle-class population and are unfair to black children or children from poor areas. Some questions on the WISC seem closely related to middle-class values (for example, "Why is it better to pay bills by check than by cash?"). In an attempt to be fairer to the poor and to blacks, some psychologists have proposed the use of questions more closely related to life in minority neighborhoods, such as, "What was Muhammad Ali's name before he changed it?"

Defenders of the tests, however, claim that the supposedly unfair items are few and far between. They point out that the tests are not identical with scholastic success; many children, white and black alike, score high on IQ scales but do poorly in their schoolwork. Creative thinking, they say, is a separate issue altogether. Nevertheless, in 1974 David Wechsler, the inventor of the WISC and WAIS, published a new test, the WISC-R, in which he replaced some questionable items. One of his stated objectives was to make the test fairer to minority groups. A recent study by one of the authors of this text, however, indicates that he has not yet fully succeeded.[2]

It is important to be aware of the controversies surrounding IQ tests because they have social, educational, and political implications. If it were true that certain kinds of people were born with a greater capacity to learn, it could have a tremendous impact on our educational system.

More government money would probably be spent on their education,   **87**
while those who supposedly had less capacity might be kept out of
college. Similarly, our system of government relies on the assumption
that all citizens can understand political issues and should, therefore, be
allowed to vote. If it was proven that certain groups of people had a
lower capacity to understand the issues, their votes might be taken away
or somehow reduced in strength.

Reliability and validity

It is a basic principle of science that, to be acceptable, a test must prove
itself both reliable and valid. Being reliable means that it comes out with
the same results on repeated use. If you earn an IQ of 120 on a given test
today, you should earn more or less the same score a year from now or
even five years from now. Otherwise, the test is like some sort of crazy
ruler that changes its length from time to time. Being valid, on the other
hand, means that the test actually measures what it is intended to measure. If a personality test indicates that you are highly introverted, there
must be other signs by which this conclusion can be judged. People who
know you would have to agree that you were very shy and not too
sociable. In other words, the test results should have some relationship
to real behavior.

So far as intelligence tests are concerned, validity is a thorny issue.
There are no absolute indicators of intelligence with which to compare
the test scores. Like courage, intelligence is a quality that shows itself in
different ways. How well we do our schoolwork, how quickly we learn
new subjects, how efficient we are in solving mental problems, how
clever we are in social situations—each of these things tells something
about how intelligent we may be, but none of them provides a final
answer.

Reliability is far less difficult to determine. It is possible to administer
the same, or an equivalent, test several times to groups of subjects to see
if their scores remain nearly the same. On the tests in use today, most IQ
scores are reliable within ten points. If you score 130 on a standardized
test this year, it is unlikely that you will ever score more than 140 or less
than 120 on the same scale, assuming that you always cooperate to the
best of your ability.

Such things as severe emotional disturbance or gross inability to
concentrate may lower a person's IQ by many points. Since the tests are
always administered by a trained psychologist, it is expected that the
examiner will take such conditions into account.

In the final analysis, any test is only as good as the tester who ad-
ministers and interprets it. The IQ score alone is hardly enough to identify a person's mental abilities. Equally important are the pattern of
subtest scores, the subject's behavior and attitude in taking the test, and
a comparison of the results with all the other test results and relevant
information about the subject's life.

88

George W. was a poor boy from a large eastern city. He was eight years old, in the third grade, and doing poorly in all his subjects. His father was a factory worker, his mother a housewife. They were worried about George's intelligence because he had never gotten better than a C or D in his schoolwork. As often as not, he played the role of class clown, doing and saying things to amuse the other children. He had been known to hide under the teacher's desk and squeak like a mouse or to fall flat on his face in order to disrupt the class.

On the WISC-R, George earned a Verbal IQ of 103, a Performance IQ of 121, and a Full Scale IQ of 112. It was clear, therefore, that he was not dull. The scores did not explain why he was doing so poorly, but they showed that the problem was not lack of intelligence.

His behavior in taking the test, however, gave a clue to the source of his difficulties. He was terribly ill-at-ease on the verbal questions. Even when he knew the answers, he would mumble and fidget with his clothing. When the examiner asked him what was wrong, he said he was tired. Yet when they switched to a design or puzzle, all his energy reappeared. From this behavior, the examiner concluded that George had become convinced (perhaps because his parents were not very verbal people) that he could not do well in a question-and-answer situation. He lost all his confidence as soon as anyone addressed him in an academic way.

These findings gave his parents and teachers the incentive to be more patient with him and to help him overcome his lack of confidence.

Personality Tests

objective tests

tests in which responses are factual and can be scored and counted

There are two main kinds of personality tests. One consists of questions about your habits, your moods, your attitudes, and your beliefs. The second consists of pictures, designs, or inkblots which you are asked to interpret. The former are called **objective tests;** the most widely used in this category is the Minnesota Multiphasic Personality Inventory (MMPI). The latter are called **projective tests;** the most famous of these are the Rorschach Technique and the Thematic Apperception Test (TAT).

The MMPI

projective tests

tests in which responses are based on the person's imagination or fantasy

The Minnesota Multiphasic Personality Inventory has been used in psychiatric clinics and mental hospitals for more than 25 years. It consists of over 500 statements to which the subject must respond TRUE or FALSE. The statements refer to different aspects of the subject's personality. For example:

1) Physical well-being (e.g., I have a good appetite.)

2) Self-concept (e.g., I am certainly lacking in self-confidence.)

3) Feelings about others (e.g., I believe I am being plotted against.)

4) Tendency toward strange experiences (e.g., Evil spirits possess me at times.)

The test was first given to people with known personality disorders. **89** Based upon their responses, a scoring key was developed. When individuals take the MMPI, their responses are matched to the key and they are rated on traits like **depression, hypochondriasis, paranoia,** and other disorders.

depression

a tendency to feel downcast and weak

While the MMPI can furnish useful information about a person, it has met with resistance from many patients. They feel the statements are oversimplified, and they find it confusing to have to answer them true or false. A statement like "I do not mind being made fun of," they rightfully point out, is ambiguous. Their feelings would be determined by the specific situation, by who was making fun of them, and by which of their characteristics was being laughed at. Responding to the statement "Children should be taught all the main facts of sex," they contend, is foolish unless the age of the child is specified.

hypochondriasis

a tendency to dwell on imaginary physical ills

paranoia

a mental disorder characterized by suspiciousness and feelings of being persecuted

The test, however, allows for such indecision. While too many unanswered questions make it impossible to score, a small number are acceptable and even expected by the testers. In any case, most patients cooperate in the test. As long as they attempt to answer honestly as many questions as they can, the pattern of their responses does shed light on their personality characteristics.

The Rorschach technique

Perhaps the most well-known of all personality tests, the Rorschach (or "inkblot test") is named for its creator. Hermann Rorschach, a Swiss psychiatrist, had noticed that different people, looking at the same cloud or design, were apt to see different things in it. To one, the cloud or design might look like an animal; to another, it might resemble a fairy castle. These differences, he thought, were no mere accident. They reflected important differences in how each person viewed the world.

Building on this idea, Rorschach made hundreds of inkblots and showed them to his patients and coworkers. After several years of experimentation, he selected the ten blots that people responded to most strongly and made his test out of them.

projection

the act of seeing in the outside world what is really within oneself

The Rorschach is called a projective test because the way a person interprets the inkblots is a **projection** of the way he or she interprets life. To put it very simply, what one sees in the blots reveals what is in one's own mental and emotional makeup.

Figure 6.1 shows some inkblots similar to those used in the Rorschach. Write down exactly what you see in them and compare your responses to those of other members of the class. You may be surprised to discover how many different things the blots can suggest to different people.

a   *b*

Figure 6.2:   Inkblots.

The problem is how to figure out what people's responses mean. If one person sees "a vampire bat" where another sees "a halloween pumpkin," what does it tell us about these people's mental states? If another person sees a series of X-rays and anatomical charts, what does that tell us about his or her state of mind? Rorschach devised a method he thought would work. In 1921, he published his ideas in a book called *Psychodiagnostics.* [3]

His method of interpretation is very complicated. It is much more than a matter of assigning fixed meanings to different responses. A response like "two little girls playing patty-cake" may have one kind of meaning if given by a ten-year-old child and another if given by a forty-year-old adult. Furthermore, interpretations are never made on a single response. It is, as we have seen in other tests, the pattern of all responses that is important. The Rorschach tester also notes every aspect of the subject's test performance: how he or she handles the cards; to what extent he or she is affected by the colors and shadings in the blots; how often he or she refers to sex, aggression, and other basic drives; and so on.

The test may reveal information on the following aspects of personality: self-control, emotionality, imaginativeness, sensitivity, anxiousness, self-concept, and feelings about others. It may also shed light on severe mental and emotional problems.

Despite its popularity, the Rorschach technique has been criticized by research-minded psychologists. They claim that the method of interpretation is not scientific because it relies too heavily on the psychologist's intuition. Those in favor of the Rorschach, on the other hand, believe that in order to understand personality we must go beyond statistical analysis. They do not think it wrong for psychologists to use intuition in their work.

A subject's pattern of responses is the basis for Rorschach interpretation—never a single response. Sometimes, however, a person may reveal an aspect of his or her problem in one dramatic image. Here are some actual examples:

"You're in a tunnel and it's all closed up." (Response given by an eight-year-old boy whose mother still feeds and dresses him and requires him to sleep in her room so she can be sure he's breathing.)

"Everything seems to be held together but the foundation is not solid." (Response given by a fifty-year-old woman who was to suffer a nervous breakdown a few weeks later.)

Such highly revealing single responses are rare, but a series of responses exposing a particular conflict are not uncommon. A six-year-old girl who had been physically abused by her parents saw four of the ten cards as something "smashed" or "broken":

"A broken butterfly."

"A smashed-up doll."

"A whole bunch of flowers broken to bits."

Her continual return to this theme arose from the feeling that she herself had been smashed or broken by her parents' harshness.

An eighteen-year-old boy saw many creatures in the blots whose sex he could not identify:

"Two natives, I don't know if they're men or women."

"A bat. Are bats male or female?"

"Two lions or maybe lionesses."

"It looks like either male or female sex organs."

His confusion over sexual identity, it was later found, stemmed from confusion about his own masculinity.[4]

The TAT

Another popular projective technique is the Thematic Apperception Test. It consists of 30 pictures which are shown to a subject, one at a time, with the following instructions: "This is a test of imagination. I am going to show you some pictures. Please make up a dramatic story for each picture. Tell what led up to the event in the picture, what is happening at the moment, what the characters are feeling and thinking, and then give the outcome."

From the stories people make up, it is possible to discover how they feel about themselves and other important people in their lives. As with the Rorschach, interpreting TAT responses is no simple matter. Psychologists trained in giving this test can come up with startling insights into their patients' private feelings, but it takes a lot of experience to become an expert.

One of the TAT pictures shows a boy gazing thoughtfully at a violin. Two stories in response to this picture might run as follows:

1) "This is a young genius dreaming of the future. He has been given this expensive violin by his parents who are poor but have spent all their savings on it. He is dreaming of the great-

ness he will achieve to show them that their trust in him was not misplaced. In years to come, he will be known as one of the finest violinists of all time."

2) "This is a boy whose parents are making him practice. He hates it and is sitting there trying to figure out how to get out of it. He feels like smashing the violin, but probably won't. He'll just mope and complain until they give up and let him quit taking lessons."

Interpretation of these stories is based on the principle that what a person sees in the pictures reflects what that person feels about his or her own life. The first story, therefore, might have been told by someone who entertains dreams of glory. The subject is ambitious and feels a need to prove to his parents that their sacrifices were not in vain. The second story, in contrast, was probably made up by someone who resents being pushed to achieve, who feels that his parents are forcing him to do things he doesn't want to do, and who believes that, if he resists long enough, they will finally let him have his way.

Figure 6.3 shows a picture similar to those used in the TAT. Following the instructions for the test, make up a story about it and compare it with the stories of other members of your class.

Figure 6.3: A picture similar to those used in the TAT.

Aptitude Tests and Vocational Interest Tests

Aptitude tests attempt to assess people's ability to do certain jobs or to succeed at certain professions for which they have not yet been trained. In other words, they try to predict how well we will do in different occupations. Vocational interest tests attempt to determine whether the things we like to do are similar to the things preferred by successful people in various fields of work. Both types of test are used by vocational counselors to help people decide what kind of jobs to look for.

Mechanical aptitude tests, clerical aptitude tests, artistic aptitude tests, and musical aptitude tests have all been used quite widely. So, too, have vocational interest tests which compare one's likes and dislikes to those of successful people in fields as varied as medicine, forestry, business, teaching, and sports.

The intention of such tests is to help us make more intelligent career choices. They are also used by large organizations to select people who are best suited for different jobs. At times they are very useful. Often, however, people who have reached the stage of seriously seeking a career already know, through their own life experience, what they do well and what they enjoy doing.

A testing session.

One of the factors involved in mechanical aptitude is called spatial aptitude. This refers to one's ability to visualize the size, shape, and relationship of figures in space. It is measured very accurately by the Revised Minnesota Paper Form Board Test.[5] Here is an item similar to those used in that test. You must choose the figure that would result if the pieces in the first square were put together.

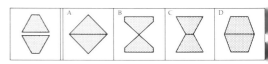

Achievement Tests

Achievement tests measure what students know about subjects that are taught in school. Weekly quizzes, midterms, and final exams are all examples of this type of test. They attempt to assess a student's grasp of a subject and to determine if he or she has learned enough to advance to the next grade or level.

Some achievement tests have been designed for broad general use. The California Achievement Tests, the Iowa Tests of Basic Skills, the Iowa Tests of Educational Development, and the Stanford Achievement Test are among the most well known. They enable testers to compare the levels of learning in different states and cities. They assist in finding the appropriate grade placement for transferring students. They are useful in identifying students with special educational disabilities who may need remedial help. They may also be employed as aids in the evaluation and improvement of teaching.

As an example of the content of achievement tests designed for national use, consider the Stanford Achievement Test. Its intermediate form, applicable to fifth and sixth grade pupils, includes questions on: vocabulary; reading comprehension; word study skills; mathematical concepts; mathematical computation; mathematical applications; spelling; language; social science; science; and listening comprehension.

Here is an item similar to those used on the Stanford Achievement Test to measure "listening comprehension." Examiner reads passage, questions and response options. "Martians who visit Earth should beware of little boys with baseball bats. Since Martians normally look like baseballs zooming toward home plate in a fast-breaking curve, they may be surprised when some enterprising child tries to hit them for a double. In fact, should they chance upon some of our better Little Leaguers, they may find themselves part of a grand-slam homer that could send them all the way back to Mars."

Q. The best title for this passage would be:

1) Current Studies in Astronomy
2) The Space Race Between the U. S. and the U. S. S. R.
3) Does Little League Help Promote Sportsmanship?
4) Up, Up, and Away: It's a Grand Slam Homer

Q. What word best describes this passage?

1) reasoning
2) advice
3) humor
4) mystery

Controversies

While intelligence tests, personality tests, aptitude tests, and achievement tests are all accepted tools of the psychologist's trade, several arguments continue to be waged about their value. Are intelligence tests unfair to certain groups of people? Are projective tests too unscientific? Do tests really measure what they are supposed to measure? Don't we already know what the tests tell us anyway? Each of these points, we have tried to indicate, is frequently mentioned in debates about the usefulness of tests.

Possibly the most profound criticism of tests, however, is that they overlook the uniqueness of the individual. When a test reveals that you are, let us say, highly emotional, all it really shows is that you are more emotional than most people of your age and sex. It fails to explain whether you are more emotional than is good for you. Neither does it explain how your emotionality serves your own life style. Similarly, a test may show how intelligent you are in comparison to your peers. It may not, however, tell whether you use your intelligence constructively or, indeed, whether you use it at all.

While these arguments expose the limitations of psychological testing, they do not disprove that the tests are useful tools. All instruments have their shortcomings. A hammer cannot be used to saw a piece of wood; an aircraft that flies at supersonic speeds cannot take off from a small airfield. Like any other manmade device, tests should be used only where appropriate, with a clear understanding of what they can and cannot do. If such is the case, then there is every reason to believe that testing will remain a part of the psychologist's repertoire of skills.

Summary

In this chapter we have discussed intelligence tests—the Stanford-Binet, the WISC-R, and the WAIS in particular. We have also described the most frequently used personality tests, both objective—the MMPI—and projective—the Rorschach and TAT. We have mentioned some other types of tests, those directed at vocational choice—aptitude and interest tests—and those used in the school system—achievement tests. We have explained their uses, their advantages and disadvantages, and the controversies that surround them.

Now, if you ever have the occasion to be tested by a psychologist, we hope you will understand what the poor man or woman is up against and treat him or her with kindness.

Class Projects

1. The IQ items we quoted in this chapter are too easy to pose a challenge to students your age. Here are a few problems similar to those you might encounter on an IQ test at your level. They might give you a feel for what it

is like to take such a test. As in the intelligence tests we have described, each set of items runs from simple to difficult.

Verbal Problems: Similarities

1) In what way are a carrot and a cucumber alike?

2) In what way are a car and a bicycle alike?

3) In what way are patience and courage alike?

Verbal Problems: Numerical Reasoning (no pencil or paper allowed)

1) You have 10 brown socks and 10 gray socks all mixed up in your dresser drawer. The room is completely dark and you want two matching socks. What is the smallest number of socks you must take out of the drawer to be sure you have a pair that match?

2) If you buy two books at $2.19 each and give the clerk a five-dollar bill, how much change should you get back?

3) Two teams are having a tug-of-war. The boys, on the average, are twice as strong as the girls. The first team consists of four boys and two girls; the second team consists of three boys and five girls. Which team should win?

Nonverbal Problems: Picture Completion

In each of the pictures in Figure 6.4, find the missing part.

Figure 6.4: Find the missing part.

1) How many different squares can you count in the following diagram?

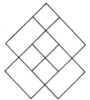

2) With three straight cuts, divide this pie into seven pieces. (The pieces need not be equal in size.)

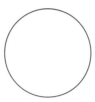

3) Draw this hopscotch diagram without taking your pencil off the paper or going over the same line twice.

As you can see, such items are not exactly what you learn in school, but their solutions require mental alertness and clear and careful thinking.

2. The question of whether certain characteristics, like intelligence, are determined genetically or environmentally—the so-called nature-nurture controversy—has long been debated. One famous example is the story of a man named Kallikak who lived in the 1800s. Mr. Kallikak had an illegitimate child by a poor and feeble-minded woman. This child and many of his offspring were also mentally deficient and some were criminals. Some time after, Mr. Kallikak married a fine, upstanding, Puritan woman. The children of this union were pillars of society, contributors to their church and their community.

Can you see how this example supports either side of the nature-nurture argument? Use it as the basis for a debate in your class. In order to more fully appreciate the complexity of this issue we suggest you argue *for* the side you would normally oppose.

3. In Figure 6.5, you will find two sets of pictures—one of males, one of females. Look them over, one set at a time, and make up a story of a person's life based on each set. You do not have to include all the pictures in your story. Just select as many as you like and build your story around them.

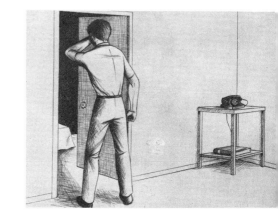

Figure 6.5

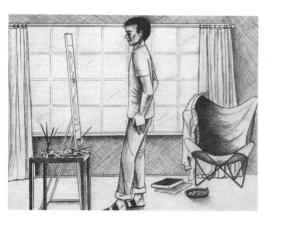

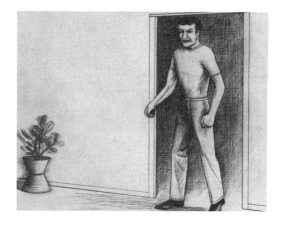

After you have completed the stories, try to analyze your responses in terms of what they tell about you. Ask yourself the following questions about the first story and then about the second.

    a) Is your story essentially happy or unhappy?

    b) Does the character in your story succeed in life or is he or she defeated?

    c) What effect does the character's family have on his or her life?

    d) What part does education play in his or her life?

    e) Does marriage play a part in your story? If so, what kind? If not, why not?

    f) Does the character have a fulfilling career? If so, what kind? If not, why not?

    g) Do inner problems interfere with his or her happiness? If so, what are they?

    h) Is your male story very different from your female story? If so, what do you think that tells about your view of men's lives as compared to women's lives?

References

1. N. J. Block and Gerald Dworkin, eds., *The IQ Controversy* (New York: Pantheon Books, 1976).
2. Paul R. Munford, "A Comparison of WISC and the WISC-R on Black Child Psychiatry Outpatients," *Journal of Clinical Psychology*, 1979, *34*, pp. 938–943.
3. Hermann Rorschach, *Psychodiagnostics* (Berne: Huber, 1921).
4. Bruno Klopfer et al., *Developments in the Rorschach Technique* (New York: Harcourt, Brace, Jovanovich, 1968).
5. *Revised Minnesota Paper Form Board* (New York: The Psychological Corporation, 1969).

Suggested Readings

1. Anastasi, Anne. *Psychological Testing.* New York: Macmillan, 1976.
2. Block, N. J. and Dworkin, Gerald, eds. *The IQ Controversy.* New York: Pantheon Books, 1976.
3. Johnson, D. *Tests and Measurements in Child Development, Handbook II.* Vol. I & II. San Francisco: Jossey-Bass, 1976.
4. Layon, R. I. and Goodstein, L. D. *Personality Assessment.* New York: Springer, 1968.
5. Sundberg, N. *Assessment of Personality.* Englewood Cliffs, NJ: Prentice-Hall, 1977.
6. Williams, Robert L. "Scientific Racism and IQ: The Silent Mugging of the Black Community," *Psychology Today*, May 1974, *8*, pp. 32–34, 37–41, 100.

The Neuroses

7

eople suffering from emotional and mental disorders have been called unstable and crazy. As these terms suggest, those who consider themselves sane and well balanced tend to look down on those who appear disturbed. They tend to pity them, fear them, laugh at them, or get angry at them for not behaving normally.

To the psychologist, in contrast, emotional and mental disorders are common human conditions that deserve careful study and treatment. They are no more shameful than a fever or a state of exhaustion. Even the custom of seeing them as forms of illness has been brought into question. The trend nowadays is to speak less of "cases" than of people reacting to their problems in particular ways.

Technically, severe emotional disorders are known as *neuroses*, while more devastating conditions involving disorders of thought are known as *psychoses*. In this chapter, we will explore the major neuroses, giving examples of each and discussing its possible causes. In chapter 8, we will discuss the psychoses in similar fashion.

When students read such material, they sometimes leap to the conclusion that they or their friends have all the problems described. We would like to advise some caution here. Before you begin to have everyone you know locked up in a padded cell, remember psychology's unwritten law: a little craziness is part of the best of us.

Mental Illness

The terms neurotic and psychotic have become household words in recent years. We all have heard them many times, but few of us understand exactly what they mean. A neurotic, we may realize, is a person suffering from anxiety, depression, or other emotional disturbances of such severity that they disrupt his or her ability to conduct a normal, happy life. A psychotic, we may gather, is a person suffering from mental abnormalities such as seeing strange things that are not there or believing strange things that are not so. If a man spends hours weeping and talking to himself, if he feels compelled to wash his hands two hundred times a day to cleanse his soul of sin, or if he believes that vicious insects are eating away his brain, we may conclude that he is neurotic, psychotic, or some combination of the two. Aside from such obvious cases, however, most people are unclear about the frequency, variety, and causes of neuroses and psychoses in our society.

According to current estimates, mental illness disables more people in the United States than all other health problems combined. One out of twelve persons now living in this country will be hospitalized because of severe neurotic or psychotic symptoms. Millions more will seek outpatient psychiatric help and, of those who do not seek it, a large percentage appear to be in need of it. In other words, "neurotic" and "psychotic" are not terms to be applied to a scattered few: they apply, to some extent at least, to a large part of the population.

In *Abnormal Psychology and Modern Life*[1], James C. Coleman clarifies the gradual way in which normal and mildly maladjusted people shade off into cases of severe neurosis and psychosis. He helps us appreciate the fact that psychological abnormalities are merely extensions of problems that all of us have known and struggled with from time to time.

organic
based on a physical or
bodily condition

In the least extreme cases, the individual is regarded as "queer" or "eccentric" but still within the bounds of ordinary, understandable human experience: here, for example, is the boy of brilliant intelligence who complains that he just can't concentrate on his studies and does inferior college work; the secretary who has persistent headaches for which the doctors can find no **organic** explanation; the painfully self-conscious young man who blushes crimson whenever he becomes the center of attention; the middle-aged Don Juan who centers his life around the conquest of women.

The difficulties may be more serious and bring a recognition that "there's definitely something wrong," as, for example, with the 25-year-old bachelor who will not accept a promotion because it involves an occasional business trip away from his mother; the college girl who is so depressed, anxious, and tearful, for no reasons she can name, that she cannot study or go to class and eventually has to drop out of school entirely; the young husband who cruelly mistreats his wife and then threatens suicide when she decides to leave him; the successful professional man who insists that he is a "miserable failure" and can't continue his work; the adolescent girls who forge checks to pay for their shopping tours; the father who wanders away from his family and is found months later in a strange community, the victim of **amnesia.**

amnesia
loss of memory

Finally, there are individuals whom everyone recognizes as obviously abnormal—the fourteen-year-old boy who has never been able to get past the second grade; the young mother who kills her illegitimate baby; the indignant young man who insists that his enemies have set up an electrical device that "controls his thoughts"; the middle-aged man who molests children; the alcoholic who cringes in terror before an "invasion of cockroaches"; and the "persecuted" paranoid who kills several innocent people he believes are "plotting" against him.

As we study the most well-known forms of neurosis and psychosis, let us remember that they are instances of human suffering and attempts to cope with problems not far removed from what all of us will probably experience in our lifetimes. In this regard, let us also shed the old-fashioned notion that mental illness is a disgrace. Far from thinking that neurotics and psychotics are inferior, weak, or "freaky" people to be looked down upon, modern psychologists believe that they span every category of human being from the most unintelligent to the most intelligent, the most selfish to the most unselfish. We see them, in short, as people like you and me who are either temporarily or chronically the victims of inner conflicts and destructive behavior patterns that cause them and those they live with a great deal of pain and misery.

The Neurotic Core

syndrome
a group of symptoms
that occur together

The neuroses have been categorized into a number of **syndromes.** However, they all share certain common features which can be called the "neurotic core."

1) *Dependency.* Neurotics usually feel unprepared to deal with life's problems. They tend to be overly dependent on others for support and guidance. Even the most well-adjusted human being has dependency needs, but in neurotics these needs loom very large. As a result, they form relationships in which they play the child, or else they try to deny dependency needs by engaging in feats of extraordinary independence.

2) *Anxiety.* Since neurotics see most situations as threatening, they experience a great deal of anxiety. As a result, they resort to many defensive maneuvers to reduce the discomfort of being "on edge."

3) *Irritability.* Continually anxious and on the defensive, the neurotic tends to overreact to ordinary, everyday problems. Mild challenges and frustrations lead him or her to blow up in anger or withdraw in resentment.

4) *Self-centeredness.* Rarely content or relaxed, the neurotic is constantly tuned in to himself or herself and his or her complaints. He or she is thus less capable of responding to other people's needs, which generally leads to strained relations and, in turn, reinforces the neurotic's view of the world as unpleasant.

5) *Lack of insight.* Even though he or she is obsessed with his or her complaints, insight into their causes is usually lacking. The neurotic is apt to blame others for his or her unhappiness and to deny responsibility for continuing it.

6) *Physical symptoms.* In addition to the psychological disorders already mentioned, most neurotics suffer from such generalized physical symptoms as fatigue, muscular tension, indigestion, excessive sweating, headaches, and heart palpitation. While these complaints may be the result of a true organic illness, in the case of the neurotic a medical examination will fail to discover organic **pathology.**

pathology
the results of a disease

Anxiety States

The most common of all neurotic syndromes is a pattern of excessive anxiety with symptoms of shakiness, nervousness, chills, sweating, rapid breathing, and frequent or constant worry. The individual may feel that a terrible catastrophe is about to happen or that his or her death is imminent, even though there is nothing in the immediate environment that other observers would rate as threatening. Such states may be mild and constant or sudden, acute, and overwhelming. In efforts to fend them off, anxiety neurotics may consume a great deal of food, alcohol, narcotics, sleeping pills, and tranquilizers. When the effects of the drugs have worn off, however, the anxiety reappears, for it is produced by problems the individual has been unable to resolve.

Some of the most frequent causes of anxiety are fear of competition, awareness of unacceptable desires in oneself, decisions involving risk of loss or failure, the reexperiencing of prior **trauma,** and anticipation of punishment for real or imagined misdeeds. While these events may produce some anxiety even in normal, well-adjusted individuals, they produce attacks of panic in the neurotic, for he or she commands very little self-confidence to balance them out.

trauma
an emotional shock

Consider, for example, the awareness of unacceptable desires. If **109** people feel that they are likable and just as good as their acquaintances, they will take such desires in their stride. Let us say that they are tempted to steal or cheat. Their moral principles may not allow this kind of behavior, but they will not feel terrible for having been tempted. If, on the other hand, they feel that they are incompetent, disliked, or inferior, the temptation to steal or cheat may throw them into a panic. Afraid that they may not be able to control themselves and convinced that this will prove how bad they really are, they may suffer a prolonged attack of worry and distress.

Consider, too, the reexperiencing of prior trauma. An anxious young woman goes to work for the telephone company and is placed under the supervision of a fussy, demanding, older woman. Anyone having to work under this person may feel slightly uneasy but since this particular employee once suffered under the control of an equally demanding mother, she experiences attacks of panic whenever her supervisor talks to her. Unconsciously, she is reliving a painful period in her past; her reactions to the supervisor are magnified by her old fear and resentment of her mother.

People who suffer excessive anxiety, whether chronically or in the form of occasional attacks, may need to discover the source of their symptoms and strengthen their feelings of self-confidence before they can control their fears.

Mary J. was about to graduate from high school. She was in the top ten percent of her class and had won a scholarship to one of the finest universities in the country. She was going to be escorted to the senior ball by a handsome and popular boy. Her parents were proud of her accomplishments and held her up as an example to her younger brothers and sisters. They had promised to reward her by giving her a summer tour of Europe. Yet Mary was extremely unhappy.

The graduation ceremonies, the honors she would receive, the social events connected with the occasion, even the trip to Europe were dreaded by the girl. When she thought about entering the university in the fall, she experienced intense anxiety, as though she were faced with a dangerous mission.

On the day before the graduation ceremony, Mary fell ill with nausea, dizziness, and shortness of breath. She asked her parents to send for the doctor since she felt too weak to get out of bed. The doctor examined her but was unable to find any medical cause for her complaints. He decided that she was fatigued from overwork and prescribed rest, vitamins, and a balanced diet. They did not do her much good. She remained ill for several weeks. When she recovered her parents concluded that it would be too risky to send her away to college.

The reasons for Mary's strange reactions were really very simple. While she seemed confident and capable on the outside, she was inwardly uncertain of her ability to live up to the expectations of her parents and teachers. She had always worked doubly hard at her studies and exerted a great deal of effort to present a friendly facade in social situations. As the time drew nearer to her graduation, however, she became more and more worried, for she felt she did not deserve all the honors she was getting. Furthermore, she feared that at college she would be shown up as a fake, unable to do well when deprived of the support of her family and lifelong friends.

Phobias

A phobia or phobic reaction is an intense, irrational fear of some particular thing or situation. Closed places, high places, open places, being alone, darkness, crowds, and dirt are some of the common items that bring on such fear reactions. Persons who suffer from phobias know very well that there is nothing especially harmful in the object or situations that upset them. Such knowledge is of little value, however, for the emotions aroused are beyond their control.

Most of us encounter frightening situations in our daily or weekly routines, but we are able to handle them without too much trouble. The phobic neurotic, in contrast, feels compelled to alter his or her normal routine of living in order to avoid the possibility of experiencing the phobia. Thus, people who are afraid of high places may refuse to visit friends or make appointments with doctors or dentists whose offices are above the first floor of a building. Peole who dread dirt may never go to the beach or the park. They engage in a great deal of planning ahead and develop escape plans to use in the event of being faced with the feared situation. If these maneuvers fail and they are forced to encounter their phobia, they may become dizzy and nauseous or be reduced to trembling and tears.

displaced

something expressed in one situation that really belongs in another

Two lines of thought regarding the development of phobias are taken by modern psychologists. In the Freudian tradition, phobic reactions are seen as **displaced** or **symbolic** forms of anxiety in which the consciously feared situation replaces or signifies an unconscious source of fear. Thus, a phobia of small rooms and other enclosing places may signify an unconscious fear of returning to the womb. The individual who suffers from this phobia may have a secret wish to **regress** to infancy, to be protected to the point of being totally enfolded in mother's enclosing warmth, and the experience of being in any closed place may awaken this wish. Since the wish in its raw form is intolerable, however, intense anxiety ensues. The only way the individual can erase it is by avoiding the situations that bring it on. In the same fashion, phobic reactions may represent underlying fears which the sufferer cannot admit. Extreme stage fright, for example, may relate to one's hidden fear that, if one exposes oneself to public scrutiny, one's secret defects will be revealed and lead to scorn and humiliation.

symbolic

representing or signifying something hidden or unknown

regress

to go back to an earlier time

In the behaviorist tradition, on the other hand, phobias are explained as the result of a neutral situation being paired with an anxiety-arousing event. Thus, a person's irrational fear of dogs in adulthood may be based on a childhood experience of being frightened by a dog. A fear of closed places may be rooted in forgotten experiences of having been punished by being locked in a small room. Rather than finding symbolic meanings in people's phobias, the behaviorist assumes that the fears were learned through unfortunate experiences.

Like other neuroses, phobias may be strengthened by the *secondary gains* or hidden rewards the sufferer derives from them. Not only sympathy and special consideration from friends and relatives, but also an excuse for avoiding unpleasant duties may be furnished by a phobia. On **111** a more subtle level, it also enables the individual to make extraordinary demands on other people and to exert more control over his or her environment than would otherwise be acceptable.

Obsessive-Compulsive Syndromes

Obsessions are thoughts a person feels compelled to think against his or her will. Compulsions are acts he or she feels compelled to carry out, even though they may make no sense. Obsessive thinking and compulsive behavior frequently occur in the same individual. Singly or in combination, they may reach such proportions that they interfere with the person's ability to lead a normal life.

Most of us, at one time or another, have found ourselves repeatedly humming a particular song. As children we may have engaged in secret rituals like trying to avoid stepping on the cracks in the sidewalk. These bits of behavior are mildly obsessive-compulsive, but in all likelihood they do not cause us any distress. The extent to which obsessive-compulsive syndroms can dominate a personality, however, is truly astounding. The neurotic may have to rehearse the phrase, "I love my brother," for example, several hundred times a day. Similarly, he or she may have to bathe or shower half a dozen times a day.

ritualizes
engages in precisely the
same act repeatedly

When the disorder takes the form of a way of life, as it sometimes does, the individual **ritualizes** every action, until he or she resembles a mechanical robot more than a human being.

Mr. W. attempted to structure his life to the ultimate. He arose every morning at exactly 7:10, shaved, showered and dressed, ate breakfast, and left the house at precisely 8:15. Arriving at work at 8:45, he maintained a rigid schedule while performing his duties as a minor administrative official. Each evening he arrived home at precisely 6:20, read the paper for 40 minutes, and had his dinner at 7:00. On Mondays and Wednesdays he spent the evening relaxing. On Tuesdays he went to the movies and on Thursdays he played chess with a friend. Fridays were devoted to his stamp collection. Saturdays he took care of home maintenance and spent the evening with friends.

After church on Sunday morning, the afternoon was devoted to golf. This weekly schedule was adhered to, year in and year out, without the slightest deviation. Mr. W's appearance was always meticulous and in his home and office, as he often said, "There was a place for everything and everything was in its place."

We all have routines in our day-to-day lives but Mr. W's schedule is so fixed that it can be called compulsive. There is no room for change of any kind. If he were to lose his job or fall in love and wish to marry, it would be disastrous. His life is ruled by the need for a rigid structure.

Obsessive thought patterns commonly deal with unacceptable primitive impulses. A young mother, for instance, may become preoccupied with thoughts about killing her children although she loves them and is devoted to their welfare. A highly moral, elderly man may become preoccupied with thoughts of yelling obscenities in public. Compulsive acts, in contrast, commonly display great concern about cleanliness, promptness, neatness, and other signs of high moral standards. Thus, a homemaker may feel it necessary to scour her house several times a week, although there is not a speck of dust or grime to be seen. A business person may not be able to sleep unless all his clothes are laid out for the next day and all the documents he may have to consult are in perfect order.

Because of these characteristics of obsessive-compulsive syndromes, psychologists believe that they come from guilt feelings and represent attempts to reduce anxiety caused by the guilt. Obsessive thoughts either show the source of the guilt feelings or create a front behind which to hide them, while compulsive acts either try to deny any inclination to wrongdoing or symbolically enact a ritual of forgiveness. The mother who has fantasies of murdering her children also feels that she would never do such a dreadful thing. Thus, her obsession both masks and reveals a deepfelt wish to be rid of the responsibility of taking care of them. Similarly, the homemaker who scours her house may be trying to disprove her fear that she is really a lazy or dirty person.

Hysterical or Conversion Reactions

mutism
an inability to speak

anorexia nervosa
a neurotic refusal to eat

A neurosis in which psychological conflicts are turned into physical disabilities, conversion hysteria includes a wide array of symptoms. Blindness, deafness, and paralysis of parts of the body may be hysterical in nature. Tremors, ticks, **mutism,** and fainting spells may also be due to hysteria. Headaches, stomachaches, nausea, chest pains, vomiting, hiccuping, sneezing, **anorexia nervosa**—every form of physical illness, in fact, from apparent appendicitis to apparent pregnancy—may be produced by hysterical neurotics.

dysfunction
something not working
properly

The symptoms are so convincing, at times, that unnecessary surgical procedures have been carried out by doctors attempting to relieve them. It is possible, however, to distinguish neurotic from actual physical illness in a number of ways. To begin with, hysterics usually describe their symptoms in a detached, indifferent fashion which seems out of keeping with the severity of the ailment. This attitude, long known as *la belle indifference,* betrays the fact that unconsciously the patient welcomes his or her illness. Secondly, hysterical **dysfunctions** are sometimes selective in the sense that supposedly blind people avoid bumping into dangerous obstacles and supposedly paralyzed people are able to move in emergencies. Besides that, the symptoms may not be in line with physiological facts: a patient's paralysis may end at the wrist or elbow while actual neural pathways are not so neatly defined. Finally, if the hysteric is hypnotized, the symptoms may be removed or shifted to other parts of the body.

Psychologists have shown that the hysterical neurotic develops a **113** physical ailment in order to avoid some anxiety or guilt-producing situation. In addition, he or she gains secondary rewards from the ailments. A combat infantryman, for instance, may develop a hysterical paralysis of his legs in order to be removed from active duty and enjoy the benefits of hospitalization. All of us have played sick, at times, to get out of doing something unpleasant (e.g., going to school). In the case of conversion hysteria, the difference is that the patient does not know he or she is creating the illness. Hysteria is not malingering. It is a matter of producing physical symptoms, often painful and debilitating, in an unconscious effort to avoid anxiety or guilt.

Hysterical disorders have been recognized since ancient times. The word "hysteria" itself comes from the Greek term for uterus; the disease was long believed to be a feminine one. In the last fifty years, however, its incidence has declined, perhaps because of our increasing sophistication about the nature of physical illness. As you will see in a later chapter, Sigmund Freud began his career as a psychoanalyst by providing a new explanation for hysteria. His discoveries regarding the cause and treatment of the disorder have been important also in reducing its occurrence in the modern world.

Neurasthenia

Neurasthenia is characterized by fatigue accompanied by a variety of aches and pains. The people most likely to suffer from neurasthenic reactions are middle-aged adults. Their major complaints are tiredness—lack of energy, feeling worn out—and bodily discomfort. They rest and sleep a lot, yet they rarely feel refreshed upon awakening. As the day wears on, their fatigue increases; but they may suddenly snap out of it when invited to participate in parties or other exciting events. Because of their aches and pains, neurasthenics are apt to take a lot of vitamins, laxatives, antacids, aspirin, and tranquilizers. None of these preparations ever cures them, but the temporary relief they obtain appears to help them a bit.

Once treated entirely by such simple remedies as rest, relaxation, physical exercise, a healthful diet, and mild medication, neurasthenia is now regarded as a neurotic condition based on such problems as hostility toward one's spouse and family or guilt resulting from a failure to achieve desired goals. Thus, the housewife who continually complains about her headaches and backaches may be expressing, in this indirect fashion, her resentment at the husband and children who shoulder her with work and responsibilities. Similarly, the businessman who feels he has "lost his pep" may be suffering from disappointment with himself over having given up his youthful dreams of a colorful, adventurous life.

114

As a rule, neurasthenics appear to be lacking in self-assertion. They are immature, dependent adults who fail to satisfy their own basic needs and then resent both themselves and others for forcing them to assume responsibilities they wish they could ignore. Their conflicts are similar to those that most of us experience from time to time. In the case of the neurotic, however, the condition becomes, in effect, a way of life.

Depression

All of us have low moods at times—hours or days when we feel blue, sad, discouraged, and pessimistic. If we should lose someone we love, either through death or because they no longer want to be close to us, we will grieve for a few days or weeks. If we fail in an enterprise that means a lot to us, we will be disappointed and miserable for a while. These are the normal kinds of depressive reactions all human beings

Inactivity and social isolation are characteristic of depressed individuals.

experience. Neurotic depression, in contrast, is either a matter of grief **115**
prolonged beyond reasonable bounds or pessimistic or indifferent
moods arising from unknown causes and lasting for months or years
on end.

The incidence of neurotic depression is greater than most of us
realize. It is estimated that one in eight people now living in the United
States will suffer a bout of depression serious enough to require
psychiatric help during his or her lifetime. Of the 50,000 to 70,000
suicides that occur in this country every year, approximately half are
committed by persons in the grip of depressive moods. Traditionally an
affliction of the middle-aged and elderly, depression is now affecting
more and more young people. "Most drug-taking," says one expert, "is
in reality self-medication for depression."

Psychologists and psychiatrists are still unsure whether severe and
prolonged low moods are the result of environmental stress, unresolved
inner conflicts, or faulty body chemistry. In all likelihood, some combination of these three factors is involved in most cases. The physiological
conditions that can cause depression are both subtle and complex, but
the fact that antidepressant drugs (i.e., "uppers") can relieve "the blues"
indicates that chemical factors are indeed at work. At the same time, loss
of a loved one, disappointment in one's career or love life, or despair
over the problems of our modern world may drive people into states of
apathy or brooding. Yet the question remains how other people, equally
aware of the horrors of war and poverty and equally beset by reverses in
love and work, manage to keep up their spirits and retain their hope.
Some psychologists assume that faith or belief in a higher power is the
key. They claim that the breakdown of religion, followed by a loss of
faith in science and technology as improvers of the world, has made us
more prone to depression today. Others, however, disagree. They contend that the central cause of depression is more closely connected with
the ways in which we handle our anger and resentments. If we openly
and directly express our negative feelings toward whoever has evoked
them, we will not become depressed, they say. If, on the other hand, we
bottle up these feelings because of fear or guilt about expressing them,
they will cause us to become depressed.

Whatever the underlying causes, it is clear that a depressed mood
involves lack of energy and enthusiasm, feelings of hopelessness and
discouragement, and a sense of having failed or of being stymied in
one's attempts to conduct an exciting, meaningful life. Such moods can
become so intense that the sufferer would rather commit suicide than go
on experiencing them. To guard against this possibility and to help the
depressed person reestablish his or her joy in living, it is necessary to
lead him or her to a hopeful, assertive outlook. While there is no guaranteed method of achieving this goal in all cases, it is encouraging to know
chemotherapy that many types of psychotherapy, as well as **chemotherapy,** are effec-
treatment through drugs tive in curing neurotic depressions.

The following excerpts from Leo Tolstoy's personal account give us a firsthand experience of neurotic depression.

But five years ago, a strange state of mind-torpor began at times to grow upon me. I had moments of perplexity, of a stoppage, as it were, of life, as if I did not know how I was to live, what I was to do. I began to wander, and was a victim to low spirits. This, however, passed, and I continued to live as before. Later, these periods of perplexity grew more and more frequent, and invariably took the same form. During their continuance the same questions always presented themselves to me: "Why?" and "What after?"

My life had come to a sudden stop. I was able to breathe, to eat, to drink, to sleep. I could not, indeed, help doing so; but there was no real life in me. I had not a single wish to strive for the fulfillment of what I could feel to be reasonable. If I wished for anything, I knew beforehand that, were I to satisfy the wish, nothing would come of it, I should still be dissatisfied. Had a fairy appeared and offered me all I desired, I should not have known what to say.

The truth lay in this, that life had no meaning for me. Every day of life, every step in it, brought me nearer the edge of a precipice, whence I saw the final ruin before me. To stop, to go back, were alike impossible; nor could I shut my eyes so as not to see the suffering that alone awaited me, the death of all in me, even to annihilation. Thus I, a healthy and a happy man, was brought to feel that I could live no longer, that an irresistible force was dragging me down to the grave.

Such was the condition I had come to, at the time when all the circumstances of my life were preeminently happy ones, and when I had not reached my fiftieth year. I had a good, a loving, and a well-beloved wife, good children, a fine estate, which, without much trouble on my part, continually increased my income. I was more than ever respected by my friends and acquaintances; I was praised by strangers, and could lay claim to having made my name famous without much self-deception. Moreover my mind was neither deranged nor weakened; on the contrary, I enjoyed a mental and physical strength which I have seldom found in men of my class and pursuits: I could keep up with a peasant in mowing, and could continue mental labor for ten hours at a stretch, without any evil consequences.

The mental state in which I then was seemed to be summed up in the following: my life was a foolish and wicked joke played upon me by I knew not whom.[2]

Psychosomatic Symptoms

While not considered exactly neurotic, there is a class of disorders whose origins appear to be psychological although their symptoms are mainly physical. People with psychosomatic symptoms endure headaches and stomachaches, muscular tension, fatigue and irritability, loss of appetite and the compulsion to overeat, ulcers, asthma, eczema, and other kinds of allergies. They are likely to surround themselves with pills, medicines, and other medical paraphernalia that indicate a preoccupation with somatic concerns although these symptoms may be the result of emotional conflicts. It is actually an oversimplification to say that certain illnesses are caused by physical agents and others by psychological stress. The human being is made up of mind and body so to some extent all disorders result from an interaction of physical and psychological events. When psychologists or psychiatrists call an illness psychosomatic, however, they mean to suggest that a major part of its origin can be traced to emotional problems.

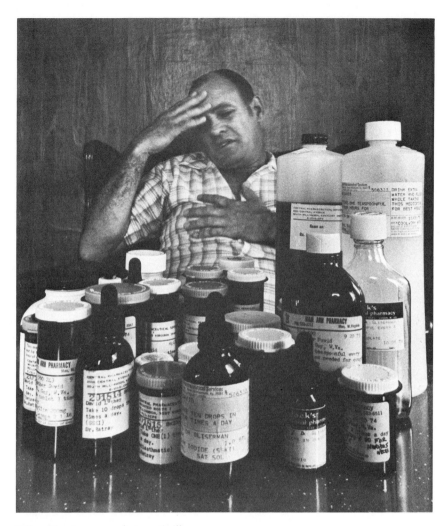

Pills will not cure psychosomatic illness.

The process by which emotional conflicts end up as physical illnesses is difficult to trace. Similar processes can be observed in our everyday behavior—when embarrassed, we are apt to blush, and when frightened to shiver. In both cases an emotional state has been turned into a physical event. On a slightly more complex level, when we are worried, we may develop a headache. When we are anxious, we may develop a digestive disturbance. A constant interplay, in fact, goes on between our psychological and bodily selves. It should come as no surprise, therefore, to discover that there are psychological components to every physiological condition from radiant health to fatal illness.

118

Character Disorders

Another class of abnormalities that is not exactly neurotic includes antisocial behavior patterns that are destructive or demeaning to other people. Both criminal acts and sexual perversions fall into this category. Law-enforcement agencies assume that fines and imprisonment are appropriate methods of attempting to reduce these problems. Many psychologists, however, believe that, either in addition to or instead of legal action, the perpetrators are in need of psychotherapy.

Crime itself is by no means a simple matter. White-collar crimes such as forgery, fraud, and embezzlement, crimes of passion such as murder, organized crime such as drug peddling and prostitution, and crime in the streets such as mugging and theft are in many ways distinct kinds of activities. The thief may have no inclination to peddle drugs, the forger may be as appalled at murder as the most law-abiding citizen. Most criminals share, however, a lack of regard for other people's welfare and a willingness to act on impulses most of us suppress.

Criminal character disorders usually have their roots in early childhood experiences. Infants have no idea of right or wrong, no regard for other people's needs, and no control over their impulses. In this sense, all infants are amoral. Most children learn, however, that respect for other people's rights results in better relations. At first in order to avoid punishment and to gain approval, and later in order not to cause others distress, they learn to restrain their selfish drives. Antisocial characters, in contrast, never seem to learn such restraint. Their inability or refusal to learn it generally stems from a home environment that has failed to teach it effectively. Parental neglect, sadistic punishment, and criminal tendencies on the part of parents are frequently found in the background of confirmed adult criminals. Whatever the specific pattern of causation, the compulsion to engage in criminal acts is evidence of deep-seated psychological disturbance and is very difficult to cure.

Nevertheless, since legal action alone has never been successful in preventing crime, it would seem that more opportunities for treatment of criminals should be provided. Even if offenders are not successfully cured, the sources of their problems may be identified. Future generations may thereby be aided to reduce the incidence of crime.

Sexual perversions, too, are many and varied. Exhibitionism (i.e., exhibiting oneself sexually in public), voyeurism (i.e., achieving sexual gratification by spying on other people's intimate activities), fetishism (i.e., becoming sexually excited by a nonsexual object such as a shoe or a glove), pederasty (i.e., sexual attraction to young boys), sodomy (i.e., abnormal forms of sexual intercourse or intercourse between a person and an animal), and rape (i.e., forcible sexual intercourse) are all specific problems ranging from passive to violent and from relatively harmless to exceptionally harmful. Those who engage in these behaviors share a tendency to perceive other people as sexual objects rather than as human beings and an inability to relate to others on a basis of mutual affection.

Like criminal disorders, sexual perversions have their roots in early childhood, but they seem somewhat easier to treat. These problems can usually be relieved if the individual who suffers from them enters psychotherapy with a sincere desire to learn how to be successful in normal sexual relations.

In many cases, however, a sexual perversion may be part of a broader neurotic or psychotic illness. The same, of course, is true of criminal behavior. In these instances, effective treatment will have to attack the neurosis or psychosis as well as the antisocial behavior.

Summary

This chapter began by distinguishing between neurotic and psychotic disorders and pointing out their frequency in our culture. Not only do neuroses and psychoses occur more frequently than you might suspect, but they happen to people just like us.

We then defined the essential characteristics of neuroses, the so-called neurotic core: dependency, anxiety, irritability, self-centeredness, lack of insight, and physical symptoms. We further described each major category of neurosis: anxiety states, phobias, obsessive-compulsive syndromes, hysterical or conversion reactions, neurasthenia, and depression. Finally, we discussed psychosomatic and character disorders. We hope this information will help you understand and sympathize with people suffering from such problems.

Class Projects

1. Have you ever had an illness that you would call psychosomatic? If so, try to recall the emotional conflicts or anxieties that played a part in producing it. If the identical conflicts or anxieties were to arise again, do you think you could find another way of handling them? Do you react with certain bodily symptoms (e.g., headache, stomachache, loss of appetite) to anxiety-arousing events such as finals? If so, can you tell why your anxiety results in those symptoms rather than others?

2. At a noisy New Year's Eve party which was becoming more and more rowdy, a shy young man developed an acute asthmatic attack. He began to wheeze, had difficulty breathing, and soon had to be rushed to the emergency hospital.

   When her only son declared his intention to move away from home, a doting mother began to experience severe chest pains leading her to suspect that she might be developing heart disease.

   A professional boxer, learning of his wife's involvement with another man, found it impossible to clench his fists.

   In each of these cases, can you detect the hysterical motivation for the onset of the physical symptoms? Write down your ideas and discuss them in class. Also consider if you, or anyone you know, ever suffered an ailment which you suspect may be neurotic in origin.

120

3. How many people do you know who have an irrational fear of insects or reptiles or other harmless creatures? Interview these individuals and try to find out why their fears arose and how they think they might be overcome.

References

1. JAMES C. COLEMAN, *Abnormal Psychology and Modern Life*, 5th ed. (Chicago: Scott, Foresman, 1976).
2. BERT KAPLAN, ed. *The Inner World of Mental Illness* (New York: Harper and Row, 1964).

Suggested Readings

1. DEUTSCH, H. *Neurosis and Character Types*. New York: International University Press, 1965.
2. GOLDSTEIN, J. J. and PALMER, J. O. *The Experience of Anxiety*. Englewood Cliffs, NJ: Prentice-Hall, 1971.
3. LINDNER, ROBERT. *The Fifty Minute Hour*. New York: Rinehart, 1954.
4. PARKER, B. A. *Mingled Yarn: Chronicle of a Troubled Family*. New Haven, CT: Yale University Press, 1972.
5. SHAPIRO, DAVID. *Neurotic Styles*. New York: Basic Books, 1965.
6. ULLMANN, L. P. and KRASNER, L. *A Psychological Approach to Abnormal Behavior*. Englewood Cliffs, NJ: Prentice-Hall, 1975.

The Psychoses

8

Psychoses are sometimes believed to be based on organic or chemical abnormalities; in this they contrast with the neuroses, which are generally seen as psychological in origin. It has been shown that some psychotics have unusual amounts of certain chemicals in their blood, and it is a well-known fact that chemical agents like LSD can produce psychotic symptoms.

Nevertheless, most people suffering from mental disorders have not been proven to have an unusual body chemistry, and purely psychological forces like grief and shock have been known to bring on psychotic states.

It seems reasonable, therefore, to think of the conditions we are about to describe as partly, if not wholly, psychological. In discussing them as such, we leave open the question of whether an organic or chemical factor may one day be found to underly them. Since they are very difficult to treat, most psychologists would be happy to learn of a pill or a diet that could cure them. Meanwhile, however, we intend to keep trying to understand the psychology of mental disorders.

psychoses

mental disorders in which the patients hear voices, see things that are not there, or entertain strange beliefs (e.g., that people are plotting against them, that their insides are being eaten away by insects, that the world will be saved if they engage in some strange ritual)

The Psychotic Core

124

We have already noted that neurotics tend to share certain characteristics. The same is true of psychotics. These characteristics are not by any means unknown among the normal population, but their occurrence is much more common among the mentally ill.

Whereas the neurotic core consists of strong dependency needs, defensiveness, irritability, self-centeredness, lack of insight, and physical complaints, the psychotic core consists of the following:

1) *a tendency to distort reality* (seeing, hearing, feeling, and believing things that are not really there)

2) *a rich and frightening amount of fantasy*

3) *inappropriate affect* (becoming enraged at situations most people would find only mildly annoying or feeling no grief at the death of a very close friend)

4) an experience psychologists call *depersonalization* (feeling divorced from one's body or removed from the actions one engages in)

Whether these characteristics are inborn or acquired is still a matter of debate, though most psychologists believe they are strongly influenced by the way we are brought up. Many children, for instance, have a rich and sometimes frightening fantasy life. They imagine monsters, ghosts, and wild animals as well as fairy-tale adventures of heroism and hidden treasures. As they grow older, they give up these thoughts and become more concerned with dating, school, sports, and the things of this world. The child who is deprived of these normal outlets, however, may well hold on to his or her fantasy life and thus move into adulthood with one of the characteristics that could lead to a psychotic problem.

In any case, it is important to understand that the components of the psychotic core are not without value. A rich stream of fantasy can help a person become creative, while depersonalization sometimes has the merit of enabling people to withstand **traumatic events.** Like the neuroses, the psychoses may be seen as attempts to cope with life's ups and downs and to maintain one's **integrity** in the face of confusing, frustrating, or demoralizing experiences.

traumatic events
very upsetting experiences that leave a person with an emotional wound

integrity
one's sense of wholeness, of being put together right

In the television drama, "Holocaust," one scene shows a young woman huddled in the corner of a boxcar in which the Nazis sent their victims to concentration camps. She is cradling her dead infant to her breast. When her friends try to take the baby away to bury it, she whimpers pathetically and insists that the child is alive. There is a wild, confused look in her eyes and she seems unaware of her surroundings.

This woman has lapsed into a psychotic state as her last defense against the terrible circumstances of her life. Unable to bear the realization that the brutal Nazis have destroyed everything that is dear to her, she has made herself believe that her baby still lives and needs her mothering.

Schizophrenia

delusions

believing things that are not so, especially about other people's evil intentions or one's own superiority

hallucinations

seeing, hearing, smelling, or feeling things that are not there

The most common form of mental illness is called schizophrenia (splitting of the mind). It includes a number of symptoms, each of which may be present to greater or lesser degree. 1) Withdrawal from reality—in other words, a loss of interest in external events—is one of the main signs. It is usually accompanied by *autism,* or obsessive preoccupation with internal sensations, moods, and fantasies. 2) A general flattening of emotionality disrupted from time to time by inappropriate emotional outbursts is common, too. 3) **Delusions** and **hallucinations** constitute the most dramatic symptoms; weird behavior in the form of strange gestures and postures is frequently displayed. 4) A lowering of impulse control and a deterioration in habits of personal hygiene round out the clinical picture.

Schizophrenic patients are often subject to visual hallucinations.

The psychosis has been divided into four major categories.

1) In *simple schizophrenia,* the patient shows a gradual withdrawal from the activities of everyday life. He or she becomes disinterested in other people, in world events, and in his or her own obligations and pleasures. Unresponsive to pleading, threats, or reasoning by family and friends, he or she seems extremely remote. Simple schizophrenics are often able to maintain themselves outside an institution, but they usually occupy such fringe positions in society as prostitutes, vagrants, and petty criminals.

2) In *hebephrenic schizophrenia,* the patient has a history of odd behavior going back to childhood. While his or her peers were acquiring social interests, he or she was becoming more and more preoccupied with inner fantasies. Inappropriate giggling and laughing, plus various kinds of speech disorders, are common in hebephrenics. Auditory hallucinations (hearing voices) and delusions of persecution (believing that people are plotting against them or purposely trying to make their lives miserable) may result in outbursts of violence. As the condition worsens, modesty is lost. The patient may smear dirt and feces on his or her body, indulge in morbid kinds of clowning, and find enjoyment in acts that repel most normal people.

3) In *catatonic schizophrenia,* patients shift from periods of excessive activity to periods of total inactivity. They may actually maintain awkward physical positions for hours, days, or weeks. They appear to be completely disconnected and must be fed, bathed, and toileted. During periods of excitement, catatonics talk and shout incessantly, pace endlessly back and forth, engage in sexual activities in public, and assault other people or attempt to commit suicide.

4) In *paranoid schizophrenia,* the patient has usually had a long history of suspiciousness and distrust of other people. He or she experiences delusions of grandeur and persecution, often accompanied by hallucinations. Paranoid schizophrenics may believe that they have been sent by God to impart the Truth to humankind, and they may actually hear supernatural voices telling them what to do. At the same time, they may believe that certain groups are plotting to keep them from carrying out God's will. Being completely involved in this delusional system, they may engage in violent reprisals against their supposed enemies. In mental hospitals, paranoid patients in exalted states maintain that they are Napoleon, Christ, or Joan of Arc, while those who are feeling anguished claim that they

These catatonic patients may maintain these frozen positions for hours.

are being roasted alive for their sins or that they are famous murderers awaiting execution on death row.

The causes of delusional thinking have been explained in different ways. One theory holds that because they feel terribly confused and insecure, paranoid schizophrenics imagine themselves very important to bolster their self-esteem. In believing that they are distinguished figures or close friends of God, they supply themselves with an uplifting sense of identity. Even delusions of persecution, according to this explanation, serve the purpose of establishing the patient's importance, for they suggest that he or she matters enough that whole groups will try to harm them.

Another theory asserts that paranoid people really feel very guilty over what they consider their terrible sins. Their delusions of persecution thus represent the punishment they feel they deserve, while their delusions of grandeur represent attempts to prove that they are justified in doing whatever they feel like doing.

128   **projection**

believing that other people have feelings and thoughts that are really one's own, or seeing "out there" what is really in oneself

Projection plays a large part in paranoid thinking. When patients see the devil tempting them to sin or hear insulting voices calling them names, it is their own feelings that are being expressed. When they believe their neighbors are banding together to crucify them, it is their own wish to suffer that is being projected. Whatever the pattern of feelings may be in each individual case, it seems clear that all schizophrenics find their environment too frustrating to tolerate, their impulses too dreadful to accept. Having an unusually free access to their fantasy, they create an imaginary world that contains the elements of their inner life.

A young woman whose husband had recently died in an automobile accident began to suspect that her sister's husband was plotting to murder her sister. He had, she believed, developed an erotic longing for her and probably thought that, if his wife were out of the way, he could seduce her. The evidence for her suspicions rested on the fact that, since her own husband's death, her brother-in-law had been unusually attentive to her and in a dream she had seen him covered with her sister's blood.

As time went on, she began to hear voices which, she felt sure, belonged to her brother-in-law and some criminals he had hired to kill his wife. Her agitation increased until she could no longer sleep. She would pace up and down in her bedroom, waiting for a phone call she was certain would come, in which he would tell her that her sister was dead and he was coming to live with her. When, after several weeks, this phone call failed to occur, she called the police and told them that her brother-in-law was criminally insane.

Most psychologists would explain this woman's problem as a projection of her longing for her brother-in-law's love combined with jealousy of her sister. When her husband was killed, they would reason, she began to envy her sister and to wish she would die. Unable to tolerate this evil wish, however, she projected it onto her brother-in-law and made herself believe he was the evil one. When he failed to do what she thought he would, she reported him to the police in the vain hope that they would somehow confirm his guilt, thereby allowing her to feel pure and innocent.

Paranoia

Whereas the paranoid schizophrenic suffers confusion that affects all areas of his or her life, the true *paranoiac* seems relatively well-adjusted within the framework of a delusional system. If a paranoiac harbors delusions of persecution, he or she may collect press clippings or other so-called "evidence" for years on end, supposedly showing that the blacks or the Jews or the Communists are poisoning our nation by putting harmful chemicals into our water supplies. If a paranoiac harbors delusions of grandeur, he or she may organize a religious cult based on his or her "divine inspirations."

Such people are sometimes successful in convincing others of the truth of their beliefs. Hitler, Stalin, and other modern dictators appear to have had strong paranoid characteristics. When linked to an unusual ability to write, preach, or propagandize, paranoia can drive people into positions of power. Since all of us have a tendency to believe that certain groups are against us, since it is tempting to conclude that all the trouble

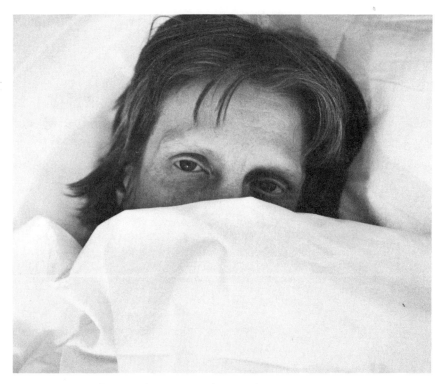

Suspiciousness is the main characteristic of paranoid patients.

in the world is caused by people other than ourselves, and since it is inspiring to join a crusade led by someone in whom we have placed great faith, we are all susceptible to the claims of paranoiacs.

The important question is how to distinguish brilliant leaders from men and women whose careers are based on delusions of persecution and grandeur. It seems safe to say that the more such leaders attack certain groups as the source of all evil and assert that they alone are faultless, the more ruthless they are in pursuing their goals, and the more intolerant they are of any form of criticism, the more paranoid they are likely to be.

Manic-Depressive Cycles

lethargy
a great lack of energy accompanied by drowsiness, dullness, and apathy

Though not as common as schizophrenia, manic-depressive conditions also constitute a major form of mental illness. They may occur as extreme mood swings from states of high excitement to states of total **lethargy.** They may also occur as prolonged states of mania or depression.

The lows and highs of manic depressive illness.

Mania itself varies widely in intensity. In the condition known as *hypomania*, patients claim to be feeling unusually happy. Their thinking is speeded up and they seem tireless. Often brilliant, witty, and entertaining, they manage to be the life of every gathering. They exhibit poor judgment, however, spending money recklessly and engaging in shameless sexual displays. In *acute mania*, on the other hand, the patient's happiness has expanded into a kind of wild **elation.** Flights of ideas are common and speech may become incoherent. Extremely irritable when provoked, acute manics may destroy furniture and attack other people. Constant activity coupled with **disorientation** in time and place characterize the manic condition at this level. In *delirious mania*, finally, patients are deeply confused, excited, and violent. Exceptionally irritable and in a state of great agitation, they may be dangerous and have to be physically restrained.

Depression, too, varies from mild dejection to suicidal fits. Depressed patients suffer a loss of energy and an overwhelming feeling of **futility.** They feel discouraged and rejected. Days or weeks may be spent in blank despair or in contemplating all the morbid aspects of life. Hallucinations and delusions occur, expressing in bizarre, dramatic form a sense of total emptiness and hopelessness.

Manic-depressive cycles may rotate on a daily or monthly basis, while prolonged mania or depression can continue for months or years. **Malfunctions** in body chemistry are frequently involved in these conditions, so treatment includes heavy doses of medication and other kinds of physical manipulation (exercise, hot and cold baths, electroshock therapy).

elation
extreme happiness and high spirits

disorientation
confusion, not knowing where you are

futility
hopelessness, feeling useless and ineffective

malfunctions
not working properly

I come now to the central feature of my whole experience. Somehow I want to find adequate words to describe the dawn of what I may call the Horrific Vision. . . . A crumpled pillow is quite an ordinary everyday object, is it not? One looks at it and thinks no more about it? So is a washing-rag, or a towel tumbled on the floor, or the creases on the side of a bed. Yet they can suggest shapes of the utmost horror to the mind obsessed by fear. Gradually my eyes began to distinguish such shapes, until eventually, whichever way I turned, I could see nothing but devils waiting to torment me. . . . They had names, too. There was the god Baal, with a cruel mouth like a slit (a wrinkle in the side of a bed), waiting to devour me as a living sacrifice. There was Hecate, who used generally to appear in pillows. Her shape was, I think, the most horrible of all. When I went out I saw devils by the hundreds in trees and bushes, and especially in cut wood, generally in serpent form. . . . Certainly I was be-

witched. But that was no new discovery, it did not frighten me more than I was frightened in any case. Then, suddenly, the answer came. Bishop Berkeley was right, the whole universe of space and time, of my own senses, was really an illusion. Or so it was for me at any rate. There I was, shut in my own private universe, as it were, with no contact with real people at all, only with phantasmagoria who could at any moment turn into devils. I and all around me were utterly unreal. . . . My soul was finally turned into nothingness—except unending pain.

Not long before my attack I had been reading James Joyce's *Portrait of the Artist as a Young Man*. The description it gives of a sermon preached by a Jesuit father on the meaning of damnation had made a great impression on me. As I sat there I could recall almost every word. "For ever," says the preacher, "for all eternity. Try to imagine the awful meaning of this. You have often seen the sand on the

132

seashore. How many of those tiny grains go to make up the small handful which a child grasps in its play? Now imagine a mountain of that sand a million miles high, and a million miles broad, and a million miles in thickness; and imagine such an enormous mass of countless particles of sand multiplied as often as there are leaves in the forest, drops of water in the mighty ocean, feathers on birds, scales on fish, hairs on animals, atoms in the vast expanse of air; and imagine that at the end of every million years a little bird came to that mountain and carried away in its beak a tiny grain of that sand. How many millions upon millions of centuries would pass before that bird had carried away even a square foot of that mountain, how many aeons upon aeons of ages before it had carried away all? Yet at the end of that immense stretch of time not even

one instant of eternity can be said to have ended. . . ."

At that moment I had reached the extremity of fear. Paroxysms of terror overcame me and I nearly jumped straight out of the window with the idea of killing myself with the broken glass. But the fit passed, and looking back I date my improvement and subsequent recovery from that moment. No imagination could produce a greater horror than that vision of infinitely increasing physical pain through astronomical time. My soul had plumbed the lowest depth.[1]

The foregoing material, written by a man suffering from manic-depressive psychosis in the depressive phase, is a beautiful description of the inner experience of a psychotic person. If you are interested in more such first-person accounts, we suggest you read some of the other chapters in the book from which this was taken.

The Medical Model

psychopathology

disorders of mental and emotional function, anything wrong with your mind or feelings

Several times in the last two chapters, we have referred to neuroses and psychoses as "illnesses" and the people who suffer from them as "patients." These terms have been used for generations. In recent years, however, psychologists have challenged their validity. Explanations of **psychopathology,** they argue, can be made in terms of various models. The notions of "illnesses" and "patients" come from a medical model. In this model, neuroses and psychoses are seen as similar to physical illnesses like heart disease or tuberculosis. They are thought to require treatment by doctors in professional offices, clinics, and hospitals. In societies other than ours, however, a supernatural model has been employed. The neurotic and psychotic, it suggests, are possessed by demonic or divine forces and need to be treated (if at all) by witch doctors, priests, or other religious persons. We believe that the medical model is superior to the supernatural, but other models may be superior to the medical.

A moral model, for example, has been proposed. It suggests that neuroses and psychoses are results of irresponsible ways of living. According to this view, all forms of psychopathology result from avoidance of such questions as, "Who am I? What is my destiny? What must I do to be happy and content with my life?" The treatment of such conditions does not require doctors and hospitals, but help in facing these important questions and taking responsibility for one's own welfare.

One of the major critics of the medical model, Thomas Szasz, has put forth a learning model which he claims is far more accurate. He writes as follows:

So-called mental illnesses may be like languages, and not at all **133** like diseases of the body. . . . Suppose, for instance, that the problem of hysteria is more akin to the problem of a person speaking a foreign tongue than it is to that of a person having a bodily disease. We are accustomed to believe that diseases have causes, treatments, and cures. If, however, a person speaks a language other than our own, we do not usually look for the "cause" of his peculiar linguistic behavior. . . . To understand such behavior, we must think in terms of learning and meaning. Accordingly, we might conclude that speaking French is the result of living among people who speak French. . . . If a so-called psychopathological phenomenon is more akin to a language problem than to illness, it follows that we cannot meaningfully talk of "treatment" and "cure." . . . I submit that hysteria is nothing other than the language of illness, employed either because another language has not been learned well enough, or because this language happens to be especially useful."[2]

Another critic of the medical model, John Weir Perry, says:

No one is more isolated than when withdrawn in an altered state of consciousness (i.e., psychosis). When one is thus prey to every psychic force, one is in desperate need of the human response of **empathy,** for which drugs are so poor a substitute as to amount to a mockery. But when the psychiatrist resorts only to medication and management to stamp out the nonrational, the "patient" quickly senses that this is not a congenial atmosphere in which to open up or a safe relation in which to reveal his actual preoccupations—so he clams up."[3]

empathy
feeling what someone else is feeling in order to understand him or her better

Later in the same work, he offers the following argument.

If I went to a friend and told him that I died last night and entered into an afterlife state right here, and that I saw the world divided into opposing forces of good and evil ready for the great cataclysm, he would reach for the phone and gently and compassionately turn me over to a hospital where they know how to stamp out such wildness of mind. But if I were more circumspect and put it that I dreamed last night that I died and so on, he and I could have a little laugh about it. . . . Or I might choose another route, radiantly recounting to him a great happening at a Sunday revival meeting, couching my experience in the commonly agreed language of a religious form, that I felt myself dying with Jesus on that rugged cross while the world was riven between the power of God and of Satan. My friend would doubtless say that this is all right for those who like it. . . . In our dreams, our religion, our poetic moments, we all have this madness in us as part of our makeup.

From this point of view, Perry argues that it is more helpful to try to understand the psychotic experience than to try to "cure" it.

Whatever model or view of mental disorders may prove to be most effective in the long run, it cannot be denied that the medical model is only one way of looking at the neuroses and psychoses. It has its advantages, for those who use it do in fact help some people overcome their problems, but it also has its drawbacks. Some of these have already been pointed out by Szasz and Perry. Another that we would like to mention is that in calling neurotic and psychotic behavior "sick," we imply that more conventional ways of behaving are "healthy." That may at times be so, of course, but the question may also be raised whether our society itself is not "sick" in certain respects. If it is—for instance, in promoting the highly competitive "rat race" many people must engage in to make a good living or in condoning tendencies to violence by spending billions on armaments and striving to build bigger and better bombs—then some forms of *deviant behavior* may well be healthier than what we accept as normal.

While the majority of neurotic and psychotic people are probably suffering because of purely personal problems, it is possible, we believe, that some of those we label "sick" are merely more sensitive and more idealistic than the rest of us. In these cases, at least, we need a very different view than that provided by the medical model.

Summary

In this chapter, we have described the characteristics of persons suffering from psychoses. We have outlined and illustrated the two major forms of mental disorder—schizophrenia and manic-depressive cycles—and have gone into detail on the dynamics of paranoid conditions. We have also presented criticisms of the medical model in an effort to get you to see that there are other ways to understand neurotic and psychotic behavior.

Class Projects

1. In common slang, psychotic people are called "crazy, cracked, nuts, screwy, out to lunch, weird," etc. Mental institutions are referred to as "loony bins, booby hatches, funny farms, and cracker factories." Try to track down or figure out the sources of these terms and discuss the reasons that so-called "sane" people seem to enjoy making fun of those who are "out of their minds."

2. A man was admitted to a mental hospital because he spent an entire day walking round and round a city block talking to himself. At each of the four corners of the block he would kneel and say a prayer to one of the four directions: north, south, east, and west. When questioned by police, he proclaimed that he was saving the world from destruction. Later, when a psychiatrist at the hospital had won his confidence, he explained that he had

had a vision that the directions were at war with one another. They were **135** threatening to pull apart and, if they did, the entire world would be torn to shreds. Only he could save the world, because it was the evil in him that had started the whole thing. Besides, he had been chosen by God to improve everything in the universe. When he had accomplished his mission, a new race of people would be born. They would all be of one color—neither white nor brown nor black, but a kind of golden bronze—and they would love and help each other all the time and never hate or fight. It would be easy to say, "This man is crazy," and let it go at that. It would also be easy to recommend medication to erase these strange ideas. We suggest, instead, that you make an effort to understand his thinking. Try to see it as a representation of his inner conflicts, his sense of guilt and his need to be "reborn" as a better, more loving person.

3. Read and discuss the short story, "Silent Snow, Secret Snow," by Conrad Aiken. It portrays a young boy sinking into a psychotic state.

References

1. JOHN CUSTANCE, "The Universe of Bliss and the Universe of Horror," in *The Inner World of Mental Illness*, ed. Burt Kaplan (New York: Harper and Row, 1965).

2. THOMAS SZASZ, *The Myth of Mental Illness* (New York: Harper and Row, 1961).

3. JOHN WEIR PERRY, *The Far Side of Madness* (Englewood Cliffs, NJ: Prentice-Hall, 1974).

Suggested Readings

1. BARRY, A. *Bellevue is a State of Mind*. New York: Harcourt, Brace and Jovanovich, 1971.

2. BRAGINSKY, B. M., BRAGINSKY, D. and KING, K. *Methods of Madness: The Mental Hospital as a Last Resort*. New York: Holt, Rinehart & Winston, 1969.

3. COLEMAN, JAMES C. *Abnormal Psychology and Modern Life*. 5th ed. Chicago: Scott, Foresman, 1976.

4. FADIMA, JAMES, and KEWMAN, DONALD. Reality of Madness in J. Fadima and D. Kewman eds. *Exploring Madness: Experimental Theory and Research*. Monterey, CA: Brooks/Cole, 1973.

5. GREEN, HANNAH. *I Never Promised You a Rose Garden*. New York: Holt, Rinehart & Winston, 1964.

6. KAPLAN, BURT, ed. *The Inner World of Mental Illness*. New York: Harper and Row, 1964.

7. KESEY, KEN. *One Flew Over the Cuckoo's Nest*. New York: The Viking Press, Inc., 1962.

8. PRICE, RICHARD H. *Abnormal Psychology*. New York: Holt, Rinehart & Winston, 1978.

Psychotherapy:
The Talking Cure

9

sychotherapy is the treatment of emotional and mental disorders. It ranges all the way from helping patients in mental hospitals return to sanity to helping normal people cope with the demands of day-to-day living. Practitioners of psychotherapy include psychologists, psychiatrists, and psychiatric social workers. Sometimes labelled "shrinks" (from "headshrinkers"), they have a challenging task: to help unhappy people uncover the roots of their suffering, express their hidden feelings, and learn better ways of living.

Can it be done? There are those who claim the entire business is a waste of time, who feel that psychotherapy does not work—or that it does not work well enough to justify the money spent on it. Fortunately (or unfortunately, depending on your point of view), the ranks of these critics appear to be dwindling. More and more people are coming to agree that psychotherapy can be effective.

There are many techniques of therapy in use today. Practitioners of each show a strong inclination to believe that their technique is superior to all the others, but most of them share certain common convictions. One of these is the notion that *talking it out*—confiding your problems to an understanding person—is bound to be helpful in itself.

This chapter will tell you how psychotherapy developed from its beginnings to its present state. It will summarize the contributions of the most important people in the field. After reading it, you should be familiar with the similarities and differences between the leading methods. You may also be able to make an informed choice, should you or someone close to you ever seek the kind of help that psychotherapists offer.

Ancient Forms of Treatment

exorcism

the practice of driving
out an evil spirit by
religious rituals

stimulants

drugs that excite you

sedatives

drugs that calm you
down

bloodletting

opening a vein and
letting a certain amount
of blood flow out

convulsions

violent muscular
spasms, often ending in
unconsciousness

**electroshock
therapy**

sending a charge of
electricity through the
brain. It also produces
convulsions and
unconsciousness

Throughout history, people have suffered from emotional and mental distress. Anxiety, depression, and the more serious neurotic and psychotic disorders we discussed in the last two chapters have always been common. Their incidence, in fact, has been much more widespread than most of us realize. Even Biblical records make it clear that madness afflicted king and commoner alike.

In ancient times, mental disorders were thought to be caused by evil demons. Religious rituals like **exorcism** and various forms of torture, including burning at the stake, were used to drive them out.

Even when doctors began to believe that such disorders were a form of illness, they did little more than prescribe **stimulants** and **sedatives** and advise their patients to get some rest. Severe mental cases were hospitalized, but the inmates of mental hospitals were treated cruelly. In many insane asylums, as they were called, the patients were beaten, starved, and chained to the walls. Nobody tried very hard to understand their plight. In fact, it was widely believed that the more painful the treatment, the more effective the cure.

Here and there enlightened people arose with sound suggestions for treating psychological problems, but few doctors followed their advice. In 1621, an English minister by the name of Robert Burton wrote a book called *The Anatomy of Melancholy.* He foresaw the trend that psychotherapy would take, for he suggested: "If then our judgment be so depraved . . . that we cannot seek our own good, or moderate ourselves . . . the best way for ease is to impart our misery to some friend, not to smother it up in our own breast; for grief concealed strangles the soul; but when as we shall impart it to some discreet, trusty, loving friend, it is instantly removed." Two hundred and fifty years were to pass, however, before such advice began to be taken seriously. During all this time, treatment consisted of **bloodletting,** sedatives, dousing patients with ice-cold water, putting them in straight jackets, or, in less disturbed cases, advising rest and relaxation.

One curious form of treatment employed in the early mental hospitals in this country was a device known as *the whirling chair.* The patient was strapped into this contraption, which was built like a modern barber chair, and whirled around until he or she became dizzy and had a fainting spell. The object of this method was to shake up the brain and induce **convulsions** that might somehow eliminate the patient's insanity. While it was not often successful, it is interesting to note its similarity to the **electroshock therapy** that is still used in many mental hospitals.

Unchaining the Insane

Near the end of the 18th century, an era of kindness toward mental patients began to develop. Phillipe Pinel, a French psychiatrist, released them from their chains, protected them from abuse, fed them nourish-

A patient being treated in the centrifugal force bed.

Pinel standing in the courtyard at the hospital of Salpêtrière, France surrounded by mental patients.

ing food, and treated them with warmth. In the United States, Benjamin Rush adopted a similar approach. In *Diseases of the Mind*, the first psychiatric textbook written by an American, he reported, "The clanking of chains and the noise of the whip are no longer heard. . . . [The insane] now taste the blessings of air and light and motion, in pleasant and shaded walks in summer and in spacious entries warmed by stoves in winter and protected from the eye of visitors to the hospital."

In the 19th century, American Quakers established several hospitals for the mentally ill, but the majority were still confined to jail-like institutions where they were beaten into submission. Dorothea Dix, a Massachusetts schoolteacher, became instrumental in the founding of more than thirty state hospitals in this country and many in Europe. Decades were to pass, however, before the principle of humane treatment would be universally accepted.

Franz Mesmer and Animal Magnetism

Treating patients with kindness was clearly a step in the right direction, but an understanding of their problems was still a long way off. Advances along this route accumulated steadily. By cataloging mental symptoms and arranging them in groups, doctors began to clarify the forms that mental illness took. By studying the conditions under which people suffered breakdowns and those under which improvement took place, they began to glimpse both causative and curative factors.

syphilis
a venereal disease that may produce degeneration of the brain

Throughout the 18th and 19th centuries, most doctors believed that mental illness was a kind of physical illness. Their investigations focused on a search for brain disease, nerve degeneration, or chemical inbalance. Although this approach made them blind to the possibilities of psychological causation, it enabled them to understand the psychoses that result from **syphilis, senility,** brain damage, and **toxic substances.**

senility
weakness of the brain due to old age

In the 1770s, however, an Austrian physician began treating nervous ailments with a strange technique he called *animal magnetism*. His name was Franz Mesmer. His career was a blend of extraordinary cures and insupportable claims. He believed he was blessed with the power to draw out certain illnesses by the touch of his hands. Like the faith healers of religious sects, he did indeed achieve some remarkable results. His methods, however, were too theatrical to win the respect of his colleagues.

toxic substances
poisons that affect the brain or the body

"In a dimly lit, thickly carpeted room smelling of orange blossoms, with soft music playing in the background, Mesmer had his patients join hands around a tub filled with 'magnetized' water. Then, clothed in a lilac cloak and waving a yellow wand, he moved amongst them, exhorting them to cast off their symptoms."[1] After heated public controversy, he was forced to leave Austria. He set up practice in France and impressed important people like Marie Antoinette, but he was finally rejected by the doctors of that nation, too.

Mesmer ended his days in obscurity. His technique was put down as **141** a sham, not by the people he had helped, but by the respectable doctors of the day. He had planted the seed, however, for what was to become a new approach to the treatment of neurosis. As years went by, the term "animal magnetism" was dropped, *hypnosis* was substituted, and doctors began to accept it as a method of treating emotional problems.

Hypnosis Becomes Respectable

neurologist

a physician who specializes in diseases of the nervous system

Almost a century later, a French **neurologist** by the name of Jean Charcot made hypnosis medically acceptable. Ignoring the stagey devices Mesmer had employed, Charcot had his patients relax and stare at a bright, moving object whose movement would tire their eyes. In an impressive monotone, he would give them the following suggestions:

> You are tired. Your eyes are heavy. Your body is relaxed. Your mind is being emptied of all thoughts, all sensations except the sound of my voice. You are falling asleep, falling asleep. Breathe deeply now, deeply and regularly. With every breath you take, count backward from one hundred. That's right, very good— 100, 99, 98. . . . Yes, allow yourself to relax. Allow your arms and legs to grow tired, allow your thoughts to drift away. You are very, very tired, but you can hear my voice. Only my voice. Relax, relax. Soon you will not be able to open your eyes unless I instruct you to.

Charcot demonstrating hypnosis.

Certain kinds of neurotics, he found, were very easily hypnotized. In response to his instructions, most of these patients, who were called *hysterics*, fell into a deep trance. In the trance, their symptoms could be made to disappear by suggestion alone. This discovery gave Charcot the notion that certain symptoms—paralysis of the limbs, stuttering, muscle spasms, and seizures—might have a mental basis.

The discovery that physical symptoms could be removed, even temporarily, by suggestion alone was a very important advance. It laid the groundwork for modern psychiatry and clinical psychology. Hypnosis itself was to occupy a minor position as a method of treatment because its cures did not always last. Its successes, however, convinced many doctors that the mind is as important as the body in certain illnesses.

The current status of hypnosis as a therapeutic technique is clouded by the fact that it has been used by entertainers to amuse and trick the public. When a psychologist, therefore, employs it, he or she runs the danger of being suspected of fraud. In point of fact, however, hypnosis has proven effective in helping such problems as overeating, smoking, anxiety attacks, and sexual disorders. While many people cannot be put into a deep enough trance to achieve significant results, hypnosis remains a useful tool in the growing array of psychotherapeutic techniques.

The Talking Cure

Pierre Janet, a psychiatrist who had studied under Charcot, took the matter a giant step forward. He discovered that in the trance many patients recalled upsetting memories that were related to the onset of their symptoms. Sometimes, in fact, they recovered from their symptoms simply by "getting it off their chest"—by expressing the painful feelings they had been storing up for years.

This discovery was crucial for the development of psychotherapy. It had been made around the same time by a Viennese doctor, Josef Breuer, but neither Breuer nor Janet pursued it far enough. It took Breuer's colleague, the bold, brilliant Sigmund Freud, to see the new vistas to which it might lead.

In 1880, Breuer had treated a young woman for paralysis of the limbs and disturbances of vision and speech. Under hypnosis, she was encouraged to talk about the onset of her symptoms. It turned out that she had nursed her sick father, and she recalled how terribly she had resented him for being ill. As she expressed her anger under hypnosis, her symptoms disappeared. She called the treatment "the talking cure."

A few years later, Breuer and Freud published a book in which they claimed that the secret of curing hysterical patients lay in getting them to express their hidden emotions. This book, *Studies in Hysteria*, was the steppingstone from which Freud was to create the world-shaking theories and techniques of *psychoanalysis*.

Sigmund Freud and the Free-Association Method

Though he first used hypnosis as an aid in the "talking cure," Freud found that it had several drawbacks. Not all patients could be hypnotized and symptoms which disappeared often reappeared or were replaced by new ones. The method he began to use instead was called free association. He instructed his patients to lie on a couch and say everything that came to mind, no matter how trivial, embarrassing, or foolish it might seem. In this manner, Freud discovered, the roots of their illnesses were eventually revealed.

Resistance

A number of curious things happened in the free-association process. For example, patients showed signs of resistance when talking about emotionally laden topics. They forgot what they were saying, changed the subject, missed their appointments, or objected to the whole procedure. Freud took these signs as indications that they were approaching the heart of the problem. The analyst's task, he felt, was to convince the patient to overcome the resistance and face the feelings, thoughts, or memories he or she was avoiding.

Transference

Patients also developed emotional reactions to their analyst. Freud noticed that some of them fell in love with him, others became so dependent that they could not make a move without his approval, and still others began to hate him.

Freud called these reactions *transference*. He felt that patients were transferring hidden feelings they had had toward their parents onto the doctor. Thus, a man who had wished to have a strong, reliable father to lean on but whose father had never fulfilled this wish, might be driven to test his analyst's strength and reliability in all sorts of ways. He might behave unpredictably, demand special favors, or even threaten to commit suicide to test the analyst's endurance. Another man who had hated his mother for treating him like a baby might imagine that his analyst was doing the same. As a result, he might become uncooperative. Observing and explaining transference reactions, Freud believed, were effective ways of helping patients overcome the childish feelings they had not outgrown.

The unconscious

In the years between 1890 and 1910, Freud created more than a method of treating neurotic disorders. He created a new view of human nature.

Although it was ridiculed at first, his view was to change the outlook of the Western civilized world.

It hinged, essentially, on his concept of the unconscious—that is, on Freud's insistence that our feelings, thoughts, and actions are often directed by forces hidden within us. A person's choice of spouse or occupation, likes and dislikes, pecularities and habits are all highly influenced by unconscious forces. And what are these forces? They boil down to childhood memories and childish needs and wishes which have never been given up. More specifically, they boil down to sexual experiences and conflicts which have never been fully faced.

To take but one example, the women with whom a young man falls in love are determined, according to Freud, by needs he cannot admit. Not the obvious needs for affection and acceptance and sex, but needs like getting even with his mother for not having loved him enough or proving that he is a better man than his father. His choices are made not so much on the basis of the woman's attractiveness as on the effect they may have on his mother and father.

Freud's view of human nature was confusing and shocking to most people. Not only did he stress the childish desires that control us and the importance of sex in all areas of life, but he drove these arguments to their logical extremes. A soldier's courage under fire might be due to a need to deny his cowardice. A priest's dedication to his calling might be furthered by his own secret sexual fantasies. Proposals such as these outraged many critics. As years went by, however, many of Freud's insights were accepted.

The meaning of dreams

Freud also suggested that dreams reveal the workings of a person's unconscious. He worked out an ingenious method of interpreting them. *The Interpretation of Dreams,* published in 1900, was a milestone in the development of his thinking. In this book, he argued that dreams are not mere fragments of thought or the results of an upset stomach but that they express important conflicts going on within the dreamer's mind. Essentially, Freud claimed, dreams are disguised expressions of hidden wishes. They provide an outlet for feelings the dreamer cannot admit.

Thus, a dream in which a friend is hurt may reveal hostile feeling toward this friend. The friend may also be a symbol for someone else, perhaps a brother or sister, whom the dreamer wishes to attack. Or a dream in which the dreamer can fly may represent a wish to be relieved of all responsibilities—"free as a bird"—in other words, to remain a child.

Therapeutic goals

Freud's method of treatment progressed from a technique for curing neurotic symptoms to a whole philosophy of life. As we discussed in chapter 3, he saw personality as made up of three psychological systems: the id, the ego, and the superego. All human behavior, he taught, can be understood as the interaction of these systems. Sometimes the id dominates, sometimes the ego, sometimes the superego. Most people tend to go to one extreme or the other; they are either too self-indulgent (id-dominated) or too unselfish (superego-dominated). The task of psychotherapy, Freud believed, was to strengthen the patient's reason (or ego) so it could maintain a healthy balance between the id and the superego.

Many other methods of psychotherapy took their cues from psychoanalysis. They attempted not merely to treat symptoms but to help people develop fully rounded personalities.

An unmarried man, 30 years of age, consulted a psychoanalyst because of a drinking problem. He had become so dependent on alcohol that he could not sleep without a few drinks and even needed one several times a day to keep up his morale.

Investigation of his background revealed that, throughout his childhood, he had been closely attached to his mother. She was a beautiful but domineering actress who had married several times, never for very long. Her son had had no meaningful relationship with any of her husbands, including his father.

Now, as an adult, he was living on his own. He had never been in love with a woman and had no close friends, male or female. In his teens, he had had some homosexual experiences, but now he claimed no interest in sex at all.

The psychoanalyst concluded that the patient's alcoholism was the result of a lifelong unhealthy pattern of living. His attachment to his mother had never been outgrown. In the absence of a father or father-substitute, he had not learned how to relate successfully to men. He avoided intimate contact with women for several reasons: few of them measured up to his glamorous mother; he was afraid to become as dependent on another woman as he had once been on her; and he could not assert his masculinity because, as a child, he had not been allowed to do so.

The drinking was seen as a substitute for human love. Unable to admit his need for another person, the patient had succumbed to a need for alcohol. Treatment of this symptom, the analyst felt, demanded extensive psychoanalysis. Other psychotherapists might have tried to cure the patient's drinking more directly, but the Freudian approach, which was finally successful, took several years.

Alfred Adler and the Will to Power

For all his brilliance, Freud was shortsighted and stubborn on certain issues. At least, that is what some of his closest associates felt. After years of working together, several of Freud's most distinguished colleagues split away from him and formed their own schools of psychotherapy.

Alfred Adler, the man who coined the terms *inferiority complex* and *superiority complex*, thought that Freud laid too much stress on sex. According to Adler, an equally important drive is the will to power—the need to assert oneself and to prove oneself as good as, or better than, others.

Adler believed that every child acquires an inferiority complex, partly on the basis of real shortcomings and partly because children are treated as inferior by grownups. Some youngsters are made to feel that

146

Large audiences meet some individuals' power needs.

they are stupid, others become convinced that they are ugly, and still others see themselves as weak or lazy. In order to undo this complex, people try to prove their superiority. Some drive themselves to obtain high grades at school, others spend much time and money on their appearance, while others seek for positions of authority.

These are normal ways of helping oneself feel superior, but neurotic symptoms serve this purpose, too. Attacks of anxiety or depression allow the sufferer to make demands on other people, to get their sympathy and attention. Lying, cheating, stealing, and bullying are also bids for superiority. When a person cannot compete successfully according to the rules of society, he or she looks for tricky ways to come out on top after all.

Therapeutic goals

Adler felt it important to acquaint patients with the nature of their inferiority feelings and help them examine the ways in which they were trying to make themselves feel superior. His observations have become common knowledge by now. Most people accept them as a matter of course, not realizing that there was a time when they were new and controversial.

Here is another case where both the inferiority complex and the superiority complex can be clearly recognized. A girl of 16 was sent to me, who had been stealing since she was six or seven and staying out at night with boys since she was twelve. When she was two years old, her parents had divorced after a long and bitter personal struggle. She was taken by her mother to live with her in her grandmother's home; and her grandmother, as so often happens, gave herself over to pampering the child. She had been born when the struggle between her parents was at its height and her mother had not welcomed her arrival. She had never liked her daughter and a tension existed between them. When the girl came to see me I talked with her in a friendly way. She told me, "I don't like taking things or running about with boys, but I've got to show my mother that she can't handle me." "You do it for revenge?" I asked her. "I suppose so," she answered. She wanted to prove herself stronger than her mother; but she had this goal only because she felt weaker.[2]

This quotation from Adler shows him focusing on inferiority-superiority dynamics to explain problem behavior.

C. G. Jung

A very different school of thought was founded by C. G. Jung. He broke away from Freud because he was interested in religious and spiritual experiences, an interest which Freud could not tolerate.

In a series of works published in the 1920s and 1930s, Jung argued that modern men and women suffer problems due to a loss of faith. We are far too **materialistic** and **rationalistic,** according to Jung. We have lost the sense of a grand design in human existence. The core of life seems meaningless to us, so we strive to acquire wealth and prestige or to lose ourselves in trivialities like watching television.

materialistic
placing a very high value on material goods, and feeling that "having things" is what life is all about

rationalistic
believing only in what can be explained by reason

What we need is to rediscover the mystery and grandeur of life, not necessarily by going back to old religious rituals, but by experiencing within ourselves the eternal truths of our nature. Though these views seemed strange at the time, because they were neither scientific nor religious in the conventional sense, it is interesting to note that, fifty years later, many psychologists are saying similar things.

Dreams, myths, and fairy tales

How are we to experience the eternal truths? The most direct path, Jung taught, is through the exploration of our dreams. Like Freud, he believed that dreams reveal the state of a person's unconscious. However, he asserted that in the unconscious there are more than hidden wishes. All the undeveloped resources of our being exist there too, like seeds in the ground needing nourishment to grow. If we give them attention, we can cultivate new feelings and insights and become more complete individuals.

Jung discovered a similarity between his patients' dreams and the themes of mythology and fairy tales. Tales and myths, he said, express in dreamlike imagery eternal human problems. They are dilemmas with which we must struggle not because we are Mr. or Ms. So-and-so but because we are members of the human race.

One such problem is the need of every young person, on reaching maturity, to break the emotional ties that held him or her attached to his or her parents. Regardless of whether the parents were kind or cruel, understanding or narrow-minded, the young man or woman is compelled to reject them for awhile in order to become independent. What happens, generally, is that for a few years the young person sees his or her parents in a very negative light; he or she becomes acutely aware of their defects and finds their concern a nuisance.

Another eternal problem is the experience of falling in love. Here the individual sees the loved one as practically perfect—attractive, interesting, clever, charming, and a continual joy to be around. He or she fails to perceive the loved one's negative qualities—the ways in which he or she is not so attractive, not so interesting, and not so clever—because the dominant need at this time is to experience perfect bliss and contentment.

Both of these problems find expression in myths and folk tales. Stories like Cinderella, Rapunzel, and Show White, for instance, portray the process of feminine maturation. In each of them a beautiful young girl is mistreated by an evil witch-mother and rescued by a handsome prince. This symbolizes the outlook and experience of countless girls in all cultures throughout history. They feel, at a certain stage of their development, that they are being mistreated or held prisoner by their mothers, and their dream of deliverance takes the form of romantic love. The fairy-tale witch represents mother when she is seen in a negative light. The handsome prince is every girl's boyfriend or husband-to-be when she is still in love with him.

Therapeutic goals

As we discussed in chapter 3, Jung coined the terms *introvert* and *extravert* to differentiate between solitary and sociable types of personalities. He did not think that either type was better than the other. Problems arise, he argued, when we are not allowed to follow our natural ways and are made to feel dissatisfied with our personality type. With regard to the "four functions" also discussed in chapter 3 (thinking, feeling, sensation, and intuition), most of us use only one or two to any significant extent. This is a common state of affairs, but we need to cultivate all four.

Jung's method of psychotherapy put emphasis on all these beliefs: the importance of personal religious experience; understanding the collective or universal aspects of our problems; and cultivating all sides of our nature. Like Freud, he found it helpful to analyze his patients' dreams; like most other schools of therapy, he encouraged people to talk out their feelings; but he was unique, for his time, in the value he placed on our spiritual needs.

The kind of dream Jung found impressive in showing his patients' religious needs is recounted below. It was told to him by an intelligent woman approaching middle age.

> I am in a great empty temple. At one end is a gigantic statue of the god. There is a tall priest in robes with me. The atmosphere is Egyptian or Chinese. We walk over the immense empty floor toward the statue at the end. Every few steps I fall on my face and the priest calls out to the god that I am coming as a penitent and he makes confession for me aloud. Our progress is slow and solemn, but in my thoughts I am very skeptical about it all. I think this is a queer kind of ritual and that the god over there is only a stone statue. We finally come to it. On each side of it there are steps and we go up these and go behind the altar. Once there and before leaving the temple I turn around to look again at the statue, and as I look it slowly turns around and looks at me. I find myself falling on my face in real awe and devotion at last, for it really is the presence of a god with absolution and grace pouring in on me.[3]

Carl Rogers and Nondirective Counseling

In the 1940s, an American psychologist, Carl Rogers, began to influence the trend of psychotherapy. He said that we all have a strong natural drive for health and happiness. Problems arise when others fail to accept us as we are and try to tell us how we should be. Rogers' method of treatment was called *nondirective counseling*, for he refused to direct his clients in any way at all. He would not give them advice, nor would he answer their questions. The counselor, he argued, should act as a mirror reflecting the client to himself or herself and offering him or her **unconditional acceptance.**

unconditional acceptance

accepting someone not because they do something of which you approve, but simply for being who they are, as a mother accepts her newborn infant

Some people found Rogers' method confusing. Since we are accustomed to have doctors, teachers, and parents tell us what to do, we think it strange when a psychologist refuses to give us any guidance. The feeling of being completely accepted, however, and the related respect for the client's ability to solve his or her own problems, proved to be highly therapeutic. Rogers' reputation grew steadily and his views have been adopted by many other therapists.

Here is a brief interchange between a Rogerian counselor and a student he was helping.

STUDENT: I think maybe next time I come in to see you, it will be something different. Maybe I'll have a little bit better idea what to talk about by then.
COUNSELOR: Would you like to come in next Friday at this time?
STUDENT: Yes, it's all right with me.
COUNSELOR: It's up to you.
STUDENT: It's up to me?
COUNSELOR: I'm here. I'd be glad to do anything I can for you.
STUDENT: All right sir, I think I'll be there.
COUNSELOR: All right.

Regarding this conversation, Rogers says:

> In this brief excerpt, much has happened. The student makes a somewhat independent statement, showing that he plans at least to share the responsibility for the use of the next hour. The coun-

selor encourages this by putting the decision about the appointment up to the student. The student, feeling this is the usual meaningless gesture, leaves the responsibility with the counselor by saying, "Yes, it's all right with me." When the counselor shows that the counseling situation really belongs to the client, the student's surprise is clearly indicated as he says, "It's up to *me?*" His whole tone changes as he then responds in a firm and decisive manner, "All right, sir, I think I'll be there"—genuinely accepting the responsibility for the first time.[4]

Since the conversation reported above does not cut very deeply into the problems of selfhood that many people struggle with in therapy, here is another excerpt from a Rogerian counseling session. The client is a young woman, a graduate student, who had been very bitter about her professors not giving her a decent education. At this point, however, she begins to achieve a new viewpoint in which she acknowledges that she must take responsibility for her own education.

WOMAN: Well now, I wonder if I've been going around doing that, getting smatterings of things, and not getting hold, not really getting down to things.

COUNSELOR: Maybe you've been getting just spoonfuls here and there rather than really digging in somewhere rather deeply.

WOMAN: M-hm. That's what I say—[slowly and very thoughtfully] well, with that sort of a foundation, well, it's really up to *me*. I mean, it seems to be really apparent to me that I *can't depend on someone else* to give me an education. [Very softly] I'll really have to get it myself.

COUNSELOR: It really begins to come home—there's only one person that can educate you—a realization that perhaps nobody else *can give* you an education.

WOMAN: M-hm. [Long pause] I have all the symptoms of fright. [Laughs softly]

COUNSELOR: Fright? That this is a scary thing, is that what you mean?

WOMAN: M-hm. [Very long pause—obviously struggling with feelings in herself]

COUNSELOR:: Do you want to say any more about what you mean by that? That it really does give you the symptoms of fright?

WOMAN: [Laughs] I, uh, I don't know whether I quite know. I mean, well it really seems like I'm cut loose, and it seems that I'm very, I don't know, in a vulnerable position, but I, uh, I brought this up and it, uh, somehow it almost came out without my saying it. It seems to be—it's something I let out.

COUNSELOR: Hardly a part of you.

WOMAN: Well, I felt surprised.

COUNSELOR: As though, "Well, for goodness sake, did I say that?" [Both chuckle]

WOMAN: Really, I don't think I've had that feeling before. I've, uh, well this really feels like I'm saying something that, uh, *is* a part of me really. [Pause] Or, uh, it feels like I sort of have, uh, I don't know. I have a feeling of *strength* and yet I have a feeling of realizing it's sort of fearful, of fright.

Rogers comments:

I hope that this illustration gives some sense of the strength which is experienced in being a unique person, responsible for oneself, and also the uneasiness that accompanies this assumption of responsibility. To recognize that "I am the one who chooses" and "I am the one who determines the value of an experience for me" is both an invigorating and a frightening realization.[5] **151**

Note that in both these interviews, the Rogerian counselor does not advise, analyze, or criticize the client in any way. The counselor simply responds in an accepting manner, allowing the client to take the lead and strengthen his or her feelings of self-determination.

Existential-Humanism, Encounter Groups, and Gestalt Therapy

existentialist philosophers

Sartre, Heidegger, Kierkegaard, Buber, etc. For an account of their teachings, see Wm. Barrett, *Irrational Man*

A movement which has been gaining followers since the 1960s takes its inspiration from the **existentialist philosophers.** It is based on the notion that our central problems stem from our inability to be our true selves and to live in the present. It rejects intellectual explanations and insists that people express their feelings as openly as possible.

Frederick (Fritz) Perls, a leader in this type of treatment, called his approach *Gestalt Therapy*. It is more often practiced with groups of patients than in private interviews. The therapist is usually very active and outspoken, trying to get the members of the group to "open up" and be as frank as they can in saying how they feel about each other and themselves.

Gestalt therapists insist that our deepest needs are to be open and authentic, to face ourselves fully, to admit all our feelings, thoughts, and desires, and to be unafraid to expose ourselves to others. They tell us to live in the "here and now," to quit dragging up the past and worrying about the future. And above all, they say, we have to take responsibility for our own lives rather than try to please other people. As Perls states in what he calls, "The Gestalt Prayer":

> I do my thing and you do your thing.
> I am not in this world to live up to your expectations
> And you are not in this world to live up to mine.
> You are you, and I am I,
> And if by chance we find each other, it's beautiful.
> If not, it can't be helped.[6]

In existential, Gestalt, or encounter groups, the sessions are often very emotional. The therapist encourages straight-from-the-shoulder reactions from everyone in the room, and he or she does not refrain from expressing feelings either. The therapist may curse or scream at members of the group or may embrace and kiss them.

One of Fritz Perls' most effective techniques was his method of dealing with dreams. Instead of having his patients free associate about them, he had them act out their dreams, either playing all the parts themselves or assigning roles to members of the group. Suppose you dreamed that an insane old witch was chasing you through a haunted house and when you screamed for help the only person who came to your aid was a three-year-old child. Perls would have had you reenact the sequence, possibly playing every part: yourself running scared, the witch chasing you, the little child, even the haunted house. His objective would have been to get you to feel every part of the dream as part of yourself and to get you in touch with the essence of your fright and with your way of coping with it.

Another technique Perls created uses two chairs facing each other. The patient sits in one and imagines that in the other sits someone with whom he or she is having trouble. The patient expresses his or her feelings toward the other person as fully as possible. Then he or she switches chairs and expresses the other person's feelings. The "encounter" is continued, sometimes with the therapist making observations on what is being expressed, until some sort of a resting point is reached.

Aloneness, choice, and being present

Perhaps the most basic problem with which we have to deal, declare the existential-humanists, is the problem of our aloneness. No matter how close we come to each other, they assert, we are each responsible for our own life. It is useless to depend on other people to bring us happiness, for no one can completely understand or solve anyone else's problems.

Our deepest dilemmas, in fact, are all unsolvable. There are no final answers, for life does not have a meaning that human beings can grasp. In the knowledge that this is so, we still must make choices about how to live. These choices—to marry a specific person, to have or not have children, to practice a particular profession, to be honest or deceitful, hardworking or easygoing, to live within the law or against it, to pursue idealistic or materialistic goals—eventually determine our fate, but there is no foolproof way to know in advance which decisions are wise and which are foolish.

What we need most of all, therefore, is moral courage: the courage to face ourselves, to declare ourselves, to make our choices as best we can, and to assume responsibility for our individual lives. And how do we acquire this courage? We have it within us; it only needs to be released. A therapist, or a friend for that matter, who cares enough and is himself or herself strong enough to reject our alibis and accept us as we are can show us the way. Whether we choose to follow it or not, however, depends on ourselves alone.

Happiness, in this view, lies in learning to be present, to give ourselves fully to the moment at hand. The past is gone; the future is uncertain; if we fail to appreciate our immediate experience, we diminish the life that is ours to live. More often than not, we do fail to appreciate it. We become so accustomed to our comforts, our achievements, our friends and our families that we take them all for granted and cease to derive much joy from them. We resent what we were deprived

of yesterday and dream of what we will accomplish tomorrow. Mean- **153**
while, the moments we are actually living through pass without our
participation.

The existential-humanist attempts to help people by getting them to
face these facts. While the philosophy that underlies this line of approach is sometimes difficult to understand, its therapeutic method is
guaranteed to evoke strong reactions.

Transactional Analysis

Another school of therapy that has gained a great deal of public attention is called *Transactional Analysis*, or T. A. for short. It was founded by
Eric Berne, the author of *Games People Play*.[7]

T. A. is more a teaching method for identifying the workings of our
minds than a probing of the unconscious or a confrontation with existential dilemmas. It works best in groups, and the manner in which these
groups are conducted seems a cross between a classroom and a therapy
session.

One of the primary virtues of T. A. is its simplicity. In language
everyone can understand, Berne and his followers reduce human problems to a few basic formulas. They speak of the brain as a kind of tape
recorder that stores information and feelings on every event in our lives.
These memories, or "tapes," become clustered into three distinct groups
which Berne calls the Parent, the Child, and the Adult.

The Parent, or parent tapes, contain everything our parents did to
us and everything they said to us in the early years of our life. They
contain, "the thousands of 'nos' directed at the toddler, the repeated
'don'ts' that bombard him [as well as] the coos of pleasure of a happy
mother and the looks of delight of a proud father." The Child, or child
tapes, contain our responses as a child to everything we saw or heard.
They contain our excitement over new discoveries, our pleasure at being
fondled and loved, our pain upon being punished, our fear of being
scolded, our confusion about the difference between what we were told
and what we experienced. The Adult, or adult tapes, contain the understanding we have gained from applying reason to the data of our experience.

Every one of us, according to Berne, can be described as an interaction of our Parent, our Child, and our Adult. In some of us, the Parent
dominates, in others the Child is in control. Regardless of which is
stronger, however, in certain circumstances each of us lapses into an
identification with one or another of our "tapes."

Clues to an identification with the Parent, as described by Thomas
Harris, one of Berne's followers, are: "furrowed brow, pursed lips,
pointing index finger, hands on hips, arms folded across chest, patting
another on the head," as well as such expressions as, "If I were you . . .
How many times have I told you . . . I can't for the life of me . . . Now

always remember." Clues to an identification with the Child are: "tears, pouting, temper tantrums, whining voice, downcast eyes, teasing, laughter, hand-raising for permission to speak, nail-biting, squirming, giggling," and such expressions as, "I wish . . . I want . . . I dunno . . . don't care." The Adult, in contrast, has a straightforward look, is curious and interested in what is going on, and uses such expressions as, "How much . . . In what way . . . I think . . . I see . . . In my opinion."[8]

The mature person, from the T. A. point of view, must know when his or her Child or Parent is in control and must strengthen the Adult to the point that it takes precedence over the other two.

An equally important part of Berne's theory has to do with what he calls *the four life positions*. These may be summarized with the catch phrases:

1) I'M NOT OK—YOU'RE OK

2) I'M NOT OK—YOU'RE NOT OK

3) I'M OK—YOU'RE NOT OK

4) I'M OK—YOU'RE OK

According to T. A., we all begin life in the first position. As infants, we have all our needs gratified by others, so we feel inadequate compared to those around us. As we develop through childhood, however, we acquire positions two and three as well. In the end, if we are to become mature and happy, we must adopt position four. This means that we must come to feel that we are adequate and so are those with whom we choose to associate.

Behavior Modification

behaviorists

Watson, Pavlov, Skinner, etc. Psychologists who study only observable behavior and object to theories about internal mental states

An entirely different mode of treatment, called behavior modification, is gaining acceptance among psychologists of a more scientific bent. It is based on the findings of the **behaviorists,** whose laboratory techniques will be discussed in the next section of this text. Behavior modifiers believe that psychological disorders can be cured by what they call **"systematic desenitization"** and **"re-conditioning."**

The terms *conditioning, operant conditioning, and re-conditioning* are central to an understanding of behavior modification. It is therefore necessary to define them here, although a more detailed discussion of them will be presented later.

Conditioning is a learning process through which a reflex action becomes attached to a previously neutral stimulus. Consider the reflex of blinking when an object rapidly approaches our eyes. If a bell were rung every time this happened, we would soon begin to blink at the sound of the bell alone. In this example, the bell would be called a conditioned stimulus, our blinking at it a conditioned response.

systematic desensitization

systematically helping a
person become less
sensitive to certain
stimuli

reconditioning

retraining a person's
habits or reactions

Operant conditioning is a learning process through which free, non-reflex behavior becomes attached to a specific stimulus. Suppose that every expression of "not feeling well" on our part were met with a show of affection from those around us. We would soon be inclined to complain about not feeling well whenever we wished to gain affection. Once again, our complaining in order to get affection is called a conditioned response.

Reconditioning is a process by which a former set of conditioned responses is eliminated and replaced by a new set.

Reward and punishment are of primary importance in the establishment and extinction of conditioned responses. A response which is regularly, or even intermittently, rewarded is likely to continue. One which is regularly punished is likely to disappear.

Behavior therapists maintain that most human problems can be explained and cured through conditioning and reconditioning. They claim it is grossly unscientific to try to overhaul a patient's whole style of living. They find it a waste of time to probe the unconscious and analyze the personality. So they simply focus on the symptoms of which the patient complains. As one of their leaders, Hans Eysenck, has said, "There is no neurosis underlying the symptom, but merely the symptom itself. Get rid of the symptom and you have eliminated the neurosis."[9]

One of the points the behavior therapists stress is that neurotic symptoms result from anxiety. Shyness, stuttering, obsessive thoughts, sexual problems—all come from some sort of anxiety. In order to cure them, therefore, it is necessary first to teach the patient to relax. This is done by having him or her practice deep breathing and engage in muscular relaxation exercises. Once the patient has learned to relax his or her body, the attack upon the symptoms is undertaken.

Patients are generally asked to list all stimuli and situations that make them feel anxious, from the most to the least disturbing. Then they are taught to overcome their anxiety, beginning with the simplest problems and proceeding systematically to the worst ones. They are told to imagine the anxiety-arousing situation as vividly as they can; then, keeping the image in mind, they are instructed to relax their entire body in the way they have been practicing. This procedure is repeated, moving up the list of problems, until they are able to imagine the things that worry them the most and still relax themselves. When this is accomplished, the next step is to confront the anxiety-provoking situations in real life and stay relaxed throughout the experience.

Let us illustrate the [behavior therapy] process through the story of a woman who suffers un-

bearable anxiety at the sight of a cat. In the course of discussions with her, the therapist has found that she is least disturbed at seeing a small kitten in the arms of a child. When treatment begins, she is asked, therefore, to imagine this sight as clearly and vividly as she can. Though she feels some anxiety, it is bearable. Still keeping the picture firmly in mind, she is instructed to relax as she has been taught. She finds that when she is thoroughly relaxed, her anxiety disappears. She repeats this exercise in subsequent sessions until she never experiences any anxiety while imagining a kitten in the arms of a child. Now the therapist asks her to imagine a slightly more disturbing situation—a kitten playing with a ball of wool, pouncing on it, biting it, and so on—while she relaxes. When this imaginary situation ceases to provoke anxiety, the therapist

156

asks her to evoke a still more disturbing image. . . . Eventually she is able to imagine with tranquility a big tomcat stalking through the grass or curled up on her bed. And finally at the end of treatment, she is able to confront cats in real life as tranquilly as she can evoke their images in the consulting room. [10]

Behavior modification is useful not only in the elimination of phobias, as described above, but in the treatment of many problems people bring to mental health centers. It has also proven effective in teaching **autistic** children to speak and schizophrenic adults to respond more appropriately to other people.

autism

a severe mental disorder of early childhood in which the child engages in bizarre ritualistic behavior and does not speak intelligibly.

In behavior modification, the focus of attention is outside the individual rather than within. Behavior therapists believe that people acquire their problems through unfortunate experiences, but they find it unnecessary to explore the beginnings of these problems. More essential, in their view, is the task of locating the *reinforcing events*—the rewards the patient gains through having the problem—and replacing them with rewards for giving up the problem.

These rewards or reinforcements are not always obvious. According to the behaviorists, a child is rewarded for having temper tantrums by his mother screaming at him to stop. While he does not welcome her screaming, he prefers it to being ignored. They will advise the mother to ignore her son's tantrums if she wishes them to stop.

When it comes to reinforcing constructive behavior, the behaviorists insist that timing is all-important. Rewards must follow the behavior immediately if they are to be effective. Promising a child some weekend fun for going to bed without a fuss is likely to have no effect at all, but kissing and complimenting him or her every time he or she climbs quietly into bed will eventually establish the desired habit.

shaping

systematically providing rewards for desired bits of behavior, until the behavior becomes automatic or habitual

Although these principles seem simpleminded in contrast to the formulations of other schools of therapy, behavior therapists have applied them to very disturbed cases with interesting results.

A 17-year-old girl was evaluated for the complaint of chronic cough and mutism [inability to speak]. The cough began four years earlier during an upper respiratory infection and gradually increased in frequency to a rate of 40 to 50 coughs per minute, stopping during sleep. Two years later she became mute. During this time, the patient had four hospitalizations. Chest x-rays, bronchograms, bronchial cultures, and laboratory tests were normal, as were electroencephalograms, skull x-ray, and brain scan. . . .

Since it was hypothesized that the patient's coughing was being maintained in part by the social and medical attention paid to it, she was hospitalized to study the cough frequency in different settings. Event recording revealed that the cough varied as a direct function of the attention she was received from others. The rate was lowest when she was sitting alone . . . and slightly higher when she was in unstructured social situations such as dayroom activities, hospital corridors, and elevators. The highest rates were in structured situations such as group and individual therapy and when she was aware that the cough was being monitored. These data supported the hypotheses. Therefore staff and patients were instructed to ignore the cough but otherwise interact normally with the patient. A gradual decrease in frequency resulted, with ultimate elimination of the cough.

The mutism was treated by **shaping,** which rewarded the patient for successive steps toward normal speech. Since she had secluded herself at home for four years, and within two weeks of hospitalization demanded to be discharged, home visits were utilized as a reward or reinforcer. She could earn home time on the weekends [by engaging in speech exercises]. As a result, six months later she was discharged from the hospital speaking fluently.[11]

The Effectiveness of Psychotherapy

The effectiveness of psychotherapy is still a hotly debated issue. It is difficult to measure how much better a person feels or how much insight he or she has gained. Furthermore, improvement during the course of therapy does not prove that the therapy did it; the patient may have improved anyway.

Each school can produce cases showing that its particular methods were effective, yet each fails to help a certain percentage of people. Freudian psychoanalysis has been criticized as unduly lengthy and costly; Jungian therapy has been said to dwell on vague, murky, "spiritual" needs while ignoring the down-to-earth problems of everyday life; Adler supposedly made too much of superiority and inferiority; Rogers is too bland and passive; Perls and other encounter group leaders have been portrayed as crude and heartless; transactional analysis has been called superficial; behavior modification has been dismissed as too mechanical. While they all have their critics, however, the field as a whole continues to flourish.

One famous therapist, in his later years, said that he believed he had substantially helped about a third of the patients he had treated in his lifetime; he had moderately helped another third; and he had not helped the final third. This rough estimate could probably be applied to each of the methods we have surveyed. At this time, no technique has proven itself significantly more effective than all the others, although certain patients appear to benefit more from one approach than from another.

Supposedly objective studies have been done to determine the effectiveness of one or another form of psychotherapy, but the investigators have generally succeeded only in supporting their own biases.[12] The enterprise of attempting to help people cope with their problems and live happier lives is so emotionally loaded, so subtle, and so dependent on individual interpretation that it remains essentially an art. In our opinion at least, it cannot yet be judged by scientific standards.

Summary

In this chapter, we have surveyed the history of psychotherapy and briefly reviewed the methods and theories of the major schools: Freudian, Adlerian, Jungian, Rogerian, Existential-Humanism and Gestalt Therapy, Transactional Analysis, and Behavior Modification. We have tried to present them in a positive light, while acknowledging that they each have their critics. We have left it up to you to consider the importance and effectiveness of psychotherapy as a whole, as we believe it is still too early to render a final answer to that crucial question.

Class Projects

1. Dreams can be used in many ways to tell us about ourselves. As an exercise in discovering what your dreams may tell about you, have each member of your class write out one dream he or she has had within the last few weeks. Then note the role of the dreamer in each person's dream according to the following categories:

   a) the dreamer is not present

   b) the dreamer is present but only as an observer
      1) the dreamer's mood is pleasant
      2) the dreamer's mood is neutral
      3) the dreamer's mood is unpleasant

   c) the dreamer is an active participant in the dream
      1) the dreamer's actions are heroic
      2) the dreamer's actions are enjoyable to him or her
      3) the dreamer's actions are neutral
      4) the dreamer's actions are distressful to him or her
      5) the dreamer is a victim

   Attempt to analyze your findings in terms of the dreamers' feelings about themselves. (Hint: the role of the dreamer, as outlined above, often reflects the person's self-concept. People who frequently see themselves as victims in their dreams, for instance, tend to feel less sure of themselves, less strong and competent, than people who see themselves as in control.) Do not, however, jump to the conclusion that you can tell anything definite about anybody's personal problems from a single dream. It would take a trained psychologist several weeks or months to arrive at sound conclusions. Nevertheless, this exercise may give you an idea of the possibilities of dream analysis as a method of psychological investigation.

2. Try the Gestalt Therapy technique of placing two chairs facing each other, seating yourself in one, and imagining someone with whom you are having problems in the other. Say everything you would like to say to that other person. Then seat yourself in the other chair and pretend you are that other person. Say everything you imagine he or she would say to present his or her point of view. See if this helps you understand the other person better than you did before and if it results in a new attitude about how to get along with him or her.

3. Design and carry out your own behavior-modification program. In addition to learning by doing, you may eliminate or reduce the frequency of one of your own bad habits.

Choose an observable item of behavior that you really want to get rid of. **159** Nail-biting, overeating, putting things off, or persistent lateness are the kinds of things you may be able to work on successfully.

Observe and record the frequency of this behavior pattern by making a mark in a special notebook every time you catch yourself doing it. Keep track of the periods of time over which you made your observations and divide the number of hours into the number of times the behavior occurred. This will give you an estimate of its average rate of occurrence.

Next, prepare a chart on graph paper on which you can record the rate of occurrence every day. Your chart should look like that shown in Figure 9.1. Compute your rate every day for three days. Let the average of these three scores comprise the baseline with which you will compare your improvement. Enter it on your chart.

Now begin a program of positive reinforcement. Reward yourself with a pleasant activity or desired treat every time your daily rate falls below your baseline, and give yourself a large reward at the end of a week of steady improvement. Additional bonuses may be forthcoming in the form of praise and admiration from your family and friends, besides which the graphic evidence of your improvement should serve as a reinforcing agent.

At the end of a month, discuss your results with other members of the class. See if you can decide who improved the most and why.

```
2.0
1.8
1.6
1.4
1.2
1.0
 .8
 .6
 .4
 .2
 .0   Baseline Rate
      M T W T F S S M T W T F S S M T W T F S S  .  .  .  .  .  .
```

Figure 9.1: Behavior Record.

References

1. FRANZ ALEXANDER and SHELDON SELESNICK, *The History of Psychiatry* (New York: Harper and Row, 1966).

2. ALFRED ADLER, *What Life Should Mean To You* (Boston: Little, 1931).

3. FRIEDA FORDHAM, *An Introduction to Jung's Psychology* (London: Penguin, 1953).

4. CARL ROGERS, *Counseling and Psychotherapy* (Boston: Houghton Mifflin, 1952).

5. CARL ROGERS, *On Becoming a Person* (Boston: Houghton Mifflin, 1961).

6. FREDERICK S. PERLS, *Gestalt Therapy Verbatim* (New York: Bantam, 1972).

7. ERIC BERNE, *Games People Play* (New York: Grove Press, 1964).

8. THOMAS HARRIS, *I'm OK–You're OK* (New York: Harper and Row, 1967).

160

9. HANS EYSENCK, "New Ways in Psychotherapy," *Psychology Today* (June, 1967), *1*, pp. 39-47.

10. Ibid.

11. PAUL R. MUNFORD, DIANE REARDON, ROBERT P. LIBERMAN, and LYNN ALLEN, "Behavioral Treatment of Hysterical Coughing and Mutism: A Case Study. *Journal of Counseling and Clinical Psychology,* 1976, *44,* pp. 1008-1014.

12. MELVIN ZAX and GEORGE STRICKER, *The Study of Abnormal Behavior* (New York: Macmillan, 1964).

Suggested Readings

1. ALEXANDER, FRANZ and SELESNICK, SHELDON. *The History of Psychiatry.* New York: Harper and Row, 1966.

2. FARADAY, ANN. *Dream Power.* Berkeley: Medallion, 1973.

3. FRANKL, V. *Man's Search for Meaning.* New York: Washington Square Press, 1963.

4. ROGERS, CARL. *On Becoming a Person.* Boston: Houghton Mifflin, 1961.

Alcohol, Drugs, and Nutrition

10

eople in every known society have used chemical agents to relax themselves and alter their states of consciousness. Burdened by inner and outer pressures, men and women have resorted to alcohol, marijuana, heroin, and the hallucinogens or "mind-expanding" drugs to reduce their stress and help them escape from harsh reality.

At the same time, people have long believed that proper diet—not only the avoidance of alcohol and drugs, but also the consumption of healthful foods and the reduction of common substances like sugar—promotes mental as well as physical well-being.

While the moderate use of alcohol is not considered a psychological or social problem, heavy drinking and the taking of illegal drugs is a cause of great concern to many citizens. Since these practices are widespread and related to such social evils as poverty, crime, and traffic accidents, many psychologists are turning their attention to the study of their causes and effects. In recent years, some psychologists are also giving serious attention to the part diet plays in mental health.

In this chapter, we will survey current psychological thinking on the uses and abuses of alcohol, marijuana, heroin, and the hallucinogens. We will discuss the problem of drug addiction. We will also present the views of psychologists on the benefits that may accrue from eating healthful foods.

It is our belief that some parents and authority figures exaggerate the dangers of taking drugs in their desire to protect and control the young. On the other hand, many young people, out of ignorance and rebelliousness, underestimate these dangers to themselves and their friends. We hope your reading of the information that follows will help you achieve a balanced view of this highly controversial subject.

164

Alcohol

While social drinking is accepted in our society, the use of alcohol in large amounts may be taken as a sign of psychological disturbance. Alcoholism, defined by the World Health Organization as "a chronic behavioral disorder manifested by repeated drinking of alcoholic beverages to an extent that interferes with the drinker's health or his social or economic functioning," is a worldwide problem of major proportions. Four percent of American adult males and about one percent of females are alcoholics.[1] Many of these people are destined to die of liver damage or to kill themselves and others as a result of drunk driving.

What causes a person to become an alcoholic? Opinions vary, but many psychologists believe that emotional conflicts stemming from childhood play a large part in the history of the disorder.

In *The Personality of the Alcoholic*,[2] Howard T. Blane represents this view when he says that **unresolved dependency needs** are paramount. According to Blane, there are basically three kinds of alcoholics: the "openly dependent," the "counter-dependent," and the "fluctuating dependent."

As an example of the openly dependent alcoholic, he cites the case of a man who was raised in a well-to-do family by parents who could only show their love by giving him gifts and money. He was a good student in elementary school, but began having difficulty in high school. Around that time, he started to drink at parties and other social occasions. He did poorly in college and finally flunked out, but he acquired a

unresolved dependency needs

ongoing needs, in adulthood, to rely on other people and be cared for like a child

Social isolation is a common consequence of chronic alcoholism.

job in a brokerage firm because he was charming and had good family connections. Meanwhile, however, he was drinking more and more. After marrying a woman with a small inheritance, he drifted from job to job, depending on her and his parents to help support him. "Unfailingly easygoing, never nasty or aggressive while drinking, he was a 'pleasant drunk.' . . . He took for granted that his wife, parents, and friends would take care of him, and repeatedly recreated the circumstances which made it necessary that they do so."

As an illustration of the counter-dependent alcoholic, Blane relates the case of a successful sales manager whose father had always insisted that his sons be self-reliant. "All childhood indications of 'weakness,' softness, tears, and so on were subjects for paternal censure." As the boy grew up, he competed fiercely in sports and, in his teens, began to pride himself on being able to out-drink his friends. As an adult, he worked his way up to an important position in a national company but, when drinking, he began to insult executives of other companies. When his firm lost business as a result of his behavior, he denied that alcohol was responsible and tried to justify his actions. Even when the pattern was repeated many times, he continued to deny that he had a drinking problem.

As a portrayal of the fluctuating dependent alcoholic, Blane presents a man who was an organizer of health services in underprivileged foreign countries. Remarkably successful when on his own and far away from home, he would always drink heavily when he returned between assignments. Soon he would run out of money and alienate his friends. Then, as he had done many times before, he would turn to his parents and, with their support, seek another job that would take him out of the country again.

Alcoholics have other conflicts, of course. Blane goes into detail about their inability to handle aggressive impulses, their low **frustration tolerance,** their inclination to deny their problems. Fundamentally, however, both he and other psychologists believe that unresolved dependency needs are crucial in driving them to their dependency on alcohol.

Whether this explanation is sufficient is open to question. Behaviorists, for instance, claim that early conditioning—as in having frequent contact with adults who rely on alcohol for relief from tension—is instrumental in creating the disturbance. *Alcoholics Anonymous* takes the stand that a chemical deficiency makes certain people more susceptible to the ravages of drink. Whatever the final answer may be, psychologists are now engaged in attempts to discover it.

frustration tolerance
the ability to remain calm and reasonable when things are going wrong

---

Here is a description of the Alcoholics Anonymous program. See if you can detect its strengths and weaknesses from a psychological point of view.

How does A. A. work? The "pigeon," a new A. A. member, receives encouragement from the

"old timer," an older A. A. volunteer who has taken him under his wing and permits, or rather fosters, an interpersonal dependency that replaces the former dependence on the impersonal intoxicant. With the new satisfactions of friendship and reliance upon a "spon-

166 sor" for help in self-control, the "pigeon" can begin to cut down on his drinking. In this fashion he can be sobered up enough to be approached through psychotherapy if he is willing to accept this further step. A. A. prides itself on its program of effecting sobriety by itself without the help of psychotherapy. It accomplishes this in part through religion: a spiritual force is invoked to help counteract the patient's sense of failure and hopelessness. Optimism is encouraged by the example of "old timers" who no longer drink and are proof to the "pigeon" that sobriety can indeed be achieved. A. A. members speak each other's language; the social barriers between professional "helper" and "drunk" do not exist. It is easier to listen to former alcoholics than to those who have never shared the brand nor suffered from the problems of drinking. A very important feature is the fact that A. A. members who are helping newcomers spend all the time necessary to protect the newcomers from drinking impulses. They make themselves available at any time, even at night, in emergencies, and wherever the "pigeon" happens to be. Another tactic is the explicit program of *Twelve Steps*, which consists of the fol-

lowing: "(1) We admitted we were powerless over alcohol—that our lives had become unmanageable; (2) came to believe that a Power greater than ourselves could restore us to sanity; (3) made a decision to turn our will and our lives to the care of God as we understood Him; (4) made a searching and fearless moral inventory of ourselves; (5) admitted to God, to ourselves, and to another human being the exact nature of our wrongs; (6) were entirely ready to have God remove all these defects of character; (7) humbly asked Him to remove our shortcomings; (8) made a list of all persons we had harmed, and became willing to make amends to them all; (9) made direct amends to such people wherever possible, except when to do so would injure them or others; (10) continued to take personal inventory, and when we were wrong, promptly admitted it; (11) sought through prayer and meditation to improve our conscious contact with God as we understood Him, praying only for knowledge of His will for us and the power to carry that out; (12) having had a spiritual awakening as the result of these steps, we tried to carry this message to all alcoholics, and to practice these principles in all our affairs."[3]

Some psychologists regard the "cures" achieved by *Alcoholics Anonymous* as no real cures at all. They say it is as abnormal to rely on the supports the organization furnishes as it is to rely on alcohol. In effect, therefore, they claim that A. A. simply substitutes one dependency for another. Besides that, they criticize A. A.'s insistence that alcoholics may not even take one drink as "substituting an antidrinking compulsion for a drinking compulsion." Nevertheless, most people feel that A. A. has done a lot of good. If the establishment of an antidrinking compulsion does in fact wipe out a person's drinking compulsion, they say, then it is "a cure to be welcomed, nourished, and encouraged as long as it is needed."[4]

Marijuana

The benefits and hazards of marijuana have been argued strongly in recent years. Though used for centuries in China and the Middle East, the drug was unknown to Western civilization until about 150 years ago. Soldiers returning from Napoleon's Egyptian campaign brought it back to Europe, and soon several artists and poets were writing beautiful, bizarre descriptions of its effects on them. Medical doctors prescribed it for a variety of ailments, but in the United States its legal use was **167** diminished and finally terminated when laws complicating its possession were enacted in the 1930s.

The experiences described by those who have gotten "high," either by smoking the plant's leaves or eating them mixed in food, are fairly **euphoria** uniform. A feeling of **euphoria,** heightened intensity of visual and auditory sensations, passivity and relaxation lasting anywhere from one to four hours, followed by drowsiness ending in dreamless sleep is the usual pattern.

euphoria
a state of great happiness and light-heartedness

Baynard Taylor, an American writer, describes a typical marijuana state as follows:

> The sensations it produced were . . . physically of an exquisite lightness and airiness, mentally of a wonderfully keen perception of the ludicrous in the most simple and familiar objects. During the half hour in which it lasted, I was at no time so far under its control that I could not, with the clearest perception, study the changes through which I passed. I noted with careful attention the fine sensations which spread through the whole tissue of my nervous fibers, each thrill helping to divert my frame of its

> earthly and material nature, until my substance appeared to be no grosser than the vapors of the atmosphere, and while sitting in the calm of the Egyptian night, I expected to be lifted up and carried away by the first breeze that should ruffle the Nile. While this process was going on, the objects by which I was surrounded assumed a strange and whimsical expression . . . I was provoked into a fit of laughter. The hallucination died away as gradually as it came, leaving me overcome with a soft and pleasant drowsiness, from which I sank into a deep kind of refreshing sleep.

Other users have described new melodic lines bursting forth from familiar musical pieces and brighter and richer colors abounding in ordinary objects. Common physiological responses include faster pulse rate, reddening of the eyes, and increased appetite. Although time slows, five to ten minutes seeming like an hour, the marijuana smoker is usually able to separate himself from his drug-distorted experience and behave in a perfectly sober manner if necessary. A few individuals, however, have shown negative reactions characterized by anxiety or panic. The difference in effect appears to be dependent on the mental state of the user. People with serious psychological disorders may be **disinhibiting** thrown, by the **disinhibiting** action of the drug, into greater distress than they normally experience.

disinhibiting
the removal of normal cautions on thoughts and acts

To date there is no evidence that marijuana is physiologically **addictive.** Investigators, however, differ in their observations on its capacity to induce a psychological dependence. Some argue that repeated usage **addictive** amounts to the creation of an escape mechanism to avoid facing the unpleasant aspects of reality, while others contend that dependency on marijuana is not as serious as dependency on alcohol. A survey of 400 chronic users at a large Western university revealed no systematic patterns of physical or mental damage and most of the subjects seemed to be in the normal range of productivity, ambition, and adjustment.[5] On the other hand, there are well-documented cases of individuals who have undergone severe mental reactions including paranoid symptoms,

addictive
a drug is addictive if reducing its intake causes the user great discomfort

social withdrawal, and memory impairment as a result of the drug. In general, the research that has so far been undertaken indicates that weak preparations of marijuana pose little threat in terms of drug abuse, while strong preparations equal hard liquor in their potential for harm.

The possession and sale of marijuana, however, is still illegal in many parts of the Western world. One consequence of marijuana use, therefore, may well be an unpleasant and expensive legal action leading to fines, probation, or imprisonment.

The Hallucinogens

Mescaline, which comes from a peyote cactus; psilocybin, a substance derived from certain mushrooms; d-lysergic acid diethylamide (LSD), from a fungus that grows on rye and wheat; and phencyclidine (PCP), a chemical concoction better known as "angel dust," are capable of producing dramatic alterations in human consciousness. They have been called "hallucinogenic," "psychedelic," or "psychotomimetic" drugs because they cause the user to experience, for a period of time, a mental state similar to that of the hallucinating psychotic patient.

One subjective experience that is frequently reported is a change in visual perception. When the eyes are open, the perception of light and space is affected: colors become more vivid and seem to glow, the space between objects becomes more apparent, as though space itself had become "real," and surface details appear to be more sharply defined. Many people feel a new awareness of the physical beauty of the world, particularly of visual harmonies, colors, play of light, and the exquisiteness of detail.

The visual effects are even more striking when the eyes are closed. A constantly changing display appears, its content ranging from abstract forms to dramatic scenes involving imagined people or animals, sometimes in exotic lands or ancient times. Different individuals have recalled seeing wavy lines, cobweb or chessboard designs, gratings, mosaics, carpets, floral designs, gems, windmills, mausoleums, landscapes, "arabesques spiralling into eternity," statuesque men of the past, chariots, sequences of dramatic action, the face of Buddha, the face of Christ, the crucifixion, "the mythical dwelling places of the gods," the immensity and blackness of space.[6]

The description above, like many of the "trips" reported by euphoric users, puts emphasis on the entrancing beauty and profoundly visionary aspects of the hallucinogenic experience. It is also common for people under the influence of mescaline, psilocybin, or LSD to undergo horrifying states of anxiety and confusion.

The "hellish" experiences include an impression of blackness accompanied by feelings of gloom and isolation, a garish modification of the glowing colors observed in the "heavenly" phase, a sense of sickly greens and ugly dark reds. The subject's perception of his own body may become unpleasant: his limbs may seem to be distorted or his flesh to be decaying; in a mirror his face may appear to be a mask, his smile a meaningless grimace. Sometimes all human movements appear to be mere puppetry, or everyone seems to be dead. These experiences can be so disturbing that a residue of fear and depression persists long after the effects of the drug have worn off.[7]

The use of LSD by a borderline psychotic personality can be dangerous since the drug can cause total psychosis. For this reason, it has been found unsuitable for mental patients even though it offers the prospect of temporary euphoria. On the other hand, LSD has been effectively combined with traditional psychotherapy aimed at weakening rigid defenses and discharging intense withheld emotions in neurotic and more or less normal individuals. Ideal subjects seem to be those with overly strict consciences and low self-esteem, or those suffering from an inability to overcome grief. The hallucinogens have also been shown to benefit the dying patient by reducing his or her pain and uplifting his or her spirits, even for periods beyond the actual drug state.

These uses, of course, require strict professional observation and control. Most LSD consumption, however, has taken place in unsupervised settings. In such cases, where environmental conditions are unstable, the user's psychological condition unknown, and the drug itself possibly contaminated with impurities, the probability of a "bad trip" is enormously increased.

The dangers of PCP are even greater.

> Psychotic reactions to PCP mimic the symptoms of paranoid schizophrenia, with hallucinatory voices and combative or self-destructive impulses. The drug can also give users a distorted sense of their own bodies; people often feel their arms or legs are growing or shriveling. Users may also suffer the loss of bowel or bladder control, slurred speech, inability to walk, jerky eye movements, and grimacing. Acute toxic reactions can last up to a week after a single dose, and the mental effects can linger for more than a month, often recurring in sudden episodes while the patient is apparently recovering. Taken in larger doses, PCP can induce seizures, coma, and death.[8]

It seems clear, therefore, that the taking of drugs like LSD, PCP, mescaline, and psilocybin for "kicks" is a risky and foolish venture, quite apart from the fact that it is illegal.

Heroin

Of all the "uppers" and "downers," mind-expanders, pain-killers, and tranquilizers that are known to our society, heroin is undoubtedly the most addictive. Derived from the opium poppy that grows in Iran, Turkey, India, and China, it is akin to morphine, codeine, and other medical preparations. The illegal sale of heroin is an underworld operation amounting to millions of dollars a year, so the demand for it by addicts and occasional users can be seen to be immense.

What makes it so desirable? We might be tempted to think that the experience of taking the drug is luxurious. In fact, that is not so.

> The addict's enjoyment of the "high" is not the enjoyment of a stirred-up, zestful state. It is not the enjoyment of intensified sensory input and excitement, not even on a hallucinatory or fantasied level. . . . It is, in fact, not an enjoyment of anything positive at all, and that it should be thought of as a "high" stands as mute testimony to the utter destitution of the life of the addict. . . . It is, in the main, an enjoyment of a nirvana-like state unpreceded and unenriched by the pleasure of getting there. It is an enjoyment of negatives. Contact with reality diminishes. Ideational and fantasy activity are decreased, often blotting out a disquieting and disturbing fantasy life that is characteristic of the unintoxicated state. . . . Addicts feel "out of this world" and content, as if all of their needs have been taken care of. . . . There is a remarkable rhapsodic description of thumb-sucking by a grown girl (quoted by Freud in his *Three Essays on the Theory of Sexuality*) which could just as well illustrate the opiate high. "It is impossible to describe what a lovely feeling goes through your whole body when you suck; you are right away from this world. You are absolutely satisfied, and happy beyond desire. It is a wonderful feeling; you long for nothing but peace—uninterrupted peace. It is just unspeakably lovely; you feel no pain and no sorrow, and ah! you are carried into another world."[9]

It is a painful commentary on the conditions of life in this country, and on the weakness of human nature, that hundreds of thousands of Americans are willing to beg, steal, and prostitute themselves, to risk imprisonment or death as the result of an overdose, in order to sustain a heroin "habit." What they are buying so dearly is nothing more than an escape from reality, yet in the ghettos of our big cities and, in recent years, in the suburbs, too, the offer often appears to be irresistible.

When you snort heroin, you know, it got a bad bitter taste, like a taste that would turn your stomach inside out. It got some way-out taste. I couldn't snort because I couldn't take that taste; so I started shooting up. Shooting up you don't get the taste; all you get is a fast rush and a boss feeling, you know, like then you got a higher kick than marijuana. You feel drowsy, sit in a corner nodding, nobody to bother you, you're in your own world, in other words. . . .

I'm twenty-three-years-old and I've been on narcotics for about six years. It was in vogue at the time; everybody was doing it. There were four or five of us; one boy had been doing it for quite a while and said, would you like to try? . . . [He] staked everybody to a free shot, and administered it and made a big adventure out of it. . . . He explained that you can steal and carry on all kinds of perverted things to get it, but at the time you're not concerned about what's going to happen later; it's what's going to happen now and the feeling you're going to achieve. And the feeling was so overpowering that it clouds your mind to any idea of going to jail, breaking society's rules, stealing, or anything like it. You don't believe it. Of the kids who took a shot at that party, all of us became addicts—only one didn't. Of the five who took shots, four of us are still addicts today, that still keep in touch and see each other, and try and play this big game of not getting caught by the police.[10]

The Psychology of the Addict

What kind of person is likely to become addicted, either to heroin or to one of the other drugs available to the public through illegal sources of supply? According to Jeremy Larner, in his introduction to *The Addict in the Street*:

> These addicts—like most addicts who are not doctors, nurses, or druggists—grew up in a crowded, lower-class neighborhood where they were introduced to heroin as teenagers. Bored and delinquent at school, they couldn't face the prospect of starting at the bottom of the social ladder. College was unthinkable, and once school was left behind, there was little to do but hang around the neighborhood, and no group with which to identify but one's comrades on the corner: in brief, no place to aspire to. Small wonder that, when asked why they started on heroin, almost every one of them included in his answer the phrase, to kill time. To be sure, they could have gotten jobs (all of them did at one time or another) and worked and saved and become respectable middle-class householders with families of their own. But frequently the model for such industry was missing; in almost every case, the subject reported no relationship or a negative relationship with his father. . . . Psychiatrists make a distinction between neurotic and psychotic illnesses. Roughly, the difference lies in the manner in which an individual denies or distorts the realities of himself and his environment. When a neurotic is confronted with a situation that provokes anxiety, his thoughts about the matter may be severely twisted, yet they still retain some reference to the circumstances as they exist. If we can speak of the neurotic as fighting reality, the psychotic by comparison is fleeing reality. The psychotic withdraws from his environment in favor of suffering or bliss within a world of his own fabrication. Now what I would like to propose is an analogy between heroin addicts and psychotics. I am not saying that addicts are psychotic per se, but that their response to anxiety moves beyond neurosis to an absolute escapism from which there is small hope of rescuing them.[11]

Not all psychologists accept this diagnosis, but the consensus would be that both social and personality factors contribute to the problem of drug addiction. A dominant view in the field holds that three levels of

An unwillingness to accept limitations and responsibilities is characteristic of drug addiction.

maladjustment can be distinguished. The first is seen in the addict's overall approach to life. He or she usually lacks a willingness to accept limitations and responsibilities. Long-range goals are avoided and there is persistent searching for immediate satisfaction and quick rewards. The second level consists of withheld anger, boredom, and tension. Despite the surface "cool" which he or she may display as a front, the addict is seen as a resentful, empty person who doesn't know what to do with his or her life. The deepest level, however, consists of an unresolved conflict between desires for godlike power and feelings of utter helplessness. The rehabilitation of the addict, it is argued, can only be accomplished by a resolution of this deepest conflict. Since taking of the drug relieves the anger, boredom, and tension that cover it, the issue is continually skirted and never fully faced.

This formulation, unfortunately, is not without its weak spots. On the one hand, its description of addicts' life styles and inner conflicts is based on information obtained after drug abuse has been established, raising the question whether these characteristics existed before addiction or were produced by the habit itself. On the other hand, its emphasis on personality factors leaves the impression that social conditions have been ignored. Regardless of the personality problems an individual may be suffering, there can be little doubt that the mere availability of addicting narcotics and the popularity of their use in the immediate neighborhood plays a role in the development of drug addiction.

Treatment

Treatments of confirmed narcotics users so far have produced only dismal results. Three methods of attack have traditionally been employed: treatment of the user's personality problems by means of psychotherapy; treatment of the addiction itself by withdrawing the drug under hospital supervision; and treatment of such results of addiction as criminal behavior, psychosis, and physical illness. None of these methods, however, has proved successful for more than brief periods of time. Most addicts, regardless of the help they have been given, tend to go back to their addiction as soon as their tensions mount.

Synanon is an organization of ex-addicts devoted to helping others by radically restructuring their lives. The Synanon program has been effective in a growing number of cases, but it demands that the addict surrender totally to the prescriptions and life style of the organization. Membership in Synanon usually involves living within the Synanon community for a period of time, working (often at menial tasks) for the community, absolutely and completely renouncing the use of drugs or alcohol in any form, and participating regularly in the so-called "game."

> The most important widely and continually used group process in Synanon is *the game*. All members participate in its process at least several times a week. In part, it is an intimate group interac-

tion situation in which a member can openly express his problems, fears, and hostilities to his fellows. . . . The game enables members to tell their fellows what they really think of them. . . . A participant in a game can be as spontaneous, creative, rigid, angry, loud, or passive as he chooses with no authority rules save one, the rule against physical violence.[12]

What actually happens in the "game" is that members hurl abuse and ridicule at one another with little restraint. To some, it seems a heartless, sadistic procedure, yet it has also been called an effective method of treatment. For many years now, Synanon has been successful in keeping large numbers of ex-addicts "clean." Unfortunately, however, its treatment methods and authoritarian structure have discouraged many onlookers. In addition, its founders have recently been accused of criminal liability with regard to threats and attacks on some of their critics. This has thrown the organization into disfavor with many psychologists.

More promising, therefore, is a government-supported "methadone maintenance program" administered by medical agencies. *Methadone* is a drug that prevents the withdrawal agonies all heroin addicts dread yet fails to produce the escape from reality that heroin provides. Addicts who take it as a substitute are able to conduct normal lives and avoid the criminal activity their "habit" formerly drove them into. A recent study by UCLA psychologists concluded that "mandatory treatment of heroin addicts is the only workable way of curbing addiction," and named methadone maintenance as the best mode of treatment available at present.[13] If laws were passed forcing all addicts in the country to enroll in the methadone program, these investigators believe a large step would be taken toward the elimination of heroin addiction.

Nutrition and Mental Health

To turn to a less distressing subject, let us now consider the role of nutrition in mental health. While most psychologists agree that proper diet is important to our physical well-being, few have so far taken a professional interest in the importance of food to our mental well-being. Those few who have, however, tend to be strong in their opinions.

In a book called *Psychodietetics*, Cheraskin and Ringsdorf claim that many emotional problems are actually produced by improper diet. They are familiar, they say, with "many cases in which a change of diet brought about remarkable recovery on the part of patients suffering from schizophrenia, alcoholism, drug dependency, psychoses, depression, and other serious problems."[14] They offer only **anecdotal evidence**—scattered cases from here and there—but they present a persuasive argument on behalf of what they call "the food-to-mood phenomenon."

Essentially, their argument states that our brains need certain essential nutrients in order to function well. Vitamin B_3, thiamin, riboflavin

anecdotal evidence

evidence based on accounts of single cases, sometimes reported second- or thirdhand, not studied under scientific conditions pantothenic acid, vitamin B$_{12}$, biotin, niacin, iodine, potassium, magnesium, threonine, lysine, and calcium are only some of the substances they list as contributing to optimal brain function. If the food we normally eat supplies the amounts we need, we will be inclined toward mental health. If we suffer a deficiency in one or more of these substances, however, we will be inclined to disorders ranging from simple nervousness to paranoid schizophrenia.

Luckily, we can provide the essential nutrients to our brains by sticking to "the optimal diet." This diet divides foods into three categories: foods to eat liberally, foods to eat sparingly, and foods to avoid. Here is a list of the most common foods in each category:

Foods to Eat Liberally
> meat, fish, fowl, eggs, cheese, milk
> fruit and fruit juice
> fresh vegetables
> whole-grain breads and cereals

Foods to Eat Sparingly
> fat (animal fat, butter, margarine, and salad dressings)
> salt
> coffee and tea.

Foods to Avoid
> sugar
> white flour
> hydrogenated fat
> food preservatives
> artificial flavoring and coloring agents

According to Cheraskin and Ringsdorf, "Of all the foods to be avoided, sugar is the most harmful. It is a prominent factor in the development of overweight conditions and diabetes, hypoglycemia, dental cavities and periodontal disease, kidney stones, urinary infarction, cardiovascular disease, intestinal cancer, diverticulosis, indigestion, hormone disorders—and mental illness."

Other physicians, psychologists, and food faddists have been equally vehement about the ill effects of sugar. Either a deficiency or an overabundance of sugar in the blood can supposedly cause irritability, nervousness, depression, anxiety, and a host of other complaints. Similarly, a low supply of certain vitamins has been blamed for various mental disorders and megavitamin therapy (administering massive doses of these vitamins to patients) has been used, with mixed results, on hospitalized schizophrenics.

Nutritionists point out that vitamin-deficiency diseases, such as rickets, scurvy, pellagra, and beriberi, are often accompanied by psychological disturbances which improve after vitamin therapy. That much is certainly true, yet the question remains whether other kinds of psychological disorders can really be helped by proper diet alone.

The basic problem in this area is that it is all too new to be judged with any certainty. There is not enough hard evidence to support the claims of the "mental nutritionists." Nor is there enough evidence to refute them. On the one hand, the cures they claim may be either exaggerated or due to causes other than the diets employed. On the other hand, our brains being part of our bodily system, it seems entirely possible that the foods we eat may be beneficial or harmful to the organ that controls our behavior.

Summary

We have surveyed the problems of alcoholism and drug abuse, presenting both the ill-effects of overindulgence in these substances and the attempts being made to cure people who are addicted to them. We have tried to be objective in assessing the pros and cons of using marijuana, but have clearly suggested that the use of hard drugs like LSD, PCP, and heroin is a foolish and dangerous undertaking.

In addition, we have presented some of the arguments for the part proper diet can play in mental health, while maintaining an attitude of skepticism about the final importance of nutrition on the mind.

Class Projects

1. We would like to make these projects as experiential as possible, but we obviously cannot suggest that any of you go out and get drunk or stoned in order to gain firsthand knowledge of the subject matter of this chapter. If some of you have already had these experiences, however, perhaps you could enlighten your class with a discussion of their benefits and drawbacks.

2. There being a great difference between occasional indulgence and drug addiction, we suggest you read and discuss *The Addict in the Streets* by Larner and Tefferteller or *The Road to H* by Chein, et al. to get a graphic picture of serious drug addiction and the problems associated with it.

3. To test the claims of the "mental nutritionists," try putting yourself on the "optimal diet" mentioned in this chapter. In particular, avoid sugar in any form. If you must use a sweetener, a small amount of honey should do. Keep it up for several weeks at least and see if you notice any changes in your mood. Here is a sample menu to use as a guide:

   An adequate breakfast: ½ grapefruit, 2 eggs, 3 oz. ham, 1 slice whole-grain bread with butter, 1 glass milk.

   An inadequate breakfast: hotcakes with butter and syrup, coffee with sugar and cream.

   An adequate lunch: 1 bowl vegetable soup, shrimp salad, 1 slice whole-grain bread with butter, 1 glass buttermilk, 1 apple.

An inadequate lunch: 1 ham sandwich, 1 soft drink, 1 piece of pie.

An adequate dinner: 4 oz. tomato juice, mixed green salad with vinegar dressing, 6 oz. roast beef, baked potato with 1 square butter, green peas, ½ canteloupe with 1 oz. cheddar cheese, 1 glass buttermilk.

An inadequate dinner: spaghetti and meatballs, salad with French dressing, white bread, pastry, coffee with sugar and cream.

References

1. WILLIAM R. MILLER and RICARDO F. MUNOZ, *How to Control Your Drinking* (Englewood Cliffs, NJ: Prentice-Hall, 1976).
2. HOWARD T. BLANE, *The Personality of the Alcoholic* (New York: Harper and Row, 1968).
3. EVA MARIE BLUM and RICHARD H. BLUM, *Alcoholism* (San Francisco: Jossey-Bass, 1967).
4. Ibid.
5. R. L. CHRISTIE, "Marijuana and Drug Abuse," *UCLA Daily Bruin*, (April 27, 1972).
6. FRANK BARRON, MURRAY JARVICK and STERLING BUNNELL, JR., "The Hallucinogenic Drugs," *Scientific American*, 1964:
7. Ibid.
8. *Newsweek*, March 1978.
9. ISIDOR CHEIN, et al., *The Road to H* (New York: Basic Books, 1964).
10. JEREMY LARNER and RALPH TEFFERTELLER. *The Addict in the Streets* (New York: Grove Press, 1964).
11. Ibid.
12. WILLIAM H. McGLOTHLIN et al., "Alternative Approaches to Opiate Addiction Control," reviewed in the *APA Monitor*, (August 1972).
13. EMANUEL CHERASKIN and W. M. RINGSDORF, *Psychodietetics* (New York: Stein and Day, 1974).

Suggested Readings

1. AMERICAN MEDICAL ASSOCIATION, DEPARTMENT OF MENTAL HEALTH. "The Crutch That Cripples," *Todays Health*, 1968, *46*, pp. 11-12, 70-72.
2. HUXLEY, ALDOUS. *The Doors of Perception.* New York: Harper and Row, 1954.
3. JACKSON, CHARLES. *The Lost Weekend.* New York: Farrar & Rhinehart, 1954.
4. JULIEN, R. *A Primer of Drug Addiction.* 2nd ed. San Francisco: Freeman, 1978.
5. RAY, O. S. *Drugs, Society and Human Behavior.* 2nd ed. St. Louis: Mosby, 1978.

178

SOME THOUGHTS OF OUR OWN

In chapter 6, we told you about the leading intelligence and personality tests being used in this country. We did not, however, address the issue that has been raised by certain groups who consider testing an invasion of privacy. Their belief is that a person's intellectual and personality attributes are his or her own business. They are afraid that test findings may be used to damage an individual's reputation. Their fears, we feel, are largely unjustified. Whatever findings a test may produce, a reputable psychologist will always keep them in strictest confidence, just as a physician does with the findings of medical tests. Besides, test findings are only one source of information about a person's abilities and disabilities. They are not by any means the only ways, or even the best ways, to tell how intelligent or dull, well adjusted or maladjusted a person may be, so the notion that they alone reveal "the awful truth" is a gross distortion of the facts.

In chapters 7 and 8, we described conditions that many psychologists consider "sick," but we pointed out that other psychologists see some of these conditions simply as unusual ways of living. Our own position on this controversy is that serious neurotic and psychotic disorders are indeed pathological and attempts should be made to cure them; milder forms of deviant behavior, however, may well be considered part of a person's uniqueness, especially if they do not interfere with other people's welfare. A person's eccentricities or unusual life style may in fact turn out to be an asset rather than a liability.

In chapter 9, we presented a whole array of approaches to psychotherapy and made it clear that, in our opinion, most of them have something worthwhile to offer but that none has so far proved much more effective than the others. A conclusion we would draw is that effort should be made to determine what kinds of therapy are best for specific problems and/or for particular types of individuals.

Finally, in chatper 10, we discussed the effects of alcohol, drugs, and nutrition on our mental well being. We have come to believe that moderate intake of alcohol or marijuana has not been demonstrated to be harmful to most people, but heavy doses of these substances and even light doses of other, more powerful drugs are injurious to our welfare. We would like to be convinced that good nutrition can play a significant role in assuring psychological health, but we do not think there is enough evidence to accept the claims of the more starry-eyed nutritionist uncritically.

Section Three

The Scientific Tradition

OVERVIEW

his section of the text reviews the scientific background of psychology. It describes some ways in which the scientific method is used to investigate human behavior, summarizes research on the classical topics of sensation, perception, and learning, and introduces you to the use of statistical measures in the evaluation of experimental data.

It also presents the controversy between Behaviorists and Gestaltists on the best way to investigate and explain human functioning. As you will soon see, this controversy is deep and long lasting. So, too, are related controversies that have received somewhat lesser exposure. *Is it best to study groups of people and try to discover their similarities or to study single individuals and try to explain their uniqueness? Is the scientific method as developed in the physical sciences the most appropriate method to use in the social sciences? Are psychologists who do not base their theories and conclusions on laboratory research still to be taken seriously?*

You may feel inclined to jump to conclusions about these questions without giving them a great deal of thought. We would caution you not to do so. Some of the foremost psychologists in the world hold opposing views, so there is much to be said on each side of these issues. If, after reading and discussing this section, you can see the complexity of the matter, you will have acquired a sophisticated outlook—and that is an achievement in itself.

Psychological Research

11

E xperimental or research psychologists are usually employed by universities. Part of their time, therefore, is spent in teaching and fulfilling other academic duties. The core of their professional activity, however, lies in the study of human and animal behavior.

Research psychologists believe that explanations of behavior based on **objective studies** are more reliable than those based on anecdotal evidence and **subjective speculation.** As a consequence, they look down on the citing of dramatic happenings to prove a point and on abstractions like "the unconscious." What they propose, instead, is the careful study of observable patterns of behavior, with conclusions drawn in a strictly logical fashion.

Because of their habit of studying the behavior of rats in their laboratories, researchers are sometimes called "rat psychologists." We should not take this nickname too seriously, however. While there may be some rats among them, there are also many eager beavers, more than a few sly foxes, and a sprinkling of silly geese.

This chapter will give you a general idea of what psychological research is all about. It will describe some of the discoveries that have been made, discuss the theories on which many studies are based, present both sides of major controversies, and acquaint you with the scope of the field. By the time you finish it, you should have a sense of what the "rat psychologists" are up to. Perhaps you will know whether you yourself would like to join their pack.

objective studies

studies whose methods are controlled, precise, and repeatable, leading to conclusions that are not influenced by personal feelings

subjective speculation

reasoning, judging, and offering opinions in the absence of hard facts

The Terrycloth Mother: A Modern Experiment

In the 1950s, a group of psychologists at the University of Wisconsin decided to investigate the origins of love in infancy. Since they could not experiment with human infants, they used baby monkeys as their subjects.

First, they built a number of wire "mothers," each equipped with a nursing bottle from which the babies could suck milk. Then they covered half of these creatures with terrycloth. The others were left with their wire structure exposed. Separated from their actual mothers, the babies were placed in cages with these mechanical mother-substitutes. Each baby monkey had equal access to a terrycloth mother and a wire mother, but half received milk from the former and half from the latter.

The psychologists found that, no matter which mother gave milk, the infant monkeys clung to the terrycloth mother much more than to her wire double. In the words of the chief experimenter, Dr. Harry Harlow,

> The two mothers quickly proved to be physiologically equivalent. The monkeys in the two groups drank the same amount of milk and gained weight at the same rate. But the two mothers proved to be by no means psychologically equivalent. . . . Both groups of infants spent far more time climbing and clinging on their cloth-covered mothers than they did on their wire mothers. . . . Moreover, as the monkeys grew older, they tended to spend an increasing amount of time clinging and cuddling on her pliant terrycloth surface. . . . These results attest the importance—possibly the overwhelming importance—of bodily contact and the immediate comfort it supplies in forming the infant's attachment for its mother.[1]

In later variations of these experiments, Dr. Harlow and his associates found that the baby monkeys, when frightened, would comfort themselves by clinging to their terrycloth mothers. Infants who were raised without a cloth-covered mother, however, were apt to panic at the slightest disturbance. When these subjects were fully grown, they were generally unable to show or accept affection from other monkeys.

These findings indicate that the comfort provided by soft, warm, bodily contact is essential in establishing an early sense of security and an ability to relate to others in an affectionate manner. Although the experiments were carried out on animals, the results are assumed to be true for humans as well.

Our purpose in starting the chapter with this example is to give you an idea of the kinds of things experimental psychologists investigate. The terrycloth-mother experiment, however, is but one of many thousands of studies covering everything from the way our eyes move

Cloth and wire mother substitutes.

during sleep and what that tells about our dreams to the effect that authority figures have on our kindness or cruelty to each other.

The field has become a beehive of activity. Practically every major university, not only in this country but in the entire world, has its psychological laboratory. Reports of research studies fill scores of journals every month, while popular magazines like *Psychology Today* translate the findings into language the public can understand. How did it all begin? We will have to go back about a hundred years to see.

The Beginnings

Experimental psychology began in 1879 when Wilhelm Wundt established the first psychological laboratory at the University of Leipzig. Trained in philosophy and physiology, Wundt and his colleagues devoted themselves to studying the nature of conscious experience. "What goes on in our head and how it gets there," is a phrase that could be used to sum up their concerns.

psychophysics

a method of research which tries to relate the physical qualities of an object or situation to how it is perceived by a person

These experimental psychologists used two methods of investigation. On the one hand, they made careful observations of the ways in which our senses feed us knowledge of the world. On the other hand, they systematically explored their own thought processes to illuminate the workings of the mind.

introspection

studying your own thoughts

Psychophysics and **introspection** were the terms applied to these two types of investigation. The former dwelt on the relationships between physical stimuli and psychological experience; the latter helped explain how trains of thought develop.

As an exercise in psychophysics, fill three pans with water so that one is rather hot, one lukewarm, and one rather cold. Soak one of your hands in the hot water and one in the cold for a minute or two. Then put both hands in the lukewarm water. You will find that, even though you know its temperature is lukewarm, the hand that was formerly in the hot water will feel cold while the hand that was in the cold water will feel hot. This is an illustration of a psychophysical principle known as **sensory adaptation.** Our sensory receptors—not only for temperataure but also for taste, smell, light, and sound—adapt to stimuli. They get used to whatever condition they are in, and new conditions are judged in comparison to the ones that preceded them.

As an exercise in introspection, let everyone in your class respond to a series of words your teacher reads out loud by writing down the first word that comes to mind on hearing each of the stimulus words. Then inspect your reactions and attempt to find principles to explain them. We can predict in advance that many of you will respond with opposites (e.g., hot . . . cold), synonyms (e.g., big . . . large), and rhymes (e.g., sing . . . ring). There will be other responses, however, that do not fit into these categories. If you can discover the associative principles by which they were formed, you will be following in the footsteps of the early experimentalists as they investigated "the association of thought," or the ways in which one image or idea gives rise to another in our minds.

sensory adaptation

the decrease of sensitivity to a stimulus after being exposed to it for a long time

The efforts of those early psychologists were important not only because of the data accumulated but also because they demonstrated that the scientific method could be used to investigate mental events. For centuries, the workings of the mind had been thought undecipherable. Now, for the first time in history, humanity's mental faculties became the object of scientific scrutiny.[2]

The Scientific Method in Psychology

The scientific method rests on five foundation stones: systematic observation, controlled conditions, deductive logic, operationally defined terms, and objectivity. Let us attempt to describe them.

Systematic observation. To make the scientific grade, an investigation must be carried out carefully, each step being thought through in advance. Whatever procedures are applied to one subject must be applied to all subjects. Thus, if one were comparing the behavior of two-, three-, and four-year-old children in a particular situation, it would not be scientific to observe the two-year-olds for ten minutes, the three-year-olds for twenty-five minutes, and the four-year-olds for seven minutes, since the time for observing in each group would not be the same. One would strive to make the periods of observation equal for each group.

Controlled conditions. All factors that might interfere with the events being studied must be identified and, if possible, eliminated. If one were studying the existence of mental telepathy between two particular persons, one would make every effort to screen out all nontelepathic avenues of communication between them (e.g., facial expressions, eye and hand movements, etc.). Otherwise, it would not be clear whether information passed from one to the other had been relayed by telepathic means or by subtle visual signs.

Deductive logic. The conclusions reached in a scientific study must be those that follow logically from the findings. A psychologist investigating humor, for example, might notice that giggling frequently expresses feelings of embarrassment. It would not be legitimate, however, to conclude that giggling is *always* a sign of embarrassment. Perhaps it is; perhaps not. The conclusion so drawn is speculative, not deductive. In order to meet the standards of science, a study would have to be done in which many subjects would be observed while giggling and asked to describe their feelings. When sufficient information had been collected, conclusions clearly based on the facts would be presented. In all likelihood, they would be expressed in comparative terms. Instead of a blanket statement like, "Giggling is a sign of embarrassment," they might resemble the following: "In children between the ages of five and ten, giggling most often accompanies feelings of embarrassment, but it also accompanies feelings of pleasurable anticipation. In early adolescence, it is most often associated with feelings toward the opposite sex. In adulthood, it tends to diminish in frequency, occurring most often when the subject is under the influence of alcohol, marijuana, or other chemical agents."

Operationally defined terms. Not only must vague expressions be avoided, but all terms must be defined in such a way as to allow them to be translated into experimental operations. It would not be scientific, for instance, to speak of studying "the nature of love," but it would be acceptable to study, "kissing, caressing, and hugging as expressions of affection." The reason is that these acts can be observed and counted, whereas the nature of love is an abstraction that cannot be tied down precisely.

Objectivity. The scientific method is concerned with facts, not with fond hopes or dreamy ideals. In order to follow it faithfully, one must put aside all preconceived notions and emotional inclinations. One must simply pay attention to what actually takes place. All findings must be recorded, whether they support the investigator's expectations or con-

188

control group

the body of subjects that experiences all the conditions of a study except the experimental procedure

tradict them. Thus, if a study that was expected to show that psychologists are among the most intelligent members of our society reveals, instead, that they are among the least intelligent, it would not be scientific to suppress the evidence, however much we might wish to do so.

The owner of a factory had been told that piped-in music would stimulate his employees to turn out much more work. He was reluctant to invest in the equipment on hearsay, however, so he hired a psychologist to study the actual effect of music on his workers' productivity. The psychologist divided a number of workers into two groups matched for skill, experience, and normal level of production. One group, called the **control group,** was allowed to continue working under the conditions to which they were accustomed. The other group, called the **experimental group,** had musical selections piped into their working area. In the first week, the experimental group's productivity soared almost 15 percent above their usual level, while the control group's remained unchanged. The experiment was continued for five more weeks. Gradually the experimental group's upsurge subsided, not quite back to the premusic level but to less than 3 percent above it.

This use of two groups, matched in all relevant respects but one, is a standard method of psychological research. It enables the experimenter to assert that the differences in the behavior being studied (in this case, productivity) are due to the differences in the **variable** being manipulated (in this case, music). Please note, however, that even in such a simple experiment, it is possible to misinterpret the results. Having found a 15 percent upsurge in the first week, the experimenter might have concluded that the piped-in music exerted a powerful influence on the workers' efficiency. Discovering that their efficiency subsided in the following five weeks, however, led him to conclude that, while the music itself did have some effect, its novelty during the first week was more important. Once the workers grew accustomed to it, its stimulation of their productivity was much less impressive.

Pavlov Discovers Conditioning

experimental group

the body of subjects that receives the experimental treatment

variable

a condition of an experiment that is changed or can be changed; an independent variable is a condition the experimenter changes, and a dependent variable is the result of the experimental procedure

In 1903 Ivan Pavlov, a Russian physiologist, embarked on a series of experiments that were to win him worldwide fame.[3]

Studying the nature of digestive fluids, Pavlov was in the habit of using dogs as experimental subjects. He fed them as part of his usual routine. One day he became aware of a curious event: the dogs, whose normal reaction was to salivate at the sight or smell of food, had begun to salivate as soon as Pavlov entered the room, before he had given them any food at all. Intrigued by this fact, he designed an experiment to explore it.

Pavlov harnessed the dogs so he could regulate their feeding and measure their flow of saliva. Just prior to giving them food, he would ring a bell. After repeating this sequence a number of times, he found that the bell alone caused the dogs to salivate. He concluded that the repeated pairing of the bell and food had somehow linked these stimuli in the dogs' reflexive mechanisms.

This process has come to be known as *classical conditioning*. To a larger extent than we realize, it governs the behavior of people as well as animals. We associate events that occur together so that we automatically expect the second when we experience the first. Thus, people who lived through wartime air raids which were preceded by sirens exhibited fear reactions whenever they heard a siren, even if they knew it had nothing to do with an air raid. Similarly, people who have had unpleasant encounters with the police find themselves expecting trouble every time they see a police officer.

The event that produces the original response (in the case of Pavlov's dogs, the presentation of food) is called the *unconditioned stimulus*. The event that becomes capable of producing the response (in this case, the ringing of the bell) is called the *conditioned stimulus*. While conditioned reactions tend to persist for some time, they will decrease and disappear if the conditioned stimulus is presented often enough without the unconditioned stimulus. This process, known as *extinction*, can be observed in the behavior of a child who is burned from touching a hot stove. For a long time thereafter, the child will avoid contact with the stove or be extra careful about touching it. If he or she has sufficient contact with it without getting burned, however, the fear will subside and vanish.

Conditioning corresponds to what, in everyday language, would be called the acquiring of habits. Simple as it seems, however, it explains a lot of things. Many psychologists believe that the ways in which we live our lives—the foods we eat, the hours we sleep, the clothes we wear, the mates we seek, the goals we pursue, the people and things we like and dislike—are all to some extent affected by conditioning. We are creatures of habit, they claim, and most of the choices we think we make out of our own free will are really controlled by the ways in which we have been conditioned to react. We may not salivate when we hear a bell, but in many respects we are not much different than Pavlov's dogs.

The Origins of Behaviorism

In the 1920s, an American psychologist by the name of John Watson founded an entire school of thought based on conditioning. Known as behaviorism, this school has flourished enormously. It has attracted thousands of followers and produced many hundreds of volumes of research. To this day, it maintains a prominent position in experimental psychology.

The famous "Albert experiment" exemplifies Watson's approach. An eleven-month-old boy named Albert was the subject. He was first shown a white rat which did not frighten him. Later, he was shown the rat again, but paired with a sudden loud noise. The child was frightened by the noise. After seven pairings, he reacted with crying and avoidance to the sight of the rat alone.

In order to test the generalization of Albert's fear, five days later he was presented with the rat, a rabbit, a dog, a fur coat, a package of white cotton, and a set of blocks. He showed a fear response to the rat, rabbit, dog, and coat, but he played freely with the blocks.

Watson argued that Albert's reactions were a model of the ways in which we acquire our likes and dislikes. In his view, such widely different things as a woman's preference for blonde, blue-eyed men or a man's distaste for rock'n'roll music would both be based on conditioning. The woman who found blue-eyed blondes attractive, he would have said, was either influenced by commercial advertisements or associated them with someone she liked in the past. The man who could not stand rock'n'roll might have heard it in the company of noisy, troublesome youngsters.[4]

Behaviorists like Watson reject the idea that the aim of psychology is the study of the mind. They focus their attention on observable behavior—on what we say and do rather than on what we think and feel. By explaining simple acts, they assert, we will learn to understand more complicated forms of behavior. Their approach is from the outside in and they purposely limit their investigations to observable, measurable events. Anything other than this, they say, is unscientific.

Some objections

A number of psychologists have always objected to this outlook. One group, known as the Gestalt school, long ago declared that the study of simple acts does not help us understand more complicated forms of human behavior. Take our reactions to a melody, whether we find it happy or sad, ugly or beautiful, harmonious or discordant. They cannot be explained on the basis of our reactions to the notes of which the melody is composed, for the melody is experienced as a whole (in German, a *Gestalt)*, and the individual notes do not strike us as happy, sad, ugly, beautiful, harmonious, or discordant. The same is true of our reactions to a painting, a poem, or another person. We do not respond to their tangible parts (e.g., to a person's eyes, nose, feet, or arms) but to their intangible wholeness. We are affected most by what philosophers would call their "essence," and this is a quality behaviorism cannot explain.

Kurt Koffka, one of the first Gestaltists, carried out a revealing experiment using hens as his subjects.[5] He spread some seed on two sheets of paper, one light gray in color, the other a darker gray. When the hens pecked at the seed on the darker gray paper, he let them eat all they wanted. When they pecked at the seed on the lighter gray paper, he shooed them away. After awhile they pecked only at the darker paper, indicating that even hens know where to find a square meal. Then, however, Koffka did an ingenious thing. He substituted new sheets of paper for the original ones, but now the lighter sheet was the same shade as the darker sheet had been previously. (In other words, the two new sheets consisted of one which was identical to the sheet from which the hens had learned to obtain food, and one which was darker than any they had seen.) The question was, from which sheet would they attempt to feed?

The hens wasted little time in debate. Without hesitation, they began to peck seed from the sheet which was now the darker. Koffka concluded that they had not learned to respond to a specific shade of gray, but to the intangible concept "darker." He took this as evidence that behaviorism would have failed to predict what happened.

B. F. Skinner: The Leader of Modern Behaviorism

Despite the objections of the Gestaltists, interest in behaviorism continued to grow and reached new heights in the 1930s and 1940s. The most influential figure in this area is a professor we mentioned briefly in an earlier chapter. His name is B. F. Skinner. He has conducted a great deal of research, some of it quite spectacular. For example, he has conditioned creatures as simple as pigeons to operate complicated electronic devices. He has also published scores of articles and several books.[6]

In the 1930s, Skinner invented an apparatus which has come to be known as the "Skinner box." It was a small, soundproof cubicle containing a bar which, when pressed, released pellets of food. A hungry rat would be placed in the box. It would ramble around and accidentally bump into the bar. Food would be released, which the animal would eat. From these accidental pressings, the rat would soon progress to a level of behavior in which it would skillfully depress the bar in order to receive its food. Skinner saw the rat's behavior in this situation as a prototype of learning. On the basis of his observations, he defined the principles of *operant conditioning*.

Operant conditioning differs from classical conditioning in that the conditioned response (in this case, pressing the bar) is something the subject does actively rather than automatically (like Pavlov's dogs salivating). The subject is conditioned to perform a definite action in order to receive a desired reward. And what makes it work? According to Skinner, the most important factor is the immediacy of the reward. In the case of the rat in the Skinner box, the food must appear just as soon as the lever is pressed; otherwise the rat will fail to make the connection between the two.

Symbolic rewards

Behaviorists have also studied the effects of symbolic reinforcements or rewards. J. B. Wolfe, for example, showed that chimpanzees can be trained to work for a token reward—a poker chip—provided that it can be exchanged for food. He devised a vending machine that delivered grapes when a poker chip was inserted into a slot. He then taught chimps to operate the machine. In one study, a blue chip was worth two grapes, a white chip one, and a brass chip zero. When the animals learned the values of the chips, they developed preferences for the blue over the white and the white over the brass. In another study, the chimps were trained to receive two peanuts when a black chip was used and water when a yellow chip was used. Wolfe found that the chimps worked for the appropriate chips depending on their states of deprivation. When hungry, they would work for black chips and, when thirsty, for yellow.[7]

In a striking analogy to these experiments, many mental hospitals

now operate on a "token economy" system.[8] Withdrawn, antisocial pa
tients are rewarded with tokens when they perform such simple acts a
making their beds, combing their hair, or keeping themselves clean
Even more complex forms of behavior can be improved by this method
The tokens can be exchanged for special foodstuffs, offgrounds passes
and other desirable items. In this way, the patients learn to behave mor
appropriately and thus begin the road back to mental health.

Symbolic or secondary rewards such as money and status influenc
the behavior of all people. The college student will work to obtain higl
grades, the businessperson to increase income, the homemaker to b
complimented by guests. In every case, their efforts may be viewed a
operant behavior resulting in desired rewards.

Operant conditioning: claims and objections

Skinner and his associates view operant conditioning as the fundamen
tal procedure for learning. Furthermore, they claim that if schedules o
reinforcement were properly managed, people could be conditioned t
change their behavior in many desired directions.

The problem of poverty in our society may be taken as a case ir
point. Skinner asserts that people who do not work hard have not beer
properly conditioned. Their predicament, he argues, will only be cure
by making the rewards they seek dependent upon their output of pro
ductive labor. If they find that hard work brings them money and othe
goods while failure to work brings them various kinds of deprivation
they will acquire the habit of working and thus end their poverty. Edu
cation too can be improved, he feels, by the application of condition
ing techniques. He advocates the use of teaching machines and pro
grammed instruction methods to aid the learning process.[9]

Many psychologists raise strenuous objections to these proposals
They feel the behaviorist view of human nature, when carried to such ar
extreme, is oversimplified. People in real life are much more compli
cated than rats, chimpanzees, or even human subjects in a controllec
laboratory setting. To assume that conditioning techniques alone car
solve intricate social problems is, to their minds, absurd. And perhap
most important, they maintain that to exclude thinking and feeling from
scientific study is to exclude the essence of that which makes us human
In their view, the study of bits and pieces of behavior does not go ver
far toward illuminating the complex problems of people in the rea
world.

Lab or Field?

Some researchers feel that the artificial conditions of the laborator
make subjects behave differently than they ordinarily would. They re

commend, therefore, that whenever possible psychological studies be **193** done in the "field"—in the natural setting in which the behavior being studied occurs.

Robert Sommer, a psychologist at the University of California at Davis, argues this position rather eloquently. "Psychology," he says, "entered the laboratory almost a century ago and has not yet recovered from the experience. . . . Too many researchers look upon field research as laboratory studies done outdoors. Rather than leave the laboratory, these psychologists have either snail-like carried their laboratories with them or tried to turn the world into an experimental chamber." After explaining that good field research is different from lab work in that it attempts to interfere with the natural setting as little as possible, he gives an example of a study he himself conducted.

hypothesis
a scientific guess that may be tested by experimentation

Some years ago, I was interested in testing the **hypothesis** that people in groups would drink faster and more than people alone. . . . My students and I visited each of the pubs in a middle-sized city, ordered a beer, and then sat down and recorded on napkins or pieces of newspaper the consumption of lone and group drinkers. We found that group drinkers drank more, not because they drank faster, but because they remained longer in the pub. . . . The reviewer of my paper expressed concern that I had not controlled the two populations, and there might have been other differences between lone and group drinkers to influence these results. Perhaps there were. I don't know. . . . There was no way that we could control whether people who entered the premises sat alone or in groups. Maybe we could have undertaken random assignment in the basement of the Psychology Department . . . but I am not sure that the results would have been valid or generalizable to any other place.[10]

His point is that while field research sacrifices the precise control of all conditions that experimentalists seem to love, it gains the advantage of observing behavior as it normally occurs. This, he claims, is much more convincing than what happens in the unnatural setting of a lab.

The importance of this viewpoint is that it strongly encourages research psychologists to get out into the real world. If they want to study the effects of crowding on the inmates of institutions, says Sommer, let them study it in prisons and mental hospitals, not by putting groups of student volunteers into a small room for a few hours. If they want to study the membership of neighborhood gangs, let them spend some time in neighborhoods where gangs really operate, not call a few representatives down to the university for interviews.

While these suggestions may seem perfectly reasonable to us, the fact is that most research has not been done in the field. Partly because of the model set by the physical sciences, partly because of their deep conviction that science can succeed only under controlled conditions, research psychologists have usually done their work in the offices, rooms, and halls of the universities in which they have been employed.

194 **Four Basic Methods**

The four most common ways of conducting psychological research are the case study method, the survey method, the correlational method, and the experimental method. Each has advantages and disadvantages in terms of the validity of its findings, how easy or hard it is to do, and its suitability to the subjects being studied.

The oldest approach is *the case study method.* A particular ability or disability in one or several individuals is studied intensively on the basis of retrospective reports. Either the subject himself or people who have known him for some time tell how the characteristic under investigation developed. In this way, it is hoped, the source or cause of whatever is being studied will be revealed. If you read biographical accounts of famous people like Beethoven, for instance, you may learn something about the conditions that gave rise to his musical genius. The disadvantage of this approach is that important events may be forgotten or distorted in the retelling. As the Gestalt therapist Fritz Perls often said, "When pride and memory battle, pride wins."

The survey method, which is widely used by political pollsters, has the advantage of studying problems by directly questioning those who may determine their outcome. It requires a carefully designed questionnaire which must be administered to a sample of people who correctly represent the population being surveyed. On the basis of these people's answers, inferences may be drawn about the opinions and potential responses of the larger population. Thus, on the basis of 500 San Franciscans' responses to the question "Who do you prefer for Mayor—So-and-so, Such-and-such, or Whatchamacallim?" pollsters can predict the outcome of the next election.

The correlational method has been employed in thousands of studies by psychologists and psychology students. It investigates the extent to which a change in one situation or event produces a change in another situation or event. The relationship between poverty and crime, between the hours of practice a team puts in on the basketball court and its ability to win games, between the number of TV shows a child watches and his or her susceptibility to headaches: all may be studied by the correlational method.

The experimental method, finally, enables psychologists to discover cause-and-effect relationships between two or more events. An experimental group and a control group, matched for such characteristics as age, sex, and educational level, are subjected to different events. The control group, for instance, may be allowed to sit in a quiet, comfortable room with interesting magazines to read for a couple of hours, while the experimental group may be put in a room where the chairs creak, loud music is being played on poor sound equipment, and carpenters are hammering on the ceiling. Coffee machines may be available in both rooms, and the frequency of coffee drinking under each of these conditions may be studied. This method, especially when applied to more important problems like the effects of new medication on psychotic patients' delusions, the results of particular instructional programs for **195** teaching gifted children mathematics, or the consequences of long periods of sleeplessness in normal adults, is considered the heart of the scientific approach in psychology.

Unfortunately, however, the experimental method encounters several problems of its own. It may be costly and time-consuming, it may require special facilities and equipment, and it is barred from investigating some events because of ethical restraints. We might like to know, for example, how certain parts of the brain control certain kinds of behavior, but we certainly could not operate on human subjects' brains simply to satisfy our curiosity.

Some research methods used by social psychologists are ingenious. One example, from the work of Stanley Milgram, is called the Lost-Letter Technique. It permits us to measure people's attitudes toward a group or organization.

The investigators drop a large number of addressed and stamped envelopes throughout a city. A person who finds one of these "lost" letters is thereby faced with the question of whether to mail it, disregard it, or destroy it. Even though there is widespread feeling among most people that one ought to mail such a letter, under certain circumstances—as when it is addressed to an organization the finder dislikes—he or she may not mail it. By using various addresses, therefore, and noting the number mailed to each address, one can assess the public's attitude toward a particular organization. This technique has an advantage over interviews and questionnaires in that it measures what people actually do, not simply what they say.

To test the technique, Milgram and his students dropped 100 letters addressed to each of two organizations they knew to be unpopular in the city of New Haven, Connecticut. The organizations were Friends of the Nazi Party and Friends of the Communist Party. For purposes of comparison, 100 letters were addressed to a popular group, Medical Research Associates, and 100 to a private party, Mr. Walter Carnap. All envelopes contained the same letter and were addressed to the same post-office box. The letters were distributed through ten districts of the city, in outdoor phone booths, on sidewalks, in shops, and under automobile windshield wipers (with a note saying, "found near car"). A few days later, the letters were returned in unequal numbers as predicted. Seventy-two percent of the Medical Research letters and seventy-one percent of the personal letters were returned, whereas only twenty-five percent of the Nazi letters and twenty-five percent of the Communist letters were returned.[11]

A study such as this, as you can see, gives information not only on people's attitudes toward the organizations mentioned, but also on the public's behavior when faced with a moral dilemma (i.e., whether to do what one knows is socially correct or what one feels like doing on the basis of one's own moral judgment.)

The Scope of Psychological Research

Regardless of researchers' preferences for working in the lab or the field, regardless of their position on behaviorism as a guiding theory, they are coming to study more and more different aspects of human behavior. It is no exaggeration to say that experimentalists now investigate everything from eyelid reflexes to artistic creativity.

Traditionally, the areas on which research was focused were sensation and perception, memory and learning. That may have been because they were easy to study, not because they were the most important things to explain. In any case, contemporary research is accumulating data on such diverse topics as dreaming, group behavior, suicide, the psychological needs of infants, problems of the aged, student cheating, effects of nutrition on IQ scores, and the ability of apes to use Ameslan (the sign language of the deaf) to communicate with each other.

In short, psychological research now takes the entire gamut of behavior as its province. As long as the item under consideration can be clearly defined and objectively investigated, psychologists are likely to study it. The field has come of age. It continually attracts more members, and the federal government spends millions of dollars annually to support its most promising projects.

In the chapters that follow, we will go into some detail about the things that were studied in the early research laboratories. In the next section, we will tell you more about the fieldwork that has been done in recent years. By the time you finish this text, therefore, you should know as much about researchers as they believe they know about you. How's that for a tradeoff?

Summary

Modern experimental psychology has its roots in the nineteenth century, when Wilhelm Wundt founded the first psychological laboratory in Germany. Although its original methods were subjective in nature, experimental psychology is now based squarely on the scientific method of investigation. Its discoveries have increased our understanding of how behavior patterns are acquired and modified. Studies by Gestalt psychologists have shed light on the ways we organize our experiences. Some researchers are working outside the lab in natural settings such as the city streets. Findings are being applied to problems people face in their everyday lives. The field is vast, growing, heavily funded, and likely to exert more and more influence on society as a whole.

Class Projects

1. In order to become more familiar with the scientific method in psychology, carry out the following experiment on the effect of distracting stimuli on learning.

random

occurring by chance

Select 20 subjects from the students in your school. Be sure to choose them in a **random** fashion (e.g., by picking every tenth or twentieth name on the student roster). Divide them into two groups matched, as closely as possible, for age, race, and sex. Have all members of both groups memorize an unfamiliar piece of poetry. Let one group (called the control group) do its memorizing in quiet surroundings. Have the other group (called the experimental group) do its memorizing someplace where there are many distracting events going on. Calculate the average length of time it takes for each group to memorize the piece without errors (i.e., the length of time it takes each member of the group divided by the number of members in the group). Compare the two groups' averages as well as the range of individual times within each group. Discuss your findings in terms of what you can logically conclude about "the effect of distracting stimuli on learning."

2. In order to acquire some familiarity with the problems involved in doing research in the field, conduct the following study of the effect of being observed on students' participation in class.

   Let each member of your psychology class act as an observer in another class that he or she attends. On the first day of the study, for an entire class period, let the observers inconspicuously record the number of times people answer questions the teacher has asked or comment on the subject under discussion. On the second day of the study, let them announce that they are making these observations as part of their psychology course, request that the people in the class behave as they normally would, and then proceed to record, very visibly this time, the number of times people ask questions or make comments. When the results have been tabulated, calculate the average number of times students participated in class when they did not know they were being observed and compare this figure with the average number of times they participated with the knowledge that they were being observed. Discuss your findings in terms of what you can logically conclude about "the effect of being observed on students' participation in class."

   Our purpose in suggesting this study is less concerned with the findings you may collect than with the experience you will have. We think you will find that unexpected events will occur that will make the task of the observers more difficult than you may have anticipated. At the same time, we think you will find that doing a study in the field poses quite an exciting challenge. So keep your eyes and ears open while doing it, and afterward discuss what you learned with the rest of your classmates.

3. Discuss the principle of operant conditioning in the raising of children. If you want to condition a two-year-old boy to use the potty when he has to relieve himself, is it better to reward him with a hug every time he does so or to wait until the end of the day to show him how pleased you are? Why?

4. A man goes shopping for a new car. After comparing several makes, he chooses a Mustang. To what extent is his choice based on the performance of the cars he examined? To what extent is it based on associations set up in his mind by the advertisers of the different brands? If he has watched a number of television commercials in which the man who owns a Mustang is well-dressed and handsome, in which pretty girls swoon at the sight of the car, and in which the roads on which it drives are free of traffic, has he been conditioned to have a positive response to Mustangs? If so, is his choice an act of free will? Is it due to what he has been led to feel will make him happy? Can it be both?

   Discuss these questions to explore the ways in which conditioning plays a part in our lives. Try to come up with other examples from the field of advertising that show how we are conditioned to have certain reactions to things without clearly understanding why.

198   **References**   1. Harry F. Harlow, "Love in Infant Monkeys," *Scientific American* (June 1959) *200*, pp. 68-74.

2. James P. Chaplin and T. S. Krawiec, *Systems and Theories of Psychology* (New York: Holt, Rinehart & Winston, 1974).

3. Ivan P. Pavlov, *Conditioned Reflexes* (New York: Dover, 1927).

4. John B. Watson, *Behaviorism* (New York: Norton, 1925).

5. Kurt Koffka, *Principles of Gestalt Psychology* (New York: Harcourt, Brace 1935).

6. B. F. Skinner, *About Behaviorism* (New York: Knopf, 1974).

7. John B. Wolfe, "Effectiveness of Token Rewards for Chimpanzees," Comparative Psychology Monograph (1936), *12*, pp. 1-72.

8. A. E. Kazdin, "Recent Advances in Token Economy Research," in *Progress in Behavior Modification: volume 1* M. Hersen, R. M. Eisler and P. M. Miller eds (New York: Academic Press, 1975).

9. B. F. Skinner, *Science and Human Behavior* (New York: Macmillan, 1953).

10. Robert Sommer, "Toward a Psychology of Natural Behavior," *APA Monitor* (January 1977), *8*.

11. Stanley Milgram, "The Lost-Letter Technique," in *Readings in Psychology Today* (Del Mar, CA: C R M, 1972).

Suggested Readings   1. Anderson, B. D. *The Psychology Experiment*. 2nd ed. Monterey, CA: Brooks, Cole, 1971.

2. Boring, Edwin. *History of Experimental Psychology*. New York: Appleton-Century-Crofts, 1950.

3. Monte, C. F. *Psychology's Scientific Endeavor*. New York: Praeger, 1975.

4. Willis, Jerry and Giles, Donna. *Great Experiments in Behavior Modification*. Indianapolis, IN: Hackett, 1976.

Sensation and Perception

12

P

sychologists have always been interested in how our senses work. Vision, hearing, taste, smell, touch, and the inner senses of balance and movement have all received careful attention. You may wonder why. They seem to be the physiologist's area of study, so it may be difficult to see what they have to do with psychology. The answer is simple: the senses are in many ways the doors and windows of the mind.

Many psychologists believe that the mind is a *tabula rasa* (i.e., a blank slate) at birth. Whatever comes into it must enter through the senses. Whether this is so or not, it must be obvious that most of our knowledge of the world is based on what we have seen, heard, tasted, smelled, and touched. The colors of the sunset and the skyline of New York, the sounds of speech and laughter, honking horns and the cries of gulls, the cold mellow sweetness of ice cream and the spicy crunch of pizza, the delicate fragrance of flowers and the powerful odor of fish—these represent only a tiny fraction of the data our senses supply.

The way in which we receive information through our senses and use it in the conduct of our lives is the topic of this chapter. If you want to tie it in to your actual experience instead of considering it just another part of a boring textbook, take some time this week to observe the workings of your own sense organs. You may be surprised at what they are up to.

At Birth and Before

Long before we are born, our senses are working. The fetus hears the throb of its mother's heart, the gurgling of her digestion, the whoosh of her breathing. The baby's body swims and squirms inside the water of the womb. It experiences pressure as the mother's belly is pressed and even greater pressure as the uterus contracts to push it out into the world.

The moment the infant emerges, new sensations assail it. Light contrasts with the darkness in which it developed; cold, with the warmth in which it was encased. There is the touch of the doctor's gloved hands, the sounds and odors of the delivery room. Eventually, the newborn experiences the fragrance of its mother's breast and the sweet, soothing taste of her milk.

All the sights, sounds, tastes, smells, and textures one's senses record are relayed to one's brain. There the process of perception is completed. Things are recognized and given meaning. A particular cluster of shapes, colors, sounds, smells, and touches becomes Mommy. A smaller, more active, and furry one becomes Rover. One's experience of the world gradually changes from what William James called "a blooming, buzzing confusion" to the recognition of people, animals, objects, and oneself.[1]

Individual Differences

autistic children

those who suffer a severe mental disorder characterized by extreme withdrawal, garbled language, and inability to relate to other people

Just as people come in all sizes and shapes, so too do we differ in sensation and perception. **Autistic children** have been found to respond abnormally to sounds. Colorblind persons lack certain parts of their visual system. People who are musically gifted can detect tiny differences in tones, while so-called natural athletes react in a superior manner to muscular cues. Each person has a unique collection of sense receptors, and each person's brain processes their messages in an individual way, so each of us perceives a slightly different world.

Nevertheless, there are common ways in which our senses operate. Psychologists have devoted their efforts to discovering what these are. In the pages that follow, we will briefly review their major findings. Finally, we will discuss the value of this information in psychology's attempts to understand the total human being.

Vision

The eye is a complicated organ that is especially sensitive to light (see Figure 12.1). Light waves reflected from objects are focused by the *lens* at the front of the eye onto the inner surface or *retina*. The receptors on the retina have two distinct shapes and chemistries. The *cones* are clustered in the center of the retina and register color. The *rods*, receptors **203** which curve to the edges of the retina, register only black and white. A complex set of muscles moves and focuses the eye, while another set of tissues keeps it moist and clean. Our visual perception, however, depends on more than meets the eye. Light sensations received by the eye are transformed into biochemical impulses which sweep along the *optic nerve* to the back part of the brain. In that part of the brain, called the *occipital lobe*, the impulses are decoded into recognizable images.[2]

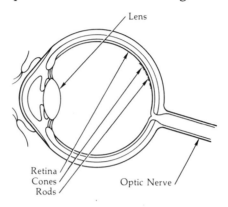

Lens

Retina
Cones
Rods

Optic Nerve

Figure 12.1: Diagram of the eye.

It may be of interest to you to learn that we all have a *blind spot* where the optic nerve joins the retina at the back of the eye. We apparently learn early in life, however, to compensate for this condition, for we do not see our visual fields with a spot missing but as though we were able to perceive them totally in a single glance. Similarly, we learn to perceive objects as we know they are rather than as their dimensions actually register on our retinas. Thus, when we view a book from different angles, different distances, or under different conditions, we do not see it as changing its size or shape or losing its colors, but that in fact is how it impinges on our eyes. Beginning art students often have to be taught "how to see"—that is, how to render objects as they actually register on the eye; otherwise, they tend to produce landscapes, faces, and figures which do not depict the specific, individualized landscapes or models they are trying to draw, but rather suggest some standardized, generalized notion of what a landscape, face, or figure looks like.[3]

What we see is further determined by what we have been taught to respond to and what we choose to see. Our culture, for example, teaches us to respond acutely to the motion of automobiles and other vehicles in our vicinity, for the very good reason that our lives may depend on seeing them in time. An African bushman, in contrast, is taught to respond to the slightest movement of grass and leaves, as the vegetation around him may conceal a wild beast of prey. He and his kinspeople are therefore likely to be much more aware of the movement of foliage than we are, while we are more aware of onrushing vehicles. Within our culture, however, there are people who at times "do not see" a car that is about to run them over. While it is difficult to prove, some psychologists assume that at least a small percentage of such people unconsciously choose not to see the car, out of a self-destructive need or an abnormal urge to be injured.

Influences on perception

The matter, as you can see, is complicated. Even when we understand how our visual organs work, we are left with many questions. Why do we not actually register everything in our visual field? Why do some people see one thing and some another, when their eyes are focused in the same direction? Psychologists who study this field have come to some interesting conclusions.[4] Although the following examples pertain mainly to vision, other senses are also subject to these influences.

Attention. In order to perceive at all (that is, to arrange the raw input from our senses in such a way as to make use of the information they provide), our attention must be aimed at certain aspects of our environment. "Tuning in" on some things and "tuning out" on others are the first order of business. The child engrossed in a TV program will not notice his siblings scuffle. And while you have been reading this page you have probably been unaware of other sensations, both visual and nonvisual, that might have distracted your attention. You have probably ignored your body's internal rumblings, the sounds of traffic outside your window, the intensity of the light by which you are reading. In other words, you have been aiming your attention at this book (we hope) in an effort to make some sense of it.

Change. Some aspects of the environment tend to attract our attention, however. Startling change is one of them. A sudden noise or the abrupt stopping of a sound that has gone on for some time, any quick movement in our field of vision, a rise or fall in temperature, are noticed more than an unvarying set of conditions. Neon signs that move, therefore, are more effective than those that don't.

Size. Large objects attract more attention than small ones. This is well known in the field of advertising, where ever-larger billboards and signs compete with one another to keep America beautiful.

Intensity. If other conditions are the same, we find ourselves attracted to the loudest and brightest stimuli. Powerful and piercing sounds are more compelling than soft muffled ones, while brilliant colors appear more prominent than pastel shades.

Individual need. Our perceptions, however, are also controlled by our needs. When hungry, we are quick to pick up any sight, smell, or sound of food. When lonely, we tend to see loving couples all around. We perceive, in other words, what we are impelled to perceive, and on the other side of the coin we become blind and deaf to things that do not mesh with our needs.

To a certain extent, this is why students often fail to learn what their teachers are trying to teach them. They do not absorb the teacher's

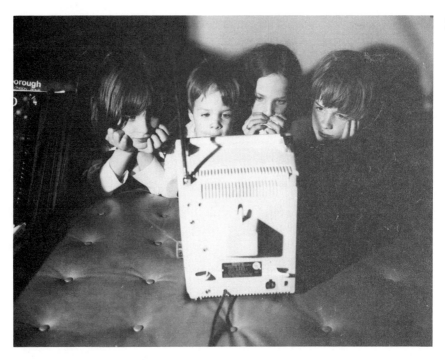

Children glued to a TV set are oblivious to what is going on around them.

words unless those words relate to their personal concerns. An effective teacher, therefore, will try to show that the subject is not a useless batch of information but something that can help students understand and enjoy their world.

Organization. We do not experience our environment as a disorganized jumble of light and dark hues, high, low, loud, and soft sounds, or hot, cold, dull, and sharp skin sensations. Quite the contrary: we grasp it as a patterned, peopled, object-filled field. Some of the principles that govern our organization of this field may be explained as follows.

Figure and ground. In reading this passage, you see the letters that form the words standing out from the page. The white space, in other words, appears as a background to the print that is on it. When addressing a person in a room filled with other people, you probably see the one to whom you are speaking as standing out from all the rest. This tendency to divide our environment into figures and grounds is perfectly normal. Yet it makes us unaware of things that are right in front of us.

Grouping. The manner in which objects are grouped influences the way we organize them. How, for example, do you see the spots below? Do they appear to be a series of dots or four groups of dots?

The *law of proximity* states that we tend to group objects together in terms of their closeness to one another. According to this law, therefore, most of you should have seen the spots above as four groups rather than a series.

Similarity. Objects that have something in common are also seen as going together. Thus, in this group of letters:

O	O	O	O	O
X	X	X	X	X
O	O	O	O	O
X	X	X	X	X

We tend to group the Xs with the Xs and the Os with the Os even though the individual Xs are closer to the individual Os than either is to its own kind.

Continuity. We tend to perceive patterns that are smooth and continuous rather than those that appear broken or discontinuous. This, for instance:

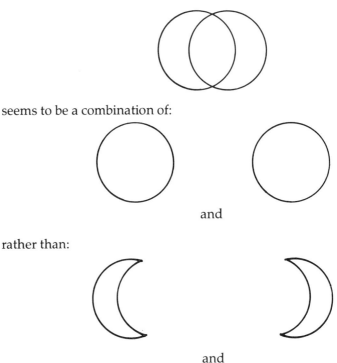

seems to be a combination of:

and

rather than:

and

Closure. We do not need a complete figure in order to perceive it as such. If small areas are missing or lines are incomplete, we tend to fill in the missing parts.

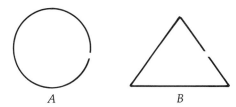

A   B

Figure A is generally seen as a circle, figure B as a triangle, even though they are incomplete. If either were flashed on a screen for a fraction of a second, observers would not even notice the gaps in their outlines and would unhesitatingly describe them as a circle and a triangle.

Judgment. The act of seeing—as of hearing, touching, tasting, and smelling—is frequently compounded by judgments about the dimensions of the things we observe or about their other attributes. We do not simply see a building, for example; we see a tall building or a squat one. We see a mighty oak or a puny sapling, not just a tree. The judgments we make, however, are not always logical. They are affected by at least three other factors: preceding sensations, adjoining sensations, and social pressures.

Preceding sensations. If you have been looking for some time at very bright colors, a medium tone will seem pale to you. The same tone will seem vivid if observed after looking at very muted shades. Similarly, an apartment will seem spacious if you have spent the preceding week in a jail cell, but it will seem cramped if you have been romping on an open beach. What we are experiencing now, in other words, is judged in terms of what we experienced a little while ago.

Adjoining sensations. We also judge the attributes of objects in relation to other objects in their immediate vicinity. Look at the following diagram, for instance. Does not circle A seem smaller than circle B? They are actually the same size, but the circles surrounding them tend to influence our judgment, as do the letters within them.

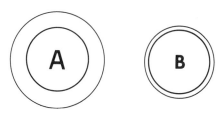

Social pressure. Some impressive experiments have shown that even such simple matters as our estimates of the lengths of lines are affected by our social climate. Subjects shown two lines of equal length, for example, were exposed to the opinions of other subjects who firmly declared the lines to be unequal. The first group of subjects tended to agree with the others and to declare the lines unequal.[5]

Can you see the relevance these findings have to the more important judgments we make in our everyday lives? When we see a work of art as beautiful, a style of furniture as elegant, a particular way of dressing as offensive, are we making up our own minds or are we being swayed by popular opinion? Psychologists believe that most of us are so anxious to be accepted members of a group that we distort our original perceptions in order to see things as the group sees them.

Hearing

Just as our visual apparatus translates light waves into images, our auditory system transforms vibrations of air molecules into sound. These vibrations can be measured in three dimensions: their frequency, their intensity, and their complexity. *Frequency* refers to the number of vibrations that occur per second. This determines the pitch or tone of a sound, more rapid frequencies producing higher tones. *Intensity* refers to the amplitude or strength of the vibrations. Thus, the harder a piano key is struck, the louder it will sound, although its tone is no different than when the key is struck lightly. *Complexity*, finally, refers to the fact that few objects vibrate at a single frequency. A piano string that vibrates at 400 cycles per second, for instance, also vibrates (with lesser intensity) at 800, 1200, 1600, and other multiples of 400. The complexity of sounds accounts for their timbre, which in turn permits us to distinguish different musical instruments or the many thousands of voices we hear over the course of a lifetime.

Enough said about what we hear, let us consider the organs that enable us to hear. Our auditory system has three major subdivisions: the *outer ear,* the *middle ear,* and the *inner ear* (see Figure 12.2).

The outer ear, that unusual appendage at the side of our head, does little more than support our eyeglasses or give us something on which to dangle earrings. Unlike other animals, we move our heads rather than our ears to collect vibrations and direct them into the auditory canal. In any case, as vibrations pass through the canal, they strike a thin membrane, the *eardrum,* which is itself set into motion. The vibration of the eardrum activates three bones in the middle ear, which in turn carry the vibrations into a structure called the *cochlea.* The cochlea, which resembles a snail, contains a fluid that is set into motion. The movement of this fluid stimulates thousands of tiny hairlike structures, each of which responds to different frequencies. They in turn generate electrical impulses that are carried to the brain, which receives and decodes them as recognizable sounds.[6]

Like visual perception, auditory perception is dependent not only on the sense organ itself, but also on the related area of the brain and the nerve pathways leading to it.

Although our hearing is not nearly as acute as that of certain animals, our response to sounds can be very dramatic. Notice what happens to you, for instance, the next time you listen to a marching band. In all

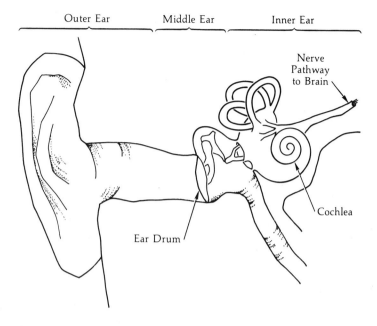

Figure 12.2:   Diagram of the ear.

likelihood, your heart will beat stronger, your muscles will tense, your breathing will become more rapid. The rumble of thunder or a loud drum roll can evoke the thrill of terror in us, while the languid murmur of a summer lake can relax us completely.

The tone of our voice is usually more indicative of our real feelings than the words we use. Have you ever been addressed politely by someone, yet felt that their politeness was merely a cover for hostility? Have you ever heard someone say they like you, yet known that their words were insincere?

As an exercise in communicating by tone alone, try repeating the phrase, "What a nice day!" in three different ways: first, as a way of letting someone know you love them; second, as a way of letting them know you hate them; and third, as an ordinary comment on the weather.

Taste and Smell

Taste and smell are closely related. Eat a piece of apple and a piece of raw potato with your nose held shut: they will seem very similar—bland, moist, crunchy, and unappetizing. When we cannot smell our food, it tastes much less distinctive. This accounts for the fact that when we have a bad cold, most things taste insipid.

The tongue is the major taste receptor (see Figure 12.3). On its surface are hundreds of little bumps called *papillae*. These papillae are also found in the back of the mouth and throat. Each papilla contains approx-

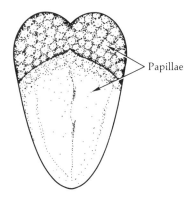

Figure 12.3: *Diagram of the tongue.*

imately two hundred taste buds, and it is the taste bud that is responsible for transmitting **gustatory** sensations to the brain. [7]

Taste buds, like other cells, are constantly dying and being replaced. As we age, however, the number of buds decreases. Older people often complain that food no longer tastes as good as it used to, while children, whose buds are more sensitive than adults', find strong, spicy foods distasteful.

The major receptors for the sense of smell lie at the top of the nasal passages between the nostrils and the throat. This area is known as the *olfactory epithelium.* As we breathe, air passing through the nasal passages comes in contact with our smell receptors, and they in turn fire nervous impulses to the brain.

In many animal species, the young know their parents and parents know their young not by appearance but by smell. Similarly, groups of animals like rats or mice share common odors that outsiders lack. Among human beings, people who eat distinctive foods, live in particular climate zones, and belong to a specific genetic group have fragrances that seem odd and at times unpleasant to members of other groups.

Our adaptation to odors is very quick. After a brief exposure to most smells and fragrances, no matter how pleasant or unpleasant they may be, we lose a large degree of our awareness of their presence. If you enter a room with a bad odor, you may be repelled at first, but after four or five minutes you probably will not notice it at all.

Previous experiences can alter our usual responses to pleasant and unpleasant odors. Pleasant associations can make an originally unpleasant odor attractive to us. Painful associations can render a neutral odor repulsive.

Do you think a stable of horses smells sweet or foul? If you loved horses and spent hours caring for them, grooming them, and riding them, how do you imagine you would feel about their smell?

n all likelihood, the more familiar you are with horses and the more you admire and enjoy them, the more invigorating do you find their odor, while the more unfamiliar you are with them and the more you distrust them, the more repellent you think they smell.

Far fewer psychological studies have been done on taste and smell than on sight and hearing. However, it seems clear that the former sensations, like the latter, operate according to physiological laws and yet are affected by psychological factors. When a taste or smell is processed in the brain, it is judged as much in terms of what we have learned of the world as in terms of what it has done to our receptors. If we have learned to love corned beef, for instance, we are apt to insist that a delicatessen smells great. On the other hand, if we had been raised in the Himalayan Andes and fed on goat's meat and milk, we would probably not like its odors at all—unless, of course, it featured "corned goat" sandwiches.

Taste and smell are also subtly attuned to our childhood memories. Perhaps this is because these senses are very keen in our early years. Have you not had the experience of biting into a piece of candy or encountering a fragrance that suddenly evoked the memory of a particular time in your past? In a classic work of literature—Marcel Proust's *Remembrance of Times Past*—the author is brought to recall an entire sequence of childhood events when he tastes a madeleine (a cookie he used to eat when he was small).

The Skin Senses

A great deal of research has been done by psychologists and physiologists to explain the sensations we experience when our skin is touched. Four separate sensations have been differentiated—pain, pressure, cold, and warmth—and to some extent linked to specific nerve endings in the skin. It has also been determined that certain parts of the body are much more sensitive than others. When two points are simultaneously touched on the surface of our backs, for instance, they must be thirty-four times as far apart as two points on our fingertips for us to be able to tell that we have been touched in two places rather than one.

Perhaps more important than this delineation of nerve endings and how they work, however, are the findings of psychologists who treat tense, anxious, or depressed clients. It has been noted that comfort and support can be communicated much more effectively by a friendly touch or warm embrace than by words alone. This is clearly a delicate matter, since professional ethics would not condone intimate physical contact between therapist and patient. It seems to be established, however, that patients can sometimes be helped as much or more by being stroked or held as by being talked to or listened to. These findings should not be

Touching is an important way of communicating friendship.

surprising. One of our earliest forms of security was being held in mother's arms; yet, until the last decade or so, most psychologists did not think of utilizing this well-known fact in their professional work.

Movement and Balance

semicircular canals

three small, liquid-filled, semicircular structures of the inner ear which contain sensory receptors for distinguishing between up-down, left-right and forward-backward

vestibular sacs

located at the entrance of the inner ear, containing the sensory receptors for maintaining the body's balance

Our awareness of the movement and position of various parts of our bodies is called *kinaesthesis*. It depends on sense organs within our muscles and tendons and is closely related to *equilibrium*. Equilibrium is our sense of balance and is governed by the **semicircular canals** and **vestibular sacs** of the inner ear. While all of this may sound rather technical and remote, our senses of movement and balance are really very important in the maintenance of our lives.

If these sensory systems were not functioning properly, we could not walk, climb, reach, grasp, or manipulate the many objects we need to sustain ourselves. Luckily, of course, few of us suffer from any serious defect in this area. Some children never manage to develop good coordination, as seen in the fact that they cannot throw or catch a ball very well and are poor at skipping rope, jumping, running, and other such activities. A sizeable number of adults, too, are notably awkward or clumsy. It is tempting to assume that such people are physiologically deficient. They may be, just as so-called natural athletes may be physiologically well-endowed. Psychological forces, however, are often significant as well.

A person's upbringing, or conditioning, may influence his or her kinaesthetic sense. Many children are brought up to cherish the life of the mind and to look down on the value of physical accomplishments. Reading, music, and the arts are looked upon with favor in their homes, while sports are scoffed at. A child's physical exuberance may be severely restricted "because it messes up the house." In some cases, children may be subtly but persistently conditioned to sit around a lot and read or watch television. After some years of such inactivity, it is entirely possible for a person to get very out of touch with his or her kinaesthetic sensations. He or she feels or seems naturally uncoordinated.

Shut your eyes and feel how you know where your body parts are. Try doing some physical exercises with your eyes shut and notice how the sensations become more acute simply because you are concentrating on them and reducing other stimuli.

Many activities, like riding a bike, playing an instrument, or bouncing a ball are governed largely by our kinaesthetic sense. Dancing, too, is an interesting example. Some people who consider themselves poor dancers have simply never learned the trick of "thinking with their feet"—that is, focusing on their inner bodily sensations rather than looking around or perceiving themselves from the outside. Good dancers often dance with their eyes half-closed, not just to enhance the romantic aspects of the situation but as an expression of the fact that they are concentrating on the inner feeling of the movements of their limbs. Try it sometime; you'll like it, and it may make you a better dancer without ever having to take a lesson.

Sensory Deprivation

Another recent finding of great interest to most psychologists is the fact that *a minimum amount of sensory input is required to maintain our normal mental stability.* In other words, we need to see, hear, and feel a certain variety of sensations to keep functioning adequately.

So-called sensory-deprivation experiments in which subjects were deprived of all sensory input for several days resulted in a decrease in their intellectual abilities and the occurrence of hallucinations and other pathological symptoms. In these experiments, the subjects were placed in isolated cubicles, their vision was reduced by translucent goggles, their sense of touch was controlled by separating their fingers with cotton and cuffing their hands with cardboard sleeves, and their hearing was subjected to nothing but the continuous hum of a ventilation fan. After a number of hours, most of them reported seeing flashes of light and hearing odd sounds. After a day or two, hallucinations of sight, sound, and touch began to occur.[8]

These results strongly indicate that, to maintain our sanity, we need the reassuring presence of the outer world relayed to us in the continual and varied impulses of our senses. This, in turn, sheds light on the problem of schizophrenia. Two of schizophrenia's notable symptoms are withdrawal of attention from the outer world and the occurrence of

An isolated human in a sensory deprivation experiment.

hallucinations. The second now appears to be a result of the first, for we know that by drastically reducing a person's awareness of the outer world we can cause hallucinations to occur. To understand this relationship more fully, more knowledge is necessary, not only about how our senses work, but about how they feed information to our brains and about how our brains create strange ideas in the absence of such information. When we process this knowledge, we will be closer to a cure of the dreadful malady of insanity.

Sensation, Perception, and Everyday Life

Knowledge of the ways in which our senses work and the effects of psychological factors on our perception of the world is of more than academic interest. It can help us evaluate the credibility of eyewitness reports of crimes. It can increase our understanding of what it is like to be handicapped. It can show us how to drive more safely. As mentioned above, it can shed light on the problem of schizophrenia and other forms of insanity. Above all, it can make us more tolerant of other people's views, for a clear understanding of sensation and perception allows us to see that the information we have in our heads has undergone a process of selection and shaping. It makes us realize, in other words, that—present company excepted—human beings do not have a direct pipeline to Truth.

Summary

Sensation is the process of experiencing the world through our senses of vision, hearing, taste, smell, touch, movement, and balance. Perception is the arranging of this raw sensory input into meaningful images and ideas. Our perception of the world around us, ourselves included, is strongly influenced by physical, social, and personal factors. Sensory deprivation, or the lack of sensory input, results in hallucinations of sight, sound, and touch. Knowledge of the workings of our senses and the factors that influence our perception of the world helps us understand why different people perceive things differently. This realization should result in more tolerance for other people's views, combined with some modesty about the "truth" of our own.

Class Projects

1. Several years ago, a popular Japanese movie, *Rashomon*, showed four people giving their versions of a dramatic event in which they had all participated. Although each one of them was telling the truth from his or her own viewpoint, they each gave a very different version of what had taken place. In this light, it may be interesting for you to try the following exercise.

   Let another class in your school be the "witnesses." Rehearse a dramatic scene that you can play out in front of that class, without giving them advance warning of what you are up to. For instance, you might have two students run into that class, both yelling and obviously upset. One of them could be holding some object, perhaps a handwritten note, which the other one is trying to get back. They could have some sort of a tussle, and then your teacher could arrive to settle the argument. When the scene is over (it should only last a minute or two), ask all the witnesses to write down exactly what occurred in as much detail as possible. In all likelihood, you will find some very odd versions of what was seen and heard.

2. In order to convince yourself that preceding sensations strongly influence our judgment of present sensations, keep one person in a darkened room for five minutes, another person in a highly lit room for the same period of time. Then bring them both into your classroom and ask them to describe the brightness of the lighting.

3. This project illustrates the ways in which our senses interact with one another and influence our perceptions.

216

Prepare:

1) Two glasses of milk, one of them dosed with food coloring to turn it yellow.

2) Two hard-boiled eggs, one colored green..

3) Two pieces of toast, one sprinkled with an assortment of food colors to make it look moldy.

4) Two glasses of orange juice, one treated with food coloring to make it black.

Serve the above foods to two blindfolded subjects who have not seen the meal. While they are eating an "experimenter" should ask them questions about the taste of each item of food. The class should observe and record their reactions. Next, remove their blindfolds and again ask them about the foods' taste and note their reactions to it. This experiment was described in American Psychological Association, Clearing House on PreCollege Psychology, *Periodically* 5 (May 1975).

References

1. WILLIAM JAMES. *The Principles of Psychology* (New York: Holt, 1890).
2. R. L. GREGORY. *Eye and Brain* (New York: McGraw-Hill, 1966).
3. H. W. LEIBOWITZ. *Visual Perception* (New York: Macmillan, 1965).
4. R. L. GREGORY. *Concepts and Mechanisms of Perception* (New York: Scribner 1974).
5. S. E. ARCH. "Effects of Group Pressure on the Modification and Distortion of Judgments," in *Groups, Leadership and Men*, ed. H. Gentzkow (Pittsburgh PA: Carnegie Press, 1951).
6. F. A. GELDARD. *The Human Senses* (New York: Wiley, 1972).
7. LAWRENCE M. ALPERN and D. WOLSK. *Sensory Processes* (Monterey, CA Brooks/Cole, 1967).
8. JOHN P. ZUBECK, *Sensory Deprivation: Fifteen Years of Research* (New York Appleton-Century-Crofts, 1969).

Suggested Readings

1. CARRAHER, R. G. and THURSTON, J. B. *Optical Illusions and the Visual Arts* Princeton, NJ: Van Nostrand Reinhold, 1968.
2. CASE, J. *Sensory Mechanisms.* New York: Macmillan, 1967.
3. COREN, S. et. al. *Sensation and Perception.* New York: Academic Press, 1979.
4. CORNSWEET, TOM N. *Visual Perception.* New York: Harry N. Abrams, Inc 1975.
5. LOCKER, J. L. ed. *The World of M. C. Escher.* New York: Harry N. Abrams Inc., 1975.
6. LUNDEL, J. *Introduction to Sensory Processes.* San Francisco: Freeman, 1978.
7. MUELLER, C. G. *Sensory Psychology.* Englewood Cliffs, NJ: Prentice-Hall 1965.
8. WEINTRAUB, D. J. and WALKER, E. L. *Perception.* Monterey, CA: Brooks/Cole 1966.

Learning About Learning

13

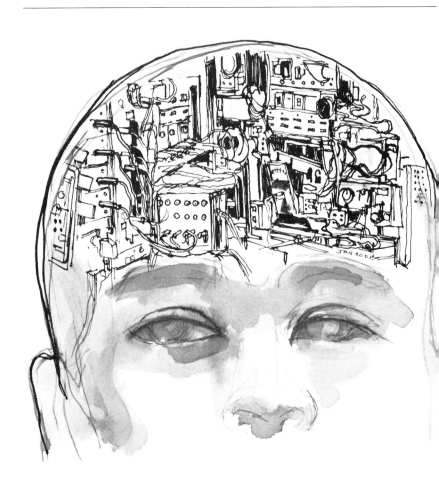

earning begins at birth and continues throughout life. The infant learns to recognize its parents, to regulate its bowels, to walk and talk and play with toys. The child learns more advanced games and how to relate to other children and adults. Then he or she goes to school, learns to read and write, and becomes familiar with a great variety of subjects. The adult learns many skills—some for pleasure, some for profit, some simply for survival. Year in and year out, we amass vast quantities of information about people, art, science, politics, religion, medicine, history, entertainment, and sports.

In a manner of speaking, our brains can be described as complex learning machines. It should not be surprising, therefore, that psychologists have spent long hours trying to understand how learning takes place.

In this chapter, we will review some of the findings they have made. We will examine several theories and present some important facts. We will concentrate on the basic patterns to which most learning appears to conform. In short, we will try to help you learn what learning is all about.

What Is Learning?

Psychologists regard learning as much more than what goes on (or fails to go on) in school. They sometimes define it as "any change in behavior as a result of experience."[1] Whether the experience occurs in a classroom, on a job, at home, or in the street is unessential. Whether the change in behavior lasts a day, a month, a year, or a lifetime is also beside the point. If you experience anything that produces a change in you, you have learned something, even though your teacher might not give you an "A" for it.

Learning, it has also been found, results in physical changes in the brain. They may be very minute, but they do in fact occur. This interesting fact was brought to light through experiments at the University of California. Psychologists there raised groups of rats in different environments: some barren and featureless, others containing many objects and passages the rats could examine and explore. The scientists later killed the grown rats and examined their brains under microscopes. The rats which had been raised in the more complex environments, and which therefore had more opportunities to learn, had developed more complicated brain structures than their deprived littermates.[2]

Even the behavior we ordinarily think of as instinctive or inborn has been shown to be affected by learning. Birds raised in captivity, for instance, who have never heard the songs of their species, will attempt to sing anyway, but their songs are often "wrong" (i.e., lacking some of the notes and inflections of the wild birds' songs). A red squirrel raised in a cage will still try to bury a nut, even in the absence of soil, but it will have more difficulty opening the nut than a squirrel who has had the opportunity to observe its elders accomplishing this feat.

The Findings and Views of the Behaviorists

Observe: a small white rat being studied by B. F. Skinner sniffs and paws about its cage. Its sniffings and pawings are aimless at first; the cage is just a cage and no part of it is more interesting than any other part. In the course of its activity, however, it happens to paw a little lever sticking out of one wall. Lo and behold! A pellet of rat food appears in a tray below. The rat of course eats it and then continues its random behavior, learning only that chicken wire is pretty much the same wherever you find it. Soon, however, it chances to strike the lever again, with the same result as before. Another pellet of food! This goes on for a little while and then the rat learns that that lever is worth pressing. We say the rat has learned this important piece of information because from now on, whenever it is hungry, it simply scampers over to the wall and has its meal delivered just like room service at a fancy hotel.

In Skinner's terms, what he has done is to *positively reinforce* a **221**
selected bit of the rat's behavior (i.e., pushing the lever), thus causing it
to occur more frequently. He might have produced the same result by
negative reinforcement—for instance, by wiring the cage to give the rat a
shock if it did not press the bar within a certain period of time. (Note
that the shock, although unpleasant, is not exactly a punishment in the
usual sense of the word. A punishment is something unpleasant we *do*
to a creature to cause a decrease in some form of behavior. A negative
reinforcement, in contrast, is something we *stop doing* when the creature
emits the desired response.) Whether positive or negative in form,
Skinner calls this kind of reinforcement and the learning it produces,
"operant conditioning." [3]

Shaping behavior. Simple operant conditioning such as we have described above works fine if what we want to teach is a simple operation
like pressing a lever. But we may want to teach rather complicated sets
of behavior that do not appear in a creature's natural repertoire. Suppose, for example, you wanted to teach a duck to play the piano. (Why
you would want to do such a strange thing is beyond us, but suppose
you wanted to do it anyway.) You could place the duck in a cage with a
toy piano and wait for it to peck out a chorus of the UCLA Fight Song,
but you would probably wait a long time. So how would you do it? Well,
you could shape the duck's behavior through operant conditioning, one
step at a time. At first, you would reinforce every move the duck made
in the general direction of the piano, either by giving it some duck food
or by saying, "Quack!" very nicely. Once the duck had learned that the
piano is the place to be, you would reinforce those responses in which
the duck looked at the piano; then those in which it touched the keys;
then its pecking of the keys; and finally its pecking of the keys in the
proper order to sound out the Fight Song. If you had enough patience
and ingenuity, you might even induce the duck to wave a UCLA pen-
nant with its tail in time to the music. Through the programmed use of
successive reinforcements, you would have turned an ordinary duck
into a football fan—or would you?

Most psychologists would insist that the duck described above has
not become a real UCLA rooter, for it performs the acts it has been
taught without understanding their significance. Furthermore, the duck
cannot transfer its responses to other situations that might call for responses appropriate to football fans. If it were given tickets to the Rose
Bowl, for example, it would probably not choose to go.

Nevertheless, behaviorists believe that even school spirit, or any
other set of complex behaviors, is the product of a long-continued series
of reinforcements. Our example of the duck was meant to be funny, but
in the case of human beings, according to Skinner, whatever attitudes
we develop are based on their having been reinforced.

Secondary reinforcement. Most reinforcement in real life is not simple
and primary, like the feeding of a rat, but subtle and complicated, like
the rewards one may get for doing well in mathematics. Skinner calls the
rewards that motivate most of us "secondary reinforcers." A secondary
reinforcer has the power to change our behavior because it is associated

The diploma is an example of a higher order reinforcer.

with a primary reinforcer. Money is the obvious example; it has value not in itself but in the things we can buy or do with it. Praise and approval are also secondary reinforcers, for they indicate that we can get what we want from those who praise us.

Conditioned learning. Systematic reinforcement, or operant conditioning, has produced some remarkable results. Children have learned to overcome serious reading disabilities by being reinforced with candy **223** and praise. Adults have learned to stop smoking by being reinforced with nauseous chemicals. And people have learned to overcome irrational fears through a form of conditioning known as *systematic desensitization.*[4] This procedure, in which the feared object or event is presented in gradually increasing doses in an otherwise supportive environment, is simply a scientific version of a technique parents have used for ages. When a child who fears the water is gradually carried into a pool by a comforting father, then encouraged to put in one foot, then both feet, and slowly helped to advance into kneedeep, waistdeep, and shoulderdeep levels, he is being systematically desensitized, although his father may never have heard of the term.

An executive in a large business corporation was so terrified of flying that she could not make business trips and was in danger of losing her job. She enrolled in a systematic desensitization program to try to overcome her fear.

The therapist or leader of the program asked members of the group, all afflicted with the same problem, to imagine what it would be like to fly in a plane. (They were sitting in his pleasant office at the time.) He had them talk about going to the airport, buying a ticket, registering their baggage, walking up the stairway to the plane, and so on. When they could comfortably imagine these specific parts of the activity, he suggested they go as a group to a nearby airport and simply walk around. Later he arranged for them to board a plane that remained on the ground, familiarizing themselves with its interior, chatting with the stewardesses, observing other planes safely taking off and landing. After several sessions in which they came into closer and closer contact with flying and become more comfortable with the idea, he arranged for the group to take an actual flight.

By the time she finished the program, the executive found that she could bring herself to fly, not with perfect comfort but with no more anxiety than most passengers experience.

Associationism

Skinnerian behaviorism, which is what we have been discussing, is the most fully developed of a group of learning theories that are classed under the general category of associationism. The principle underlying all of them is that behavior, attitudes, and ideas are learned through association with other behavior, attitudes, and ideas. In other words, if you pair two **stimuli** often enough, the two will become linked in a person's mind, so that one will thereafter suggest the other.

stimuli

any noticeable changes in the environment; anything that affects us in any way at all

It should be clear that we do indeed do much learning this way. If we want to learn the Spanish word for dog, for example, we repeat, "perro—dog," "perro—dog," a few times until the sound or sight of the one word suggests the other. This process is sometimes called "rote learning."

The first systematic studies of rote learning were done by the German experimenter Herman Ebbinghaus. He had his subjects memorize nonsense syllables like "ZUK" or "GIK" and noted the process by which they were learned. He discovered that the time it takes to learn a particular syllable is related to the total number presented; the more bits you have to learn, the longer it takes to learn each bit. He also discovered that items learned in this way will be retained for a day or two and then forgotten.[5] This finding has implications for real life situations like cramming for an exam. It really works, it suggests, if what you are cramming is data you can memorize and if you don't care how soon after the exam you forget it all.

Later students, expanding on Ebbinghaus' work, discovered that items in the middle of a list are learned more slowly than those at the beginning and end. They also found that later learning may interfere with earlier learning and vice-versa, especially if the subjects being learned are similar. You would be well advised, therefore, when studying two things on the same day, to select very different subjects (e.g., math and history) rather than very similar ones (e.g., psychology and sociology.)

If you want to get higher test scores, consider these findings from a study on learning, memory, and sleep.

Four groups of subjects learned the same material. Then group 1 slept eight hours and, on awakening, took a test on the material learned. Group 2 slept eight hours, remained awake for eight hours, and then took the test. Group 3 stayed awake for eight hours and then took the test. And group 4 stayed awake for eight hours, slept eight hours, and then took the test.

Which groups remembered the most? Groups 1 and 2, who retained 82 percent and 86 percent of what they had learned respectively. Group 3 retained 64 percent and group 4 retained 59 percent. It seems, therefore, that when sleep immediately follows learning, retention is best even if a period of waking activity occurs before testing.[6]

So, in preparation for your next test or quiz, try reviewing the material to be learned just before retiring for the night.

The man on whose theories associationism rests was a British philosopher by the name of John Locke. Locke coined a classic phrase when he called the human mind a "tabula rasa" (i.e., a blank slate). Other thinkers of his time believed that we are born with "innate ideas" of self, time, space, and God. Locke, however, argued that everything that enters the mind comes in through the senses. He thereby gave psychology the task of figuring out how simple sensations and perceptions are combined into complex ideas. Modern behaviorists and associationists still discredit the notion of innate ideas, but the debate about how complex ideas are formed has never been settled to everybody's satisfaction.

Wilhelm Wundt, whose name we mentioned in a previous chapter, was one of the first psychologists to attempt to isolate the elementary perceptions from which complex ideas are formed. If you had been a subject in his laboratory in the 1880s, you might have had an experience like this. Professor Wundt holds up a pencil and asks what you see. "A pencil," you proudly reply. "No!" the professor shouts, breaking the object in his rage. "You do not see a pencil. That is an idea that someone has taught you. What do you actually *see?*" Gradually getting the point, you tell him you see a long yellow object sharpened at one end with a black tip. He smiles, for he has gotten across his view that even such a common thing as a pencil is a complex idea made up of several simpler ideas put together.

Associationists, to put it briefly, believe that learning is nothing but the association of ideas. Sensations and perceptions that occur at the same time, or closely following one another, are combined by the mind, and that is how all our thinking proceeds. It is a bold, controversial standpoint, and one that opponents refuse to accept.

Gestalt Psychology

A rival school of thought, about which you have also heard, is called Gestalt psychology. Members of this school deny that all learning stems from simple associations. The human mind, they insist, is much more than a receiver and combiner of experience. It is active; it transforms experience and casts it into new forms. In fact, it adds something crucial to the input of the senses—something that comes from the mind itself.

You can easily perform an experiment that will make clear what the Gestalt psychologists are talking about. Just find a movie marquee or a sign with a series of lights that flash on and off one after the other in such a way as to create the impression of a moving line of light that continually goes around the sign. What is moving? The lights are standing still; all they are doing is flashing in a prescribed order. And yet you see movement. You see it so clearly that you have to concentrate rather closely on one part of the sign in order *not* to see it. Where is the movement?

The movement is in your head. You may say your eyes have played a trick on you, but it is a very valuable trick. It is the same trick that enables you to recognize a human face in a few lines drawn by a cartoonist, that permits you to understand the principles of mathematics rather than just repeating that $2 + 2 = 4$. It is the ability to perceive or create Gestalts—larger patterns, forms, or wholes that unite otherwise disconnected phenomena.

Gestalt psychology began with the very experiment you have just perfomed. The German psychologist Max Wertheimer was riding on a train, observing the countryside and thinking about thinking. It suddenly occurred to him that no combination of simple associations could explain how the mind perceives motion. He promptly got off the train and returned to his laboratory, where he set up a series of experiments with lights that flashed on and off in a dark room. His subjects reported seeing, just as you saw, apparent motion where in fact there was none. Wertheimer concluded that this apparent motion, which he called "the phi phenomenon," was a property that originates in the mind itself.[7]

Furthermore, Wertheimer argued, our minds perceive objects as they perceive motion, not as a bunch of sensations but as a unified whole.

From earliest infancy, we engage in a continual attempt to make sense of the world around us. This attempt is active and creative, not passive and automatic. Associationist theory simply fails to do justice to this aspect of thinking.

Insight. Gestalt psychologists believe that learning of any sort other than simple rote memorization involves insight—that is, a sudden reorganization of perceptions into a more satisfying whole. They contend that this process occurs not only in humans but in some of the higher animals as well.

One of Wertheimer's students, Wolfgang Kohler, made use of his confinement on the island of Tenerife during World War I to study the behavior of chimpanzees.[8] In a crucial experiment, Kohler tantalized his most intelligent subject, a chimp named Sultan, by placing a banana outside the cage beyond the animal's reach. Inside the cage he placed several hollow bamboo sticks, each too short to reach the banana. Sultan had already learned to use a single stick as a tool, but he had never been required to use more than one. In order to get the banana this time, he would have to perceive a new relationship between the sticks.

Kohler describes the moment of truth:

> Sultan first of all squats indifferently on the box, which has been left standing a little back from the railings; then he gets up, picks up the two sticks, sits down again on the box and plays carelessly with them. While doing this, it happens that he finds himself holding one rod in either hand in such a way that they lie in a straight line; he pushes the thinner one a little way in the opening of the thicker, jumps up, and is already on the run toward the railings . . . and begins to draw the banana toward him with the double stick.

Productive Thinking. Wertheimer believed that people learn new ideas in the same way, with a sudden flash of insight. In order to investigate this hypothesis, he visited elementary school classrooms where children were being taught basic geometry.

He watched a teacher explain how to find the area of a rectangle. Once the children learned to multiply the base by the altitude, the teacher went on to explain how to find the area of a parallelogram by dropping two perpendicular lines, proving congruence of the triangles thus created, and treating the new figure as a rectangle.

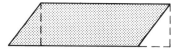

After the teacher had shown them what to do, the pupils went to work on their assigned problem. They dropped lines, found areas, and provided the proud teacher with large amounts of positive reinforcement. But Wertheimer was not satisfied. As he watched the pupils dropping their lines, he wondered if they knew why they were doing so. Did they understand the structure of the problem, or were they dropping lines simply because the teacher had told them to? He decided to find out.

Wertheimer went to the blackboard and drew:

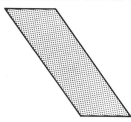

One child immediately protested, "We haven't had that yet." Others dropped lines like this:

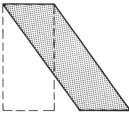

Some pupils, however, saw that Wertheimer's parallelogram was merely the teacher's original one turned on end; they either rotated their paper or solved it as it was:

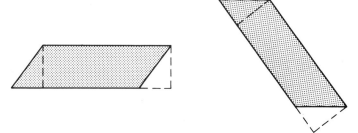

The teacher, angry and embarrassed, berated the psychologist for setting the children too hard a problem. He had missed the point of the demonstration, and Wertheimer was kind enough not to make it for him. Most of the children had learned only to mimic the teacher's behavior—to follow his instructions without understanding why. Those who had gained insight into the problem had done so without help from him.

Wertheimer later presented this problem to children as young as five. He wanted to see how they would proceed without help from a teacher. One child took a pair of scissors, cut off the end of the parallelogram that was "too much" and stuck it onto the end that was "not enough."

Another took the whole parallelogram, bent it into a ring with the ends fitted together, then made a vertical cut down the middle to turn it into a rectangle.

This, said Wertheimer, was truly productive thinking. The children had understood the pattern of the problem and had formed an insight which enabled them to solve it. Their delight at their solutions came from their realization that they had mastered a difficult challenge. No external reinforcement was necessary. They didn't even get a banana—but the point is, they didn't care.

Summary

There are two basic ways in which psychologists attempt to explain learning. The first, preferred by behaviorists and other associationists, sees it as an automatic process in which the mind records bits and pieces of information and combines them into more complex ideas simply by virtue of their occurring at the same time and place. This kind of learning is sometimes called trial-and-error. Psychologists who favor this view also see the motivation for learning as dependent upon external rewards or reinforcements. We learn, they would say, because it gets us something: praise, status, money, affection, or good grades in school.

The second viewpoint, preferred by Gestaltists and others who stress the importance of creative thinking, sees learning as an active process in which the mind reorganizes the information it receives and sometimes comes up with brand new ideas. The essential experience involved here is insight—that happy moment when we feel like shouting, "Aha! I see it all now!" From this view, the motivation for learning is internal. It is due to the inherent pleasure of solving a problem or mastering a task that formerly had us stumped.

As far as the authors of this text are concerned, both views have much to recommend them. At times our learning does seem to be governed by groping, chance happenings, and external rewards. At other times, it seems to be governed by insight and the pleasure of understanding how things fit together. We see no reason why we must accept one theory over the other. In fact, we believe the psychologist's job is to clarify the ways in which both kinds of learning interact with each other.

Class Projects

1. Here is an exercise in trial-and-error learning, from which you may learn several things. To do it, you must first construct a "finger maze" out of wood, using the diagram shown in Figure 13.1 as a blueprint. Let the base be a square piece of plywood, 12" by 12". For the walls of the maze, use wooden molding approximately ¼" thick by ½" wide. Glue the molding in place (on its edge) according to the diagram.

   When the maze is completed, try the following experiment. Choose several subjects who have not seen the maze and seat each one before it, blindfolded. Placing each subject's figure at the entrance, instruct him or her to find the way to the exit. Note the number of times he or she bumps into each blind alley (that is, stubs his or her finger against walls, A, B, C, D, E,

F, G, H, I, J, or K). Rerun the exercises until the subject gets through the **229** maze without error. When all subjects have succeeded in learning the maze, count the number of times each blind alley was entered and plot the results as follows.

	Subject #1	Subject #2	Subject #3	Etc.	Totals
Entered A					
Entered B					
Entered C					
Entered D					

Plot the totals on a sheet of graph paper as a learning curve.

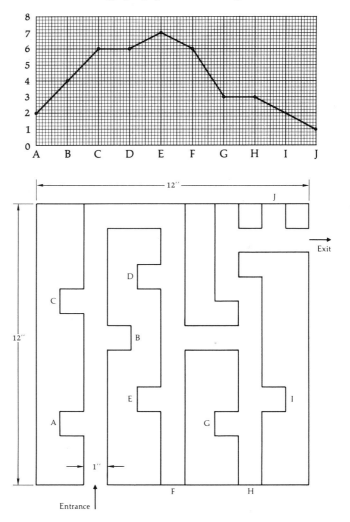

Figure 13.1: Blueprint for a maze.

Now try to answer these questions. What parts of the maze are learned soonest? What parts take the longest to learn? Can you offer an explanation for these findings?

You may also wish to ask your subjects to describe how they learned the correct route through the maze. Did they all take the same approach? If so, what does that tell you? If not, what does that tell you?

2. Here is a braintwister that requires a flash of insight for its solution:

Add a single line to this figure
to make it equal 6:   IX

Hint: try to discard your assumptions about what a line looks like as well as about what the figure represents. When you get the solution, explain how you figured it out. What does that tell you about insight learning?

3. The following classroom demonstration will provide an illustration of "shaping behavior." Choose a volunteer subject who is willing to have his or her behavior shaped. Ask the subject to leave the room while the class decides on the precise behavior to be developed. This could be sitting in a specified place, picking up a particular object, assuming a particular pose, etc. Next a shaper or experimenter should be chosen. This person will provide reinforcement or feedback by means of hand clapping whenever the subject makes a move in the direction of the target behavior. The reinforcement should follow the desired behavior as soon as possible and come from only one person.

References

1. E. R. HILGARD and G. H. BOWER, *Theories of Learning* (New York: Appleton-Century-Crofts, 1966).
2. CHARLES BELL, *Learning,* unpublished thesis, Antioch University West, Los Angeles, 1974.
3. B. F. SKINNER, *The Behavior of Organisms: An Experimental Analysis* (New York: Appleton-Century-Crofts, 1938).
4. JOSEPH WOLPE, *Psychotherapy by Reciprocal Inhibition* (Palo Alto, CA: Stanford University Press, 1958).
5. HERMAN EBBINGHAUS, *Memory,* trans. H. A. Ruger and C. E. Bussenius (New York: Teachers College, Columbia U., 1913).
6. J. L. MCGAUGH, "Facilitation and Impairment of Memory Storage Process," in *Anatomy of Memory,* ed. D. Kimble (Palo Alto, CA: Science and Behavior Books, 1965).
7. MAX WERTHEIMER, *Productive Thinking,* revised by Michael Wertheimer (New York: Harper, 1959).
8. WOLFGANG KOHLER, *The Mentality of Apes* (New York: Harcourt, Brace, 1925).

Suggested Readings

1. BEADLE, M. *A Child's Mind.* New York: Doubleday, 1970.
2. BOWER, GORDON R. "Analysis of a Mnemonic Device," in *Psychology For Our Times,* Philip Zimbardo and Christina Maslach eds. Glenview, IL: Scott, Foresman, 1977, pp. 132-139.

3. BROWN, R. and MCNEILL, D. "The Slip of the Tongue Phenomena", *Journal of Verbal Learning and Verbal Behavior,* 1966, *5,* pp. 325-337.

4. HILGARD, E. R. and MARGUIS, D. *Conditioning and Learning.* New York: Appleton-Century-Crofts, 1959.

5. LOFTUS, G. R. and LOFTUS, E. F. *Human Memory: The Processing of Information.* New York: Wiley, 1970.

6. NORMAN, D. *Memory and Attention.* 2nd ed. New York: Wiley, 1976.

7. ROSS, J. and LAWRENCE, K. A. "Some Observations on Memory Artifice," *Psychonomic Science,* 1968, *13,* pp. 107-108.

8. SMITH, W. I. and ROHRMAN, N. L. *Human Learning.* New York: McGraw-Hill, 1970.

Numbers Count

14

ou learned in a previous chapter what sorts of things research psychologists study. We mentioned that these studies utilize the scientific method and try to look at behavior in an objective manner. In most cases, the data collected are *quantified* which is to give them numerical value or to translate them into sets of numbers. These numbers are then analyzed statistically. In this chapter we will introduce you to some of the statistical methods employed by researchers and give you examples of their use in actual practice.

Please don't be afraid that you are going to have to memorize long mathematical formulas. Our intention is simply to acquaint you with a few statistical techniques that psychologists often use. So hang in there—it won't hurt a bit.

The Bell-Shaped Curve

More than a hundred years ago, a Belgian mathematician by the name of Quetelet was impressed by the discovery of a pattern in the ways people differ. Physical characteristics such as height and weight, he noted, are not spread throughout the population in a random manner. When large enough groups of people are studied, their measurements fall into an orderly series of a most particular kind. When many people's measurements are arranged from lowest to highest in what is called a *frequency distribution* (i.e., a graph which shows how often each score occurs), the visual pattern that usually results is shaped very much like a bell. Over the years, this pattern has come to be known as the bell-shaped curve of distribution.[1] As an illustration of the bell-shaped curve in the distribution of a physical characteristic, Figure 14.1 is an actual compilation of the chest sizes of several thousand soldiers.

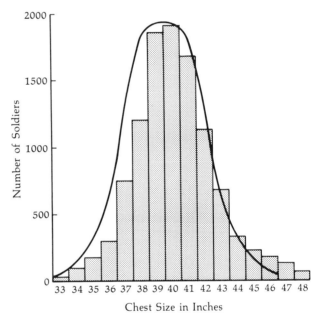

Figure 14.1: Chest Size in Inches.

It may seem odd that such characteristics as height, weight, and chest size, when studied in the masses, should form a symmetrical pattern. The fact becomes even more striking when we learn that the outcome of games of chance produces the same result.

When dice, for example, are thrown many thousands of times, the frequency with which the various numbers come up inevitably approximates the pattern of the bell-shaped curve. Even those of us who are not great mathematicians should be able to deduce the possible results

A typical distribution of height and weight among four first graders.

when a pair of dice are thrown. There is only one way to make the number 2 (1 + 1), but there are two ways to make the number 3 (1 + 2; 2 + 1), and three ways to make the number 4 (1 + 3; 3 + 1; 2 + 2). Following this pattern, there are four ways to make the number 5, five ways to make the number 6, six ways to make the number 7. Then there are five ways to make the number 8, four ways to make the number 9, three ways to make the number 10, two ways to make the number 11, and one way to make the number 12. Adding up these possibilities, we find that there are thirty-six possible results when throwing dice. If all possible results were to occur in thirty-six throws, the number 7 would come up six times. The numbers 6 and 8 would come up five times each; the numbers 5 and 9 four times each; the numbers 4 and 10 three times each; the numbers 3 and 11 two times each; the numbers 2 and 12 once each. Because of this pattern, we say there are six chances out of thirty-six that throwing a pair of dice will result in the number 7. There are five chances out of thirty-six for each of the numbers 6 and 8, and so on. Of course, in reality thirty-six throws will rarely reveal this pattern, but thirty-six hundred or so should reveal it quite vividly.

Figure 14.2 is a frequency distribution of this pattern based on thirty-six hundred throws.

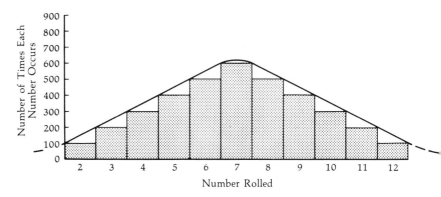

Figure 14.2:   Frequency Distribution.

If you want to try this out in class, arrange to have a pair of dice thrown several hundred times (360 might be an easy number to work with) and see how closely the outcome approximates the distribution shown in Figure 4.3.

If one or two of the numbers occurs much more frequently than the graph suggests they should, you may be playing with unbalanced dice. In order to check this out, run a second series of throws to see if your findings repeat themselves. If they do, the chances are that you have a "loaded" pair of dice. (We will not now instruct you on how to use those dice to play for money, as it might be said that we were straying from our academic role. Sorry about that.)

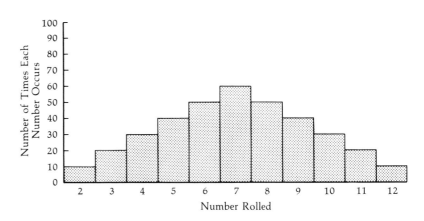

Figure 14.3:   Distribution of numbers thrown on a pair of dice.

The bell-shaped curve is so common that many psychological instruments (IQ tests, for example) are purposely designed to conform to it. As an illustration, Figure 14.4 shows a distribution of scores on the Stanford-Binet Intelligence Scale.

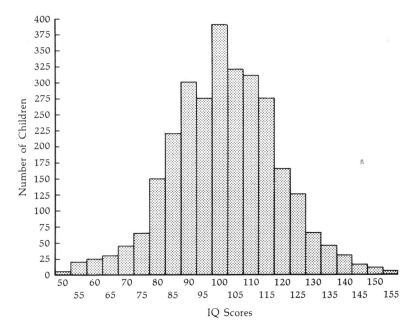

Figure 14.4: Distribution of Stanford-Binet IQ scores.

The early investigators were so impressed with the recurrence of the bell-shaped curve in the measurement of human traits that they came to believe there was some kind of universal law behind it. As more and more investigations were made, however, it became apparent that psychological or behavioral traits do not always yield a bell-shaped curve. Some distributions are *skewed*, which means there is an unusually large number of high or low scores, while others are *peaked* (high in the middle), and still others are *stretched out* (flattened).

Describing Distributions

In describing any set of scores mathematically, it is essential to report two characteristics: the *central tendency* or average score of the distribution and the *variability* or range of scores. With this information, we can rest assured that we have a mental picture of the group's major traits. If we were told, for example, that a certain athletic team's average height was 6'6'' and their range of heights ran from 6'1'' to 6'11'', we would have no doubt that we were dealing with a group of very tall people— more likely a basketball team than a basket-weaving team. If we were told that a group of students had an average IQ of 120 and a range of IQs from 45 to 180, we would know that we were dealing with a group including both intellectually impaired and gifted individuals, though on the whole we could say the group was fairly bright.

Computing central tendency

There are three ways of computing central tendency.[2] The one that is used most often is called the *arithmetic mean*. It is calculated by adding all the scores together and dividing by the number of people in the group. The other two methods are called the *median* and the *mode*. The median is simply the middle score in a distribution and the mode is the score that occurs most frequently. To find the median, scores are arranged in ascending order from lowest to highest. Then by counting up this scale, the point is found where there are an equal number of cases above and below. When a distribution has an odd number of cases and the middle score occurs only once, the median is easily found (e.g., in this distribution: 2, 3, 4, 6, 7, 8, 9, the median is 6). When a distribution contains an even number of cases, the median is calculated as the half-way point between the two middle scores (e.g., in the distribution: 2, 3, 3, 4, 5, 7, 7, 9, the median is 4.5). There is an additional calculation for distributions where the middle score occurs more than once. However, we will not burden you with it. We did, after all, promise that this wouldn't hurt.

The mode is, happily, the easiest measure of central tendency to determine. You simply count how often each score occurs, and the one that occurs most often is the mode. (In a distribution where each score occurs only once, of course, there is no mode. A distribution that has two separate most common scores is called bimodal.)

In a distribution that is a perfect bell-shaped curve, the mean, median, and mode are identical. Since few distributions are so perfectly balanced, however, investigators decide which measure to use depending on the purpose of their investigation.

Child	Allowance		Child	Allowance
Calculate the mean, the median, and the mode for this distribution representing the weekly allowances of ten children.			4	.35
			5	.50
Child	Allowance		6	.50
			7	.50
1	$ .25		8	.50
2	.25		9	1.00
3	.25		10	2.00

Computing variability

As there are three ways to estimate the central tendency of a distribution of scores, there are two ways to estimate its variability.[3] The simplest is the *range*. It is calculated by subtracting the lowest score from the highest. The range of a set of scores gives us valuable information about the group who made the scores. For example, if one group of students earned grades on a particular test ranging from 95 to 105, while another group earned grades from 60 to 140, the average of each group might be 100, so we might be led to think that they were very similar. The difference in their range of scores, however, sets them clearly apart. In the first group the gap between the worst and best students' scores is a difference that doesn't make a difference, but in the second group the gap is very significant. Teachers, for instance, would be well advised to use very different methods of teaching the high and low people in the second group, whereas all the people in the first group could probably be taught successfully with one approach.

The disadvantage of the range as an indicator of a group's variability, however, lies in the fact that a single high or low score carries too much weight in the final estimate. For example, in a group of one hundred tenth-graders, ninety-eight weigh between 100 and 150 pounds, while one weighs 79 and one weighs 265. It would be misleading to characterize the group as weighing from 79 to 265, even though these are the actual extremes.

The other measure of variability, which is both more complex and more reliable, is called the standard deviation. The *standard deviation* is a kind of average of all the deviations from the mean score of a distribution (the average of the average). Since the calculation for the standard deviation is rather complicated, we will not present it here. It is, however, an important part of statistics and you should be aware of its existence.

Measures of Relationship

In order to determine the relationship between psychological or behavioral traits, researchers often wish to compare one set of scores to another. Political pollsters, for instance, may wish to determine the relationship between religious affiliation and voting preference in a certain voting district. Clinical psychologists may wish to discover the relationship between loss of a loved one and suicide. You yourself may be interested in the relationship between body build and popularity. A *scattergram* is the simplest way to look at these relationships.[4] Here is a scattergram which relates children's IQ scores to their ability to master algebra. It is based on two scores from each child: one from an IQ test and one from an algebra test. Having collected the following scores:

Child	IQ	Algebra Test
Mary	95	74
Joe	110	83
Jane	112	84
Jim	99	73
Howard	126	90
Suzie	105	78

Anna	140	98
Paul	133	84
Martin	98	80
Trudy	107	88
Norma	118	82
Don	100	90
Al	127	81
Sally	111	85
Andy	121	92
George	131	95
Joyce	135	95

We plot them on a sheet of graph paper, placing a dot at the intersection of each child's pair of scores, as shown in Figure 14.5.

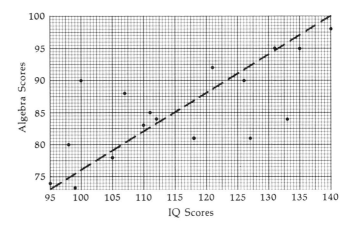

Figure 14.5: Scattergram.

If the relationship between IQ and algebra mastery were perfect, all the dots would touch the diagonal line, for the higher a child's IQ, the higher his or her score on the algebra test. We do not, however, have a perfect relationship here (nor is one ever found in real life). What the scattergram reveals is a fairly close correspondence between two variables (as you can see, the dots tend to fall near the diagonal line).

Statisticians call the relationships measured by scattergrams *correlations*.[5] Whether estimated casually in this way or by more precise and complicated statistical means, correlations are as important as any other statistical procedure in psychological research. Understanding any aspect of human behavior almost always means relating it to something else—either another piece of behavior by the same individual or a force **241** exerted on the individual by the environment.

Correlating one event with another frequently leads people to make faulty conclusions about the way the events are related. For instance, when B follows A there is a tendency to believe that A caused B simply because of the order of their occurrence. This is called the *post hoc* fallacy of logic and is illustrated by the following example.

For centuries the people of the New Hebrides made the observation that healthy people had lice and sick people did not. Although the observation was accurate it led them to the faulty conclusion that lice made people healthy. It was eventually learned that almost everyone had lice, which was normal for those particular living conditions. However, when anyone developed a fever (which could have been induced by the lice) the insects deserted their host's body because it became too hot for comfort.[6]

This example of reversing and confusing cause and effect is quite common.

Sampling, Significance, and Chance

The research psychologist believes that the behavior of large groups of people can be predicted from the behavior of much smaller groups. (From a study of 50 infants who react to a loud noise by being frightened, conclusions might be drawn regarding the "startle reflex" in all infants. From the reactions of 200 men and women to a series of jokes and cartoons, inferences might be made about the sexes' sense of humor.) The accuracy of these predictions is dependent upon two factors: the representativeness of the sample (that is, the small group used in the study) and the significance of the scores on which the predictions are based.[7]

Representativeness

Suppose you were attempting to anticipate the outcome of an election for student-body president by polling the preference of a number of the students. It stands to reason that you would interview representatives of all major groups: men and women, all ethnic groups, age groups, etc. Similarly, when psychologists intend to make predictions about the behavior of a certain group or population, they are careful to select a sample that is typical of that population.

Significance

Let us say that you were studying the possibility that drinking grapefruit juice raises people's IQs. You gave an initial IQ test to a group of 50 subjects, had them drink a quart of grapefruit juice a day for three solid months, and then administered another IQ test. Let us further say that your group's mean score on the first IQ test was 105, while the mean score on the second was 108. Could you conclude that their IQs had in fact been raised?

In order to answer that question, you would have to determine the significance of the scores you had collected—in this case, the significance of the difference between a mean IQ of 105 and 108. What this amounts to is figuring out, by complicated statistical techniques, how likely it is that such a difference could have occurred by chance alone. If it seems that chance is responsible, then the difference is not significant. If it does not seem that chance is responsible, your experiment may very well have hit upon a new source of intellectual stimulation.

Chance

For those of you who have now decided to forget psychology and take up a life of gambling, we still have something to offer. Imagine you are flipping a coin with a fellow gambler. Each time you flip the coin you bet $1,000 on the result (heads or tails). You have been betting tails and you have lost ten times in a row. Do you think your chances of winning (on tails) next time are very great? Well, you're wrong (and if you're not careful, you'll be broke too). A coin has no memory and is, therefore, just as likely to come up heads this time as every time before. The fact is that what gamblers call chance, and psychologists call the law of probabilities, refers only to an infinite number of events or at best to a very large number. If you threw your coin several hundred thousand times, you could feel confident that, in the long run, approximately an equal number of heads and tails would come up. For now, however, your sample is too small.

If you read research reports, you will come upon such expressions as, "These findings are significant at the .05 level," or, in rare cases, "at the .01 level." This means that the results being reported would have been expected by chance not more than five times out of 100 (or, in the latter case, not more than one time out of 100). These are considered significant findings. On the other hand, if you found that the possibility of your results being due to chance was thirty out of one hundred, you would have to conclude that they were not significant results.

A Word to the Worried

Many students find statistics frightening. We hope this brief introduction has allayed any fears you might have. You can think of statistics as a game. Like chess or Monopoly, it has its own language and set of rules. Once you have mastered these rules—which, we admit, takes some time and effort—you can play with the best of them. As a matter of fact, when you know statistics through and through, you can do what professional statisticians do: decide which measures you want to use and then sit back and let a computer do the work.

A researcher collecting data.

Summary

In this chapter, you have been introduced to some of the simpler statistical concepts used by psychologists. Simple as they are, however, they form the basis for an evaluation of a great deal of psychological research. The bell-shaped curve; measures of central tendency (the mean, the median, and the mode); measures of variability (the range and the standard deviation); measures of relationship (scattergrams and correlations); and measures of significance are frequently used in psychological studies. The point of it all is to make our conclusions as precise and logical as we can, and nothing is more precise and logical than the language of mathematics.

Class Projects
1. Construct a bell-shaped curve based on the height or weight of the students in your class. Remember the sample size has to be fairly large, so if your class is small, ask other students to participate. You will find, we fearlessly predict, a few extremes at either end of your scale of measurement (very tall, very short, very light, very heavy), but most people will fall somewhere in the middle.

2. Construct a scattergram to show the relationship between two variables. How about the number of hours spent studying for an exam to the score obtained on the exam? Ask all the students in your class to note how many hours they spend studying for the next exam. Then note their grades. Plot a graph that lists hours on the side and grades across the bottom. Place a dot at the intersection of each individual's performance. Draw a line through the graph from the lower left corner to the upper right corner. See how closely the dots follow this diagonal line. What conclusions can you draw

References

1. J. P. GUILFORD, *Fundamental Statistics in Psychology and Education* (New York: McGraw-Hill, 1956).
2. R. B. MCCALL, *Fundamental Statistics for Psychology* (New York: Harcourt, Brace & World, 1970).
3. W. J. DIXON, *Introduction to Statistical Analysis* (New York: McGraw-Hill, 1969).
4. S. ISAAC and W. B. MICHAEL, *Handbook in Research and Evaluation* (San Diego, CA: Edits Publishers, 1977).
5. F. F. ELZEY, *A First Reader in Statistics* (Monterey, CA: Brooks/Cole, 1967).
6. D. HUFF and I. GEIS, *How to Lie with Statistics* (New York: Norton, 1954).
7. N. M. AGNEW and S. PYKE, *The Science Game: An Introduction to Research in the Behavioral Sciences* (Englewood Cliffs, NJ: Prentice-Hall, 1969).

Suggested Readings

1. ELZEY, F. F. *A First Reader in Statistics.* Monterey, CA: Brooks/Cole, 1967.
2. KIMBLE, GREGORY A. *How to Use (and Misuse) Statistics.* Englewood Cliffs, NJ: Prentice-Hall, 1978.

SOME THOUGHTS OF OUR OWN

On the issues we said were implicit in this section, the authors of this text tend to hold opposing views. One of us, as we have already told you, sees the theories and methods of Behaviorism as the most substantial in the field. The other is more impressed by the arguments of the Gestaltists and claims the Behaviorist view of human nature is too mechanical and superficial.

In line with this difference, one of us feels that laboratory research should be the foundation of psychological progress, while the other believes that clinical findings and introspective accounts of personal experience may be equally revealing.

We both agree, however, that studies of single individuals and investigations of groups of people can complement each other in furthering our understanding. The field of psychology is still too young, we would assert, to eliminate any of its serious practitioners in favor of those who may take a different approach.

Finally, while we agree that the scientific method appears to be the most reliable way of investigating human behavior, at least one of us holds open the possibility that this method in the social sciences may evolve into something different than it is in the physical sciences.

Section Four

Human Beings in Groups

OVERVIEW

ection one of this text presented material from areas of the field that are usually known as *developmental psychology* and *personality theory*. Section two reviewed techniques and findings from *clinical psychology*. Section three discussed methods and data from *experimental psychology*. This section describes the approaches of *social psychology* and *educational psychology*.

These latter areas, unfortunately, have so far held out more promise than they have delivered. Many people believe that psychology should be able to make significant contributions to the improvement of our educational systems and our widespread social problems. It has in fact made some such contributions—but not nearly enough.

Learning disabilities in young children, disruption of schoolroom activities by rebellious or uncooperative youngsters, and lack of motivation for academic achievement are only a few of the unresolved problems in our schools. Poverty, violence, and racial strife are only some of the serious problems that beset our society. Psychologists are working to understand and alleviate these sources of distress, but we must admit that they are all still rampant.

Less controversial topics like the effect of group membership on behavior and the ways in which attitudes are formed have also been studied. In the next few chapters, we will tell you what has been found.

Social Patterns and Pressures

15

acked in a football stadium, watching a close-fought game, have you ever found yourself screaming your lungs out? Have you felt at such times that your team was made up of fair, admirable players, while the opposition was a bunch of mean, dirty lunkheads? Have you observed other fans who at first seemed like pleasant people, and then, after hearing them root for the other side, decided that they were loud-mouthed morons? And have you finally, after your team won, found football to be a wonderful sport and everyone connected with the game to be a likeable person after all?

If you have done these things or anything like them, you have displayed a well-known set of psychological characteristics. *Conformity, prejudice, attitude change,* and *attraction:* these terms refer not only to your behavior during that football game, but to four broad areas of human experience. They are of special interest to the social psychologist, because they appear to be the result of social pressures.

How do human beings behave in groups? How is the individual influenced by the groups to which he or she belongs? How are our personal habits, our likes and dislikes, our feelings toward other people and toward ourselves, formed and molded by social forces? And when these forces produce something bad—like prejudice, sexism, violence, or apathy—what can be done to improve the situation? These are the primary concerns of social psychology and the topics we will cover in the next two chapters.

Social psychology is a field of immense importance. Yet it has not flourished to the extent that clinical and experimental psychology have. We will try to uncover some reasons for this sorry state of affairs and to suggest some remedies. If social psychology were doing as well as experimental and clinical, we would all be living in a better world—or at least have a clearer understanding of why ours has as many problems as it does.

People in Groups

There are many different kinds of groups. Some, like mobs, crowds, and audiences, exist for a very brief period of time, while others, like families and nations, endure for most people's lifetimes. Some, like people waiting for a bus, are leaderless, while others, like a college class, have a designated leader. Social psychologists investigate the formation and behavior of groups, the effects groups exert on their members, the forces that promote individuals to positions of leadership, and the influence that different kinds of leaders have on their followers.

There are at least four distinct ways in which members react to group standards of conduct: by *conforming, cooperating, competing,* or *rebelling.*[1] Psychologists have studied conformity more fully than the other three; we will tell you some of the things they have learned. First, however, we would like to describe each way in more detail.

1) When we conform to a group's standards of conduct, we adopt the group's rules or expectations and do as they dictate. If we join a club, we may wear its emblem, attend its meetings, and associate mainly with people the club considers appropriate. We do this uncritically, often unthinkingly, because we want to be part of the group.

2) When we cooperate with a group's standards of conduct, we adopt them more intelligently. We question what we are doing and decide that it is in our best interest to go along with the group. On an athletic team, for instance, we may subdue our desire to be the star of every game in order to further the goals of the team as a whole. We retain some measure of individuality, however, by playing our position in our own unique style.

3) When we compete with a group's standards of conduct, we challenge them while remaining part of the group. In our schools, for example, we may argue about the grading system and try to bring about reforms in the ways the schools are run.

4) When we rebel against a group's standards of conduct, we not only challenge them but refuse to accept them. This may result in expulsion from the group, but the person who has taken a rebellious stance cares less about being a member of the group than about changing or even destroying it.

The effects of leadership

The onset of World War II raised psychologists' interest in the effects of leadership on group behavior. An ingenious professor by the name of Kurt Lewin decided to investigate it in the following way.[2] He formed clubs of boys which were each appointed an adult leader. One-third of the clubs were conducted in an *authoritarian* fashion: all policies were determined by the leader, who remained aloof from the group except when demonstrating what they were to do. One-third of the clubs were conducted in a *democratic* fashion: all policies were determined by group discussion and the members were free to work with whomever they chose. Finally, one-third were conducted in a *laissez-faire* fashion: there was complete freedom for each individual to do what he liked, while the leader supplied information but took no part in making or fostering policies.

Observation of the groups revealed that, under authoritarian control, activities proceeded smoothly but unhappily. Hostility was very frequent and it was directed toward scapegoats within the group rather than toward the leader. Under the democratic system, members liked their leaders and generally tried to do their best. In the laissez-faire situation, interest in group activities lagged and little constructive action was taken.

These results were taken to support the democratic system as the best way to run groups if your goal is a combination of productive activity and members' happiness. If you want only productivity, you may be better off to have a stern commander.

Studies like this are of obvious importance in helping us understand how people feel and behave in groups. Our nation's welfare depends upon people's feelings and behavior in family groups, school groups, work groups, and all the many other groups of which the country is composed. Therefore, as much work as possible needs to be done to help us conduct the kinds of groups that will satisfy the nation's primary needs.

Conformity

In 1951, Solomon Asch reported an experiment in which subjects were asked to compare the lengths of lines. They were shown diagrams like that in Figure 15.1 and asked which line, A, B, or C, corresponds most closely to the length of line X. The subjects were interviewed in groups of six, but unknown to one member, the other five members were ac-

X   A   B   C

Figure 15.1:   Conformity experiment.

complices of the experimenter. Although it was obvious to everyone that line B corresponds most closely to line X, the accomplices always stated that line A was the correct choice. When the real subjects' turn came to state their choice, the majority of them also picked line A.[3]

This experiment can be taken as a classic illustration of conformity. It indicates that most people, under the pressure of group opinion, will misrepresent their own judgment to fit in with the majority. (Interestingly, when given the opportunity to record their choices secretly, far fewer subjects echoed the majority opinion). We may infer that the imagined reward of being liked by the group, or the fear of antagonizing them, is strong enough to make many people disbelieve—or at least disavow—what they see with their own eyes.

If this example seems remote from everyday life, consider its bearing on eyewitness reports of accidents and crimes. It has been found that, where there is doubt as to exactly what took place, many witnesses will swear they saw what most others say *they* saw.

Conformity extends far beyond our judgments of what we see. It is a factor in the clothing we wear, the food we eat, the movies we attend, the furnishings we choose for our homes, and the automobiles we drive. Every aspect of our lives is influenced by our need to feel part of a group. Be it a family, friendship, political, racial, or socioeconomic group, most of us try hard to fit in. We are afraid to be considered an outsider or an oddball. Without realizing what we are doing, we make continual adaptations to the standards and expectations of the groups to which we wish to belong.

The history of clothing styles makes it vividly clear that people are willing to endure extreme discomfort in order to feel accepted by the in-group of their time and place. In ancient China, for example, the practice of binding women's feet in order to conform to the ideal of a dainty foot caused a dislocation of bones that was sometimes so severe that the women were forced to hobble for the rest of their lives. For hundreds of years in Europe and America, a tiny waist was considered beautiful, so women squeezed themselves into tight-laced, stiff-boned corsets, frequently suffering fainting spells or cracked ribs as a result. And in the Victorian era, men wore high celluloid collars that caused both muscular tension and skin abrasions.

Are there certain kinds of people who conform more than others? In Asch's experiment, women conformed more than men, less intelligent people more than highly intelligent people, and those with low self-esteem more than those with high self-esteem. These findings have been borne out by other studies. We may conclude, therefore, that people who are used to asserting themselves and those who have experienced success are less likely to conform. Contrariwise, people who have occupied secondary positions and are compliant are more likely to subdue their own opinions with respect to those of the majority.

Is it always undesirable?

Up to this point, we have been portraying conformity as a kind of surrender to the rule of the crowd. But that is its negative aspect. There are situations in which conformity acts as a positive social force without harming the individual. Consider, for example, the eating customs of our society, from the ways we prepare and serve our food to the ways we sit at table and consume it. By conforming, we perpetuate a style in which most people feel comfortable and enjoy their meals. Suppose we were to gorge ourselves in total disregard for other people's feelings or to snatch food from each other like animals. Dining out would probably be much less of a pleasure, let alone entertaining guests in our homes.

In the same way, our conformity to customs enables us to live in relative security and orderliness. We rely on customary ways of driving cars, writing letters, building homes, greeting friends, addressing strangers, learning trades, and so on. Widespread nonconformity would lead to confusion and chaos.

Suppose that in the future you were to take a trip to Mars. Your companions on the spaceship are all experienced astronauts, while this is your first visit to another planet. When you land on Martian soil, three purple creatures with orange fur hop up to meet you. Your companions immediately stick out their tongues and stand on one foot. Do you think you should follow their example? Why?

What relevance does this fantasy have to questions of conformity and nonconformity? If you don't know, try to find a purple friend with orange fur to discuss it with you. If that doesn't work, forget it and get on with this chapter.

Compliance, identification, and internalization

Social psychologists have identified three levels of conformity which differ in their performance and strength. The first and weakest level is called *compliance*. The sole motivation for compliance is to obtain a reward or avoid a punishment. Suppose you were a dictator who threatened to kill the citizens of a conquered country if they dared to criticize you or failed to salute you. Chances are the citizens would all keep their mouths shut and salute whenever you went by. In private, however, they might very well say uncomplimentary things about you. At the level of compliance, people do not believe in the behavior they are forced to demonstrate. They are therefore likely to change very quickly when they get the chance.

A stronger level of conformity is *identification*. Identification grows out of the desire to be like a person or group, either because they seem attractive or because identifying with them brings certain rewards. If a singing star you admire wears rhinestones and frizzy hair, you may feel inclined to do the same. If a powerful motorcycle gang wears leather jackets and hobnailed boots, you may decide to wear them too. Identification also occurs on a wider scale. Minority groups will sometimes adopt the customs and values of the majority in order to gain the advantages the majority appears to enjoy. In the early part of this century, for instance, European immigrants to this country began to dress and talk like those who ruled the land, partly to avoid being laughed at and partly out of admiration and envy for the achievements the native born had made.

The strongest and most permanent level of conformity is called *internalization*. It occurs when an individual perceives the values of a group as right and proper. The group's behavior is regarded not merely as the way they happen to do things but as the best way, or at least a very good way, to do them. In this situation, the individual does not just adopt the outward manner of the group. More significantly, he or she accepts and believes in the basic truth of the group and therefore makes its way of life his or her own.

In most cases, however, all the values of a group are not internalized lock, stock, and barrel. One selects those values that seem most impressive or meet one's own needs most directly. Consider, for example, your relationship to your family. In all likelihood, there are some things your family stands for that you do not accept and therefore have not internalized—its views on spending money, perhaps, or on dating and staying out late. There must be other things, however—its politics, perhaps, or its religious views—that you have accepted because you consider them right and good.

Having distinguished these three levels of conformity, social psychologists point out that most behavior involves all three. We may obey the speed limit, for instance, because we want to avoid a fine (compliance), our driving instructor obeys it (identification), and we accept it as the safe and therefore right thing to do (internalization).[4]

Attitude Formation and Attitude Change

We live in an age in which we are bombarded with communications. Advertisements, speeches, news reports, editorials, films, and plays—even popular songs—often carry a message of some sort about the world and the people in it. These communications influence our opinions and attitudes in a variety of ways. We may, for example, hear an environmentalist speak about how selfish the oil companies are, how much money they are making, and how they are ruining our natural resources. Then we may view a television commercial that tells us what wonderful things the oil companies do and how careful they are to protect our environment. Who and what do we believe? Social psychol-

Magazines depict stereotypes that we may try to emulate.

ogists have made many studies of questions like this and have come up with some interesting conclusions.

To begin with, they have found it important to differentiate opinions and attitudes. By an opinion, they mean what an individual believes to be a fact. It is, in other words, an intellectual belief, such as the belief that California produces more oranges than Florida, which can be disproven simply by producing accurate data. An attitude, on the other hand, refers to something more ingrained. It consists not only of an intellectual belief but also of an emotional reaction and a behavioral tendency leading to some sort of action.[5]

An attitude, in fact, is usually a judgment. It perceives things as good or bad, positive or negative. Thus, if I have a positive attitude toward dogs I will believe them to be excellent pets (opinion), feel happy in their presence (emotion), and wish to buy one for myself (behavior). If I have a negative attitude toward sales people, I may think they are schemers (opinion), feel uncomfortable in their presence (emotion), and try to avoid them (behavior).

Opinions and attitudes are both learned, but once an attitude has formed, changing it is very difficult. Our attitudes, we feel, are part of us, so we do not give them up easily. How did we acquire them in the first place? If we can provide an answer to that question, we will be closer to knowing how to change them.

Communication is a major part of attitude formation and change.[6] There are three essential elements to any communication: the source (who says it), the message (what is said and how it is said), and the audience (to whom it is said). The qualities of each of these elements are important in determining the effectiveness of the communication and the likelihood that it will become part of the audience's attitudes.

It would seem logical to assume that the source, to be effective, should be an expert on whatever he or she is talking about, but in fact that is not the case. As every advertising agency knows, movie or sports stars can sell us anything from fruit juice to shaving cream. They can, in other words, influence our attitudes toward products not because we believe they know much about them, but simply because the endorsement of a famous or attractive person sets up a positive association in our minds.[7]

Attractiveness, however, is not the only quality that works. At times sincerity, real or staged, is even more effective. Consider the kind of television commercial that shows an average housewife defending her favorite household product, only to see it fail before her very eyes. When she states her conviction that the new product is even better than the one she used to love, we too are inclined to feel that way.

When we turn to the nature of the communication itself, we find several different aspects important in its power to influence our attitudes. Not only the logic of the argument—which in fact does not have much persuasive power—but also such public-speaking devices as persistent repetition, clever turns of phrase, making the audience laugh, or, if possible, making them cry, usually help to a great extent. In addition it has been found that some audiences—notably those who are less educated and poorly informed—respond more favorably to a one-sided argument, while others—those who are more educated and well informed—respond most favorably to a two-sided argument in which the point is made only after the opposing view has been examined.

It has also been shown that most audiences have a tendency to accept either the first or the last argument presented, rather than those stated in between. The deciding factor is the time that elapses between the end of the first argument and the beginning of the last. If we hear two arguments immediately following one another and are asked to react without delay, no advantage accrues to either. If we hear one, then a week elapses, then we hear the second, and then, after another week's lapse, are asked for our reaction, there is still no advantage to either. If, however, we hear the first argument, wait a week, hear the second, and immediately afterward give our reaction, we are more likely to favor the second. And if we hear the first, then the second, then wait a week before giving our reaction, we are more likely to favor the first.[7]

It may seem odd that factors such as time and whether the speaker is **257** a movie star or made us laugh should influence our judgment of the rightness of a point of view, but so it is.

Perhaps of greatest importance in forming and changing attitudes is our need to maintain inner peace and harmony. Suppose you were an avid gumchewer. If some authority on teeth told you that chewing gum would give you a few extra cavities a year, what would happen? You would most likely feel uncomfortable and try to resolve the problem, either by forgetting what you had been told, putting down the authority by deciding that cavities are not that bad, or perhaps promising to cut down on gum chewing. The point is that you would probably find a way to reduce the discomfort set up in you by the clash between your liking gum and the information that it is bad for your teeth.

Cognitive dissonance

An impressive theory of human behavior has been created to explain situations like the above. It is called the theory of *cognitive dissonance* and has made its author, Leon Festinger, famous in psychological circles. According to Festinger,[9] dissonance—an uncomfortable feeling of disharmony like that of hearing a musical chord with some wrong notes in it—occurs when we are faced with two or more opposing bits of information.

"The surgeon-general says that smoking causes cancer, but I like to smoke." "I think of myself as an intelligent person, but I just made a stupid blunder." "I supported a recently elected government official who has just been found guilty of accepting a bribe." Each of the above examples would produce the feeling Festinger has described. Furthermore, according to his theory, our discomfort would cause us to justify our behavior through self-persuasion. In the case of smoking, for example, we might say, "I know lots of people who smoke and don't have cancer," or, "We all have to die eventually," or, "I like to live dangerously." In the case of the government official, we might say, "Well, he was okay when I voted for him, but then he changed," or, "The newspapers probably exaggerated the whole thing," or, "So who's honest anyway?"

Dissonance-reducing behavior is defensive behavior. It is a way of maintaining a positive self-image and not feeling stupid. What is most interesting is the extent to which we do it and how far we will go to keep it up. Whenever we see, hear, or do anything that could make us uncomfortable we engage in such behavior.

To test this theory out on yourself, make three broad columns on a sheet of notepaper. Head the first one, "My spontaneous behavior," the second, "Dissonance-producing information," and the third, "Dissonance reduction." Then note, for one full day, the ways in which this sequence occurs. For instance, you might start the day by putting on a cotton t-shirt. That would be noted under spon-

The jolt that this photo provides comes from the cognitive dissonance resulting from stereotyped ideas about nuns which conflict with the scene shown.

taneous behavior. You hear or read a weather forecast for cool temperatures (dissonance-producing information) and decide to wear something else. Your dissonance reduction would be to resolve the conflict by saying the t-shirt was dirty anyway or by checking the temperature in hopes of proving the forecast wrong. If you are both honest and perceptive, you should have quite a long list before the day is over.

Please note: the mere fact that we have made **259** that last statement has already set up the possibility of another dissonance in you. You are either going to feel compelled to produce a long list in order to feel "honest and perceptive," or you are going to feel the need to disagree with us, or you are apt to find some other excuse to allow you to not make a long list and still consider yourself honest and perceptive.

Attraction

At the beginning of this chapter, we talked about the ways in which individuals relate to groups. But what leads us to join groups in the first place? In the case of our family, race, or nation, we of course have no choice, but in friendship and social groups a strong factor seems to be the attractiveness of the other members.

Psychologists, accordingly, have studied the question of why we like certain people and want to be with them. Why do we choose certain friends and not others? Do "birds of a feather flock together," or do "opposites attract?" These issues, which appear so simple on the surface, have been found to be affected by more factors than most of us are aware of.

Similarity of values, attitudes, and beliefs, as we might expect, tends to make people like each other, but we are even more likely to be drawn toward someone with a different set of values, if he or she indicates a liking for us. While being with people who agree with us and confirm the rightness of our beliefs makes us feel intelligent, we feel appreciated for our very selves when a person with a different viewpoint likes us despite our differences. And that, it seems, is what we most crave.

We are also drawn toward people who are competent, able, attractive, or talented, in the hope that their abilities will rub off on us or because their acceptance of us as a friend shows that we have something on the ball as well. If a person is exceptionally successful, however, we may not like him or her quite as much. His or her success makes us feel inferior, and our envy interferes with our admiration.

In the early stages of his presidency, John F. Kennedy seemed like Mr. Perfect—a young, handsome war hero with a beautiful wife and attractive children, rich, bright, witty, and exceptionally competent. Yet his popularity increased after the Bay of Pigs fiasco in which he made the worst political blunder of his career. It is probable, according to some social psychologists, that his mistake made him seem more human, more like someone with whom the average person could identify.

In a revealing experiment, students were asked to listen to tapes of supposed contestants on the "College Bowl Quiz Show" and rate the impression each contestant made on them. The tapes were actually contrived to give the following impressions: 1) a near-perfect person; 2) a near-perfect person who commits a clumsy act (spilling a cup of coffee on himself); 3) an average person; and 4) an average person who commits a clumsy act. The results were clear cut. The contestant who made the most favorable impression was number 2, a superior person committing a blunder.

Praise is another important factor in attraction, but we need to feel that the praise is justified, or at least not too self-serving, before it will make us like the people who praise us. If they are too obviously insincere, we will not be attracted to them even though we may cherish their compliments.

A less well-known factor is described in the "gain-loss theory" of attraction. This theory makes the point that an increase of any reward (such as having people like us) is more important than the reward itself. Thus, winning the love of a stranger means more to us than continuing to enjoy the love of someone who has liked us for a long time. In the same vein, losing the love of a close friend is more painful than meeting a stranger who does not care for us, simply because the loss in the former case is greater.

The Status of the Field

Whether these and other findings of social psychology are incontestable is open to question. Human behavior, whether performed individually or in groups, is such a complicated matter that no simple line of investigation can explain it. Nevertheless, the attempt to shed light on the forces that control us is a valuable enterprise. The problems that social psychologists study—why we like certain people, how attitudes are formed and changed, how group standards affect our lives, how styles of leadership influence group behavior, and so on—are certainly of interest.

Why then, to take up a point we made in the introduction to this chapter, has this field not grown as fast as clinical and experimental psychology? In an article published in 1975, Alan C. Elms states, "Social psychologists once knew who they were and where they were going." Now, however, many people in the field are undergoing "a crisis of confidence."[9] They are neither convinced of the merit of the work they are doing nor clear about the best directions to pursue. According to Elms, this has happened for a number of reasons. First, it is much more difficult to conduct research on social problems than had been anticipated. Second, social psychology lacks a unifying theory that would give it the direction it sorely needs. (Cognitive-dissonance theory seemed promising for a while, but it has not proved powerful enough to cover the wide range of issues the social psychologist investigates.) And third, increasing pressure has been put on the field to become relevant—that is, to focus on issues like racism and sexism which are of paramount importance today.

While the call to relevance is welcome, it raises ethical questions that are hard to resolve. When a scientist studies matters about which many people have very strong feelings, he or she may feel strongly inclined to come up with results that will please (and to suppress findings that might displease) certain influential groups. In other words, the social psychologist is hard put to remain objective when he or she is tampering with explosive, emotionally loaded issues.

In the opinion of the authors of this text, this is the obstacle on which the field has been stumbling. If it investigates neutral topics about which nobody cares very much, social psychology finds it easy to remain scientifically respectable. If it investigates highly charged, relevant issues, it becomes subjected to all sorts of political pressures.

Some psychologists prefer the peace and quiet of exploring uncontested areas of human experience and behavior. For our part, however, we like to see the field poke its nose into every nook and cranny of the human scene—particularly those nooks and crannies in which people have vested interests in suppressing the truth. Our next chapter, therefore, will present the findings social psychology has made on such issues as racism and sexism, violence and crime, social apathy and social activism. Some of you may find some parts of it upsetting, but we doubt that many of you will be bored.

Summary

In this chapter, we reviewed four ways in which we react to group standards and expectations: conforming, cooperating, competing, and rebelling. We also pointed out that group behavior is differently affected by authoritarian, democratic, and laissez-faire leadership. We discussed three levels of conformity to social pressures: compliance, identification, and internalization. Our attitudes and opinions, we explained, are formed and changed by communication processes. When there is a conflict between our beliefs and our perceptions of reality, we experience "cognitive dissonance," which we try to resolve in different ways. Our attraction to other people, we reported, can be predicted by their similarity to ourselves in terms of values and attitudes. Finally, we made the point that social psychologists are themselves influenced by society with respect to the problems they choose to investigate.

Class Projects

1. How many groups do you think you belong to? Five? Ten? Well, we'll bet you belong to more than ten. Try listing them, beginning with your sex group, your family group, your age group, your peer group, and then going on to your nation, your race, your religion, your school, and your classes. Don't forget any social clubs, athletic teams, or neighborhood gangs of which you consider yourself a member.

When you have listed them all, try to decide if you relate to each in a conforming, cooperative, competitive, or rebellious manner. Then think about the ways in which each group reacts to you. What does it tell you about yourself as a group member and about the ways in which groups treat their members?

2. In order to test the effect of conformity on clothing styles, try wearing an outlandish outfit one day. Without giving anyone an explanation, put on a combination of things that nobody ever wears in your community. Then note the looks and remarks directed at you during the day to see if their intention is to "get you back in line."

3. A person arguing against his or her self-interest is usually very effective in persuading an audience to accept his or her views. To test this principle, write a speech supporting the idea that women in your school be given more privileges (such as the privilege to have their own football team or to use the football field whenever they want to). Have this speech delivered to different groups by female speakers and male speakers. Have the audiences note, on slips of paper, their agreement or disagreement with the argument presented. (Do not tell them the purpose of your study, and make sure your male speakers present the argument as sincerely as your female speakers.) You should find that the male speakers were more effective in persuading people to accept the argument, simply because it seems more sincere for a man to be arguing a woman's cause than for a woman to be doing it herself.

4. In order to explore the proposition that it is very difficult to conduct an objective study on a heated social issue, choose a topic that is very controversial in your community. Poll the public's views on it by conducting a door-to-door survey or by interviewing people in the street. Ask each person interviewed to express his or her view of the matter, telling them that you intend to publish the results in your school paper. Besides recording the responses you collect, keep a record of everything that is said to you, either by your subjects, your teachers, your friends, your family, or anyone else, which you feel represents an attempt to influence you to come out with results that would please them. Note, too, your own internal reactions when you collect responses that uphold your personal views and when you collect responses that conflict with your views. Discuss your findings in class.

References

1. W. W. Lambert and W. E. Lambert, *Social Psychology* (Englewood Cliffs, NJ: Prentice-Hall, 1964).

2. K. Lewin, R. Lippitt and R. White, "Patterns of Aggressive Behavior in Experimentally Created Social Climates," *Journal of Social Psychology, 10,* (1943): pp. 271–299.

3. S. Asch, "Effects of Group Pressure Upon the Modification and Distortion of Judgment," in *Groups, Leadership, and Men,* H. Guetzkow ed. (Pittsburgh, PA: Carnegie Press, 1951).

4. M. Argyle, *The Psychology of Interpersonal Behavior* (Baltimore, MD: Penguin, 1967).

5. M. B. Smith, J. Bruner, and R. White, *Opinions and Personality* (New York: Wiley, 1956).

6. C. I. HOVLAND, I. L. JANIS and H. H. KELLY, *Communications and Persuasion:* **263** *Psychological Studies of Opinion Change* (New Haven, CT: Yale University Press, 1953).

7. Ibid.

8. C. I. HOVLAND, W. MANDELL and E. H. CAMPBELL, "The Order of Presentation in Persuasion," in *Yale Studies in Attitude and Communication,* vol. 1, ed. Carl Hovland (New Haven, CT: Yale University Press, 1957), pp. 551–552, 555.

9. L. FESTINGER, *A Theory of Cognitive Dissonance* (Evanston, IL: Row and Peterson, 1957).

10. A. C. ELMS, "The Crisis of Confidence in Social Psychology," *American Psychologist 30* (1975), pp. 967–1002.

Suggested Readings

1. ARONSON, E. *The Social Animal.* New York: The Viking Press, 1972.

2. BROWN, ROGER. *Social Psychology.* New York: The Free Press, 1965.

3. KRECH, DAVID and CRUTCHFIELD, RICHARD S. *Theory and Problems of Social Psychology.* New York: McGraw-Hill, 1948.

4. NEWCOMB, THEODORE M., TURNER, RALPH H. and CONVERSE, PHILIP E. *Social Psychology.* New York: Holt, Rinehart & Winston, 1965.

5. PROHANSKY, HAROLD and SEIDINBERT, BERNARD, eds. *Basic Studies in Social Psychology.* New York: McGraw-Hill, 1948.

6. ZIMBARDO, P. G. and EBBLESEN, E. B. *Influencing Attitudes and Changing Behavior.* Reading, MA: Addison-Wesley, 1969, ch. 20.

7. WORCHEL, S. *Understanding Social Psychology.* Homewood, IL: Dorsey Press, 1979.

Social Issues

acism, sexism, violence, and *apathy:* these are the social issues we will discuss in this chapter. They are topics about which people have very strong feelings. Because of this, some social psychologists have avoided studying them. The attitude of these psychologists holds that it is next to impossible to be scientifically objective about such explosive issues. Another group, however, takes the opposite viewpoint. They believe the most important thing psychologists can do is grapple with the things that cripple our society, and they rate the four issues we have named high on their list of priorities.

Racism and sexism are two forms of prejudice, so we will discuss them in that context. After reviewing the factors that create and perpetuate prejudice, we will see how they apply to one race's (and one sex's) mistaken judgments and mistreatment of another.

Violence and apathy are pathological extremes. They represent two opposite, but equally undesirable, reactions to social pressures. We will tell you what psychology has discovered about them. Then we will ask you to consider how these problems can be helped.

If racism, sexism, violence, and apathy were wiped out, our world would be a better place. Psychologists, like most other people, wholeheartedly agree with this statement. Some of them, however, call it a dreamy ideal. They say it will never be achieved. After you have read this chapter, it may be interesting to see how many of you lean toward that viewpoint, and how many, in contrast, think these problems can be eliminated. We suggest you debate your views.

Prejudice

266

Prejudice—a hostile, derogatory attitude directed against all or most members of a group—is common all over the world. English people have traditionally been prejudiced against the French, while the Irish have been prejudiced against the English. Hindus and Moslems in India are prejudiced against each other, and members of both groups have always been prejudiced against Untouchables. In South Africa, a national policy is based on white prejudice against the blacks. Jews have been a target of prejudice throughout recorded history, and they in turn have entertained prejudicial opinions of non-Jews. The story of humankind, in short, is laced through and through with people hating and degrading other people because they belong to a different racial, religious, or social group.

Some questions psychologists have tried to answer are: Why is prejudice so widespread? What causes some people to be more prejudiced than others? What effect does prejudice have on members of the attacking group and on members of the target group? And how can prejudice be reduced or eliminated? We will now attempt to summarize their major findings.

Most prejudice, it has been found, is based on irrational feelings. The prejudiced person may claim to dislike members of a certain group because of bad qualities they supposedly possess. However, examination of his or her thinking will reveal a lack of factual knowledge, a store of misinformation, and a tendency to generalize from very little data. The prejudiced Englishman, for instance, may claim that the French are all liars and cheaters. But when questioned he will admit that he has only known three or four French people in his life and has visited France only once on a weekend excursion.

Studies by social psychologists have shown that many people look for *scapegoats* on whom to blame the failures and frustrations of their own lives.[1,2] Unwilling to shoulder the responsibility themselves, they pick on the Jews, the blacks, or whatever group is handy enough to be cursed as "the cause of all the trouble in this world." Having a scapegoat allows them to vent their resentments while avoiding the hard task of facing up to their personal failings.

The prejudiced person, it has also been found, tends to be an *authoritarian personality*—one who believes that the strong must rule the weak, that the young should obey their elders, that some people are innately more capable than others, and that human society works best when its leaders control the welfare of the group. Such a person may pay lip service to the principles of democracy. He or she may even profess to be a great upholder of the democratic system. However, when it comes down to actions rather than words, the authoritarian personality does not allow others to run their own lives but rather tries to control them either openly or secretly.

Some other characteristics common to prejudiced persons are a tendency to see the world as an unfriendly, unsafe place and an inclination

to believe that people are selfish, dishonest, and aggressive. Prejudiced 267
persons also tend to have an anti-intellectual bias; they fear that too
much learning is harmful rather than helpful. Most important, perhaps,
they have a hard time with ambiguity. They tend to oversimplify human
behavior and see it as either good or bad. It makes them uncomfortable to admit that an act may be both good, bad, and something in
between, depending on why it was done, when it was done, who did it
to whom, and who is evaluating it.

If we were totally candid, every one of us would have to admit to
some form of prejudice. The problem is widespread because it satisfies
deep human needs. Looking down on people who look, act, or think
differently than us is a way of bolstering our pride and denying our
doubts about the manner in which we live our lives. Claiming that
members of another group are stupid, selfish, lazy, dishonest, lustful,
greedy, or vicious allows us to feel that we are free of those unacceptable
characteristics. And lumping all the members of a social group into a
single category is a way of simplifying reality, of avoiding the strain of
dealing with the complexity of human nature. Few of us can do without
these mechanisms altogether, and the more insecure we are the more we
resort to them to reduce our own anxieties.

Prejudice allows the members of the attacking group to feel self-
righteous. It causes members of the target group to feel inferior, but in
response they often develop target groups of their own. So it goes. Hate
begets hate, simplification begets more simplification. We defend ourselves with bigotry and lull ourselves with half-truths. How much easier
than facing reality in all its unsettling complexity.

"Japanese are hard-working." "Jews are shrewd." "Germans are stiff." "Texans are braggarts." "New Yorkers are rude." "Mexicans are lazy." "Blacks are dishonest." "Italians are emotional." "Swedes are remote." "Arabs are furtive." "Chinese are inscrutable." "Farmers are simple." "City-dwellers are nervous." "Soldiers are brave." "Politicians are liars." "Psychologists are nuts."

Each of these opinions represents a form of prejudice. Have you not, however, subscribed to some of them at times? Whether you have or not, can you admit that, while some members of groups may very well share certain characteristics, there is always a great deal of variation within the group? Can you see that even if, on the whole,

New Yorkers tend to be rude, some New Yorkers are undoubtedly more polite than some San Franciscans? Can you see that the same must be true of any such generalization?

If you can acknowledge, and not forget, that within every sizeable group in this world there are many different kinds of individuals, you may be on your way to overcoming prejudice. On the other hand, you may "know better" and still distrust or hate certain groups. Why this is so and what more it takes to eliminate prejudice altogether will be discussed a little later in this chapter. Meanwhile, we just wanted you to get a feel for the ways in which you yourself may be host to prejudiced feelings.

Racism

A particularly virulent form of prejudice in this country resides in the
negative, degrading attitudes of whites toward blacks. Lazy, shiftless,

cowardly, unintelligent, dishonest, and animalistic are only some of the terms that have been used to express this attitude. Even worse than what they have been called, however, is the treatment blacks have had to endure at the hands of prejudiced whites. Discrimination in employment, housing, education, even in the use of public facilities: the list is long and, by now, well known.

Psychologists have studied the problem from many different angles. They have found that the kind of racism which is characterized by open hostility and name-calling is usually practiced by the type of person we described as prejudiced: authoritarian, suspicious, anti-intellectual, and prone to see people as either good or bad. They have also found, however, that a more subtle kind of racism—an attitude that does not see blacks as inferior but supports efforts to keep them in their place—is practiced by many persons who consider themselves fair and open-minded.[3] These people generally vote against black candidates for public office, oppose affirmative action programs, and oppose desegregation in housing and education. They justify their actions on a nonracial basis, but the consistency of their stand suggests that they are really aginst the whole idea of blacks getting ahead in our society.

Some whites practice discrimination without intending to do so. They seek to hire blacks as servants but rarely invite blacks into their homes as friends, not because they look down on them but because it would be unconventional to do otherwise. These people unwittingly help to perpetuate a racist society by being too fearful or too unimaginative to do something different than their relatives and friends.

Another interesting pattern of behavior is known as "reverse discrimination." It occurs when whites, afraid of being accused of prejudice, treat blacks more favorably than they treat other whites in the same situation. A study of this pattern was done in Canada in 1971.[4] Forty restaurants whose policy required their male customers to wear ties were used as the sites of the study. Two couples—one white, one black—visited these restaurants at the same hour on the same day of the week. In each case, the female member was properly dressed but the male wore a turtleneck sweater instead of a shirt and tie. The object was to see if there would be any difference in the frequency with which the whites and the blacks were refused service on the basis of the male's improper attire. The results were startling. The whites were refused service almost three times as frequently as the blacks. This was taken to indicate that the restaurant managers, fearful of being unjustly accused of racial prejudice, were more willing to overlook a breach in their dress code on the part of blacks than on the part of whites.

As if this were not complication enough, it has also been shown that some blacks, when they get the chance, discriminate against whites and against other blacks as well. The picture of racism in the United States today, therefore, is a mixture of many different kinds of behavior. Nevertheless, if we believe in the proposition that all are born equal, we must oppose discrimination wherever we find it.

Overcoming racism

Since the early 1960s, vigorous legal efforts have been made to curtail racism in this country. While psychologists applaud these efforts, they are often more concerned with the prejudiced feelings and thoughts on which racist behavior is based. Overt action, they say, can be legally curtailed, but the law cannot be used to control people's minds.

Actually, there is some controversy among psychologists on this score. One group believes that when people are forced to behave fairly and see everyone else behaving fairly, too, they gradually come to believe that this is the proper way to behave. This group also points out that when blacks are given the opportunities for better education, more adequate housing, and higher scale employment, they will prove their competence and thereby dispel the prejudiced views that some whites have held against them.

Another group of psychologists, in contrast, feels that direct and immediate efforts should be made to modify prejudiced feelings and thoughts. They recommend the use of the mass media—television, radio, magazines, and newspapers—to disclose the injustice and mistaken beliefs on which racism feeds. They contend that close interpersonal relations—blacks and whites working together, learning together, and socializing on a free and equal basis—are effective in reducing prejudice. And most important, they argue that efforts to teach the very young to see each other as individuals, not as members of this or that racial group, will pay off handsomely in years to come.

Race differences are insignificant to kids having fun.

An interesting device psychologists have used to promote better understanding between members of different racial groups is called the "culture assimilator." A culture assimilator is a training technique designed to reduce conflicts between individuals from different cultural backgrounds. It has the trainee read descriptions of incidents involving people from other cultural backgrounds and helps him or her to understand these incidents from their point of view.

In a study sponsored by the U. S. Army, black and white officers and enlisted men were exposed to such a technique.[5] They read 100 paragraphs describing incidents in the army. After each, they were asked to choose (from four options) the best explanation of the incident. Here is a sample: "The white CO of a racially integrated unit tried to recommend promotions on the basis of his men's work and proficiency scores. After the list of promotions was posted, a black Spec 4 entered his office and asked why he had not been promoted. The Spec 4 claimed that he had fairly good scores and asked the CO to review his decision. The CO was surprised at this behavior, but promised to give some attention to the complaint. Upon reflection, the CO noted that promotion reviews were requested much more frequently by blacks in his unit than by whites. The CO was puzzled and surprised by this realization.

Why did more blacks than whites request reviews of promotion decisions?

Option 1. Blacks feel they won't be given a promotion unless they ask for one.

Option 2. The CO was prejudiced and promoted more whites than blacks.

Option 3. Blacks are troublemakers more often than whites are.

Option 4. Many blacks hope to get promotions they don't deserve by intimidating their COs and getting them to give in to avoid being called "prejudiced."

When a trainee chose option 1 as the best explanation, he was told that that was correct and given the following explanation: "Many blacks feel that a good mark record alone is not sufficient for a promotion. They feel that unless they call attention to their case, it will not be acted upon." When a trainee chose any one of the other options, he was told that that was wrong and given an explanation such as the following: "There is no evidence to support this. Reread the incident and select another response."

After finding the correct response to all 100 incidents, the trainees were found to have a better understanding of the behavior of members of the cultural group to which they did not belong. The technique helped them learn how to put themselves in another person's shoes and see life from that other person's point of view. It was concluded that the culture assimilator can be used effectively to reduce prejudice between blacks and whites.

Sexism

A widespread form of prejudice that has gone on for centuries is sexism—the evaluation of the female sex as weaker, less intelligent, less competent, less objective, and less capable of leadership and independence than the male. Because of this attitude, which has been held by many men and many women as well, females throughout the ages have been deprived of opportunities for advancement and self-expression in fields as diverse as business, art, politics, medicine, and theology. They have been underpaid and forced to do menial jobs, denied recognition of their talents, and generally made to feel second-rate.

Even psychology, in years past, was filled with scholars who were convinced that women were inferior to men. There were those who contended that because the female brain is usually smaller than the male

it was less capable of intellectual accomplishment. There were also those
who observed that women were unable to think independently, had
strong inclinations to be mean and untrustworthy, and spent a good deal
of their time in an emotionally unbalanced stated. And as late as 1914,
the respected researcher Edward Thorndike offered the opinion that
"women in general are thus by original nature submissive to men in
general."[6]

Notions of feminine inferiority may be acquired in different ways.
On the one hand, they are taught. We are brought up in a culture that
tells us from birth that boys are robust, girls delicate, that boys are
adventurous, girls fearful, that boys are aggressive, girls passive, and
that boys will grow up to be leaders, girls only their helpmates. We are
inclined to absorb very early the lesson that the female sex is less
adequate than the male. On the other hand, these notions may be culti-
vated by men who are insecure about their own masculinity. Such men
give themselves a lift by downgrading women and parading about in the
illusion that they belong to the "stronger sex."

These false ideas and the discriminatory practices they foster have
been under increasing attack in recent years. The Women's Movement
has set out to eradicate the abuses to which females have been subjected
throughout history. It has already accomplished a significant amount of
"consciousness raising" and positive social change. Because of the efforts of distinguished women like Betty Friedan, Gloria Steinem, Bella
Abzug, and Shirley Chisholm (to name but a few), we seem to be making progress toward greater equality and justice for all people.

Unfortunately, however, some champions of women's rights have
fallen prey to the very disease they set out to cure: sexist prejudice. Just
as eminent men like Thorndike promoted prejudiced views of women,
these eminent women have promoted prejudiced views of men. Lumping all men together as out to dominate their mates, ignoring the contributions of men like John Stuart Mill who fought for women's rights
over a hundred years ago, and disregarding the many male-female relationships that have always been conducted in a spirit of mutuality, they
use the male sex as a scapegoat on which to blame all human problems.

The irony of this turn-of-events underscores a simple but important
point we wish to make about prejudice: it is difficult to avoid. The
temptation to view some group of people as inferior or evil and to abuse
them, dominate them, or blame them for our misfortunes is very great.
Resisting it means being able to recognize the differences among individual human beings and being willing to assume responsibility for
whatever part of our problems is of our own making. That, it seems, is
rather hard to do.

It can be done, however, and psychology as a field tries to help us do
it. Evidence of psychology's concern with sexism can be found in the
many books and articles now being published on the problem. The
Summer 1976 issue of the *Journal of Social Issues*, for example, is devoted
completely to this topic.[7] Its contents include research reports and essays on the social attitudes toward women that were held in ancient

times. It contains articles on ways of measuring equality between the sexes, fear of success in women, ways of using power to influence other people, and the role of motherhood in a woman's life. Finally, the development of female competence is discussed.

In an article entitled "Images of Woman," Jean Hunter points out that in ancient times there were three main images of feminine nature: "woman as inferior, woman as evil, and woman as love object."[8] The Greeks, she says, "insisted on the low worth of women. . . . Athenians excluded women from any political, intellectual, or social life. Shut away in separate quarters, having little contact with anyone outside her own household, the Athenian woman had no legal status and was for her entire life under the tutelage of her nearest male relative." The story of Adam and Eve, she adds, attributes the evils of the world to a woman, for it is Eve who first succumbs to the temptations of the serpent. Side by side with these negative images, however, woman was also seen as someone to adore. "Among the ancient Hebrews, deep affection between husband and wife was common. The Song of Solomon is a beautiful love song, clearly showing that passionate attraction between male and female was accepted in Jewish society. . . . During the eleventh century there arose the chivalric or courtly love tradition. Here woman was at once the object of man's passion and the purifying and elevating force that inspired a man to excellence." She does not attempt to explain these contradictory views, but goes on to say:

> In modern times women increasingly have challenged prevailing conceptions of their role and worth. The first real challenge began with the Renaissance when some humanists and educated women suggested that females too had minds to be trained. It continued in the seventeenth century when the French *precieuses* opposed the traditional subordination of the wife and when radical English puritans claimed for women the long-lost spiritual equality once preached by Jesus. In the eighteenth century women intellectuals insisted on their right to be heard and one, Mary Wollstonecraft, attacked the whole structure of female inferiority while at the same time rejecting the image of woman as pure and protected. Finally, in the nineteenth century, modern feminism was born.

In another article entitled "Women and Power: Toward a Theory of Effectiveness," Paula Johnson asks: "What do the following have in common? (a) A young woman pleads teary-eyed with the detective to help find her missing brother because she just doesn't know what to do. (b) The wife wants the husband to take her to Hawaii; she doesn't tell him, but puts travel brochures all over the house. (c) Mrs. A lets Mr. A know he can sleep on the couch if he won't let their son go off to college."[9] Her answer is that all three scenarios show how women use power by acting incompetent, by making their points indirectly through suggestion, and by withholding love. These methods, she points out,

Women are now entering fields traditionally reserved for men.

emerge from and reinforce the image of feminine inferiority. They result from a social system in which the use of power is seen as belonging to the male. "In order to change this system," she says, "we need to provide women with wider access to more forms of power."

This author and others go on to discuss the different ways in which members of one sex try to obtain satisfaction from members of the other sex. They sketch a broad picture of human beings engaged in what

James Thurber called "the war between men and women." This conflict is conducted on many fronts, using numerous tactics, involving a lot of mixing with the enemy—sometimes funny, sometimes stupid, sometimes useless, sometimes tragic.

The writings of psychologists reflect the complexities of sexism. It is by no means restricted to men having power over women and making them feel inferior. Many women claim the sexes are inherently different and criticize the Women's Movement for trying to persuade females to be more like males. Many people of both sexes dominate other people unfairly. Many proclaim one attitude in public and practice another attitude in private. And many discriminate without even realizing it.

Overcoming sexism

As with racism, an important part of the problem lies in our inability to focus on people as individuals: John Smith or Mary Jones rather than Male or Female. Another part lies in our inclination to blame our unhappiness on other people. Yet another part lies in the reluctance of those in power to give up their power. Underlying it all, perhaps, is the need people have—or believe they have—to control other people's behavior. It stems from the mistaken notion that to have my way I cannot let you have yours. This notion is especially false when what we are after is each other's affection, understanding, and respect. Yet many people cling to it as they cling to all the feelings and ideas that keep prejudice alive.

What then can we do to overcome sexism? Some psychologists suggest broad-scale solutions. Let the media—television, radio, the movies, and the popular press—portray women as intelligent, competent, stable, and capable of leadership. Let the nation give them greater opportunity to occupy positions of power. Let families be run more equably, with women having as much right to go out to work as men and husbands sharing domestic duties with their wives. Above all, let us bring up our children to feel that, boy or girl, they all have equal rights to aspire to whatever goals attract them.

Those of us who deal more with individuals than with groups feel something else is needed, too. We are all for social changes that would equalize the sexes' status and self-esteem, but we believe the struggle must be fought in our hearts and minds as well.

One of the thorniest problems we see is that people who "know better" often continue to feel threatened by or contemptuous toward the opposite sex. And people who are forced to behave decently toward those they devalue do not necessarily begin to like them better. Hopefully, however, psychologists now have some understanding of how feelings can be changed. Here is a formula that often works.

> Give people the opportunity to express their feelings
> openly in words. Let them express them to the people at
> whom they are directed. Listen fully to what everyone has
> to say. Encourage people to explore the source of their

feelings in their past experience. If these feelings seem **275**
unfounded or exaggerated, reason with such people in a caring
but persuasive manner. Help them to find different ways of
dealing with those they resent or fear. Check to see how
the new ways are working out. Repeat the whole process
as often as necessary. Expect only small and gradual
gains.

It is clearly not a simple solution. We do not believe any simple solutions
are effective in changing deep feelings. We do have confidence, however, that such an approach can be used to combat sexism in prejudiced
individuals.

Violence

To psychologists, the issue of violence includes the following questions.
What kind of people engage in violent acts? What experiences, past and
present, make them inclined to do it? Is aggressively harmful behavior
natural to human beings? What kinds of social conditions tend to foster
it? What can be done to reduce violence in our communities, our society,
and the world at large? We think it fair to say that we have fairly good
answers to all but the last and most important of these questions.

Regarding the kinds of people who engage in violent acts, many
psychologists agree that they are either chronically overcontrolled individuals who build up explosive moments of rage or chronically undercontrolled individuals who have a lifetime history of harmful behavior.

The overcontrolled type often seems entirely harmless. He or she
may be quiet, meek, and solitary. Neighbors and other acquaintances
may see him or her as a pleasant, if somewhat stiff and guarded, person.
After he or she has gone on a rampage, however—killing innocent
people, perhaps, in an orgy of gunfire—evidence of violent impulses
may be found. Collections of weapons, photographs of mutilated
bodies, Nazi insignia, and plans to destroy certain groups of people are
occasionally discovered among such a person's possessions. It becomes
clear, then, that this person was not meek at all. He or she was merely
successful in keeping his or her violence hidden.

The undercontrolled type, on the other hand, seems a bully from
childhood on. He or she gets his or her way by intimidating other
people, either through threats and beatings or by being so explosively
unstable that everybody tiptoes around for fear of incurring his or her
wrath. What is sometimes found in such persons is not a lot of anger but
an absence of feeling toward their victims. They do not hate the people
they prey on; they just couldn't care less. This makes them particularly
dangerous, for the only thing that keeps them in line is fear of getting
caught. The minute they want something—say, your money or other
possessions—and think they can get away with it, they will do anything
to achieve their ends.

How did they get that way? What experiences, past and present, provoke such people to rob, rape, assault, or murder? One of the most consistent findings psychology has made on this question is that people who act violently have either observed violence at close quarters or have been victims of violence themselves.

Child abusers, for instance, are usually found to have suffered similar abuse when they were children. Their parents punished them by beating them, starving them, locking them up in dark closets, or tying their hands and feet. Now they do the same to their children. It may be a case of modelling: that was the example their own parents set, so that's how they think a parent behaves. It may also result from displaced aggression, much as the man who is pushed around at work may come home and abuse his wife.

A study by Ulrich and Azrin illustrates this maneuver in animals. [10] Two rats were placed in a chamber containing a floor grid that could be electrically charged. In the absence of any unpleasant electric shocks, the rats showed no aggression toward each other. When shocks were delivered through the floor grid, however, the rats began to attack each other. A conclusion we can draw is that pain provokes hostility. When we are unable to attack the source of our pain, we will be inclined to attack a substitute.

The frustration-aggression studies of Dollard, et al. also make this point. [11] When their subjects were forced to endure many hours of unpleasant idleness, and especially when they were criticized and made to feel inadequate, they began to turn on each other. Perhaps you have noticed the same thing in your own reactions to your family. When things are going well for you, you may be lovely to everyone. When you have had a particularly bad day, however, are you not more likely to snap at your family and friends?

This brings up the large question of corporal punishment of children. Some psychologists contend that spanking or slapping children is a form of violence and should be forbidden, regardless of the children's misbehavior. In punishing one's children this way, they say, we give them the message that "might makes right." We indicate that hitting others is an acceptable act, and we set up in them the desire to get even by hitting somebody else.

Another source of aggressive behavior, according to many psychologists, is the depiction of violence on television. The average American child watches more than twenty hours of television a week. Since many popular programs feature murders, assaults, and other kinds of mayhem, viewers are led to feel that beating people is a more-or-less normal thing to do. "Television desensitizes children to violence in real life," observes University of Mississippi psychology professor Ronald Drabman. "They tolerate violence in others because they have been conditioned to think of it as an everyday thing." [12]

In fairness, it must be said that this is still a debatable point of view. Some psychologists maintain that viewing violence on television helps drain off our own aggressive impulses. However, the majority appears

to accept the notion that it makes us far too willing to condone harmful   **277**
acts as a normal part of the American way of life.

Konrand Lorenz, the noted **ethologist,** thinks aggressive behavior is
natural in human beings. In his book, *On Aggression,* he offers substantial evidence that throughout the animal kingdom the instinct to protect
one's own territory leads creatures to fight off takeover efforts of others
of their species.[13] This instinct, he says, is not lost in humans. On the
contrary, natural selection makes it more than likely that the best
fighters will survive.

At the same time, however, we share with other animals an instinct
for species survival. Not only do we ourselves wish to prosper but, deep
within us, we want those with whom we identify to prosper as well.
Belonging to a strong group makes us stronger too, so we all have a need
to eliminate infighting in the groups to which we belong. Even the criminal, as is well known, demands loyalty from the mob. Juvenile delin-
quents expect protection from their gang, although they may be totally
vicious when dealing with rival gangs.

ethologist

a person who makes a
scientific study of animal
behavior.

Overcoming violence

The instinct for species survival may be the basis on which we can
combat violence in our communities, our society, and our world. If we
can foster a sense of belonging, first to our own neighborhoods, then to
our cities and towns, then to our country, and finally to the world, we
will reduce people's tolerance for violent behavior. Psychologists have
found that it is easiest to hurt or kill a person one feels is "not one of us."
Indeed, many muggers and murderers fail to see their victims as human
beings like themselves. Snipers and bombers carry out their destructive
acts more readily because of the physical distance between them and
their targets. The more we can get the human community to feel connected, therefore, the more we may lessen the incidence of harmful acts.

This grand plan, while admirable, may be too impractical by itself.
What we also need, it seems, are more concrete suggestions for things
we can do here and now. Psychologists agree that the social conditions
of poverty, overcrowding, and exploitation (e.g., being paid low wages
for hard labor) make most of the sufferers angry. It should be apparent,
then, that improving these conditions would reduce the likelihood of
violence. Occurrences like the Watts rebellion in Los Angeles, in which
thousands of people burned and looted their neighborhoods, could
probably be averted if the residents' living conditions were more comfortable and satisfying to them. Meanwhile, we must pay attention to
contributing factors like the violence shown on television and the beating of children by their parents. If these things can be decreased, the
problem may be eased.

When we come to the pathological types who become random killers
and criminals, more individual attention seems necessary. What we
need first are better ways of identifying such persons early. Perhaps

through observation at school and by educating parents to be alert to certain behavior patterns, we could begin to locate the potentially violent child before he or she has had a chance to do anything too destructive.

If this were done, we would of course need techniques for helping that child overcome his or her anger and/or remove its source, express it in nonharmful ways, and develop more compassion for other people. As of now, it must be admitted, we are only groping toward the perfection of such techniques. There is no reason to doubt, however, that they will eventually be developed. When that time comes, psychological treatment of disturbed individuals will make its contribution to the reduction of violence in our society.

Apathy

A much less dramatic issue exists in the growing number of people who simply don't care what happens to our society and, in extreme cases, to themselves. The current term for such an attitude is "alienation." It denotes a state of mind in which a person feels indifferent to his or her environment and even more detached from his or her feelings. Such people have been vividly described in novels like *The Stranger*. [14] Real-life cases of this sort and the social problem they represent are discussed by Kenneth Keniston in his book *The Uncommitted*. [15]

Keniston begins by presenting a portrait of alienated youth—college students, brought up in successful homes, who are down on everything our culture stands for. To make clear the extent to which alienation departs from society's norms, he offers the following contrasts.

alienated outlook	*values of American culture*
low view of human nature	human nature basically good
repudiation of intimacy	closeness, togetherness
rejection of group activities	teamwork, social-mindedness
futility of political activities	usefulness of political activities
pessimism about future	optimism about future
universe chaotic and meaningless	universe orderly and purposive
appearances are misleading	appearances are trustworthy
intolerance, scorn for people	tolerance, respect for people
self-contempt	self-confidence
rejection of success	drive to succeed

This type of person, he goes on to say, is not just a case of abnormal personality. He or she is a natural outgrowth of the flaws in our social systems. "The mere presence of a body of misfits," says Keniston, "tells us something about the faults of a society."

The empty booth reflects increasing voter apathy.

To a lesser extent, alienation or apathy may be observed in many walks of life. The low percentage of voters who turn out for national elections says something about the lack of confidence many people have in our leaders. The disinterest that many people show in problems like integration, pollution, and population control is another example of not caring what happens on a national scale.

Apathy is a condition similar to that of "learned helplessness" in which individuals simply give up when they could be happier if they tried. They come to believe that they can have no effect on improving their lives and seem to resign themselves to accept whatever happens to them. This concept comes from learned-helplessness experiments with animals. Dogs received painful electric shocks in two different situations. First, they were given numerous painful electric shocks from which they could not escape. Next, these dogs, as well as dogs who were never shocked, were placed in an avoidance apparatus. Painful shocks could be avoided by their learning to run to another compartment of the box when they heard a warning tone or saw a light come on. The two groups of animals behaved very differently. The ones who had never been shocked became upset when they received the first few shocks but quickly learned to run to the safe area. In contrast, the dogs who had previously been unable to escape shock made no effort to run, but instead passively accepted the punishment.

The behavior of these animals has been used as a model for explaining depression in humans. People seem to experience painful anxieties as a result of events they are powerless to control (e.g., inflation, war, racism, unemployment). Their helplessness in the face of these situations is then automatically transferred to situations which they could control if they tried but instead passively accept.[16]

280

Most psychologists agree that widespread apathy is a symptom of something wrong in the body of society. Measures to overcome it, however, have hardly begun to be formulated. Studies like Keniston's, which at least diagnose the illness, are invaluable as starting points, but cures remain to be found.

It seems to the authors of this text that the validity of the alienated outlook must first be squarely faced. To what extent, we must ask, are people not to be trusted? To what extent are close relationships doomed to failure and unhappiness? To what extent are appearances misleading? To what extent are group activities a waste of time? Only as we grapple with these issues and come to see, perhaps, how the fabric of our lives can be made more genuine, may we learn what it will take to upgrade the commitment of members of our society to the American way of life.

Summary

This chapter was devoted to the social issues of racism, sexism, violence, and apathy. Psychologists have discovered certain personality patterns of prejudiced persons and the reasons they cling to their prejudices. They have also shown that there is a tendency for all of us to hold prejudicial attitudes at one time or another. Racism and sexism are two major forms of prejudice that have resulted in various ethnic, racial, and sex groups being discriminated against. Psychologists have developed methods for reducing racial and sexual prejudice by means of education, mass communication, and bringing conflicting groups together. Violence and apathy, opposite behaviors, also pose a serious threat to our society and have been subjects of concern to psychologists. Some of the conditions that cause and maintain these behaviors have been discovered in both the laboratory and in real-life settings. These findings suggest ways in which these problems can be resolved but much more remains to be done.

Class Projects

1. To test the extent to which television programs promote sexist images of men and women, watch a specified number of programs (and/or commercials) and note the number of men and women who fall into the following categories.

	Men or Boys	Name of Program or Commercial	Women or Girls	Name of Program or Commercial
Intelligent				
Competent				
Stable				
Courageous				

Men or Boys	Name of Program or Commercial	Women or Girls	Name of Program or Commercial

Able to lead

Foolish

Incompetent

Unstable

Fearful

Unable to lead

Discuss your findings with respect to specific programs and, if you like, send a copy of your conclusions to the sponsors.

2. To explore the degree of apathy in your school or neighborhood, compose a petition for some local improvements you feel are needed. Make a sign telling what you are for (e.g., new equipment in the science lab, better lighting on street corners, or more efficient bus service) and set up a stand at which you will ask people to sign your petition if they agree with you.

    Count the number of people who walk by and ignore you as compared to the number who take a moment to discuss the issue with you.

3. Read and discuss *The Stranger* by Camus for the light it sheds on the type of person who doesn't care about the things most of us find important.

4. Read and discuss *Portrait of the Assassin* by Gerald R. Ford for the light it sheds on the type of person who might set out to murder one of our national leaders.

References

1. GORDON ALLPORT, *The Nature of Prejudice* (Cambridge, MA: Addison-Welsey, 1954).

2. HOWARD EHRLICH, *The Social Psychology of Prejudice* (New York: Wiley, 1973).

3. JOHN McCONOHAY and JOSEPH C. HOUGH, JR., "Symbolic Racism," *Journal of Social Issues 32* (Spring 1976): pp. 23–46.

4. D. G. DUTTON, "Reactions of Restaurateurs to Blacks and Whites Violating Restaurant Dress Requirements," *Canadian Journal of Behavioral Science 3*, (1973): pp. 298–302.

5. DAN LANDIS et al. "Can a Black Culture Assimilator Increase Racial Understanding?" *Journal of Social Issues, 32* (Spring 1976): pp. 169–184.

6. STEPHANIE SHIELDS, "Functionalism, Darwinism, and the Psychology of Women: A Study in Social Myth," *American Psychologist, 30* (July 1975): pp. 739-754.

7. DIANE N. RUBLE, IRENE H. FRIEZE, and JACQUELYNNE E. PARSONS, eds., "Sex Roles: Persistence and Change," *Journal of Social Issues 32* (Summer 1976).

8. JEAN HUNTER, "Images of Woman," *Journal of Social Issues 32* (Summer 1976): pp. 7–18.

9. PAULA JOHNSON, "Women and Power: Toward a Theory of Effectiveness," *Journal of Social Issues 32* (Summer 1976): pp. 99–110.

10. R. E. ULRICH and N. H. AZRIN, "Reflexive Fighting in Response to Aversive Stimulation," *Journal of Experimental Analysis of Behavior, 5* (1962): pp. 511-520.

11. J. Dollard, et al., *Frustration and Aggression* (New Haven, CT: Yale University Press, 1939).

12. "What TV Does to Kids," *Newsweek* (February 21, 1977).

13. Konrad Lorenz, *On Aggression* (New York: Bantam, 1967).

14. Albert Camus, *The Stranger* (New York: Knopf, 1946).

15. Kenneth Keniston, *The Uncommitted* (New York: Harcourt, Brace & World, 1960).

16. S. F. Maier, M. E. P. Seligman and R. L. Solomon, "Pavlovian Fear Conditioning and Learned Helplessness: Effects on Escape and Avoidance Behavior of (a) the CS-US Contingency and (b) the Independence of the US and Voluntary Responding," in *Punishment and Aversive Behavior,* B. A. Campbell and R. M. Church, eds. (New York: Appleton-Century-Crofts, 1969), pp. 299–342.

Suggested Readings

1. Allport, Gordon. *The Nature of Prejudice.* Reading, MA: Addison-Wesley, 1954.

2. Bem, Sandra L. and Bem, Daryl J. *"Homogenizing the American Woman: The Power of the Unconscious Ideology"* in *Psychology for Our Times,* eds. Philip Zimbardo and Christina Maslach. Glenview, IL: Scott, Foresman, 1977, pp. 303–314.

3. Bennett, J. L. *Before the Mayflower.* New York: Macmillan, 1966.

4. Camus, Albert. *The Stranger.* New York: Knopf, 1946.

5. Cohen, Arthur. *Attitude Change and Social Influence.* New York: Basic Books, 1964.

6. Flaubert, Gustave. *Madame Bovary* translated by Francis Steigmullen, in *Psychology for Our Times,* eds. Philip Zimbardo and Christina Maslach. Glenview, IL: Scott, Foresman, 1977, pp. 297–300.

7. Ford, Gerald R. *Portrait of the Assassin.* New York: Ballantine, 1965.

8. Hyde, Janet and Rosenberg, B. G. *Half the Human Experience: The Psychology of Women.* Lexington, MA: Heath, 1976.

9. Nettler, Gwynne. *Explaining Crime.* 2nd ed. New York: McGraw-Hill, 1978.

10. Varela, Jacobo A. *Psychological Solutions to Social Problems.* New York: Academic Press, 1971.

11. Sue, S. and Wagner, N. *Asian Americans: Psychological Perspectives.* Palo Alto, CA: Science and Behavior, 1971.

Psychology in the Classroom

17

**W**hen you think of a school psychologist, you may imagine a person doing anything from giving IQ tests and sending students off to remedial math to holding rap sessions on sex, drugs, and child care. There are thousands of school psychologists in the United States, but the use that is made of them by school administrators is varied.

Depending on his or her abilities and opportunities, the school psychologist may contribute to the management of children with special problems, help establish new methods of instruction, conduct research on the educational process, or even attempt to overhaul the entire school system.

Some school systems employ a large corps of psychologists. Others have few or none on their staffs. Some schoolteachers strongly believe that psychologists can aid them in their work. Others feel they have little to offer. In this chapter, we will discuss a number of the actual functions performed by psychologists in our schools. Using real-life examples, we will try to give you a picture of what has been done. Then you can decide for yourselves what value there may be in school systems hiring specialists from this field.

History and Philosophy of Schools

Schools are a recent invention in the history of the world. A couple of centuries ago, there were special training programs for the trades and professions. Young doctors, lawyers, and priests attached themselves to masters and served long apprenticeships, while other aspiring professionals gathered together and learned in small groups. Universal education in places especially set aside for that purpose is a relatively modern innovation.

Economically, schools are part of an affluent society. Schools belong to a society that can afford to educate its young for many years before sending them out to work. Politically, schools reflect a nation's desire to influence its citizens in such a way that they will uphold the prevailing system of government. And socially, they tend to educate to a cultural norm: that is, to produce people who accept the values of the dominant social group. Children who grow up in a small tribe in Africa or Polynesia are taught how to hunt, fish, plant, cook, make weapons, build shelters, and interpret life according to the values of their people. Likewise, we who grow up in America are taught both the practical skills and the sets of beliefs our educators think we will need to adapt to this environment.

Some educational psychologists are critical of the school system as seen in this light. They say it serves to perpetuate old ways of living rather than to prepare people to create new and better ways. Others, however, contend that until we acquire the traditional knowledge, beliefs, and skills of our society, we are in no position to make effective improvements. The debate remains open. We will return to it at the end of this chapter, for it is not merely academic. The way we conceive of education in the large sense is important in determining just what our schools will try to accomplish.

Many educators see formal learning as the accumulation of knowledge. Others see the school years primarily as a time for acquiring effective study habits—for learning how to think clearly, collect information, and evaluate different interpretations of the facts. Still others conceive of school attendance as an opportunity to learn how to interact with peers, profit from the experience of teachers, and discover one's own central talents. While these concepts overlap, the extent to which a particular school emphasizes one or another view determines the use it makes of the psychologists it employs. Schools that emphasize the acquisition of knowledge rely on psychologists who are specialists in methods of assessing achievement. They develop and carry out testing procedures that determine how effectively students are learning and teachers are instructing. If the school's focus is on how knowledge is gained, rather than on what is learned, the psychologist's major task is to join in the development of curricula designed to increase the ability to think critically. If the primary concern is on understanding one's self and others, the psychologist's work tends to be in the area of helping students and teachers deepen their understanding of themselves and others by means of individual and group counseling.

Adjustment and Behavior Problems

Children misbehave. One kindergarten child cries all the time, afraid to leave home and the arms of his mother. Another cowers in the corner of the classroom, sucking on her thumb, while another jumps up and down, climbs on the furniture, and refuses to participate in group activities. All these children distract the other students, upset their teachers, and disrupt the flow of education. Whereas in the old days they may have been sent home or punished, in many schools nowadays they are referred to the school psychologist.

He or she is expected to evaluate the child's problems and suggest a solution. The evaluation process may involve observation of the child in class, conversations with the child, the teacher, and the parents, testing, and in some cases referral to other specialists such as the pediatrician, speech therapist, or eye clinic. Solutions might include medical treatment, individual or family counseling, removal to a special class or therapeutic setting, or training the teacher to cope with the child's specific problem.

Let us take a look at the case of Earl, a hyperactive second grader. According to the psychologist who was consulted on the case:

> Earl was in almost continuous motion in the classroom and impossible to control unless he was in the immediate presence of the teacher. Easily distracted, he would work at his lessons for only short periods of time and then leave his desk and wander about the room. Occasionally, he would literally move his desk through the classroom. For no apparent reason, he would hit, pinch, or hurtle himself into a group of children and, as a consequence, demolish the group. Although the other children occasionally found his behavior amusing, by and large they avoided him.

In this case, the psychologist decided to concentrate on Earl's symptoms in the classroom and reduce their intensity by using behavior modification. He constructed a small apparatus containing a lightbulb, a counter, and a candy dispenser. Earl was given a book and told to pay attention to it. For every ten seconds he concentrated on his book, the light would flash, the counter would click, and a piece of candy would drop on his desk.

When Earl had shown interest in this machine, the psychologist taught the teacher how to use it. She then made this announcement to the class:

> Earl has been having some trouble in learning things here in school because he is always moving around. This is a magic teaching machine that is going to teach Earl to sit still so that he can learn like other children. Each time the light flashes on, it means that Earl has been sitting still. It also means that he has earned a piece of candy. The counter here will keep score. At the end of the lesson, we will take the candy and divide it up among all of you. If you want to help Earl earn the candy, you can do so by not paying attention to him when he is working.

The conditioning sessions began at the same hours each day and continued for about four weeks. At first they lasted five minutes, but by the end of fifteen sessions they were extended to thirty minutes. Earl sat reasonably still during silent reading, art, oral reading, and arithmetic. Soon from 60 to 100 candies were dispensed each day. Earl was praised by his fellow students. They offered him encouragement during breaks and applauded him at the end of his successful sit-still performances. Earl felt great and everyone, of course, loved the candy.

The psychologist found that Earl lowered his average of hyperactive responses per minute by nine. His teacher stated that his hyperactive behavior had noticeably decreased both in class and on the playground, while his mother reported that he now had friends from school. He made progress in remedial reading and in general seemed a happier child.[1]

288 Once maladaptive behavior like Earl's has been brought under control in one situation, an attempt is made to generalize the improvements to other situations. In Earl's case, steps would be taken to improve his behavior at home and in the community in general. Either his parents or other responsible adults would dispense rewards for specific target behaviors in a fashion similar to that employed in the classroom. Since the ultimate goal would be for Earl to function well without the artificial help of candy reinforcers, they would gradually be withdrawn. Instead of receiving a reward for every desired act, he would soon receive one for every second such act, then for every third such act, and so on until the rewards could be eliminated altogether. While this gradual withdrawal of candy reinforcers was happening, Earl would be receiving praise and other such natural rewards for his improved behavior. These reinforcers would then suffice to keep him behaving in a more normal manner.

Not all school psychologists would use conditioning procedures like the one used for Earl. Some prefer to help students release their feelings and get their troubles off their chest. Some psychologists make efforts to establish better relations between students and teachers, counsel the students' parents, or refer them to other experts. No matter what technique the psychologist uses, however, success depends on the cooperation of the student, the parents, the teacher, and even—as in Earl's case—the student's classmates. The school psychologist has special knowledge of human behavior and how to influence it, but not a magic bag of tricks to change the world.

Assessment of Mental Ability

Not all children learn at the same rate, nor can all children learn every subject equally well. Accordingly, many schools have special programs for the gifted, for slow readers, for the mentally retarded. Many teachers divide their classes into faster and slower groups, so the slow will not impede the progress of the fast nor the fast frustrate and shame the slow.

If children are to be guided into appropriate learning placements, an objective assessment of their intellectual abilities would seem useful. For this reason, group tests such as the *California Mental Maturity* scale are routinely administered in many school districts. As we discussed in chapter 2, there is a great deal of debate on the fairness of intelligence tests, especially when given to non-English-speaking, minority, or culturally different youngsters. Nevertheless, they do measure abilities that correlate well with academic achievement in our schools, so despite their faults they provide at least a rough guide for appropriate placement.

Many people are opposed to including IQ scores in students' records. They feel that such information may be used to keep children out of activities they would like to try or, in some cases, serve as a basis for labeling a particular child "mildly retarded," "dull," or below average. As we shall see from the following case, however, IQ testing may also help children get the most out of their school experiences.

Wendy was a small, pretty girl who, at age nine, could barely read. She was shy and withdrawn, had few friends, and because of her reading problem had fallen far behind in her schoolwork. Her third-grade teacher, like her second-grade teacher, had decided that she must be dull, and her mother was inclined to agree. An active, aggressive businesswoman, the mother had sadly concluded that her timid, retiring daughter just didn't have the brains to compete with children her age. Both she and Wendy's teachers were prepared to recommend that the child be removed to a class for the mentally retarded. As a matter of procedure, however, Wendy was seen by the school psychologist who administered a number of tests. Her scores on the IQ test, as it turned out, were highly uneven: very low on those subtests that were based on reading, but fairly high on those that depended only on abstract reasoning and imagination. As a result, the psychologist concluded that the child was not dull at all. Her inability to succeed at school was due to much more complicated factors, one of which, as you may have guessed, was her mother's lack of understanding of her daughter's sensitive nature. In any case, the recommendation that was made was not to remove Wendy from her class but to involve both the girl and her mother in psychotherapeutic treatment.

Diagnosis and Treatment of Learning Disabilities

Educational and school psychologists frequently conduct remedial programs designed to help students who have difficulty in learning. These programs are aimed at children of average or above-average intelligence who are failing to progress very well in basic subjects like reading and arithmetic. The causes for such difficulties have been found to fall, by and large, into three categories: *organic, educational,* and *emotional disorders.*

An organic condition that can cause a learning disability is known as *irregular perceptual development.* This means that the inborn capacity to perceive, remember, and reproduce sensory material does not develop at a normal rate. Children who suffer from this condition are late in learning to walk and talk and awkward in muscular coordination. It seems that some area of the brain does not mature as rapidly as the rest. While they may be quite intelligent, these children do not learn to do certain things very well. They may not, for instance, remember words from the way they look, though they may remember them from the way they sound. Sometimes they do not learn very easily in this way either. The remedial specialist might try another approach, perhaps through the sense of touch. Some children who fail with other techniques make progress when they are required to trace words with their fingers. What they seem to remember best is neither the look of a word nor its sound, but what it feels like to write it.

While the method that works best for certain children may seem odd in comparison to the methods that are normally used in most of our schools, it is important to remember that not all children learn most easily in one standard way. Rigidity in teaching, therefore, creates problems for many students who might learn much more in more flexible situations.

In the last generation or two, a striking change took place in the teaching of reading in the public schools. The *sight* or *look-say* method replaced the *sound* or *phonetic* method. The latter consists of teaching the sounds of letters first, then showing how they are built up into words (e.g., c–a–t says "cat"). The former consists of teaching words or phrases immediately and only much later showing that the phrase is made up of words and the words of letters. A second-grade pupil being taught by the look-say method may be able to read the sentence, "There once was a cat who liked mice," and yet not be able to tell what the "c" or "l" sounds like. While this method has proven effective with some children, it leaves others floundering in its wake.

The most common causes of learning disability, however, are neither organic nor educational. They are based on emotional problems that have become linked with schoolwork. Academic learning is not unrelated to the rest of the child's life. It takes place in the context of his or her relationships with other people and feelings about him or herself. Many aspects of self-concept relate to learning. One obvious aspect is the sense of achievement that successful schoolwork can produce. The child who learns well is praised by teachers and parents. Adults assume that every child desires such praise and is willing to make strenuous efforts to obtain it. Such is not always the case. Some children do not want to succeed and others want to gain the recognition without making the effort to obtain it.

Even if a learning disability begins as the result of some nonemotional cause, it eventually acquires emotional overtones. Repeated failure will give the most well-adjusted child an inferiority complex plus a distaste for learning. What tends to develop is a mixture of poor skills, negative attitudes, and feelings of inadequacy. The educational or school psychologist who undertakes to help children with learning disabilities must understand the interrelationship of all these factors. Tutoring or treatment programs must be designed to take them into account.

If a little girl is resentful of her parents, she may find an outlet for her feelings by frustrating their hopes. They dream of her graduating from Harvard; she fails grade two. If, on the other hand, she is too anxious to succeed—perhaps because the only way she can rate in her family is by making As—she may foul herself up by her excessive tension. And if she has been lulled into the mistaken belief that she can earn the recognition she needs by putting on a front and acting charming and sweet without producing any real work (a belief that some parents foster by the way they conduct their own lives), she may fail to learn much at school and never grasp the reason why.

Group Counseling

Group counseling is sometimes offered to normally functioning students to help them meet developmental problems. Most boys and girls, for instance, experience anxiety about relating to the opposite sex. Dis-

A group counseling session.

cussions led by a sensitive psychologist can help young people feel more comfortable in their relationships. Many graduating high-school seniors are anxious about seeking employment. Discussions of the problems to be met and overcome in this endeavor can be helpful, too.

In conducting these kinds of meetings, the school psychologist is doing something that a teacher or counselor might do as well. As a matter of fact, the school psychologist's activities often overlap those of other school personnel. As in any closely integrated team, many duties are interchangeable, although individual members have their own particular areas of expertise.

One technique that psychologists use is known as *role-playing*. In this technique, students are encouraged to act out various life roles as though they were engaging in them in earnest. The problems involved in applying for a job, for example, are explored by having one student play the role of applicant, another the role of prospective employer. In acting out these parts in the classroom, the students experience their own anxiety and confusion and display their ways of coping. The discussion that ensues is enlightening for both participants and observers. The challenges involved in the situation can be identified and the strengths and weaknesses of various solutions can be evaluated.

Research on Educational Problems

A contribution psychologists can make to the improvement of education lies in doing research on specific aspects of learning. Many such studies have been carried out. Let us consider two examples.

1. *Programmed instruction* is a method of organizing the material to be learned into small, manageable units. Students cover the material at their own pace. Questions are asked frequently, requiring student responses. These responses are immediately confirmed or corrected. Programmed materials can be presented to students by means of teaching machines, mechanical devices that automatically process the student's responses and provide confirmation or correction as needed.

School personnel have frequently reacted negatively to the introduction of mechanical devices into the classroom. They say the process is dehumanizing, they fear that in time they may be replaced by machines, and they warn that students are becoming targets of exploitation by profit-making corporations. Their fears and warnings may have a good deal of substance to them, but research that has been done comparing modes of instruction (e.g., television teaching versus face-to-face teaching) has shown that, in some courses at least, the mechanical mode results in more learning than the conventional, face-to-face encounter.

The data accumulated on programmed instruction are not by any means exhaustive. Nor are teaching machines always more effective

Programmed instruction.

than live teachers. The issue, therefore, is far from settled. Philosophical questions, such as the differential effect of being taught by human beings rather than by electronic or mechanical devices, remain to be debated. Nevertheless, the findings of psychological research tend to focus the discussion on emerging facts rather than on personal bias.

2. Several studies have probed another aspect of the educational process: the effect of *teachers' expectations* on students' actual achievement. Robert Rosenthal and Lenore Jacobson, for instance, investigated the relationship between first- and second-grade teachers' beliefs about their pupils' innate intelligence and the pupils' actual improvement on a test of general intelligence.[2] Their procedure began by testing the entire population of an elementary school with Flanagan's Test of General Ability, the scores of which can be translated into IQ scores. The alleged reason for testing was to identify "academic bloomers"—children with hidden academic ability which would likely show itself later in the school year. The teachers, therefore, were given the names of pupils who supposedly would demonstrate "unusual intellectual gains during the academic year." In reality, these names were selected randomly, without regard to the test scores. Rosenthal's and Jacobson's aim was to see if the teachers' expectations alone would produce improvement in the children. Nothing more was done to the teachers, the pupils identified as "bloomers," or the rest of the students in the school. Eight months later the intelligence test was readministered and the students' new scores were compared with their original scores.

The results were remarkable. Children whom the teachers expected to make rapid gains did exactly that, while the others showed much less improvement. Of interest, too, was the fact that younger children made greater gains than older ones. The authors proposed the following explanation to account for their findings. "Younger children have less well-established reputations so the creation of expectations about their performance is more credible. . . . Younger children may be more susceptible to the unintended influence exerted by the expectation of their teacher. . . ."

Whatever the mechanics of the process, however, this study appeared to make clear that teachers' expectations alone could affect pupils' intellectual growth. (We say "appeared to" because other psychologists subsequently criticized the procedures used in the study and expressed doubts about its validity.)

Reevaluating Schools

As you have seen, most educational psychologists devote their time to investigating and helping solve problems that students encounter in school. Some radical thinkers, however, have raised the question whether the entire system is not itself a problem to be solved. While they are not officially psychologists, their views are closely related to topics of interest to educational psychologists. The views cited in the following paragraphs had their main impact in the 1960s, so some people feel they are dated. However, perspectives expressed in the past have, in some measure, influenced what is happening in education today. Those criticisms which led to change are being reviewed and reevaluated, while others are still the subject of debate.

Ivan Illich, a Viennese pastor, worked in the slums of North and South America. Having observed the struggle that emerging nations face when they attempt to make education compulsory, Illich says, "Universal education through schooling is not feasible." It is economically impossible for poor countries to send all their children to school. Besides, he says, compulsory schooling divides society into castes and isolates things children learn in school from things they learn from their friends and families. False standards of intelligence are established and diplomas erroneously equated with competence.

Instead of schools as we know them, Illich proposes "learning webs" whereby people who want to acquire a skill can contact those who can teach it to them. Let us say that you plan to travel to Mexico this summer in your VW van. For this trip, you would like to learn how to speak Spanish to the people you will meet and how to fix your car if it breaks down. As a typical student in this country, you would probably be in bad shape. Having taken German I or French I last year, you might not be able to get into a Spanish class. Even if you did, it probably would not specialize in traveller's Spanish. Also, since you took Auto Shop last year and learned how to fix an old Chevy, your chances of learning how to repair your VW are undoubtedly very slim. According to Illich's system, on the other hand, you would simply phone up a central registry and within days you would be hiring a Mexican immigrant to talk to you in Spanish and to teach you some of the essentials of Mexican life as well. Meanwhile, you would sign up for an apprenticeship and work in a VW mechanic's shop until you could handle most of the repairs your van might eventually need.

You would pay for this special schooling with vouchers supplied by the government. In other words, they would supply you with money to buy the education you need, rather than giving it to school districts to teach you things you don't care about. You would decide what you need to learn and how you would go about learning it. The government would simply help you acquire the education you want.

Illich is not against learning in structured environments, but he is against people being restricted to school buildings for many long years on end. Schools as we know them, he says, are boring, degrading, and financially disastrous. Our society and all its children would be better off if we did away with our present school system and replaced it with an altogether different one.[3]

A. S. Neill was not a philosopher, but an English schoolmaster. After extensive psychological training and work with emotionally disturbed children, he created a special school called Summerhill. Summerhill was and is a place where Neill's unusual views on education could be put into practice. A small boarding school in the English countryside near the sea, its pupils range in age from five to sixteen years. Academic subjects are taught, and craft rooms, music, theater, and mechanical tools are also available. The main thing about the curriculum, however, is that no one is obliged to do anything at all. Every child has the right to choose what he or she will learn and how and when he or she will learn it. A young artist may spend months working on a piece of sculpture while a teenager who wants to prepare for college crams for the entrance exams. A group of students may decide to take a bicycle trip to a nearby town while another group spends the day watching television.

Summerhill's students and staff are entirely self-regulating, for Neill firmly believed that trouble starts when one person tells another person what to do. Decisions regarding the running of the school, therefore, come from democratic group discussions, where even Neill, like each individual child, had only one vote. The rules of the place are mainly concerned with people respecting each other's rights and feelings, but aside from that the children develop as they themselves see fit. In Neill's words, "The difficult child is the child who is unhappy . . . and at Summerhill, children's unhappiness is cured, and, more important, children are reared in happiness."[4]

A system such as Neill's, it should be clear, places great faith in young people's ability to guide their own lives, in contrast to the traditional view that adults need to guide their children's behavior until the children are old enough to understand the implications of the choices they make. Which approach will prove better in the long run remains to be seen, but at the present time it can be said that a small but persuasive group of educators would like to scrap the traditional system or at least make substantial changes in it.

Another such educator is John Holt. Trained in this country as a regular teacher, he too has adopted a radical view of schooling and its problems. As he sees it: "Most children in school fail. . . . Most students fail to develop more than a tiny part of the tremendous capacity for learning, understanding, and creativity with which they were born. . . . They fail because they are afraid, bored, and confused."

Holt puts the blame on grownups.

> We adults destroy most of the intellectual and creative capacity of children by the things we do to them or make them do. We encourage children to act stupidly, not only by scaring and confusing them, but by boring them, by filling their days with dull, repetitive tasks that make little or no claim on their attention or demands on their intelligence. Worse yet . . . we present ourselves as if we were gods, all-knowing, all-powerful, always rational, always just, always right.[5]

He too wants a much more flexible, nonauthoritarian school system. Rather than teachers and administrators telling students what to learn, Holt, like Neill and Illich, feels that the students' own interests should direct their learning activities.

Those who are skeptical of the views of Holt, Neill, and Illich maintain that learning cannot always be a happy and carefree experience. To acquire knowledge and skill in any subject requires effort, they contend. Education entails study, practice, and mental and physical exertion. Rather than give in to children's desire to play around, therefore, we need to seek more and more effective ways to motivate them to work. A child who would like to play the piano, for instance, cannot hope to master it by simply playing when the spirit strikes. We must be prepared to practice long and hard, for hours and days and weeks and years, or there is simply no chance that we will become virtuosos. Good schooling, they say, inevitably evokes some anxiety, boredom, and strain. Of course it should also result in the pleasures of accomplishment, but to believe that a sound education can be gotten without strenuous effort is to believe in fairy tales.

Regardless of which point of view you adopt, our educational system allows for divergent opinions. This, we believe, is one of its greatest assets. We are encouraged to discuss and disagree; critical voices are neither censored nor ignored. In this way, educators engage in ongoing attempts to evaluate their programs and increase the effectiveness of their efforts.

Summary

The role of the psychologist in education, it should be clear, is about as diverse as psychology itself. Research, testing, counseling, and evaluating: the school psychologist may undertake a great variety of activities in his or her endeavor to be a productive contributor to the learning process.

Some schools still find that they can conduct their business without psychological assistance, but they are becoming fewer every year. The vast majority of school districts in the United States now employs one or more psychologists and makes frequent use of their expertise. It can be said, therefore, that the school psychologist is fast becoming an indispensable part of the educational team.

In this chapter, the history and philosophy of formal education were briefly reviewed. The role of the school psychologist in relation to an individual child was demonstrated. Other duties such as testing, treating learning disabilities, and conducting research were illustrated. In addition, proposals to redesign educational systems were discussed.

Class Projects

1. Set up a role-playing situation in which several members of your class are vying for a place on a school athletic team. Let two or three others play the coaches who are to decide who gets the spot. Have the applicants leave the room and come in one at a time for their interveiws. The interviewers should ask the applicants why they want to be on the team, what they think

they can do for the team, and what their experience has been in athletics. **297**
The applicants should try to answer in a fashion that shows they are confident of their abilities.

Observe and discuss the ways in which they attempt to present their case. See what conclusions you can come to regarding the effectiveness of various ways of petitioning for a position.

2. Recall your own experience in learning something new. Did you learn it by yourself or did someone teach you? If you had a teacher, did he or she tell you what to do or encourage you to figure it out by yourself? How did you feel about the learning process? How did you feel about the accomplishment?

3. Invite your local school psychologist to visit your class and describe his or her professional duties. If he or she has the time, perhaps you could arrange to take some group tests or to engage in a group counseling session. The experience of doing these things personally is often more enlightening than merely reading about them.

References

1. G. R. PATTERSON, "An Application of Conditioning Techniques to the Control of a Hyperactive Child," in *Case Studies in Behavior Modification*, ed. L. P. Ullman and L. Krasner (New York: Holt, Rinehart & Winston, 1965).

2. ROBERT ROSENTHALL and LENORE JACOBSON, *Pygmalion in the Classroom* (New York: Holt, Rinehart & Winston, 1968).

3. IVAN ILLICH, *Deschooling Society* (New York: Harper and Row, 1970).

4. A. S. NEILL, *Summerhill* (New York: Hart, 1960).

5. JOHN HOLT, *How Children Fail* (New York: Dell, 1971).

Suggested Readings

1. HOLT, JOHN. *How Children Fail.* New York: Dell, 1971.

2. NEILL, A. S. *Summerhill.* New York: Hart, 1960.

3. LEONARD, GEORGE B. *Educational Ecstasy.* New York: Dell, 1968.

4. SAMPLES, ROBERT E. "Learning with the Whole Brain," *Human Behavior*, February 1975, pp. 15-23.

5. HANEY, CRAIG, and ZIMBARDO, PHILIP. "Social Roles, Role Playing and Education: On the High School as Prison", *Behavior and Social Science Teacher*, 1, 1973-74.

SOME THOUGHTS OF OUR OWN

Psychology, we believe, could make important contributions to the betterment of our society, not to speak of our schools, if it were not for the following factors. First, the establishment is too firmly entrenched to be easily dislodged. Old ways of doing things have a tendency to continue simply because it seems safer to most people to go on repeating old patterns of behavior than to risk trying something new. Second, psychologists are suspect in certain quarters. They are thought of as "pointy-headed intellectuals" or radical rabble-rousers rather than as serious scientists committed to social improvement. Third, groups in positions of power derive great benefit from the status quo. While they may proclaim their support for efforts to rid our society of poverty, prejudice, and crime, they are often unwilling to give up the benefits they derive from these very conditions. Finally, psychologists themselves are part of the prevailing system; therefore, much as they may want to bring about change, they tend to obstruct it through their own ingrained habits and beliefs.

Nevertheless, there are signs that psychology has had at least some minor impact on our social welfare. Reduction in racial prejudice, more permissive classroom environments, improved relations between police officers and the public they serve, attempts on the part of corporations to better the emotional climate in which their employees work—such events are at least in part a result of psychologists' efforts.

The fields of educational and social psychology will flourish when we, the public, allow them to flourish. If we believe they can help us, we are more apt to let them help us. They, of course, have to win our confidence. In order to do so, they must come up with more impressive contributions than they have so far produced. The authors of this text believe they will.

Section Five

Frontiers of Investigation

OVERVIEW

here are many areas in which psychologists are breaking new ground. We have chosen three we thought would interest you: the role of *humor* in human functioning, the dynamics of *creativity*, and the possibility of *extrasensory perception*.

Humor and creativity were largely ignored by most psychologists until the 1960s. Extrasensory perception was investigated as early as the 1930s, but it remained a taboo for respectable psychologists until very recently. Each of these phenomena, we feel, bespeaks the inspiring potential of the human mind. Each of them leads to a contemplation of our flexibility, our adaptability, and our capability for growth.

What makes us laugh and what good does it do us to see the funny side of life? What encourages our creativity and what are the hallmarks of creative genius? What kinds of extrasensory perception have been shown to exist and what kinds remain to be proven? These are a few of the questions this section of the text attempts to answer.

The Sense in Humor

18

 n at least one respect, psychologists bear a close resemblance to human beings. They claim to be intelligent, but their behavior is sometimes foolish. Psychological investigators, for example, have spent years ignoring one of our most distinctive and delightful traits—our sense of humor. They have studied our pain and suffering, our aggression and hostility, our growth, our learning, our group identification, and our sexuality, but they have paid little attention to our ability to laugh.

Now we ask you: can a profession that tries to explain human nature afford to overlook the giggle? Can it disregard the modest chuckle and neglect the mighty guffaw? These are only a few of the weighty questions we will soon elucidate.

Are we kidding? Well, you be the judge. In this chapter, we will provide a survey of the theories and findings that have been amassed on laughter and humor. Not many psychologists have devoted time to the subject. Those who have done so, however, have made some interesting observations. We will attempt to summarize their work.

So sit up and glue your eyes to the page. Wipe that smile off your face and look glum and scholarly. We intend to take humor seriously and we don't want to catch you enjoying it.

304

Before we study what psychologists have said about humor, we thought we would review what humorists have said about psychology.

> Conversation at a cocktail party:
> "Are you a psychologist?"
> "Why do you ask?"
> "You're a psychologist."

> A psychiatrist says to his patient:
> "After all these years, you still feel guilty?
> You should be ashamed of yourself!"

Figure 18.1

Figure 18.2

A lady visits an analyst to discuss her husband's problem.
"It's terrible," she says. "He thinks he's a horse. He lives in the stable, he walks on all fours, and he even eats hay. Please tell me, doctor—can you cure him?"
"Yes, I believe I can. But I have to warn you, the treatment will be long and expensive."
"Oh, money's no object. He's already won two races."

Jokes, and cartoons like those shown in Figures 18.1 and 18.2, suggest that psychologists and psychiatrists are not as perfect as they might like to appear. This is not surprising. One of humor's age-old functions is to reveal people's defects and shortcomings. The person who is the butt of a joke may find its point jarring; the joke itself may be a gross exaggeration; still, there is often a measure of truth in comedy. It reminds us, at least, that no one is beyond criticism.

A Purely Human Trait

One characteristic that sets human beings apart from other creatures is a sense of humor. A sort of laughter has been observed in chimpanzees, but it is stimulated mainly by tickling and horseplay. The ability to recognize absurdity and to be amused by it, on the other hand, is common to all human cultures. Every known society has its fund of jokes and witticisms. Comedy is enjoyed by all normal people from early childhood to old age.

Not only is humor a distinctively human trait, it is also an important one. Most psychologists agree that laughter and humor help us cope with life's problems. Understanding how our sense of humor works and how to improve it, therefore, is obviously of value. For many generations, psychology contributed little to this goal. In recent years, however, a number of works have appeared that give evidence of a growing interest in the subject.[1,2,3,4,5] They examine such questions as the following. How are humor and laughter related to intelligence? How are they related to aggression, anxiety, and other personality characteristics? What is humor's role in different cultures? Did the early American Indians, for instance, laugh at the same sorts of things we laugh at today? What is humor's potential as a therapeutic agent? Can it help us maintain our sanity? If so, how does it do it?

As we review the theories and findings that have so far been put forth, we will attempt to answer some of these questions.

Types of Humor

The many things that make us laugh fall into several standard categories. To a greater or lesser degree, these categories occur in almost every culture on the face of the globe. With examples, the categories may be listed as follows:

Nonsense and word play

Q. Why did the moron tiptoe past the medicine chest?
A. He didn't want to wake the sleeping pills.

Q. What did the Martian say when he landed on Earth and found we had switched to the metric system?
A. Take me to your litre.

Q. How do you drive a baby buggy?
A. Tickle its feet.

Insult

Q. Why did God make man before He made woman?
A. So He could learn from His mistakes.

Q. Why did God make man before He made woman?
A. Because He didn't want any advice on how to make man.

Ribaldry (dirty jokes)

CENSORED

Morbidity (sick humor)

Little Willy hung his sister.
She was dead before we missed her.
Willy's always up to tricks.
Ain't he cute? He's only six.

"Momma, momma, I don't like my brother."
"Shut up and eat what I give you."

Wit and wisdom

A forty-year-old man marries a twenty-year-old girl. When his relatives frown at the difference in their ages, he says, "It's no problem at all. When I look at her, I feel ten years younger and when she looks at me she feels ten years older. So you see, we are perfectly matched."

A man meets his friend on the street. "How's it going?" asks the friend.
"It could be worse. My house burned to the ground."
"Oh, that's terrible."
"No, not so terrible. You see, I was heavily insured."
"Oh, that's wonderful."
"No, not so wonderful. My wife died in the fire."
"Oh, that's terrible."
"No, not so terrible. I have since remarried, and my new wife is sweeter and prettier than the first."

"Oh, that's wonderful."

"No, not so wonderful. You see, my neighbor is a handsome man and my wife spends a lot of time visiting him."

"Oh, that's terrible."

"No, not so terrible. As it happens, he also has a lovely wife, and when my wife visits him, his wife visits me."

"Well then, that is wonderful."

"No, like I told you before—not wonderful, not terrible, it could be worse."

Theories of humor attempt to explain what it is about these things that makes us laugh. Their aim is to clarify the essence of humor and help us understand the part it plays in our lives.

The Incongruity Theory

The other day, on entering a library, one of the authors of this text had an amusing experience. His eyes scanned a shelf labeled RECENT BOOKS, but what his mind registered was DECENT BOOKS. His so-called brain clicked through a deductive process. The rest of the shelves, he thought, must be filled with INDECENT BOOKS! He found the thought so funny that he almost laughed out loud.

Now why was he amused?

Two centuries ago, the philosopher Immanuel Kant observed that laughter is "an affection arising from a sudden transformation of a strained expectation into nothing." This insight was expanded by another philosopher, Arthur Schopenhauer, into the *incongruity theory of humor.* According to this theory, we laugh whenever we are led to expect one image or idea and then suddenly are presented with another.

Thus, Kant and Schopenhauer might have said that on entering the library our author was prepared to find shelves of books arranged according to the typical classifications. His momentary fantasy that the place was stocked with pornography sprung a surprise on his expectations. That surprise was what made him smile.

There is incongruity, it seems, in practically every humorous happening. The standard form of the joke illustrates this clearly. Jokes almost always lead us along one avenue of thought and then, with the punch line, jolt us out of it.

Three men lay dying in a hospital ward. Their doctor, making rounds, went up to the first and asked him his last wish. The patient was a Catholic. "My last wish," he murmured, "is to see a priest and make confession." The doctor assured him he would arrange it and moved on. The second patient was a Protestant. When asked his last wish, he replied, "My last wish is to see my family and say goodbye." The doctor promised he would

Would these legs be as funny in a Mardi gras parade?

have them brought and moved on again. The third patient was, of course, a Jew. "And what is your last wish?" the doctor asked. "My last wish," came the feeble, hoarse reply, "is to see another doctor."

Here the element of surprise or incongruity is obvious. We are led to consider the conventional responses to life's final ebb—to make confession, to take leave of one's loved ones. Then, in a moment, we are jerked around to consider a new outlook altogether. Our expectations have, without a doubt, been tricked. Kant and Schopenhauer would appear to have hit the nail on the head.

But have they? The outlook expressed by the last patient is not entirely incongruous. It is unexpected, unconventional, and impolite, but in the end it may make more sense than the supposedly sensible requests. "My last wish is to bake an apple pie," would have been more surprising but not nearly so witty or laughable. By the same token, had the author of this text imagined that the library was stocked with fresh fish instead of books, the effect would have been more bizarre but less funny.

The Superiority-Aggression Theory

Those who disagree with the incongruity theory say that its aim is too intellectual. It ignores the emotional content of humor: the expressions of lust, greed, hostility, contempt, and rivalry that put meat on the bones of comedy.

Another leading theory, in contrast, aims directly at the emotional side of humor. The philosopher Thomas Hobbes stated, "The passion of laughter is nothing else but sudden glory." His colleague Alexander Bain claimed that, "The occasion of the **ludicrous** is the degradation of some person or interest possessing dignity." Stephen Leacock asserted that, "Laughter begins as a primitive shout of triumph." Underlying all those statements is the belief that humor is essentially competitive or hostile. This viewpoint has been labelled the *superiority-aggression theory of humor.* It asserts that whenever we laugh we feel superior to someone else.

ludicrous
laughably absurd

satire
a literary work in which vice, folly, and stupidity are held up to ridicule

Is the superiority-aggression theory better than the incongruity theory? Let us see.

A child asks his teacher, "What's the difference between a mailbox and a garbage can?" When the teacher says, "I don't know," the child replies, "Then I'll never ask you to mail a letter." Is the jest aggressive? Yes, we must agree it is, for it enables the child to make the teacher seem stupid. Similarly, the joke about the doctor and the dying men disparages the dignity of the medical profession, and our author's fantasy in the library poses a challenge to the stodgy atmosphere that supposedly prevails there.

parody
an imitation of someone else's artistic creation, but treating it in a funny or nonsensical manner

Now that he's got the degree, he can afford to jest.

caricature
a deliberately distorted
picture of a person,
exaggerating their
defects to make them
look funny

If we cast about in the wide seas of laughter, we will come across many examples that support the superiority-aggression theory. **Satire, parody,** and **caricature** all thrive on the exposure of someone's weaknesses; insults are the common fare of popular comics; and political car-

Figure 18.3

toons are sometimes savage in their ridicule of our elected officials. Even the cartoon in Figure 18.3 illustrates the theory's point.

Who will deny that our pleasure is enriched by the sense of superiority it gives us? Jokes like this, in which some poor soul is revealed as even more stupid than we are, tempt us to agree that the essential motive behind our laughter is to downgrade others.

But is it really so? Is humor just a form of competition? If it is, then what do we say to those rare but wonderful times when we laugh at

Figure 18.4

ourselves? Not only students of humor but all normal persons can recall times when they were amused at their own shortcomings. That fact alone raises a doubt about the superiority-aggression theory.

A second doubt is raised by the joy of nonsense humor. Consider the cartoon shown in Figure 18.4. Is it not a fine example of humor? And is not this couplet by Ogden Nash funny too?

> When called by a panther,
> don't anther.

Even foolish riddles contain their measure of mirth. For instance:

> Q. How are an elephant and a plum alike?
> A. They're both purple—except for the elephant.

Whatever our age, we may smile at these quips. Yet whom do they attack? We may admit to hostile impulses against our oppressors, against pompous people and restrictive institutions, but few of us (we hope) have a need to put down jockeys, panthers, elephants, or plums.

The Liberation Theory

The superiority-aggression theory, like the incongruity theory, explains an important part of humor, but neither of them explains the full range of the subject. Neither, in addition, comes to terms with the most important quality humor possesses—its ability to lift our spirits, to lighten our hearts, to inject vitality into a drab or gloomy mood.

Is there then a more comprehensive theory? Is there a concept that fits the entire range of things that make us laugh? Is there an explanation that makes sense of the fact that wit and comedy are delightful experiences? Yes. The selfsame author of library renown has proposed such a theory.[1] In order to become familiar with it, let us return to the scene of his confusion. Why was that slip-of-the-brain, from RECENT BOOKS to DECENT BOOKS to INDECENT BOOKS, so enjoyable?

As the author remembers it, he was feeling overworked as he entered the library that day. He had gone there to search out some material for this text. The prospect of working all afternoon depressed him. He saw no way out; he was there and the work had to be done. In that fleeting fantasy, however, his imagination furnished him with respite. If only things were different, it suggested; if only the shelves were filled with pornographic material—lusty novels, bawdy farces, sly limericks, and unprintable cartoons—what an afternoon he could have!

In a proper, serious, but restrictive situation, sex reared its lovely head. Our author's foolish notion compensated for his workaday routine. His imagination sprung him free. The experience suggests what may be called a *liberation theory of humor.* This theory claims that the most fundamental function of humor is its power to free us from the burdens and restrictions under which we live our lives.

According to the liberation theory, humor gives us moments of freedom from our psychological bonds. That is the secret of humor's success. In the fully flowered peal of laughter, routine ways of thinking and feeling are dislodged, new mental connections are created, cats are let out of bags, sacred cows are kicked in their behinds, and noses are thumbed at authorities. The pristine individual leaps forth, unbeautifully, in his or her birthday suit—and that is the reason it feels great.

Research: Difficulties and Discoveries

Whatever theory they accept, psychologists agree that extensive research still needs to be done on humor. In the last twenty years, many minor studies have been made, but no major series of investigations has so far been conducted.

The researcher labors under a number of handicaps. In the first place, it is difficult to measure anyone's response to humor. Asking subjects how well they like a printed joke or cartoon is at best a crude procedure. Attempting to rate their mirth by watching their facial expressions is not much better. In the second place, a research lab is hardly the place to observe humor in its natural state. Subjects find it hard to be spontaneous. The comic material presented to them often seems artificial. The entire set-up resembles the dissection of a flower; in examining its parts we destroy its beauty.

Despite these handicaps, some studies are very interesting. In 1956, **315** for example, John Doris and Ella Fierman designed an experiment to explore the relationship between anxiety level and response to humor.[6] An anxiety questionnaire was administered to 419 Yale men and 197 Connecticut College women. Extreme groups of "high anxious" and "low anxious" subjects were selected. These subjects were shown 18 cartoons. Six cartoons had previously been rated by a group of psychologists, psychiatrists, and psychiatric social workers as high in aggressive content. Six had been rated high in sexual content. The remaining six had been rated high in nonsense content. The subjects' vocal and facial responses to the cartoons were rated by the examiners on a scale ranging from disapproval to pronounced pleasure. The subjects personally indicated their response to each cartoon on a scale ranging from "Very Much Disliked" to "Very Much Liked." There were two examiners, one male and one female, and 56 subjects: 14 "high anxious" men, 14 "high anxious" women, 14 "low anxious" men, and 14 "low anxious" women.

Two results stood out clearly. First, there seemed to be a relationship between the subjects' anxiety level and their enjoyment of aggressive humor. The "high anxious" subjects liked the aggressive cartoons far less than the "low anxious" subjects. Second, this difference was more pronounced when the experimenter was of the opposite sex to the subjects. Males tested by a female and females tested by a male scored differently than males tested by a male and females by a female.

These findings allowed the researchers to draw two conclusions. People's liking for aggressive humor is affected by their anxiety level; the more anxious they are, the less they like it. At the same time, the interpersonal context in which the humor is introduced is influential. People who like aggressive humor like it more when it is presented to them by someone of their own sex; people who dislike aggressive humor dislike it more when it is presented to them by someone of the opposite sex.

inhibition
the holding back of our natural feelings or the inability to express ourselves freely

Another study, published in 1967 by David Singer, Harry Gollob, and Jacob Levine, investigated the effect of **inhibitions** on the enjoyment of aggressive humor.[7] Two hundred and sixteen male undergraduates were divided into two groups. The first group was asked to rate reproductions of five etchings which portrayed the brutal and sadistic treatment of innocent victims. The second group was asked to rate five etchings of pleasant social scenes. The exposure of the first group to the brutal pictures, it was presumed, would mobilize their feelings of outrage and horror.

After they rated the etchings, the subjects were each given a booklet of twelve cartoons. Four cartoons contained no aggressive content, four portrayed mild aggression, and four depicted acts of high interpersonal aggression. The subjects rated each cartoon on a scale from "not at all funny" to "extremely funny."

Subjects who had been exposed to the brutal etchings enjoyed the highly aggressive cartoons much less than subjects who had been exposed to the pleasant etchings. The investigators concluded that the wish to be aggressive increases people's enjoyment of aggressive humor; when that wish is inhibited or reduced by showing them the terrible results of aggressive behavior, people's enjoyment of aggressive humor is lessened.

Finally, two enterprising psychologists in Wales have carried out extensive studies of children's laughter in small-group social situations.[8] Antony Chapman and Hugh Foot equipped a mobile van with stereo and television in a comfortable playroom whose occupants they could observe through a one-way screen. Their general procedure has been to drive the van to a schoolyard and, with the consent of parents and teachers, invite children in in pairs or occasionally in threes. The children are either shown Tom 'n Jerry and Woody Woodpecker type cartoons on the television or allowed to listen to comic stories and songs on the stereo. The psychologists observe the children's reactions through the one-way screen, recording their smiles and laughter in a systematic fashion.

Having done this kind of study for many years with hundreds of children, Chapman and Foot point out that it is very important that the children do not suspect they are being observed. Knowledge of being observed severely inhibits laughter, both in children and adults. When they think they are alone, however, the children tend to react as they would at home.

A number of results have emerged from these studies. Primarily, they have shown that both smiling and laughter are increased by the presence of a companion, especially if this companion does a lot of laughing and smiling, if he or she sits close to the subject, looks the subject in the eyes, and touches the subject in a friendly way. Girls tend to laugh and smile more in the presence of a boy than in the presence of another girl, while boys' smiling and laughing is not affected by the sex of their companion.

The implication is obvious. Laughing and smiling are, in large part, social responses, and they are highly affected by the social situation in which the individual finds him or herself.

Laughter in Cultural Contexts

Laughter and humor occur in every known human society. What we find funny may differ from one culture to another; the styles in which comedy is clothed may change from one epoch to another, but the categories of the ludicrous remain impressively constant. Nonsense and absurdity; puns and plays-on-words; stupid actions and remarks, especially when made by those who claim to be intelligent; ridicule of persons of higher status; ribaldry and double-entendres; and philosophical and political wit are among the most enduring, universal phenomena that people all over the world find amusing. We may infer that humor functions in the same way for Americans as for Russians, and that illiterate primitives enjoy a good joke no less than sophisticated men and women.

It is interesting, however, to study the humor that predominates in certain cultural contexts. What becomes the primary source of laughter for a group of people tells us something about their central concerns and their ways of coping with life.

The Jewish people who resided in Eastern Europe in the eighteenth and nineteenth centures formed a close-knit community under the scourge of oppression. They were barely tolerated, frequently discriminated against, and periodically massacred by the Russians, Poles, and other nationalities among whom they lived. In the face of such treatment, they retained their dignity, their optimism, and their belief in themselves. How they were able to do so is a question of importance for anyone who cares about oppressed minorities and human survival. That their religious convictions enabled them to endure their sufferings seems indisputable. It is probable that their sense of humor helped keep them afloat as well.

In some stories they pictured themselves outwitting their oppressors. In others they made fun of their own **idiosyncracies.** Two examples of the former run as follows:

idiosyncracies

peculiar characteristics or quirks of behavior

> A Jew is condemned to death for failing to
> salute the Czar. "Since in all other respects
> you have behaved like a decent person,
> even though you are only a lousy Jew," says
> the Czar, "I will demonstrate my clemency
> by allowing you to choose the manner of your
> death." To which the condemned man replies,
> "For a compliment like that, Your Highness,
> I will show my gratitude by saving your
> soldiers the trouble of killing me. I
> choose death by old age."

> A Jew meets a Nazi officer in the street.
> Clicking his heels, the Nazi snarls, "Schwein!"
> To which the Jew bows politely and replies,
> "Cohen. Pleased to meet you."

Two examples of the latter are:

> Three Jews are lined up before a firing squad.
> The captain steps up to the first and says,
> "Do you want a blindfold?" "All right," replies
> the prisoner. The captain asks the same question
> of the second prisoner and he too accepts the
> blindfold. When the captain asks the third man
> if he wants a blindfold, however, he says, "No."
> Whereupon the second Jew turns to the third and
> whispers, "Take the blindfold. Don't make trouble."

> A Jew is quarreling with his partner. "You
> thief! You liar! You swindler!" he shouts.
> "I'm just as honest as you!"

How could two such opposing forms of humor help an oppressed group maintain its self-esteem? When the Jews portrayed themselves outwitting their oppressors, they indulged in a comic fantasy that "little guys" all through the course of history have enjoyed. When one group of people oppresses another, the underdogs always resort to wit as one way of relieving their feelings. It is a universal gambit; students all over the world make fun of their teachers, employees of their employers, citizens of their leaders. By imagining ourselves capable of making fools of the people who, in some respect, control our lives, we give ourselves a lift.

More perplexing is how the humor the Jews directed at themselves was also helpful. Making fun of one's own idiosyncracies would seem to be a put-down of oneself, but in fact that is not so. In one way or another, we all have done some laughing at ourselves. Perhaps we have made fun of our looks, our intelligence (or lack of it), our awkwardness in social situations, or whatever. If we have done so, we may sense that laughing at ourselves is a way of accepting ourselves—accepting ourselves with all our faults. In the act of laughter we affirm that we can be joyous in the midst of our problems. Thus, when the East European Jews made light of their flaws and failings, they were engaging in a therapeutic exercise. They were liberating themselves from false pride and replacing it with an affirmation of their true, imperfect selves.

Afro-Americans have also known the scourge of oppression. Outright lynching and physical assault on black people were practiced for many years. Until recently, widespread discrimination resulted in the improverishment and degradation of black citizens in this country. In this context, it is instructive to note a particular kind of humorous interchange that many blacks have engaged in for generations. The activity, in one form, is known as *signifying;* in another form, it is called *playing the dozens.* It consists of a ritualized verbal contest. The participants—two boys, for the most part, but sometimes two girls—boast, brag, and insult each other and each other's family in a kind of rough rhyming doggerel.

Using expressions like, "I might not be the best in the world, but I'm in the top two and my brother's getting old," the players try to best each other at bragging. When it comes to insulting each other's family, the jibes are usually directed against the participants' mothers. "Your momma wears G. I. boots," is among the mildest of the insults used.

What do these contests accomplish? Black psychologists tend to agree that they are a kind of initiation into adulthood. The only way to win the dozens is to "keep your cool." By boasting and bragging, a youngster bolsters his self-esteem. By insulting his peers while shrugging off the insults directed toward him, he learns both to dish it out and to take it. Thus, this hostile-humorous game prepares ghetto children for coping with the degradation they may experience as members of our still-imperfect society.

Do you and your friends ever use humor as a way of relieving your anxieties or raising your self-esteem? Do you make fun of your teachers, ridicule police officers, or laugh at other people whom you consider your oppressors?

If your teacher (the tyrant) will allow it, discuss the jokes and wisecracks you have enjoyed along this line. See if you can understand the ways in which they have helped you feel better about your social position.

Humor as a Therapeutic Agent

Psychologists who treat people with emotional problems have noted that their patients' sense of humor can be affected in various ways. Some, for example, try to laugh their troubles off. Making light of problems is a defense for such people whereby they avoid taking a clear, hard look at what is going on within themselves. More often, emotionally disturbed people lose their sense of humor altogether. Then, rather than laughing off their troubles, they take them so seriously that they magnify their importance in their lives.

From time to time, troubled people use humor in a truly therapeutic way. An after-dinner speaker who is suffering from stage fright says, "As soon as my teeth stop chattering, I'll begin my speech." A woman who has been having difficulty holding a job, getting along with her husband, tolerating her children, and keeping her weight down says, "I don't have but one problem—me." A man who is terrified of being drafted says, "I have a medical disability that should keep me out of the army. No guts." All of these people are helping themselves feel a little better by setting their problems in a humorous light. They do not deny what is troubling them; they simply describe it in a way that makes it less devastating.

Some psychologists use humor as a therapeutic technique. A young woman, for example, came to see a psychologist for the first time and said, "I'm really scared to be here. I know I need help, but I have heard that therapy can harm you. Some of my friends say their therapists practically destroyed them!"

"Well, you're in luck," the psychologist replied. "I have already destroyed my quota for this week." This facetious answer may not seem like the sort of thing a psychologist should say, but in fact it was very helpful. The patient laughed, her anxiety was reduced, and she got the point that her fears were exaggerated.

It is a risky procedure to kid another person when he or she is emotionally upset. Your kidding may be interpreted as a lack of sympathy for their distress. If you can make it clear, however, that you really care, and that all you are trying to do is help them see that they are going overboard, the humorous approach can be very effective.

The examples we have so far given are rather superficial, but humor can be deeply therapeutic when it amounts to an attitude of philosophical detachment. Such an attitude is rarely evident in ordinary jokes and wisecracks, but one classic Jewish story portrays it very well.

A wise old rabbi lay dying, so his disciples
lined up next to his deathbed to catch his
final words. They arranged themselves in
order from the most brilliant pupil to the
dumbest. The brilliant one bent over the
dying man and asked, "Rabbi, rabbi, what are
your final words?"
"My final words," murmured the old man, "are . . .
life is a river."
The disciple passed it on to the fellow next
to him and the phrase traveled like wildfire
down the line. "The rabbi says life is a
river . . . the rabbi says life is a river."
When it reached the oaf at the end, however, he
scratched his head. "What does the rabbi mean,
life is a river?" he asked
That question traveled back up the line.
"What does the rabbi mean life is a river . . .
what does the rabbi mean life is a river?"
When the star pupil heard it, he bent over
again. "Rabbi," he begged, for the old man
was breathing his last, "what do you mean,
life is a river?
And the rabbi, shrugging, croaked, "So it's
not a river!"

People who are like this rabbi are in touch with the soul of humor. They can recognize the meaninglessness of even their profoundest thoughts and shrug off the insufficiency of their ultimate wisdom. Such an attitude is therapeutic because it represents the humility of a person who does not have to be right to be content.

The more we see the foolishness of taking ourselves too seriously, the more able we are to use our sense of humor as a therapeutic agent. At this level, laughter becomes not a sign of mere amusement but an indication that we are maintaining a modest and balanced outlook. Our sense of humor, in other words, becomes a source of self-help—and, lord knows, we can use all the help we can get.

Summary

In this chapter we have done our best to destroy your sense of humor. By reviewing philosophical and psychological theories of the ludicrous, summarizing several research studies, and showing you how humor operates within certain cultural contexts as well as in psychotherapy, we have tried to convince you that it is a grave and serious subject deserving of scholarly scrutiny. From now on, whenever you hear a joke, we want you to analyze it. Whenever you feel like smiling, we want you to **321** wonder why. And most important, whenever you hear people laugh, we want you to package them neatly and mail them to us for immediate examination.

Class Projects
1. Have each person in the class relate one of their favorite jokes. Attempt to classify them under the following headings: nonsense humor; hostile wit; ribaldry; philosophical humor; political or social satire; sick humor; ethnic jokes. Some stories will be difficult to classify; some will fit into two or more categories. When you have arranged them as well as you can, however, try to see what your class's favorite categories reveal about your anxieties, concerns, and outlooks on life.

2. Read and discuss the works of some of our leading national humorists: e.g. James Thurber, Woody Allen, Art Buchwald, Jules Feiffer, Ogden Nash. What makes them funny? Do they instruct us as well as amuse us? Why does each one of them appeal more to some people than to others?

3. Consider the phenomenon of self-directed laughter. How many of you are capable of laughing at yourselves? Under what circumstances are you most likely to do it? What topics do you find so touchy that you cannot laugh them off? Do you think you would profit from becoming more capable of doing it?

References
1. HARVEY MINDESS, *Laughter and Liberation* (Los Angeles: Nash, 1971).
2. JACOB LEVINE, ed. *Motivation in Humor* (New York: Atherton Press, 1975).
3. WERNER MENDEL, *Celebration of Laughter* (Los Angeles: Mara Books, 1970).
4. JEFFREY H. GOLDSTEIN and PAUL E. MCGHEE, eds. *Psychology of Humor: Theoretical Perspectives and Empirical Issues* (New York: Academic Press, 1972).
5. ANTONY CHAPMAN and HUGH FOOT, *Humor and Laughter: Theory, Research and Applications* (New York: Wiley, 1976).
6. JOHN DORIS and ELLA FIERMAN, "Humor and Anxiety," in *Motivation in Humor,* ed. Jacob Levine (New York: Atherton Press, 1969).
7. DAVID SINGER, HARRY GOLLOB and JACOB LEVINE, "Mobilization of Inhibitions and the Enjoyment of Aggressive Humor," in *Motivation in Humor,* ed. Jacob Levine (New York: Atherton Press, 1969).
8. ANTONY CHAPMAN and HUGH FOOT, *Humor and Laughter: Theory, Research and Applications* (New York: Wiley, 1976).

Suggested Readings
1. MINDESS, HARVEY. *The Chosen People?* Los Angeles: Nash, 1972.
2. FEINBERG, LEONARD. *The Secret of Humor.* Atlantic Highlands, NJ: Humanities Press, 1978.
3. MINDESS, HARVEY. *Laughter and Liberation.* Los Angeles: Nash, 1971.

Creativity

19

hile modern civilization has placed a high value on creativity for several centuries, psychologists have made it an area of study only in recent years. The creative act is difficult to pin down. For that reason, perhaps, it was virtually ignored both by researchers and theorists until the last few decades. Occasional observations were made by sages like Freud and Jung, but the vast majority of psychologists simply turned their attention to other things.

Now, a growing body of data suggests that creativity can be subjected to psychological study. Research has been undertaken to discover what inspires creative geniuses and to learn what would help us all become more creative. First-person accounts of creative achievement have also proven enlightening.

In this chapter, we will present a survey of theories and findings about creativity in the arts and sciences. We will look at the nature of the creative person, the creative process, and the creative experience. Finally, we will have a word to say about creativity in the classroom.

If we manage to handle this task in a creative fashion, perhaps we will leave you not only informed but also inspired. Having studied creativity in others, you may feel inclined to become more creative yourself.

The Creative Person in the Arts

A prime example of the creative person in our culture is the artist. Painter, sculptor, composer, poet, novelist, dramatist: these people seem to command a high degree of creativity. Indeed, their lifework depends on it. Studying them, therefore, would appear to be a good way of learning about the creative personality.

Is there, in fact, a definable artistic personality? If so, is it born or made? What enables or compels a person to become a creative artist? What inspires him or her to produce the particular paintings, poems, music, or stories he or she composes? Art critics, historians, biographers, and philosophers have pondered these intriguing questions. Psychologists too have tried to answer them.

Frank Barron and his associates at the University of California have conducted studies of artistic personalities.[1,2] In one of their projects, they gave a group of professional writers (56 men and women who had attained distinction as poets, novelists, and nonfiction authors) a battery of psychological tests. In addition, they explored the writers' family backgrounds, their styles of living, their habits, and their beliefs. The writers' behavior was also directly observed by the investigating team. From the data they collected, Barron came to the following conclusions:

1) As a group, creative writers have a high degree of intelligence. They all possess a high, but not necessarily phenomenally high, IQ. In order to be a successful creative writer, then, it seems that one must have superior intelligence. Exceptionally superior intelligence, however, does not appear to make much difference.

2) Creative writers value intellectual and cognitive matters. They like to use their brains, to discuss philosophical issues. They are concerned, in particular, with ultimate questions such as the essence of human nature, the goals of humanity, and the relation of human beings to the cosmos.

3) They value their independence. They tend to be strong-minded individuals who believe in themselves and resist direction from others.

4) They are verbally fluent and can express their ideas effectively.

5) They enjoy esthetic impressions. They are tuned in to beauty, rhythm, grace, and style, not only in literature but in music, art, and life as a whole.

6) They tend to have a rich fantasy life. Not only do they dream profusely, but they report frequent mystical experiences: seeing visions, hearing voices, feeling presences that cannot be explained.

7) Their motivation for writing is high enough to withstand criticism, failure, poverty, rejection, and self-doubt. Most of the people Barron studied had endured long periods of privation and failure. They had not attained status easily. Despite the hardships they had known, however, they had not abandoned their creative goals.

8) As a group, they are both "more sane and more insane" than the average person. They are keenly aware of personal and social problems that the average person denies or ignores, yet they also entertain fantastic notions that would normally be taken to indicate a divorce from reality.

Some of Barron's findings are surprising. They suggest that qualities quite different from what we think of as "normal" are common among creative people. Not only does the creative person have a stubborn enough belief in his or her calling to reject the opinion of others, but he or she is receptive to fantasy experiences that many would find odd or bizarre.

Aspects of Barron's data call forth the venerable notion that creative genius is related to madness. Many great writers, painters, and musicians were in fact tempestuous, eccentric individuals. The phenomenon of inspiration itself is an unusual, mind-blowing experience. As a result, there has long been a point of view that holds that artistic geniuses are generally very disturbed personalities.

Sigmund Freud's views

catharsis

getting relief from emotional problems by expressing them fully

In a series of essays, Sigmund Freud took the position that the artist suffers neurotic conflicts that are projected into his or her work. Freud saw art as a kind of **catharsis** by means of which the troubled person releases emotional tension and gains recognition in the process. In a study of Dostoevsky, for example, Freud examined the Russian novelist's fascination with violent, murderous characters.[3] This fascination ran through Dostoevsky's works, culminating in his final masterpiece, *The Brothers Karamazov*. In this story, a lecherous, miserly father is murdered and each of his sons is suspected of the crime. Freud suggested that Dostoevsky's motivation for creating the story came from the fact that his own father was murdered when the writer was still an adolescent. (The elder Dostoevsky was, in fact, a lecherous, miserly man who was killed by his serfs.) According to Freud, this tragic event set up a lifelong guilt complex in the novelist, for as a boy he must have wanted to see his father dead and yet must have felt terrible when the deed was actually done. Freud's analysis maintains that Dostoevsky spent the rest of his life trying to discharge his guilt and resolve his mixed feelings through his writing.

Freud's view of art as catharsis has led to many studies of writers, painters, and composers in which the attempt is made to track down the

Figure 19.1: The Cry, *by Edvard Munch*

personal problems that motivate their work. Understandably, many artists have opposed this view, claiming that it undermines our appreciation of art and degrades the creative process. Regardless of these objections, however, most psychologists agree with Freud that personal conflicts of one sort or another frequently find expression in works of art.

The famous Norwegian painter, Edvard Munch (1863–1944), wrote, "Disease, insanity, and death were the angels which attended my cradle and since then have followed me throughout my life." His powerful painting, *The Cry,* (Figure 19.1) seems an apt expression of the inner torment that was a frequent part of his experience.[4]

C. G. Jung's views

C. G. Jung, on the other hand, took a very different stand on creativity. The creative artist, he maintained, is a kind of prophet who foresees the direction in which a society is moving and expresses it in his or her work. Essentially a very sensitive individual whose antennae pick up the signals in the air which the rest of us cannot decipher, the artist keenly feels the unconscious needs of the time. According to Jung, he or she puts into words or pictures the feelings that others are dimly aware of but cannot yet clearly express.

In *Brave New World,* a novel written in 1932, Aldous Huxley correctly foresaw both the technical accomplishments and the dehumanizing effects of the scientific age in which we live today.[5] He conceived of the world of the future as a place in which test-tube babies have become a major industry, not to help parents who are unable to produce a child in the normal way, but to provide scientifically designed citizens for a totally controlled society. It sounds like an ominous forecast, but there are those who believe we are moving steadily in that direction.

A third view

alienation

feeling alone and isolated, cut off from meaningful contact with other people

The two views—the artist as neurotic and the artist as prophet—are not necessarily mutually exclusive. It is often the case that artists are driven to express their personal problems which, in turn, reflect the problems that many people are experiencing as well. There is also a third view that deserves attention. J. Middleton Murry, a brilliant literary scholar, wrote, "An artist, great or small, works for the salvation of his own soul above all other things." To translate this statement into psychological language, we may say that in their creative works artists are frequently trying to find solutions to their problems, to arrive at a level of understanding that will give them peace of mind.

T. S. Eliot, one of the greatest poets of the modern age, clearly illustrates all three views mentioned above. In *The Waste Land,* his major poem, he profoundly expressed the sense of **alienation** and meaninglessness that was to become a hallmark of our modern era. The poem was written in 1921, yet it rendered a view of life that was only to become commonly held thirty or forty years later.

April is the cruellest month, breeding
Lilacs out of the dead land, mixing
Memory and desire, stirring
Dull roots with spring rain.[6]

A feeling of desolation, of loss of faith and hope in humankind, pervades the poem. Jung woud certainly have said that this is an example of the artist

T. S. Eliot.

foretelling a state of mind that many people would experience in years to come.

Ironically, however, Eliot himself had something to say about the writing of *The Waste Land* that lends support to Freud's position. "Various critics have done me the honor to interpret the poem in terms of the contemporary world. . . . To me it was only the relief of a personal and wholly insignificant grouse against life; it is just a piece of rhythmical grumbling."[7] Perhaps he is being too modest, but the fact is that *The Waste Land* was composed while Eliot was recuperating from a nervous breakdown for which he had been sent away to a sanitarium. It seems quite clear, therefore, that at least part of the desolation he pictured in the poem was due to his own personal problems.

It is the progression of Eliot's writing, finally, that appears to support Murry's view of the artist working for the salvation of his soul. *Ash Wednes-*

day, a poem he wrote in 1930, ends with these lines:

> Blessed sister, holy mother, spirit of the fountain, spirit of the garden,
> Suffer us not to mock ourselves with falsehood
> Teach us to care and not to care
> Teach us to sit still
> Even among these rocks,
> Our peace in His will
> And even among these rocks
> Sister, mother
> And spirit of the river, spirit of the sea,
> Suffer me not to be separated
> And let my cry come unto Thee.

Like a prayer, the poem expresses Eliot's search for salvation and peace of mind. It was a search which ended happily with his gradual but complete acceptance of the Anglican faith.

On a lesser scale, of course, artistic creativity can be little more than a pleasant enhancement of one's ordinary routine. It can also be the practicing of a craft in which one is unusually proficient. For artists who devote their lives to their creative pursuits, however, it sometimes amounts to an awesome, life-or-death commitment.

The Creative Person in the Sciences

Creativity extends to other fields than the arts. Science, for example, attracts creative geniuses, too. Are the people responsible for important scientific achievements characterized by any particular set of attributes? Anne Roe, Raymond Cattell, Frank Barron, and other psychologists have conducted studies designed to answer this question. They have tested, interviewed, and given questionnaires to leading scientists and have analyzed the biographical descriptions of former scientific giants. By these means, they have tried to discern the qualities that typify creative scientists.

In his book, *Creative Person and Creative Process*,[2] Barron summarizes their findings.

If we list the traits found in one study after another, this unified picture of the productive scientist emerges:

1) High ego strength and emotional stability

2) Strong need for independence and autonomy

3) High degree of control of impulse

4) Superior general intelligence

5) Liking for abstract thinking . . . comprehensiveness and elegance in explanation

6) High personal dominance . . . forcefulness of opinion

7) Rejection of conformity pressures in thinking

8) Detached attitude in interpersonal relations

9) Special interest in . . . pitting oneself against the unknown

10) Liking for order and exactness with an interest in the challenge . . . of disorder.

The results are not surprising. They portray the creative scientist as a highly intelligent, controlled but forceful person who is more interested in his or her work than social activity or "having a good time." Creative scientists are revealed as essentially nonconformist with a strong belief in themselves and their own powers of judgment. The popular image of the dedicated scientist is supported by Barron's research. Clearly, however, the "mad scientist" that lurid fiction describes at times is not a valid image.

A contemporary Nobel-prize winning biologist, Max Delbruck, sees himself and his associates in a more picturesque and surprising light. Leading scientists, he told a UCLA audience in 1972, are sometimes childlike in their naivete and frequently ill-informed about world affairs. Absorbed in their work, they neglect families and friends. Laypeople are prone to consider scientists much more intelligent than they in fact are. The major quality that distinguishes them, according to Delbruck, is an obsessive, untiring preoccupation with the scientific problems with which they are involved. Admittedly, they are capable of perceiving relations and of reasoning in a way that the nonspecialist can follow only with difficulty. Delbruck asserts, however, that their achievements are due less to brilliance than to dogged perseverance.

Whether Delbruck's observations are more compelling than Barron's, or vice versa, remains to be determined. Biographical accounts of famous scientists like Albert Einstein, however, seem to indicate that both are valid. People who knew him well have described Einstein as a complex mixture of brilliance and naivete, intellectual independence and nonconformity, kindness mixed with inability to sustain close relationships with many people, and a lifelong, obsessive preoccupation with relativity theory.[9] The same qualities appear among other creative geniuses in the realm of science. Depending on their biographers' bias, they can be pictured equally well as unusually wonderful people or as peculiar neurotics.

Albert Einstein.

The Creative Process in the Sciences

As legend has it, Karl Friedrich Gauss, a mathematical genius, performed a neat trick of arithmetical ingenuity when he was only six. The children in his class had been taught to add. As an exercise, their teacher had asked them to add all the numbers from one to ten. As the other children plodded along, figuring $1 + 2 = 3 + 3 = 6 + 4 = 10$, little Gauss announced, "The sum is 55." The astonished teacher asked him how he had arrived at the answer so quickly. He pointed out that in the series, $1 + 2 + 3 + 4 + 5 + 6 + 7 + 8 + 9 + 10$, the two end numbers always equal 11. Thus, $1 + 10 = 11$, $2 + 9 = 11$, $3 + 8 = 11$, $4 + 7 = 11$, and $5 + 6 = 11$. Gauss had seen that there were five pairs equalling eleven and had deduced that five elevens make 55.

This feat can be called a creative achievement, for the child who executed it departed from the conventional method he had been taught. He perceived a pattern of relationships his classmates had failed to notice and utilized this pattern to solve the assigned problem more quickly than anyone else. The feat highlights what may be the essence of the creative process—perceiving a pattern in events that other people fail to recognize. In its simplicity, however, it does not fully represent the creative process at a more advanced level of operation.

Archimedes, the Greek philosopher, was ordered to solve a vexing problem by Hiero, the king of Syracuse. The king had received a beautiful crown, supposedly of pure gold, but he suspected that it was adulterated with silver. He asked Archimedes to determine the purity of the metal without marring the crown by scratching its surface or cutting it up. Archimedes pondered long and hard, but he could not come up with a way to test the metal. Then, as the story goes, he took a hot bath to relax. The moment he immersed himself in the water, the solution occurred to him. Leaping out of the tub stark naked, he ran down the road to the palace, exclaiming, "Eureka! I have it! I have the answer!"

Now what did the philosopher perceive? Those who know the story (or who are themselves ingenious thinkers) will recall that water rises as a body is immersed in it. Not only does it rise, of course, but it rises a certain distance proportionate to the volume of the body. What Archimedes saw, as he lay in his bath, was the fact that he could immerse the crown in water and, by measuring the volume of water displaced, determine the exact amount of material in the crown. Then, by weighing the crown, he could easily tell if it was pure gold, since the weight of gold per unit volume was already known (or could be determined very simply).

This achievement illustrates the creative process in its full-fledged form. It begins with a perplexing problem and ends with an elegant solution that can be applied to analogous problems as well. In between, the process itself appears to consist of several stages. These stages have been named and described as follows:

Preparation: in this first stage of the creative process one ponders the problem, refers to whatever knowledge one can accumulate on the matter, and tries to solve it logically and systematically.

Incubation: one becomes fatigued if the preceding effort fails and attention is temporarily shifted to other things; yet the problem continues to be a preoccupation.

Illumination: in a sudden flash of insight, occurring when one least expects it, the solution becomes clear.

Verification: then one spends some time working out the details or the specific steps that would have to be taken, but by this stage one is sure that the answer is at hand.

Henri Poincaré, the great French mathematician, described the incubation and illumination stages of the process in recounting how he made certain mathematical discoveries.

> Just at this time, I left Caen, where I was living, to go on a geologic excursion. . . . The incidents of the travel made me forget my mathematical work. Having reached Coutances, we entered an omnibus to go someplace or other. At the moment when I put my foot down on the step, the idea came to me, without anything in my former thoughts seeming to have paved the way for it, that the transformations I had used to define the Fuchsian functions were identical with those of non-Euclidian geometry. I did not verify the idea; I should not have had time as, upon taking my seat in the omnibus, I went on with a conversation already commenced, but I felt a perfect certainty. On my return to Caen, for conscience' sake, I verified the result at my leisure. Then I turned my attention to the study of some arithmetical questions without much success. . . . Disgusted with my failure, I went to spend a few days at the seaside and thought of something else. One morning, walking on the bluff, the idea came to me, with just the same characteristics of brevity, suddenness, and immediate certainty, that the arithmetic transformations of indefinite ternary quadratic forms were identical with those of non-Euclidian geometry. . . . Most striking is this appearance of sudden illumination, a manifest sign of long, unconscious, prior work.[10]

The Creative Process in the Arts

The process of artistic creativity is, in some respects, as varied as the poets, painters, and composers who embody it, but certain basic features tend to reappear in all accounts. In the creative arts, as in the sciences, a close collaboration of conscious effort and unconscious inspiration seems to characterize the process.

Mozart's melodies, it has been said, came to him as if by magic, while Beethoven's manuscripts give evidence that he laboriously reworked his themes. Yet both men—in company with all major artists—really meshed both inspiration and perspiration in their musical compositions. Hard work alone is not likely to result in creative accomplishments, but neither is improvisation alone. A combination of labor and fantasy, the experience of carrying the work and of being carried by it, appears to be most characteristic of the creative process.

Amy Lowell, the noted poet, puts it this way.

> Let us admit at once that a poet is something like a radio aerial—he is capable of receiving messages on waves of some sort; but he is more than an aerial, for he possesses the capacity of transmut-

ing these messages into those patterns of words we call poems. . . . A common phrase among poets is, "It came to me." So hackneyed has this become that one learns to suppress the expression with care, but really it is the best description I know of the conscious arrival of a poem. . . . The subconscious is, however, a most temperamental ally. Often he will strike work at some critical point and not another word is to be got out of him. Here is where the conscious training of the poet comes in, for he must fill in what the subsconscious has left, and fill it in as much in the key of the rest as possible. . . . This is the reason that a poet is both born and made. He must be born with a subconscious factory always working for him or he can never be a poet at all, and he must have knowledge and talent enough to putty up his holes. . . . Let no one undervalue this process of puttying; it is a condition of good poetry.[11]

In more personal detail, Robert Crichton has published a revealing essay on his writing of the novel, *The Secret of Santa Vittoria*.[12] "The only thing I ever wanted to accomplish in life," he says, "was to write a good novel." Despite this desire, for many years he refrained from sitting down to write. Then one day a friend told him the story of a small Italian town where the people had hidden one million bottles of wine from the German army during World War II. "Someone should write that," the friend said. Crichton decided to do it. He went off to Italy to collect background material. When he returned, he sat down at his desk and tried to behave like a writer should. But he could not get started. He found himself avoiding the actual writing, until, as he tells it:

There finally came a time when I could no longer find a believable excuse not to begin. I even announced the fact to my family and friends. "Tomorrow I begin." I made it easy on myself. I vowed I would write exactly one page for a week. This shouldn't frighten anyone and at the end of the week I would be like a colt let out to his first pasture.

But I couldn't do it. All day I sat at my desk and I wrote one word. "If." Toward evening I wrote the word in pencil so that it covered the entire page. The next day I wrote "So now I begin" and never got further than that. The day after I tried the reliable weather and date technique. "On a cold blustery morning in May 1943, on the sunless eastern slopes of the Apennines, spring was coming hard."

After that I quit. I rented an office away from home not to inspire creativity but to hide from those who could see me doing nothing for hours on end. . . . I came under the idea that if I could get one good opening sentence, the keynote, and get it down right, the rest of the book would unravel itself from there. . . .

One afternoon I realized I was never going to write the sentence and once I understood that I arrived at the idea of disowning art. I had become so self-conscious about style and craft that I had become incapable of reading or hearing words any longer. When I said them they sounded strange and when I put them down on paper they looked strange. I recall writing "This book begins" and then stopping because the word book looked wrong. What kind of a word was book? An indefinite word. It could be a checkbook or the Bible. Volume was better. Journal even better. "This journal begins. . . ." Too pompous. But I couldn't go back to book.

In this way the day went. It was possible to fill a wastebasket in a day and never write over four different words. I always used a clean fresh sheet for a clean fresh start. With every empty sheet there was hope and failure. On this afternoon, however, I began to write the story of Santa Vittoria in the form and style of a Dick and Jane first reader. "There is a little town on a hill called Santa Vittoria. It is in Italy. The people in the town grow grapes to make wine. . . ."

Now the pages were piling up and I felt good. It was silly, considering the manuscript was one that I would have shot someone over before allowing him to see it, and yet the feeling was real. In the end I had several hundred pages filled with one-syllable words and while I pretended to disown the pile of paper it meant a great deal to me. It was no good but at last I had something which was no good. . . .

A week later I cut the manuscript to 125 pages and in the process something strange happened to it. In the starkness of its naked simplicity the book became mysterious in tone. . . . I had the bones of a book. The problem now was to flesh out the skeleton. I was still afraid to begin but not as much as before. The first act of creation is the terrifying thing and once this is done, it now seems to me, no matter how badly, something menacing has been overcome.

Interestingly enough, Crichton went on to complete the novel and had it accepted for publica-

tion. Then, while making a few revisions the publisher had requested, he found himself rewriting the entire book once more.

> I had meant to work until lunch but when I stopped I was surprised to find out it was five o'clock and I had written 42 pages. I had no sensation of having worked hard. I intended to stop the next day but I didn't. I wrote 35 pages that day and I knew that evening I was going to redo the whole book. . . . The word I have found for the experience was *immersion*. It is something I intend to work to find again. Previously I had worked on the book and at the book but all at once I was immersed in the book. The book seemed to be carrying me instead of me pushing it. It was a very rare sensation. The book was much more real than anything else in my life then. . . . At the end of 23 days I finished a manuscript which, when published, occupied 447 reasonably tightly printed pages. The following day, while walking down Madison Avenue, I collapsed in the street.

We have quoted at length from this essay because it represents an unusually frank account of the ups and downs of the creative process: the intermingling of desire and resistance, the task of overcoming a sustained block, and the way in which, after much conscious effort, the unconscious seems to take over. Even the incident of Crichton's collapse is not unique. /Albert Einstein and other creative geniuses reportedly suffered bouts of physical breakdown after completing major enterprises. Creativity, it seems, can require an immense expenditure of energy.

The Creative Experience

A flash of insight or a sudden perception of beauty or harmony lasting no longer than a fraction of a second is sometimes referred to as a creative experience. Such an occurrence does not involve the sustained attention or the demanding labor that has been described as part of the creative process. Yet there is no reason to deny it the status of a creative event. If we knew more about such moments and what makes them happen, we would probably be closer to unraveling the mystery of creativity as a whole.

Full-fledged creative experiences, however, seem to pass through a sequence of stages that occur with predictable regularity. At first there is a sense of agitation or restlessness. After groping for a means of expression, one finally connects with one's mood; then the hidden sequence of thoughts or feelings rises to the surface. Uplifted and enlightened, one finds relief and satisfaction in the creative expression. The experience ends in exhaustion. Possibly in retrospect there is some disillusionment with the paltry results when one recalls the excitement of the experience itself.

Consider the following subjective report by a music student and amateur composer:

The only time I ever write music is when I am extremely depressed. This depression is brought on usually when I feel communications have broken down between myself and others. This lack or inability to express my feelings, or the pain of loneliness, is an important factor in my writing. It is this factor which turns me toward the piano, in search of another form of communication. I don't want to say that when I write music it is merely a therapeutic working-out of personal frustration. While this is in part true, there is much more involved: basically a love of music which dates back to my early childhood.

Going step-by-step through an account of what it is like for me to write music, as I described earlier, [it] starts out with a depressed feeling. To relieve my depression, I go to the piano and get out something dreary like Wagner and start to play. Somehow this particular time it just doesn't do it. I pound the keys furiously, then slam the piano shut. This always happens without fail as a prelude to my writing. However, it is not until this point that I decide to write. Upon making the decision, I feel elated and excited to begin.

At this point, I have a sort of ritual I go through. First I get out my composition book and two freshly sharpened pencils. Then I make a large pot of Chamomile tea with honey in it and set it on a tray by the piano. When this is done, I'm ready to start composing. I usually begin by playing some chord progressions until some combination or pattern feels good. When this happens, it's not so much like I'm creating but more like the melody is already in the piano and I'm finding it on the keyboard. I play with different patterns and rhythms until it is a true expression of what I am feeling. When this

happens, I start to put down on paper the melody which is taking shape. Sometimes I can go right through and never come to any real difficulty. Much of the time, however, I work for a couple of hours and come to an impasse. As I work and rework some passage, I become more and more frustrated. The harder I try at these points, the worse it becomes. I have found that, if I come to an impasse, the best thing to do is to discontinue my efforts and relax or get involved with some other endeavor. Most of the time it is very late, so I just go to bed. Sometimes my unconscious plays an important role. For instance, I will give up writing a piece, feeling totally thwarted, and then when I'm not thinking about it at all, a melody comes to me. I have even awakened from a sound sleep with the missing part of a song I was working on.

When I complete a song, it is a peak experience for me. I get elated. Then I play it over and over again, listening carefully and feeling exactly what the music is saying. I am pleased with both myself and the composition. When returning to play the song a day or two later, however, it usually holds little meaning for me. Rarely do I like it well enough to play it for other people.

This change in attitude about my music baffles me. It is strange that something so intense as the feelings that motivate me to compose, and the totality of involvement while composing, could turn to apathy. Perhaps the reason is that, when I am composing, I am expressing a deep emotion and the expression itself is enough to bring me satisfaction. Then later I judge the composition not on its value as a personal expression but on its merits as a piece of music, and it usually fails to measure up to what I consider good music. Maybe this is the difference between just writing music and being a Beethoven or a Mozart. [13]

While the disillusionment our composer reports seems discouraging, **337** it must be remembered that neither she nor other creative artists allow it to stop them from trying again. The essential value of creativity is in the process itself. The final result is secondary, even though one may dream of creating masterpieces.

Creativity in the Classroom

Before we leave this fascinating area of psychological inquiry, it seems appropriate to give some consideration to the problem of creativity in the classroom. Our schools and colleges have been criticized as squelchers of creativity. It has been asserted by more than one disillusioned teacher that the kind of education most of us receive discourages original thinking. Our schools, it is said, reward rote learning and conformity; they either disregard or openly punish unusual lines of thought, for the student who "marches to a different drummer" represents a threat to the comfortable **status quo.**

status quo
the way things are at the present time

As every one of us can attest from his or her experience, there is truth in these allegations. Yet school systems differ and within every school there are classrooms in which the atmosphere is more encouraging. The problem, then, for those who want to see creativity promoted in our educational institutions, is how to cultivate the spread of such a favorable atmosphere.

A study done in 1960 indicates that creative thinking is increased when students are reinforced for producing novel ideas. The experimenter, I. Maltzman, gave subjects a word-association test, but he repeated the stimulus words six times in a row, requiring a different response each time. In this way, he forced his subjects to go beyond the first associations that came to mind and create unusual ones. When these people were later given a test of creative thinking, they scored higher than a control group who had not done the word-association test.[14]

Jacob Getzels and Philip Jackson, Clark Moustakas, and E. Paul Torrance are among those psychologists and educators who have studied the matter of creativity in the classroom. Getzels and Jackson have demonstrated that highly creative children are often different, in important respects, than high-IQ children. Furthermore, while teachers reward the high-IQ child who achieves good grades, they find the creative youngster troublesome.[15] If they could be convinced to reward the highly creative child as well, our schools might produce more creative people.

Moustakas has argued that authenticity in teachers—their ability to be themselves, to trust their own judgment, to cast off their official roles and meet their students openly—encourages creativity in students.[16]

Torrance, finally, has spelled out specific ways in which creativity can be nurtured in our schools and colleges. "Success orientation," he says, "when greatly overemphasized, is inimical to creative growth because creative ways of learning involve experimentation, taking risks, making mistakes, and correcting them." Therefore, he suggests, success seeking should be muted in favor of exploring new and different ways of doing things. Besides that, "teachers should be alert to look at behavior disapproved by the norm group for signs of creative potential."[17]

If the exhortations of leaders such as these have any effect, we may look forward to school systems of the future in which creativity will receive more encouragement than it has enjoyed in the past.

A Word of Warning

The change, however, is not likely to advance very rapidly, for creativity is not just a colorful, exciting characteristic we all can applaud and appreciate. It may seem that way on the surface, but its implications—in the arts, the sciences, the schools, and in everyday life—are deeper and more disturbing than we care to admit.

The very fact that creative solutions are called for implies that present ways of doing things could be bettered. To opt for creativity, then, is to admit that the ways you and I think and feel, the ways we conduct our lives, and the standards employed by those who teach the arts and sciences or run our schools are imperfect and in need of improvement. That, unfortunately, is an admission many people are unwilling to make.

Summary

The creative person in the arts appears to be one who is strong-willed and independent, who enjoys esthetic impressions, who has a rich fantasy life, whose motivation is very high, who is in Barron's words "more sane and more insane" than the average person. High intelligence is common, but exceptionally high intelligence is not essential. The creative person in the sciences is also forceful and independent, has a high degree of self-control, superior general intelligence, a liking for abstract thinking, a detached attitude in personal relations, and a special interest in pitting him- or herself against the unknown.

The motivation for creating works of art and, perhaps to a lesser degree, achieving scientific breakthroughs is often more complicated than the artist or scientist would avow. In Freud's view, art is a kind of catharsis through which the artist achieves emotional relief. In Jung's view, the artist is a kind of prophet who foretells the direction in which a society is heading. In Max Delbruck's view, scientific achievements are due less to brilliance than to obsessive perseverance.

The essence of the creative process, in the sciences at least, lies in **339** seeing a pattern of facts that others have failed to recognize. The process typically goes through four stages: preparation, incubation, illumination, and verification. In the arts, as much perspiration as inspiration goes into the making of a masterpiece.

Creativity has not been fostered in the traditional classroom setting, but in recent years some psychologists and educators have been making suggestions for improving this unfortunate state-of-affairs.

Class Projects

1. To experience the creative process in your own mental operations, try to solve the puzzles shown in Figure 19.2.

(a)

Without lifting your pencil from the paper, draw a straight line consisting of four segments that runs through every dot in this diagram.

(b) A   EF HI KLMN   T VWXYZ
        BCD G J   OPQRS U

There is a logical reason for reproducing the alphabet in this form. What is it?

Figure 19.2

2. Think of as many uses as you can for such objects as a brick or a tin can. Offer a prize to the person in your class who comes up with the most answers and for the person who, in the opinion of the class, comes up with the most unusual answers.

3. Using the diagrams shown in Figure 19.3 as part of your picture, try to draw something that no one else in your class will think of.

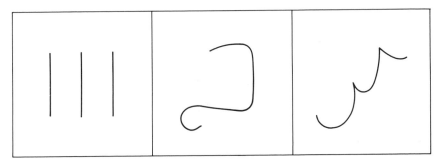

Figure 19.3

4. Close your eyes and visualize a doorway. Try to see it as clearly as possible. Then imagine yourself stepping through the doorway to whatever lies beyond it. Write down your description of the doorway and what you saw or encountered when you went through it. Let several members of your class read their accounts out loud. You should be impressed by the diversity of scenes such a simple exercise produces. It is an example of the infinite capacity of our imaginations.

5. Most of us learned, in early childhood, a particular method of making paper airplanes. We tend to repeat that method, with little variation, throughout the years. In order to exercise your creativity, try to make a paper airplane in an original manner. Keep in mind the aims that it should both fly well and look interesting. (If you are interested in pursuing this activity, get a copy of *The Great International Paper Airplane Book*, in which are reproduced prize-winning paper airplanes submitted to a contest held by *Scientific American* in 1967.)

References

1. FRANK BARRON, *Creativity and Psychological Health* (New York: Van Nostrand, 1963).

2. FRANK BARRON, *Creative Person and Creative Process* (New York: Holt, Rinehart & Winston, 1969).

3. SIGMUND FREUD, "Dostoevsky and Parricide," in *Collected Papers* (New York: Basic Books, 1959).

4. MUNCH, EDVARD, "Geschrei," in Werner Tim (ed.) *The Graphic Art of Edvard Munch*. New York Graphic Society, 1972.

5. ALDOUS HUXLEY, *Brave New World* (New York: Harper and Brothers, 1932).

6. T. S. ELIOT, *The Waste Land and Other Poems* (New York: Harcourt, Brace, 1934).

7. HARRY TROSMAN, "T. S. Eliot and the Waste Land," *Archives of General Psychiatry 30* (May 1974): pp. 709-717.

8. T. S. ELIOT, *The Waste Land and Other Poems* (New York: Harcourt, Brace, 1934).

9. PETER MICHELMORE, *Einstein: Profile of the Man* (New York: Dodd, Mead, 1962).

10. JACQUES HADAMARD, *The Psychology of Invention in the Mathematical Field* (Princeton, NJ: Princeton University Press, 1945).

11. AMY LOWELL, "The Process of Making Poetry,' in *The Creative Process*, ed. Brewster Ghiselin (New York: Mentor, 1952).

12. ROBERT CRICHTON, "On the Secret of Santa Vittoria," in *Afterwords*, ed. Thomas McCormack (New York: Harper and Row, 1968).

13. JUDITH KAMPEN, UCLA student, quotation from a class project, 1970.

14. I. MALTZMAN, "On the Training of Originality," *Psychiatric Review 67*, (1960):

15. JACOB GETZELS and PHILIP JACKSON, "Family Environment and Cognitive Style," in *Explorations in Creativity*, ed. Ross L. Mooney and Taher A. Razik (New York: Harper and Row, 1967).

16. CLARK MOUSTAKAS, "Creativity and Conformity in Education," *Explorations in Creativity*, ed. Ross L. Mooney and Taher A. Razik (New York: Harper and Row, 1967).

17. E. PAUL TORRANCE, "Nurture of Creative Talents," in *Explorations in Creativity*, ed. Ross L. Mooney and Taher A. Razik (New York: Harper and Row, 1967).

Suggested Readings

1. GHISELIN, BREWSTER. *The Creative Process*. New York: Mentor, 1952.

2. GOERTZEL, V. and GOERTZEL, MILDRED G. *Cradles of Eminence*. Boston: Little, Brown, 1962.

3. MAIER, N. R. F. *Problem Solving and Creativity in Individuals and Groups*. Monterey, CA: Brooks/Cole, 1970.

4. JOSEF P. HODIN, *Edvard Munch* (New York: Praeger, 1972).

5. STORR, ANTHONY. *The Dynamics of Creation*. New York: Atheneum, 1972.

ESP: Fact or Fiction?

20

mental telepathy

transfer of thought from
one mind to another

clairvoyance

seeing or hearing
something out of the
range of one's sense
organs, sometimes
thousands of miles away

precognition

knowing something is
going to happen before it
happens

ouched in the head," is how most psychologists have judged those who dabble in the occult. Mind-reading, spiritualism, astrology, and the like have seemed to attract the "lunatic fringe" of our society. In 1971, however, on the Apollo 14 mission to the moon, one experiment was concerned with what is now known as "extrasensory perception" (ESP). During that flight, astronaut Mitchell attempted to establish telepathic contact with four persons on earth. Mitchell has been quoted as saying that the results of the experiment exceeded all expectations.

ESP is beginning to command a rising level of interest in scientific circles. Not only in this country but also in Russia and elsewhere, the number of scholarly publications on the subject has increased dramatically. Yet even today in many departments of psychology, ESP is laughed off as the playground of self-deluded fools.

This chapter will present an objective account of the evidence for and against ESP. The major subdivisions to be considered are **mental telepathy, clairvoyance, precognition, psychokinesis,** and **spiritualism.** After reading the material we have collected, you may wish to express your own views on the matter. On the other hand, you may decide to contact some friendly spirits and see what they have to say.

Mental Telepathy

psychokinesis

mental control of
physical events

spiritualism

communication with
the dead

Mental telepathy is the transfer of thought from one person to another without overt communication. Certainly the most investigated form of ESP, it is also the most believable. Many people who make no claim to extraordinary mental powers presume to have had experiences of this nature. "I was just thinking of him when he rang me up on the telephone," they will say. Or, "My friend and I have the very same thoughts at the very same moment." Or, "I knew exactly what she was going to say before she said a word."

These events, they assume, give evidence of mental telepathy. If alternative explanations are offered—that the events were mere coincidences or that their memory has distorted the actual sequence—they strongly object. The happenings seem too convincing to be dismissed so lightly. Such experiences are listed by ESP investigators under the heading, "spontaneous data."

Spontaneous data includes reports of strange experiences from everyday life and statements by people who claim to possess some kind of unusual mental power. The trouble with such information, from a scientific standpoint, is that it depends on the claimants' memory and truthfulness. Most reputable psychologists consider it unreliable. There are many reasons, they say, why people may wish to believe, or to have others believe, that they have had extraordinary mental experiences. Scientific investigators therefore insist that formal proof be produced before mental telepathy can be accepted as a fact.

The following events were reported in a book published in England shortly after World War II.[1]

1. Only this summer [1944] a naval officer told me of one of his men who came to him in great agitation, asking to be put on shore at the first possible opportunity, as he knew positively that his home had been wrecked by bombs and his eldest child killed. No information from ordinary sources had reached him, but his impression proved to be true.

2. A friend and I were picnicking in a Sussex hayfield, having left the car at the side of the road. Presently, we heard footsteps approaching, and the tapping of a stick, first on the roat, and then against the metal part of the car. At that moment, I became aware of a battlefield scene and of a young man wearing a trench helmet. In a few minutes, an elderly man came and leaned on the gate which led into our field. I wondered if there would be any connection between him and the battlefield scene which flashed into my mind. So I spoke to him and found that he was a blind policeman, retired, and living in the neighborhood. I asked him if he had served in the war and he said that he was too old, but that a young son of his had been killed in the war, and he had a photograph of him at home in which he wore a trench helmet. I did not tell him of my impression. It seemed strange to me that the mere passing of this man along the road should bring to my mind such a scene; unless, possibly, he had been thinking of his son at the time.

Such accounts are taken by some as evidence of mental telepathy and clairvoyance, while to others they seem mere coincidences.

Looking for proof

The search for formal scientific proof began in 1882 when the British Society for Psychical Research was founded by a group of scholars from Cambridge University. They decided that: "The time had come to set up a learned society to examine those faculties of man, real or supposed, that appeared inexplicable to science."[2] The presidents of the society have included a prime minister, three Nobel laureates, ten fellows of the Royal Society, and many physicists and philosophers.

The work of the British Society has inspired many other researchers. From 1932 to the present, J. B. Rhine and his associates at Duke University have been studying extrasensory perception under controlled experimental conditions. They have systematically explored the phenomena of mental telepathy, clairvoyance, precognition, and psychokinesis. In the pages that follow, we will give you several examples of their studies.

One of Rhine's main procedures uses a pack of so-called ESP cards. These specially manufactured cards are marked with one of five designs: a circle, a square, a cross, a star, or a set of wavy lines. Thousands of subjects have been studied. Typically, two persons participate at a time: a sender and a receiver. They are either separated by an opaque screen, seated in different rooms, or housed in different buildings. The sender (in mental telepathy experiments) turns up one card at a time and concentrates on the design in an attempt to communicate the image to the receiver. The receiver, notified automatically when each card is turned up, tries to guess the image the sender is seeing. The guesses are recorded. After a number of tries—sometimes as many as several thousand—the results are statistically evaluated.

The probability of a correct guess made by chance alone is one in five, or twenty hits in a hundred tries. It is a relatively simple matter to weigh these odds against the actual scores achieved, and Rhine's results have consistently exceeded chance expectations.

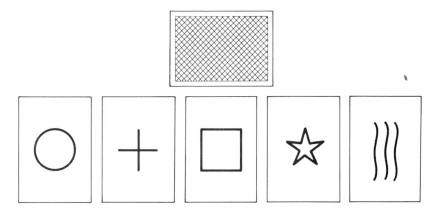

His first results, published in 1934, contained the record of 85,000 card-calling tries. The overall score averaged 28 hits instead of 20 out of 100 guesses. Occasionally, he has had subjects make as many as 25 correct guesses in a row. The odds against these scores occurring by chance alone are astronomical.[3]

Rhine's procedures appear to rule out the possibility of the sender transmitting information to the receiver in any customary way. The existence of mental telepathy (and, as we will soon see, clairvoyance) would seem, therefore, to have been proven. For several decades, however, doubt was expressed by many psychologists about the validity of his statistics, the foolproofness of his system, and even his personal honesty. Rhine himself considered the following alternative explanations for his findings: chance, fraud, incompetence, unconscious sensory perception, and rational inference. Although he came to the conclusion that he had eliminated these possibilities, critics have attacked his work on these very issues.

To check for errors, other experimenters have tried to duplicate Rhine's experiments. The results are mixed. It is possible to read the literature and find support for whichever position you are inclined to take. For example, when Rhine's experiments were repeated by W. S. Cox at Princeton University, no evidence for ESP was found. On the other hand, Rhine's results have been duplicated, at times even more impressively, in research centers around the world. Many skeptical, tough-minded scientists have therefore come to believe in mental telepathy and clairvoyance. E. J. Eysenck says,

> Unless there is a gigantic conspiracy involving some thirty university departments all over the world, and several hundred highly respected scientists in various fields, many of them originally hostile to the claims of the psychical researchers, the only conclusion the unbiased observer can come to must be that there does exist a small number of people who obtain knowledge, existing either in other people's minds or in the outer world, by means as yet unknown to science.[4]

Demonstrating in the lab that mental telepathy exists was a giant step forward. Discovering the laws that govern its operation, however, has turned out to be an even more difficult task. From the studies that have been done, it seems that boredom and worry reduce one's ability to use telepathic powers. Enthusiasm, on the other hand, increases it. Researchers, however, have not been able to create the precise conditions that will guarantee how well any particular person will perform. Telepathy remains a capricious phenomenon that flickers on and off rather unpredictably.

Other experiments in telepathy

Thelma Moss, an ingenious psychologist at UCLA, has studied the conditions governing various forms of ESP. From anecdotal reports, she identified several factors that were almost always involved. First, the sender and the receiver were usually related. They may have been husband and wife, parent and child, or close friends. Rarely were they strangers. Second, the sender was usually in a highly charged emotional situation. A life may have been in danger or the sender may have been engaged in some other highly stimulating experience. At the same time, the receiver was usually in a relaxed state of mind, sometimes sleeping, sometimes dozing.

Moss designed a series of experiments in which these conditions could be evaluated.[5,6] Pairs of subjects were selected, some of whom were related, others of whom were strangers. Relaxed on a comfortable bed, the receivers free-associated while the senders were exposed to emotionally arousing stimuli (e.g., in an episode labelled "fear," the senders heard an eerie musical composition interlaced with heartbeats, groans, and gasps, climaxing with a scream while a slide of a venomous snake was flashed on a screen). The results were astounding. The receivers' free-associations reflected the senders' experience much more often than one would expect by chance alone. At times the correlation was uncanny. One sender, for example, was exposed to slides depicting Disneyland rides—cable cars, Matterhorn, Mad Teacup, etc. The receiver reported, "So many things. The Swiss Alps, especially the Matterhorn. And those little cable cars. Then ice cream cones, little boys. But mostly the Matterhorn." When another sender was viewing slides of changing colors, his receiver reported, "I see the colors of the flag, but not really the flag . . . just stripes of red, white, and blue, then all colors . . . red speckled with yellow."

One condition presumed to be important did not prove significant. The closely related pairs did no better than the strangers.

Moss has carried out several variations on this design. She has used groups of senders and receivers rather than single pairs. She has had her subjects separated by as much as 6,000 miles. Regardless of the variations, her results have been uniformly better than chance. In the course of her investigations she has unearthed some provocative data. She has repeatedly verified her original finding that, in the laboratory situation at least, strangers can communicate telepathically just as well as close relatives. Also, she has found that, of all types of subjects, highly creative people (e.g., professional artists) do far better than any other group both in sending and receiving telepathic communication.

Accounts of spontaneous data from daily life indicate that the majority of such experiences occur as dreams. Now that science has devised ways to study sleep and dreams with **electroencephalographic equipment,** these occurrences, too, are being studied in the lab.

electroencephalo-graphic equipment
equipment to monitor and record brain waves

For the past ten years, at Maimonides Hospital in Brooklyn, New York, Montague Ullman and Stanley Krippner have been conducting studies of telepathy in dreams. Their subjects are asked to sleep in the laboratory for about a week. Each night, electrodes are placed on the subject's head to obtain physiological indications that the subject is dreaming.

Dream laboratory at Brooklyn's Maimonides Hospital.
The subject is hooked up to an electroencephalograph.
The connection between Alpha waves and extrasensory
perception is being observed.

When the subject begins to dream, another person (the sender) concentrates on a randomly selected painting. He or she attempts to "send" this image to the subject for the duration of the dream. Once the dream is over, the sleeper is awakened and asked to describe what he or she dreamed. This sequence is repeated each time the subject falls into a dream state; only one painting, however, is used for an entire night. In the morning, the subject is asked to summarize all the dreams he or she had that night.

After this phase of the experiment is concluded, the subjects' dream reports and the actual paintings used are given to research assistants to assess how alike they are. Their assessments are statistically evaluated. In a number of these experiments, results well above the level of chance were achieved. This has led the experiments to conclude that their subjects have indeed received the image sent to them telepathically.[7]

Clairvoyance and Precognition

Clairvoyance refers to the ability to see things that are not in sight; precognition means knowing something is going to happen before it happens. Both are forms of ESP that have been reported by psychic societies and individuals throughout history. Neither, however, has been given much credence by hard-headed rationalists.

Early in his career, Rhine reported an experiment which, as he says, "was something of a turning point or a milestone" with respect to scientific evidence of clairvoyance. Here is his description of it.

Pratt and I had as our principal subject a student, Hubert E. Pearce, Jr. Pearce was instructed to try to identify the order of cards in a pack of twenty-five, with the card faces hidden from him. He knew the five symbols or suits (star, circle, square, cross, and waves) that were on the cards, and either recorded his response or called it aloud. His scoring was sufficiently high to indicate the operation of something more than chance. Then the test procedure was modified to increase the safeguards against error or sensory cues. The cards were completely screened from view and even removed to another room; but even after these precautions were added, Pearce (and other later subjects like him) continued to score at a rate of success that was significantly above that to be expected from chance alone. . . . Chance alone would give, in a series of sufficient length, an approximate average of five hits or 20 percent. Pearce, an outstanding subject, would average from six to eleven hits per run (that is, from 24 to 44 percent) at an experimental session. Several times, however, in runs of twenty-five trials, he got a score of zero; that is, he missed every card in the deck. Once, too . . . he scored a perfect run of twenty-five successive hits. . . .

In this experiment . . . the aim was to set up conditions thoroughly adequate to exclude all the factors that could produce extrachance

scores except ESP. Pratt [Rhine's assistant] handled the target pack of cards in one building, while Pearce was located in a reading cubicle across the quadrangle in the stacks at the back of the Duke University Library. Thus he was situated approximately 100 yards away from the cards.

At the start of each session, before Pearce departed for his cubicle, the two men synchronized their watches. After he left, Pratt shuffled the cards and placed the pack at a left-hand corner of his table. At the agreed-upon starting time Pratt removed the top card and, without looking at it, placed it face down on a book in the middle of the table and left it there for a minute. He then removed the card, still keeping it inverted, to the right-hand corner of the table and immediately picked up the next card and put it on the book. . . .

Two runs through the pack were made per day and the total series consisted of 12 runs or 300 trials. The number of hits expected on a theory of pure chance was 20 percent of 300 or 60 hits. Pearce obtained a total of 119 hits. . . . A score as large as this one of 119 hits in 300 trials would be expected to occur by chance only once in a quadrillion (1,000,000,000,000,000) of such experiments; we knew, therefore, that every reasonable man would, without further argument, join us in dismissing the chance explanation.[8]

Arthur Koestler, an eminent scholar, reports an equally impressive series of experiments that seem to prove the case for precognition.

In 1934, Dr. Soal, then a lecturer in mathematics at University College, London, read about

Rhine's experiments and tried to repeat them. From 1934 to 1939 he experimented with 160 persons who made altogether 128,350 guesses with ESP cards. The result was nil—no significant deviation from chance expectation was found. . . . Soal was on the point of giving up in disgust when a fellow researcher, Whately Carrington, suggested to him that he check his reports for "displaced" guesses—that is, for hits not on the target card but on the card which was turned up before it. . . . Soal reluctantly undertook the tedious labor of analyzing his thousands of columns of experimental protocols and was both rewarded and disconcerted to find that one of his subjects, Basil Shackleton, had scored consistently on the next card ahead—i.e., precognitively—with results so high that chance had to be ruled out.

Soal now set out on a new series of experiments with Basil Shackleton. . . . The results were statistically so significant that the Professor of Philosophy at Cambridge, C. D. Broad, felt moved to write: "There can be no doubt that the events described happened and they were correctly reported; that the odds against chance coincidence piled up to billions to one; and the nature of the events, which involved both telepathy and precognition, conflicts with one or more of the basic limiting principles of physical science."[9]

If in fact clairvoyance and precognition do occur, no matter how infrequently, then, as Professor Broad implies, our current scientific explanations of the world are challenged to the very core. How can certain persons receive, with their mind's eye, objects and events out of their range of vision? How can these or other persons foretell events that have not yet taken place? Either the human mind is a far stranger instrument than we imagine or our concepts of time and space need radical revision.

Physicists and Psychics

In *The Roots of Coincidence*, Koestler takes pains to show that leading physicists, without any reference to ESP, have already radically revised their ideas of space and time.

Einstein's theory of relativity, to which Koestler makes reference, disproves many long-held beliefs about the universe. With illustrations both humble and sophisticated, and with brilliant mathematical reasoning, Einstein proved that both space and time are relative. In certain circumstances, he found, their properties are not at all what common sense expects.

Koestler's explanation for calling on physicists like Einstein is to make one particular point. The fact that clairvoyance and precognition require us to revise our common-sense view of the world should not be held against them. Modern physics has also required, and is already supplying, such a revision. Perhaps what we need to do is learn to think in new ways.

Perhaps. But then again, perhaps we need to be on guard against the seductive attractions of ESP. Those scientists and scholars who remain unimpressed by psychic research point out that many experiments have failed to find any evidence of mental telepathy, let alone clairvoyance and precognition, while many so-called sensitives have eventually been shown up as frauds. The amazing ways in which stage magicians can fool us is well-known, they observe, so who is to say that we are not being tricked by the proponents of ESP? The notion that

underlies all this criticism is that no claim of evidence for ESP is accept-   **351**
able if a more natural explanation can be produced.

Psychokinesis

The nonscientific literature has always included reports of very weird happenings. Pictures fall off the wall and clocks stop at the moment of somebody's death. Furniture moves about the room and crockery shatters without being touched. These phenomena are thought to be the work of occult forces constellated by certain spiritual conditions.

Scientific psychologists, as we would expect, have been loath to take these reports seriously. Such an eminent person as C. G. Jung did believe in them, however, and researchers at Duke University have engaged in experiments related to such happenings. Since the underlying factor appears to be a matter of mental states affecting physical objects, they have carried out a series of studies to see if people can influence the throw of a set of dice by mental concentration alone.

The dice are thown either singly or in lots of six, first by hand from containers and later by rotating cages. The effects of possibly faulty dice are eliminated by having the subject concentrate on each of the faces in turn. In more than a half million throws so far recorded, the willed face has come up significantly more often than chance would allow.

"My sister, Anna, was psychic from early childhood. We had an agreement that whoever passed over first would attempt to give the other some signal of survival. My sister died unexpectedly and her passing was a great loss to me. We had been close friends from early childhood. On my return from her funeral, I entered my office at the college where I was to hold a conference with a senior on the subject of William James' *Varieties of Religious Experience*. It was a warm, sunny afternoon in mid-October. As the student sat down in the chair by my desk I suggested that I tell her something about the religious experiences of my sister. The moment I uttered the word 'Anna' there was a report as though a small pistol had been fired, and the inkwell was cut down through the center. The student, apparently in great fright, arose and backed away, asking what had happened. She was so upset that she asked to be excused and allowed to return another day. I took the inkwell and washed it. Returning to the office, I had a vivid experience which I have had but twice in my life. A voice said distinctly, "Is this clear-cut evidence?" Then I recalled that I had said to my sister in years past, "If you ever give evidence of survival, make it clear-cut." There were no slivers of glass. The inkwell was cut so cleanly that I rubbed my hand against each side. . . ." (Dr. Ralph Harlow, as quoted in Rhine[8])

The phenomenon demonstrated in these experiments is now called psychokinesis (or PK). It implies, of course, the power of the mind to influence physical events without an intermediary action. While this possibility appeals enormously to those who favor the likelihood of magic, it is distinctly distasteful to rationalistic individuals. Mental telepathy has already become acceptable and many psychologists can begin to imagine ways to explain it. Clairvoyance and precognition seem dubious but, considering the time-space revisions most physicists accept, perhaps they will become conceivable too. Psychokinesis, however, still seems like a throwback to the age of superstition.

Spiritualism

Yet psychokinesis is not by any means the most far-out member of the ESP family. Several other things vie for that honor, the most publicized of which is the supposed existence of ghosts and other representatives of the departed. So-called mediums have long claimed the ability to contact the dead and convey their messages to the living. Ordinary people, too—as Dr. Harlow's experience (quoted above) clearly indicates—have at times seen apparitions and heard voices that they believe have come from beyond the grave. And recently the distinguished psychiatrist, Elisabeth Kübler-Ross, whose international reputation is based on her compassionate treatment of dying persons and their families, has publicly expressed her conviction that she has seen evidence of life after death.

Here at last, however—despite all these claims—even the most broad-minded scientist tends to maintain heavy skepticism. To our knowledge, at least, no respectable research has been directed at spiritualistic happenings. Most psychologists are quick to point out that reports of such events are often made by persons in confused mental states. The wish to remain in contact with one's deceased loved ones may be so great that it leads grieving people to delude themselves. Furthermore, professional mediums are regularly revealed to be charlatans, psychotics, or a combination of the two.

The Future of ESP Research

ESP is a treacherous and explosive subject. Most people experience difficulty when trying to be objective about it. Typically, we are all either believers or disbelievers. What, then, are psychologists of the future likely to do about it?

The acceptance of ESP research over the past several decades may yield some clues. When Rhine began his experiments in the 1930s, he was virtually ostracized by the profession. Now, in the 1970s, universities all over the world are conducting ESP studies. It seems safe to predict that more scientific inquiry will be undertaken in the years to come.

conceptual models
ideas or images of the
way things are

Arthur Koestler argues that modern physics itself is providing **conceptual models** whereby the possibility of ESP can be calmly contemplated. If Koestler's argument takes hold, we may assume that the rationalistic prejudice against ESP will continue to evaporate.

Suppose one facet of ESP is proven beyond any doubt, however. We **353** need not jump to the conclusion that all other facets will inevitably follow suit. It is a far cry from mental telepathy to psychokinesis, and farther yet to communication with the dead.

Naive acceptance

occultism

belief in mysterious happenings beyond human understanding

Some people today uncritically accept every form of **occultism** as valid. Astrology is a prime example. It makes the assumption that everyone born under a certain sign shares certain personality characteristics (e.g., Aquarians are calm and modest, Geminis are deceptive). Given a moment's thought, that assumption must be seen as foolish. Consider the millions of people who are born under the same astrological sign. Some are born into wealth, others into poverty. Some are raised by doting parents, others by neglectful ones. Some are highly intelligent, others are feeble-minded. Some are conditioned from childhood to be economical and hard-working, others are encouraged by family circumstances to be lazy and self-indulgent. To believe that, despite these circumstances, some mysterious power of the stars renders all Leos, Capricorns, Virgos, and so on basically alike, seems naive. On careful examination, most psychologists believe, the characteristics ascribed to the various signs are simply those that everyone shares to greater or lesser degree.

The naiveté of uncritically accepting astrology's claims, however, is not the main issue. All of us find it hard to deal with uncertainty. It is harder still to accept responsibility for our personality traits. We are therefore prone to swallow a fatalistic explanation, such as astrology provides, and to become attracted to a creed that promises to reveal our future.

A balanced view

Like astrology, ESP as a whole inhabits the realms of wishful fantasy. It lures us away from dealing with the hard, cold facts of life. As such, it represents a haven for the immature. On the other hand, our common sense notions of reality are sadly limited. Studies of ESP, at the very least, remind us that there is more to existence than reason readily comprehends.

Gardner Murphy, a psychologist whom no one would accuse of naiveté, has long advocated ESP research.[10] To ensure, however, that such research contributes to the body of scientific knowledge, he recommends the following guidelines.

1) Experimental studies with built-in controls should be emphasized instead of informal, anecdotal reports.

2) The experiments should be carried out according to the prevailing psychological methods and the statistics used should be standard to most psychological research.

3) Experiments should be devised to quantify ESP (i.e., make it measurable and predictable).

4) Psychologists should work in collaboration with biologists, physicists, and mathematicians.

5) ESP research should be evaluated in terms of the light it sheds on the nature of science itself.

Murphy's stance comes down to that rarest of attitudes: hard-headed open-mindedness. What he suggests, in effect, is that we accept nothing uncritically, but that we also dismiss nothing just because it runs counter to our prejudices.

The roots of the controversy

Whatever the final truth of the matter, we should be aware that there are strong inner forces pulling us in both directions. Our inclination to believe that ESP exists is fed by our wish to believe in magic. If only the world were not ruled by natural laws, something in us yearns, then anything would be possible. Great accomplishments, exciting adventures, fairy-tale romance, even immortality: if ESP is true, it opens a door into the infiinte and keeps alive our poetic hope that there is more to life than working hard and growing old.

Our inclination to disbelieve, in contrast, is fed by our common fear of the unknown. The irrational and unpredictable are upsetting to our logical minds because they suggest that we cannot control our destinies. If ESP is a fraud, the skeptic in us senses, we can relax in the normal framework of an orderly universe that reason can explain.

The controversy, therefore, is not based solely on the state of the evidence. The evidence, as we have seen, is fragmentary, and it will probably be many years before it is more complete. Besides that, even scientists are not unlikely to focus on those findings that support their own beliefs and ignore or forget those findings that contradict them. Whether we choose at present, then, to call ESP fact or fiction depends as much on whether we are more susceptible to our magical wishes or to our logical faculties as it does on our serious study of the data.

Summary

In this chapter, we have presented findings and arguments regarding mental telepathy, clairvoyance, precognition, psychokinesis, and spiritualism. Some of the findings were anecdotal reports by laypersons who believed they had had extraordinary experiences. Other findings were collected in laboratories under strict experimental conditions. Arguments in favor of ESP make reference to the changing conception of time and space that physical scientists have come to accept. Arguments against ESP always rest on the conviction that it doesn't make sense. They are also buttressed by suspicion of fraud or, at the very least, self-delusion on the part of mediums, psychics, and the like. The final truth about ESP remains, however, to be determined; at this date we must admit that it is still a confusing, though terribly interesting, subject.

Class Projects

1. You may wish to conduct an experiment along the lines of Dr. Moss' work. Begin by collecting four sets of stimuli, each of which should provoke a strong emotional reaction. (You could, for example, attempt to evoke the emotions love, hate, fear, and disgust. For love, you could show slides of romantic couples, accompanied by a popular song celebrating the bliss of falling in love, and for the other emotions you could also use combinations of slides and music or sound effects.)

   Select a group of senders and a group of receivers, none of whom should know in advance what your stimuli consist of. Decide upon alternating periods of activity and relaxation—for instance, there might be four three-minute periods of stimulus separated by seven minutes of rest. Let the receivers relax in a comfortable, quiet room. Have them, at the specified intervals, attempt to "pick up" what the senders are experiencing and write down the thoughts or images that come to their minds. Meanwhile, during these specified intervals expose the senders to the stimuli you have prepared. Let the order in which you present the four sets of stimuli be chosen at random, so that nobody knows in advance which emotion will be evoked at which time. Have the senders also write down their thoughts and images as they look and listen to each set of stimuli.

   At the end of the experiment, you will have a sequence of four descriptive statements from each sender and each receiver. Have these statements transcribed and sorted. Put together all the senders' statements for interval 1 (i.e., when they were exposed to the first set of stimuli); for interval 2; for interval 3; and for interval 4. Likewise, put together all the receivers' statements for interval 1; for interval 2; for interval 3; and for interval 4.

   Now you can do two things: (a) compare the appropriate batches informally to see if any striking correspondences show up; (b) select a group of independent judges who know nothing about the experiment and have them attempt to match the senders' statements with the appropriate receivers' statements. By chance alone, the judges could be expected to correctly pair up statements from *one* of the four intervals. Calculate the results to see if the correspondences perceived are significantly better than chance.

2. As a contrast to the experiment outlined above, collect some samples of supposed ESP and try to find natural explanations for them. If you or one of your friends, for instance, recalls a "prophetic" dream or a strangely meaningful sequence of events, have it thoroughly described in all its details and then try to see if it can be explained without resort to supernatural forces.

3. If anyone in your community has gained a reputation as a "psychic," invite him or her to your class to discuss his or her "gift." While the aim of your meeting should be to determine the validity of the person's supposed powers, we know we don't have to remind you that, as your guest, he or she deserves to be treated with respect.

In all probability, you will find that it is very difficult to rule out (or rule in) the factuality of claimed ESP experience. Pursuing these projects, however, should sensitize you to the problems encountered by professional ESP researchers.

References

1. L. Margery Bazett, *Beyond the Five Senses* (Oxford: Blackwell, 1946).
2. Arthur Koestler, *The Roots of Coincidence* (New York: Random House, 1972).
3. J. B. Rhine, *The Reach of the Mind* (New York: Sloane, 1947).
4. H. J. Eysenck, *Sense and Nonsense in Psychology* (Hammondsworth, England: Penguin, 1958).
5. Thelma Moss and J. A. Gengerelli, "Telepathy and Emotional Stimuli," *Journal of Abnormal Psychology, 76,* (1967), pp. 341–348.
6. Thelma Moss, Alice F. Chang and Marc Levitt, "Long Distance ESP: A Controlled Study," *Journal of Abnormal Psychology, 76* (1970), pp. 288–294.
7. Montague Ullman and Stanley Krippner, *Dream Telepathy: Experiments in Nocturnal ESP* (Baltimore: Penguin, 1974).
8. J. B. Rhine, *New World of the Mind* (New York: Sloan, 1947).
9. Arthur Koestler, *The Roots of Coincidence* (New York: Random House, 1972).
10. Gardner Murphy, "Parapsychology," in *Taboo Topics*, Normal Farberow, ed. (New York: Atherton Press, 1963).

Suggested Readings

1. Chance, Paul. "Telepathy Could Be Real," *Psychology Today,* 1976, *9,* pp. 40–44.
2. Child, Irvin L. "Extrasensory Perception: A Humanistic Approach." In *Humanistic Psychology and the Research Tradition: Their Several Virtues,* Irvin Child, ed. New York: Wiley, 1973.
3. Koestler, Arthur. *The Roots of Coincidence.* New York: Random House, 1972.
4. Leshan, L. *The Medium, The Mystic and The Physicist.* New York: The Viking Press, 1974.
5. McCain, G. and Segal, E. *The Games of Science.* Belmont, CA: Brooks/Cole, 1969.
6. McConnell, R. *ESP: Curriculum Guide.* New York: Simon & Schuster, 1970.
7. Ibid. "ESP and Credibility in Science." *American Psychologist,* 1969; 24, pp. 531–538.
8. "Mind and Supermind," *Saturday Review,* (February 22), 1975.
9. Rhine, J. B. and Pratt, J. G. *Parapsychology: Frontier Science of the Mind.* Springfield, IL: Thomas, 1974.

SOME THOUGHTS OF OUR OWN

The subjects discussed in these last three chapters are highly interesting but hard to pin down. They lend themselves more to armchair speculation and anecdotal evidence than to scientific research. Yet, as we have shown, respectable studies on each of these topics have begun to accumulate. Were the members of our profession more daring and more innovative, we would probably have even more research along these lines.

It is our opinion that psychology needs not only to till the ground it has already sown, but also to open up new areas of investigation, if it is to explore the entire range of human endeavor. Let us not, therefore, shrink away from the frontiers of knowledge. Let us not be afraid to probe and assess experiences and acts that have never before been measured. It may take years of groping in the dark, but our willingness to tackle such elusive subjects as humor, creativity, and ESP may make the difference between the evolution and the stagnation of our field.

Appendix 1:
The Nervous System,
the Brain,
and the Endocrine Glands

ll human behavior, thinking, and feeling is mediated by bodily organs—in particular, the nervous system, the brain, and the endocrine glands. In this appendix, we will briefly survey the physiology of these organs. We will describe the structure of the nervous system and the brain and specify the psychological functions each part performs. We will then do the same for the endocrine glands.

Brief as it is, this survey should give you some understanding of the ways in which our minds are dependent on our bodies. We have already touched on this topic in earlier chapters (see especially chapter 12, Sensation and Perception). It is our purpose now to deal with it in greater detail.

We will also include a report on recent findings in "split brain research." This is one of the exciting new developments in the field of physiological psychology and we believe you will be interested to learn about it.

The brain is the organ of the mind. This statement can be accepted, with some qualifications, as indicating that all mental functions—recognizing, remembering, learning, imagining, and reasoning—take place in the brain and depend on its welfare. Fortunately, it is a durable organ and well-protected by the skull.

The brain may be described as a highly organized, highly specialized collection of **neurons.** Like our country's intelligence network, which is composed of many departments, our brains contain sections concerned with decoding information received from our senses, sections concerned with processing this information and making decisions, and sections concerned with sending our muscles into action.

neurons
cells that receive and transmit nerve impulses

Before we begin our study of the nervous system and the brain, let us look at **359** the structure of the neurons that compose them.

The Neuron

The neuron consists of three parts: the *soma* or cell-body, the *axon*, and the *dendrite*. Neurons have many axons and dendrites. Here is a diagram of a typical neuron:

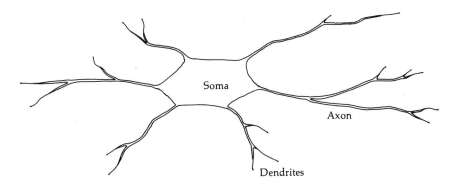

Not all neurons look alike, however. They vary in size, shape, composition, and the speed at which they transmit information.

How does the neuron transmit information? When excited, one neuron releases chemicals that are picked up by other neurons. This chemical message travels across a tiny gap known as a synapse. The chemicals are known as neurotransmitters and are located in tiny sacs called *vesicles*. These vesicles are on one side of the synapse only, since information is always transmitted in one direction. When activated, the vesicles dump their chemical into the synapse; if the message is strong enough, the information is picked up by neighboring neurons and relayed along.

The process is strengthened and speeded up by drugs known as stimulants (or "uppers"); it is weakened and slowed down by tranquilizers (or "downers").

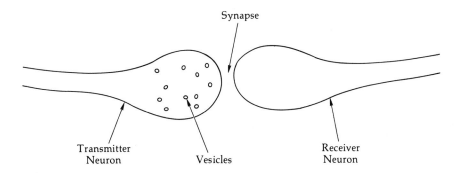

The Peripheral Nervous System

The nervous system may be divided into two parts: the *central nervous system (or CNS),* so named because it is located in the center of our body, and the *peripheral nervous system,* so named because it branches outward from the spinal cord to the surfaces of our body.

The peripheral nervous system is itself subdivided into two parts called the *somatic nervous system* and the *autonomic nervous system,* while the autonomic nervous system is subdivided into two more parts called the *sympathetic nervous system* and the *parasympathetic nervous system.*

The somatic nervous system regulates striped muscle activity, such as the movement of our limbs. The autonomic nervous system regulates our viscera or "gut reactions." The sympathetic system is excitatory and tends to fire as a whole. It produces impulsive, "fight or flight" reactions when we are challenged or threatened. The parasympathetic system, in contrast, is inhibitory. It produces relaxation and the saving of bodily energy.

Since such psychological disorders as phobias, anxiety reactions, and temper tantrums involve an overabundance of sympathetic nervous system activity, methods of reducing this activity and evoking the relaxing effects of the parasympathetic system can be of great help. Such methods are available today, based either on the administration of certain drugs or on the techniques known as biofeedback. Meditation, too, enables some people to modify the activity of their sympathetic system and enhance the activity of their parasympathetic system.

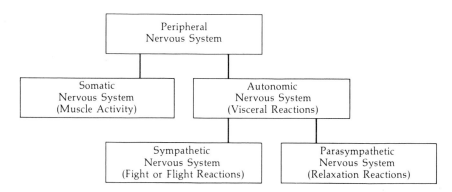

A conceptual diagram of the peripheral nervous system.

The Central Nervous System

The central nervous system consists of three major parts: the *spinal cord,* the *brain stem,* and the *forebrain.*

The spinal cord, running the length of the back and protected by the skeletal vertebrae, maintains a liaison between body and brain. It channels sensations of touch, movement, and temperature to our control centers and carries directing impulses back to our limbs and internal organs. If the spinal cord is severed, as **361** sometimes happens in cases of physical injury, the person may be paralyzed or unable to control certain bodily functions. He or she may go on living in a disabled state, but it is very rare for such a condition to be healed.

The brain stem, which is the section between the spinal cord and the forebrain, contains two important areas. One is called the *reticular formation*. It is the center for waking and sleeping. The other is called the *cerebellum*. It serves in motor functioning and balance. Damage to the brain stem can severely incapacitate a person, while even a sharp blow (such as the well-known "rabbit punch") can render the victim unconscious.

The forebrain contains the *pituitary gland,* the *thalamus,* the *hypothalamus,* the *limbic system,* and the *cortex.* The pituitary is the master gland in the body; it regulates the secretions of all other glands. The thalamus is primarily concerned with relaying sensations, while the hypothalamus controls such basic drives as hunger, thirst, and sex. The limbic system plays an important role in the release of our emotions, while the cortex contains the areas where most of our thinking takes place.

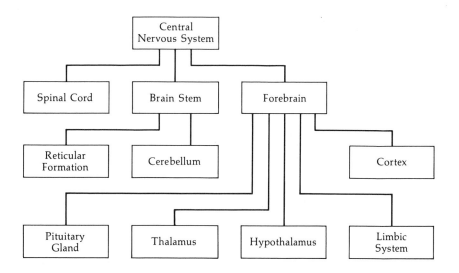

A conceptual diagram of the central nervous system.

The cortex can be divided into right and left hemispheres or into four lobes that are fairly distinct in their functioning. The *frontal lobe* regulates reasoning, speech, and motor activity. The *parietal lobe* regulates bodily sensations. The *temporal lobe* is the center for hearing and the *occipital lobe* is the center for seeing.

In describing the brain's major psychological functions in these terms, we are oversimplifying the matter, for in fact there is more overlap of duties than we have indicated. Nevertheless, on an introductory level, our descriptions are fairly accurate. They indicate, as you can see, that the physiological structures of the nervous system and the brain control our psychological reactions in a rather specialized fashion.

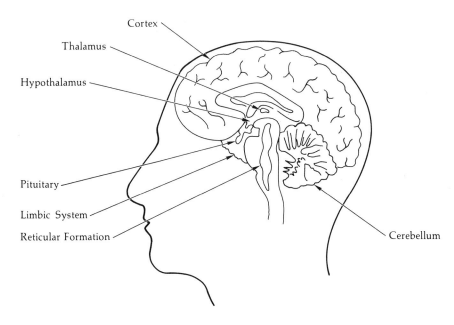

Cortex

Thalamus

Hypothalamus

Pituitary

Limbic System

Reticular Formation

Cerebellum

A cross section of the human brain.

In performing brain surgery where the patient is anaesthetized but conscious during the operation, it has been found that stimulating specific areas of the brain with a weak electrical impulse produces specific types of response. When the occipital lobe is stimulated, the patient has visual sensations; when the temporal lobe is stimulated, the patient has auditory sensations; and so on. It has also been found, interestingly enough, that stimulation of certain areas of the cortex can revive entire scenes of forgotten memory, much as is done under deep hypnosis.

The Electrical Activity of the Brain

electrodes

metal discs that conduct electricity

The activity of the brain can be recorded by placing **electrodes** on the scalp and connecting them to a machine that transcribes electrical impulses into wave patterns on a sheet of graph paper. The result is known as an *electroencephalograph* recording or an *EEG*.

Since normal brain activity produces characteristic patterns, unusual patterns can be used to detect abnormalities in the brain. The EEG is administered, therefore, whenever the existence of a brain tumor, epilepsy, or other abnormal condition is suspected.

One of the normal patterns of brain activity is known as the "alpha wave." Whenever this wave is dominant, the person whose brain is producing it experiences a sense of relaxation and contentment. Attempts have been made to train

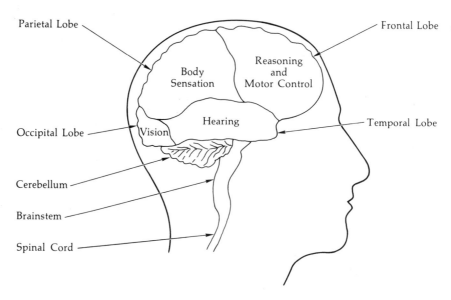

Parietal Lobe

Frontal Lobe **363**

Body
Sensation

Reasoning
and
Motor Control

Occipital Lobe

Vision

Hearing

Temporal Lobe

Cerebellum

Brainstem

Spinal Cord

*The four lobes of the right hemisphere of the cortex. The left
hemisphere can be similarly divided.*

people, by the use of biofeedback techniques, to produce more alpha waves, and
they have met with some success.

EEG research has also led to interesting discoveries about our sleeping
rhythms. Two patterns have been found to occur with regularity: delta waves,
which are characteristic of dreamless sleep, and electrical activity which is similar to that we produce when awake, known as REM (or rapid eye movement)
sleep. Most of us tend to go through cycles of 80–85 minutes of delta waves
followed by 10–15 minutes of REM sleep. Newborn babies, however, spend
most of their time in REM sleep, while adults spend only 20–25 percent of their
sleeping period in REM sleep.

People who are deprived of REM sleep display such disturbances as irritability, tension, and memory loss. It has been hypothesized, therefore, that we need
this type of brain activity, during which we usually dream, to work off our
tensions and renew our vitality.

The Endocrine Glands

There are two types of glands in our bodies: *exocrine glands,* such as tear ducts,
sweat glands, and saliva-producing glands, and *endocrine glands* which secrete
their substances (called hormones) directly into the bloodstream.

The *pituitary,* as we have already said, is the master gland which controls the
functioning of all the other glands. About the size of a hazelnut and located at

metabolism

the physical and
chemical processes by
which living tissue is
produced and
maintained

the approximate anatomical center of the head, it is a very powerful organ. It secrets a growth hormone as well as a set of hormones that stimulate the activity of the other endocrine glands.

The *thyroid* is located in the neck and controls the rate of **metabolism** in our bodies. An excess of thyroid production can cause a person to become high strung, restless, and irritable, while a deficiency of thyroid production can bring about listlessness and depression.

The *parathyroids* are located below the thyroid. They regulate our calcium and phosphorous levels, which are important to the nerve transmission process we described earlier in this appendix.

The *adrenal cortex*, located on top of the kidneys, secretes adrenalin, which is intimately involved in furnishing us with energy to cope with stress.

The *gonads*, or sex glands, serve many functions. Not only do they regulate our sexual behavior, but they help produce such secondary sexual characteristics as pubic hair, muscular strength, fatty deposits, and female breasts.

The *pancreas*, located underneath the stomach, contains the *Islets of Langerhans*, which produce insulin. This hormone is crucial to the regulation of blood sugar. Both diabetes, a serious disease, and hypoglycemia, which can be accompanied by emotional instability and apprehensiveness, are due to abnormalities in blood sugar level.

On the whole, then, our endocrine glands and the hormones they produce affect our emotional and mental well-being in a host of ways. Some of the common psychological problems from which people suffer—anxiety, depression, irritability, and sexual maladjustment, to name but a few—may at times be traced to deficiencies in endocrine functioning.

Split Brain Research

The right and left hemispheres of the brain are connected by a bundle of nerve fibers named the *corpus callosum*. These fibers act as messengers, enabling the hemispheres to communicate with each other.

Occasionally, because of abnormal brain functioning such as severe epileptic seizures, the corpus callosum is surgically severed. Thus, the brain is actually split into two discrete units. The left hemisphere continues to receive information from the right side of the body and the right hemisphere continues to receive information from the left side of the body, as is the case for a normal brain, but the two hemispheres are no longer able to communicate with each other. In cases like these, scientists have been able to study the workings of each hemisphere alone.

The usual procedure involved in this kind of research is to seat the subject in front of a screen. Images or words are flashed on the far side of the screen so only one eye, and therefore one hemisphere, can detect the image. Since the hemispheres are no longer capable of cooperating in the processing of information received from the sense organs, only the information stored in the receiving hemisphere is available to the subject.

The results of these experiments have shown that the dominant hemisphere (which is usually the left for right-handed persons and the right for left-handed persons) contains the language and writing centers of the brain. It is also the **365** locus for reasoning, emotional expression, and mathematical deductions. The subdominant hemisphere, on the other hand, seems to be more in charge of drawing and mapping abilities, spatial relationships, and the recognition of musical melodies.

Some psychologists have gone so far as to call the dominant hemisphere the center for logic and science and the subdominant hemisphere the center for intuition and art. But that may be an over-generalization.

Research in this area is continuing, as is research on brain functioning in general. It will undoubtedly yield fascinating results and help us in our continuing efforts to clarify the relationship between the human mind and body.

Suggested Readings

1. PLOTNIK, R. and MOLLENAUER, S. *Brain and Behavior.* San Francisco: Canfield Press, 1978.
2. TEYLER, TIMOTHY J. *A Primer of Psychobiology.* San Francisco: W.H. Freeman and Co., 1975.

Appendix 2:
The History and Future of Psychology

hen we are living in the present, why should we look back into the past? Why try to predict the future when it is at best uncertain? Historians tell us that today's events are determined by yesterday's, so knowing what happened in the past puts us in a better position to understand what is going on now. And even a guess at what is likely to happen tomorrow must be of interest to anyone who plans to live that long.

But there is another reason for acquiring a historical perspective. It helps us gauge the value of what we ourselves are involved in. All of us—psychologists and nonpsychologists alike—share a tendency to overrate whatever we are doing at the moment. Be it work or study, a friendship, a romance, an examination, or a football game, the mere fact that it is happening now makes us feel like our life depends on it. If we recall, however, that the things we thought were all-important last year have proved to be but tiny currents in the stream of our lives, we attain greater objectivity.

Not until the 19th century did psychology become a science, and not until the 20th did it become a helping profession. Before psychology was born as a separate field, the study of human nature was carried on by writers like Shakespeare, churchmen like St. Augustine, and philosophers like Schopenhauer. These thinkers came up with deep insights into the workings of the mind, but they created neither a systematic method of studying human behavior nor a scientific technique for treating the mentally disturbed.

In this appendix, we will trace the growth of psychology out of its philosophical roots and indulge in some speculations about where the field may be heading. We will restrict our speculations to the next thirty or forty years, a period of time in which most of you will still be young **367** enough to care. If our visions of the future seem strange, please remember that the things we do today would probably have seemed outlandish to our grandparents.

Genius or Zeitgeist?

How does a field of study arrive at any given stage of its development? What determines the problems it investigates, the methods it uses, the theories it holds dear, the discoveries it makes? There are two points of view on this matter.

One explanation for the development of new ideas is the *great man* approach. It suggests that the genius of outstanding individuals lies at the root of all major progress. Copernicus in astronomy, Newton in physics, Priestley in chemistry, Pasteur in medicine, Freud in psychology: these people's brilliant insights and amazing deductive powers, according to this point of view, controlled the direction their fields were to take not only during their lifetimes but for centuries afterward.

A second approach, however, disputes this first explanation. The *Zeitgeist* or *spirit of the time* theory maintains that the needs and knowledge of an era make it certain that someone will come up with particular discoveries or programs. The invention of the microscope and the need to halt the spread of fatal diseases, it suggests, made Pasteur's discoveries inevitable. The use of hypnosis in unearthing hidden thoughts plus the need to correct the Victorian era's taboo on sex paved the way for Freud.

You will be glad to learn that we do not intend to argue a case for either one of these approaches. We will simply assume that both the spirits of the times through which it has passed and the inspirations of the geniuses who have been involved in it have made psychology what it is today. Very likely, that same interplay of factors will determine what the field will become tomorrow. But which came first, the genius chicken or the Zeitgeist egg, we will let you decide for yourself.

Soul and Mind: Out of Date

For many a century, philosophers and theologians, poets and dramatists believed that the essence of a human being was what religion had termed the soul. Modern psychology accepts no such notion. Even mind is a dubious term in the field today. Both these concepts, soul and mind, are intangible; they can neither be observed nor measured. As a result, psychologists who think of themselves as scientists want no truck with them.

There is some irony in psychology's rejection of these concepts. The field was begun by people who were interested in nothing less than the nature of the soul. It was furthered by people who were interested in nothing less than the workings of the mind. Yet any psychologist who speaks in these terms today is looked down upon as an unclear thinker. (It may not have escaped your attention that the authors of this text have used the term "mind" fairly frequently throughout the book. You may conclude that we find it useful and meaningful and don't mind being called names by our colleagues.)

The Greek Philosophers

Perhaps the earliest figures akin to modern psychologists were three of the classical Greek philosophers: Democritus, Plato, and Aristotle. Their theories dwelt heavily on the nature of human nature. Let us review their points of view.

Democritus' thinking was far ahead of his time. He conceived of the entire world as being composed of tiny particles, or atoms, in constant motion. The interaction of these particles, he felt, could explain everything that existed and happened, including the soul. The particles comprising the soul, he surmised, were exceedingly small and smooth, but they were material and could not survive the death of the person to whom they belonged. This notion met with disapproval during Democritus' lifetime. It anticipated by many centuries, however, the materialistic outlook that was to become influential with the rise of science in the eighteenth century.

Plato, in contrast, insisted on an absolute distinction between body and soul. This point of view, held by most religious thinkers too, is known as *dualism*. Plato contended that the soul is both immaterial and immortal. Capable of understanding the world of ideas, the soul enables us to comprehend such things as beauty, goodness, and truth. An interesting aspect of Plato's theory was his belief that the soul develops throughout our lifetime. When we are young, he taught, our souls are hampered by our animalistic drives. As we mature, however, we become more capable of thinking clearly and appreciating higher values.

Many people consider Aristotle the first "real psychologist." Dissatisfied with Plato's separation of body and soul, he stressed the unity of human nature. At the same time, he distinguished between our *structural qualities* and our *functional qualities*—how we are built and what we can do. Without reducing the soul to a part of the body as Democritus had done, Aristotle's theory bridged the gap between our material and immaterial characteristics. The outlook his teachings engendered, called *monism* in contrast to dualism, has become the point of view of most psychologists today.

Aristotle wrote about human experience and behavior in a very detailed way. Whereas Plato was content to speak in broad generalities about things like the ideal of perfection, Aristotle focused on the daily activities of eating, sleeping, and dreaming, the psychology of men and women, the workings of memory and learning, the development of self-control, and the problems involved in interpersonal relationships. He even named the five senses: sight, hearing, taste, smell, and touch.

These early philosophers studied the psyche as a scholarly pursuit. They used speculation and reasoning rather than objective measurement. Yet they produced fruitful insights, many of which we still accept.

The Middle Ages

The 5th to the 15th centuries in European history are sometimes referred to as the Middle Ages. Learning, teaching, and intellectual advances went into decline during those hundreds of years. The Church was powerful; wars were plentiful. Plague and pestilence ravaged the countrysides. Art, architecture, and handcrafts were highly developed and great cathedrals were built. Discouraged or forbidden, however, were the pursuit of free thought and its application to the problems of the world. All knowledge was held to come from God, and the Church set itself up as the distributor of truth. Ordinary men and women were denied the privilege of reaching their own conclusions about questions of right and wrong. Knights, ladies, and serfs were in style, but scientific minds were not. In fact, when brilliant people like Copernicus dared to challenge the Church's teachings on how the universe was constructed, they were imprisoned, banished, or executed.

Dualistic thought came into its prime during this period, for the Church believed that the body lacked value in itself and that the soul gained release only at death. Emphasis was laid on preparing one's soul for Heaven rather than enjoying one's existence here on earth.

The Renaissance

It was not until the sixteenth century that important changes began to take place in people's conceptions of themselves and their lives. Led by the famous Dutch thinker Erasmus, an ever-increasing number of scholars began to study the ancient Greek classics and to rely on their own powers of observation and deduction. These people called themselves *humanists*. They came to stress the dignity of the human race. They contended that it is we ourselves who decide whether to turn toward salvation and the good life, not God who arbitrarily decides to save us from sin.

The effect of this kind of thinking was to give the ordinary person a higher opinion of himself or herself, as well as to turn people's attention to the improvement of life on this earth.

At the same time, the spirit of science was beginning to take root and bear fruit. Copernicus hypothesized that the earth and other planets move in circles around the sun. Tycho Brahe constructed telescopes and other instruments to scrutinize the heavenly bodies. Kepler improved on Copernicus by demonstrating that the planets' orbits around the sun are elliptical rather than circular. Gilbert, Galileo, and others promoted the scientific method of discovering natural laws. Finally, the great genius Isaac Newton clarified the world's understanding of mass, motion, force, space, and gravity.

With this upsurge of intellectual achievement, universities enjoyed a new era of growth. Travel routes were opened and explorations of distant lands fired the excitement of the citizenry. The whole world seemed a vast, uncharted wilderness just waiting to be discovered.

Near the end of the sixteenth century, the English physician Harvey proved that blood circulated through the body, and the Dutch scientist Leeuwenhoek perfected the microscope. The stage was set for developments in biology. Soon the attention of the foremost thinkers of the time would be devoted not only to the physical universe but also to the world of living creatures. All life forms would be studied, from germs and other microscopic organisms to plants and vegetation, insects and animals, and the human race itself.

Descartes and Locke

In the seventeenth century, two men—one French, the other English—developed such powerful philosophies that they literally changed the way in which people in the Western world conceived of themselves. Although their teachings differed on many important points, they shared a rebellious stance against all earlier philosophizing. They also shared an intense desire to bring the thinking of their times into line with the methods and findings of science.

René Descartes, the French genius, was born in 1596. He was educated in a Jesuit College where he majored in both the humanities and mathematics. By the age of sixteen, he was showing signs of physical frailty which were to keep him an invalid for the better part of his life. Luckily, however, he had inherited enough money to support what was to become a life of scholarly study, much of it spent in bed. His most advanced work was done in Holland, a country more receptive to freedom of thought than was France at that time. For a period of years, in fact, his books could not be sold in his homeland because he was considered to be an atheist.

Perhaps most significant for the yet undeveloped science of psychology was his attempt to solve *the mind-body problem* which had plagued philosophers for centuries. What is the relationship between mind and body? Are they two distinct entities and, if so, how do they interact? Descartes, like Plato long before him, saw no common ground between the body and the mind. He adopted, in other words, the dualistic outlook that Aristotle had attempted to overcome. Within that framework, however, he greatly clarified his generation's understanding of the workings of both parts of the human being.

The body, he argued, obeyed purely physical laws. Its operations could be explained in mechanical terms, almost as if one were speaking about a marvelously complicated machine. The mind (or soul), on the other hand, was free, unmeasurable, and immaterial, yet it interacted with the body through the pineal gland. Descartes had picked this site as it was the only unitary location he could find in the two-hemisphered brain. "This gland," he wrote, "is variously affected by the soul. . . . It impels the spirits which surround it toward the pores of the brain, which discharge them by means of the nerves upon the muscles." The mind, however, had higher functions as well, which were independent of the body. These were the functions of reason, choice, and will. It was in those functions that our humanness resided.

Descartes' formulations may appear naive to us. Yet his insistence on examining human nature and explaining the human body in a purely scientific fashion helped promote the rise of modern medicine. Similarly, his emphasis on reason rather than faith as our greatest human attribute contributed to the birth of psychology as an objective field of study.

"Cogito, ergo sum." I think, therefore I am. Descartes developed his entire system from this one, now famous, statement. What the statement recognized was the human being as a thinking creature, as the rational animal, the only organism that is capable of reason and free will. It was, in many ways, a much more modern concept than had ever been expressed. Combined with his views on mind-body interaction, on the brain as the location of the mind, on the workings of the nervous system, it made Descartes one of the grandparents of contemporary psychology.

John Locke, the British genius, was born in 1632. A doctor by profession and a philosopher by inclination, he came to exert an influence comparable to that of Descartes. As interested in the mind as was his French counterpart, he viewed its workings differently. Descartes had defined two types of ideas—innate and acquired. Locke maintained that there was no such thing as an innate idea. The only source of knowledge, he said, was experience or learning. At birth, the mind is a *tabula rasa:* a blank state containing nothing but the potential to collect and organize information fed into it by the senses.

Locke held that there were two kinds of human experience, one deriving from sensation and the other from reflection. From each of these sources ideas may arise, and ideas are the elements of consciousness. Ideas combine to form trains of thought in a manner he called "the process of association." *Associationism,* or the study of this process, soon became an engaging field of endeavor. The earliest psychological laboratories devoted a great deal of time to experiments on how ideas are combined.

The great Greek philosopher, Aristotle, had surmised that there were three principles governing the association of ideas: similarity, contrast, and contiguity. In other words, one idea suggests another if the two have something in common (similarity), if they are opposites (contrast), or if they occurred together in one's earlier experience (contiguity). Thus, if you think about your mother, your thoughts will probably go on to other mothers or motherhood in general (similarity), to your father (contrast), or perhaps to something your mother often said or a particular dish she used to prepare (contiguity).

Experimental psychologists in the nineteenth century used the word-association technique to investigate these principles. The experimenter read a list of words to the subject, who was instructed to respond to each word with the first word that came to his or her mind. The principles were upheld. To a stimulus word like "hot," for example, the most common responses were "heat," "fire," "burn" (similarity); "cold," "chilly," "freezing" (contrast); "sweat," "pepper," "sun" (contiguity); and "tot," "cot," "pot" (similarity again, but this time based on the sound of the word rather than its meaning).

The Blossoming of Experimental Psychology

Although rudimentary efforts at using the scientific method to explore the workings of the senses and the mind had been made in Britain, France, and Italy, it was a group of Germans who accomplished the most productive studies of the nineteenth century.

Johannes Muller's *Handbook of Physiology*, one of the classics of the time, applied the experimental methods of physics and chemistry to the study of the human organism. It also summarized all the significant research that had been done and proposed the doctrine of specific energy of nerves. According to this doctrine, a given nerve ending always produces the same sensation—heat, cold, pain, or pressure—because each nerve has its own kind of energy.

The attention given to this concept led to research on localized functions of the brain. Marshall Hall found that animals who had been decapitated continued to move about for some time when parts of the animal were stimulated. He concluded that different types of behavior depend upon different parts of the nervous system, not all of them being controlled by the brain itself. Pierre Flourens perfected the technique of extirpation, or systematic removal of parts of the brain and spinal cord. It was discovered that this procedure would change the behavior of the organism in specific ways, depending on the section removed. Paul Broca performed autopsies in an attempt to locate the parts of the brain that were responsible for certain defects. He was successful in defining the speech center of the brain, and to this day it is called "Broca's area." Gustav Fritsch and Edward Hitzig found that sending weak electric currents into the brain resulted in various motor responses. Electrical stimulation was a far less drastic method of investigation than extirpation. Two highly dedicated researchers forged the link between these physiological discoveries and the brand new science of experimental psychology. Their names were Ernst Weber and Gustav Fechner. They came to be known as the founders of *psychophysics*—the study of the relation between physical stimuli and psychological responses.

Weber was a gifted experimenter. His studies resulted in the first truly quantitative law in psychology. He and Fechner determined the exact mathematical proportion that a stimulus must be increased for our sense organs to register a difference. In doing so, they laid the groundwork for attempts to quantify human behavior—to study human beings as physicists and chemists study inanimate matter.

Wilhelm Wundt

In the history of any field, there is frequently a person who excels at taking the findings and theories of the time and welding them into a unified approach. This master synthesizer usually receives credit for founding an important movement. Wilhelm Wundt was such a person. Intelligent, knowledgeable, and ambitious, he set out to found the science of experimental psychology. Over the course of a long career, he succeeded completely.

Wundt had taught the first formal course in physiological psychology at Heidelberg, Germany. Upon moving to Leipzig in 1875, he established a laboratory that would be known internationally. Scholars and scientists from many parts of the world studied there. In time, Wundt's disciples became the leading psychologists of Europe and America. He was the much admired "Meister" of his day, and his approach to psychology dominated the field for many generations.

Wundt's approach was called *structuralism*. It can best be described as a search for the basic elements of consciousness. Wundt insisted that the functions of sensation and perception be studied in laboratory settings under carefully controlled conditions. His aim was to trap the elements of consciousness by having trained subjects report on the effects of various stimuli immediately after the experience had registered on their senses. His goals were three. First, he wished to analyze conscious experience (such as seeing and smelling a flower) into its basic components (the perception of yellow, perhaps, and softness, fragility, and a perfumey fragrance). His second and third goals followed from the first: to determine the manner in which these components became connected and to discover the laws that govern the process. You can see that Wundt was putting together and following up on the notions of those who had preceded him. In addition, however, he was perfecting a novel method for examining these notions systematically.

In pursuing this kind of investigation, Wundt was not interested in what would later be known as individual differences. He was striving, instead, to discover universal laws according to which the human organism operates. What was significant about his work in the end was not the findings of his experiments but his development of a scientific methodology for performing them.

Hermann Ebbinghaus

One of the most remarkable figures in the history of experimental psychology, Hermann Ebbinghaus, trained himself, carried out a long series of experiments using himself as his only subject, then published his findings in an epoch-making book. *Über das Gedächtnis* (*on Memory*) appeared in 1885 and immediately established the fact that higher mental processes, such as memory, could be subjected to experimental investigation.

What Ebbinghaus had done was examine, in a totally systematic fashion, the way in which memory worked. In order to distinguish the difference between remembering meaningful and meaningless facts, for instance, he invented the *nonsense syllable*. Then he memorized lists of nonsense syllables and equally long stanzas of poetry. It took him an average of nine readings to memorize a stanza of poetry and an average of eighty readings to memorize a list of nonsense syllables. He concluded that meaningless material is approximately nine times as hard to learn as meaningful material.

The nonsense syllables Ebbinghaus invented were composed of two consonants with a vowel in between. *Lef, bok, yat, sil, nem,* and *rel* are typical examples. He felt he had memorized a list completely when he could repeat it perfectly after a given period of time—say, twenty-four hours. The same, of course, would be true of a stanza of poetry. His studies revealed the fact that meaningful material, like poetry, is not only learned more quickly than meaningless material, like nonsense syllables, but is also retained much longer. Several days after memorizing a list of nonsense syllables, he would begin to forget them, whereas he would remember the same poems he had learned for weeks or months.

These findings have important practical implications. If you are required to learn information that seems rather meaningless to you, you would be well advised to make it meaningful. Try to see its relationship to your own life or to something you care about. That way you will learn it much more quickly and remember it much longer.

Ebbinghaus, we may say, took Wundt's approach to psychology and extended it to the study of mental operations that Wundt had not investigated.

Darwin, Galton, Pavlov, and Freud

Wundt's approach was historically important for yet another reason. It provoked a rebellion among psychologists who felt that his methods were inadequate and his experiments meaningless. Without Wundt to fight against, some of the thinkers of the nineteenth and twentieth centuries would have had nothing to fight for. We will discuss *functionalism*, the most direct revolt against Wundt's structuralism, a little later in this chapter. First, we must digress to acknowledge the contributions of four great geniuses, each of whom had a particular approach to the investigation of human behavior.

Charles Darwin is known, of course, as the founder of the theory of evolution. As such, his work is in the domain of biology, but it influenced the science of psychology as well. Darwin's theory led Freud and others to conceive of human nature as an attempt to civilize our animal instincts. The scope of psychological inquiry was thereby broadened to include all those conflicts that arise out of the clash of our bodily impulses and our "higher" aspirations.

Darwin's cousin, Francis Galton, was especially concerned with the investigation of individual differences and hereditary genius. He believed that individual greatness follows family lines and that high intelligence is inherited. Modern psychology has since deemphasized the importance of heredity in intelligence, but Galton's careful collection of data to support his claim is still respected. He contributed to the movement to turn psychology away from abstract speculation toward the collecting of hard facts.

In Russia, meanwhile, Ivan Pavlov was making scientific history. As we discussed in an earlier chapter, he discovered that living creatures—not only dogs, on whom he experimented, but also human beings—acquire basic habits as a result of what he called *conditioning*. A natural response (like the dogs' salivating at the sight of food) becomes paired with an arbitrary stimulus (like the sound of a bell which is rung every time they are fed). After a while, conditioning occurs: the arbitrary stimulus alone begins to produce the original response.

It took several generations for the importance of Pavlov's discovery to impress the majority of psychologists. Today, however, there is not a professional in the field who would deny that a great deal of human behavior can be explained on the basis of conditioning theory.

Sigmund Freud's contributions were no less important than Pavlov's, but they were much more startling. A Viennese physician with a special interest in "nervous disorders," Freud developed *the theory of the unconscious* as the source of mental and emotional problems. He shocked the upright citizens of his day by exposing the sexual basis of neurosis. Eventually, he made a profound attempt to explain the roots of normal as well as abnormal behavior. Crime, art, religion, and other significant arenas of human endeavor came under Freud's scrutiny. By the time his career was at its height, in the 1920s and 1930s, he was as famous and influential as any psychiatrist has ever been.

Today Freud's theories are questioned in many quarters. A long-range as- **375** sessment will undoubtedly find that, while he had amazing insight into many hidden aspects of human nature, he was also in error at times. Nevertheless, his writings and teachings expanded the scope of psychological inquiry more widely than anyone else had ever done.

William James and Functionalism

The school of thought that rebelled most directly against Wundt's structuralism became known as functionalism because it laid emphasis on the functions or processes of the mind rather than on its contents. William James was a leader in this movement. To search for the elements of consciousness, he said, was useless. Our minds are not composed of bits and pieces of experience. They are a flowing, living unity.

"The stream of consciousness," a famous phrase used by James, catches this outlook most succinctly. The human mind, he taught, is like a river, constantly flowing forward, sometimes rapidly, sometimes sluggishly. Like a river, the mind carries its contents along with it, all blended and mingled in indissoluble combinations. If we could dip a cup into anybody's stream of consciousness, we would come up with a sampling of its contents. We would not, however, have a clue to the overall path the stream was taking unless we could stand back and observe it in wider perspective.

James found the human being most interesting in his or her ability to change, adapt, and express the power of will. A person, unlike an animal, can plan and choose and resist basic impulses if it seems practical to do so. Besides making our lives much more complicated than those of the lower creatures, this ability makes it possible for us to engage in more progressive activities than feeding, sleeping, and mating. Psychology, James insisted, must investigate these progressive activities—literature, art, philosophy, religion—instead of spending all its time on the simple acts of sensation, perception, and memory.

Behaviorism from Watson to Skinner

In the 1920s, a strong personality in this country began to criticize all preexisting systems of psychology. His name was John Watson and he was influenced by several developments. For one, a movement called "logical positivism" was growing in philosophy, which claimed that valid knowledge is obtained only by observation, never by introspection. For another, the discoveries of Pavlov on conditioning were becoming widely known. Finally, strides were being made by a group of psychologists who called themselves "learning theorists." In line with these events. Watson fostered an approach that was to dominate the field of psychology right up to the present time.

That approach, already discussed at several points in this text, is known as *behaviorism*. Its basic tenet is that observable and ultimately measurable behavior is the only proper subject for psychology—not subjective experience, introspective reports, or intangible moods and feelings. The behaviorists' goal is to turn psychology into a respectable science instead of an offshoot of philosophy or a domain for romantic dreamers.

The uncontested leader of modern behaviorism is B. F. Skinner. His ingenious experiments on the conditioning of pigeons and other animals, his invention of the "Skinner box" and other devices for experimentation, and his brilliant exposition of the behaviorist position in numerous books and articles have won the respect of thousands of psychologists. Most univeristy departments of psychology today are dedicated to the behaviorist approach. Even the field of psychotherapy, which was long the stronghold of nonbehaviorists, is beginning to yield a place for behavior modification.

operant conditioning

a training system in which the subject is conditioned to perform a definite action (see Chapter 11)

During World War II, Skinner designed a guidance system for air-to-ground missiles that was run by pigeons! Using **operant conditioning,** he taught the pigeons to peck at targets projected on a visual screen. The pigeons were housed in chambers within the missile. As the missile approached its target, the target would appear on the screen and the pigeons' pecks, translated into guidance commands, would keep the missile on course. The amazing system worked, but the military refused to accept it—not because it meant the sacrifice of a certain number of pigeons, but because they could not place their confidence in what seemed to them a weird technique.

Humanism: The Latest Trend

A vocal minority of psychologists have always opposed the behaviorists. Back in the 1920s and 1930s, *Gestalt psychology* objected to what it saw as an oversimplification of human behavior. Higher levels of thinking, Gestalt psychologists contended, were ignored by the behaviorists, who preferred to see human beings as little more than animals.

In the field of psychotherapy, similar objections have been made against Freudian psychoanalysis. Many therapists have felt that it reduces us to conflicted, neurotic creatures and ignores our potentials for growth.

During the 1960s and 1970s, a movement took shape which has been called "the third force" in psychology. Providing a balance to what its proponents see as the deficiencies of both behaviorism and psychoanalysis, it has come to be known as *humanism*. Abraham Maslow, Rollo May, and Carl Rogers are among the leaders of the humanist movement. They profess great interest in subjective experience and inner growth. They focus on immediate, gut-level feelings and our capacity to make improvements in our lives. Choice, will, and decision making are important elements in their world view. They even give a great deal of credence to transpersonal or spiritual awareness, thus broadening psychology's domain beyond the boundaries within which behaviorists and psychoanalysts feel comfortable.

Summing It Up

Psychology, we may say, began with a group of Greek philosophers. Their theories were partly an outgrowth of religious notions about the soul and partly an anticipation of scientific interest in observable behavior.

After the hiatus of the Middle Ages, psychology began to pick up steam. **377** More philosophers contributed useful insights and, in the nineteenth century, a group of experimentalists turned the field into a science.

At the end of the nineteenth century and the beginning of the twentieth, psychoanalysis and psychotherapy added another important dimension. The field became, as it is today, not only a science but also a healing profession.

Various viewpoints have always contended for dominance. Introspection versus observation as the best source of knowledge, heredity versus environment as the prime shaper of human character, monism versus dualism, structuralism versus functionalism, humanism versus behaviorism versus psychoanalysis: each has had its eloquent spokespersons, each has had its day in the sun, and each has contributed to the evolution of this burgeoning, vital discipline.

Our age has been called "the age of psychology." More and more people are entering the field, either as researchers, as teachers, as consultants, or as practitioners of psychotherapy. It remains, as it has been from the start, a hotbed of controversy and a fascinating area of study—which is hardly surprising, since its essential subject is us.

So Where Do We Go from Here?

Two hundred years ago, no one knew there was going to be such a field as modern psychology. Two hundred years from now, it may have served its purpose and been superseded by something we cannot imagine. Any attempt to predict the directions it will take in the next generation or so is bound to be risky. Only a fool—or two—would try it in print. So here we go. In our opinion, this is what will happen in the next 30 or 40 years.

1. The field has steadily become more intricate and there is no reason to believe that it will be simpler in the future. In 1975, there were thirty-six separate divisions within the American Psychological Association. Each one represented a particular area of interest and investigation. Personality and social psychology, developmental and educational psychology, clinical and experimental psychology, the psychology of women and community psychology, psychopharmacology and psychology in the arts: the list grows and grows. In all likelihood, it will go on growing. Many diverse interests, many schools of thought, many ways of studying and of helping human beings: this is the patchwork picture that psychology will present for many years to come.

2. An ideological split, moreover, will continue to exist. On the one hand, there are those who see the field as a science whose main business should be to collect and interpret data on human behavior. On the other hand, there are those who see it as a profession whose main goal is to help suffering humanity. In public, these two factions will coexist as they do today. Privately, however, each will continue to think it represents the more valuable part of psychology.

3. Within the scientific community, the likelihood is that experimentation will direct itself more to issues having social relevance. Findings that will enable us to curtail pollution, prevent violence, diminish crime, and eliminate racism, sexism, and poverty will command more respect for the psychological researcher. If anyone, in fact, should come up with a totally effective, yet humane,

procedure for ending any one of these social ills, he or she will be known as another Pasteur—a scientific benefactor of all humankind.

4. Computer technology will enable the science of psychology to operate on a vaster yet more refined scope than has heretofore been possible. There will still be those, however, who will choose to probe such esoteric areas as altered states of consciousness, ESP, intelligence in lower forms of life, and perhaps, in time to come, communication with the inhabitants of other solar systems.

In June of 1966, R. Allen and Beatrice Gardner acquired an infant female chimpanzee and immediately set about attempting to teach her to "speak." For a medium of communication, they used American Sign Language, or Ameslan. . . . Using a gestural rather than a spoken language was a stroke of brilliance that their chimp, named Washoe, acknowledged by the rapidity with which she acquired signs. . . . Washoe's first word was not "mama" or "papa" but "more," a sign made by repeated touching of the fingertips. . . . When she left Nevada five years later she knew 160 words, which she used singly and in combinations in a variety of conversational situations.

The success that the Gardners, their former assistant Roger Fouts, and other psychologists have had in teaching apes sign language calls for a major change in our conception of our relationship to the so-called lower animals. It shows us that apes, at least, are capable of much more communication and thought than we had formerly believed. It suggests, therefore, that we are closer to the animal kingdom than many of us care to admit.

Important as they are, scientific breakthroughs are not without their amusing aspects. The following incident is a nice example.

> Washoe was outraged at the holding cage that was her temporary home. Grabbing the bars, she rocked back and forth. She would occasionally emit a series of hoots that eventually erupted into deafening screams. Alternating with these screams . . . she would touch her thumb to her mouth or make a series of quick signals when someone she recognized passed by. One handler was working in the vicinity of the cage. After ignoring several of her requests for drink and escape, he noticed that before gesturing his name, Washoe was making a sign he did not recognize. She would hit the top of her palm to the underside of her chin. He asked another handler what the sign meant. It was the gesture meaning "dirty." Washoe was saying, "Dirty Jack gimme drink." She had learned the word that meant "soiled," but now she was mad enough to swear.[1]

---

5. Within the therapeutic community, the three leading movements—psychoanalysis, behaviorism, and humanism—will continue to vie for prominence. While we live today in an age in which the effects of the environment and the exercise of will are seen as decisive in shaping our lives, in years to come there will be a reemergence of interest in the genetic and biological bases of behavior. Eventually, psychoanalysis, behaviorism, and humanism will be joined by a fourth and possibly fifth distinct viewpoint. Meanwhile, there will be attempts to merge them all into one grand explanation of human nature and human behavior. If anyone succeeds in fashioning such an explanation, he or she will become as famous as Freud.

6. Many specific kinds of therapy—like biofeedback and holistic healing—will burst into prominence, then fade back into the mass. In time, eclectic therapy will prevail; practitioners will no longer think of themselves as Freudians or Jungians, behavior modifiers, transactional analysts, or Gestalt therapists, but all will attempt to combine the best of each system into a repertoire of therapeutic techniques.

Biofeedback is a process of learning how to control automatic or reflex regulated body functions. According to its proponents, the ordinary person can "learn to exert voluntary control over skin temperature, over heart rate, over blood pressure, over muscle tension, over brain waves, or over any internal biological function capable of being monitored. And he can learn how to normalize disturbed body activities."[2] The claim may be exaggerated, but there is already enough evidence to suggest that there is a fair amount of truth to it. When people are hooked up to simple thermometers, gauges, and other devices that show them what is going on in their bodies, they can sometimes, through concentration alone, change these bodily processes according to their wishes. The exciting implication of biofeedback is that there is more to the old idea of "mind over matter" than modern psychologists have so far believed.

The average person can demonstrate to himself the biofeedback phenomenon by using an or-

dinary thermometer. . . . He can tape the thermometer bulb to the fat pad of the middle finger with masking tape, making sure of good contact but no constriction of circulation. After five or so minutes of quiet sitting, preferably with the eyes closed, note the temperature of the finger. Then, while sitting quietly, repeat a few autosuggestion phrases to yourself, slowly, such as, "I feel relaxed and warm," "My hand feels heavy," "My arm feels heavy," "My hand feels warm," "My hand feels warm and relaxed," "I feel calm and relaxed." Repeat the phrases slowly, allowing the suggestion to take effect, then go on to the next one, and then repeat the series. Every five or ten minutes, take a reading of the finger temperature. Most people will show a rise in finger temperature after ten to twenty minutes, some increasing their finger temperature three to five or even ten degrees. . . . With repeated practice, everyone can learn to increase finger temperature by using mental activity."[3]

7. The medical model of mental illness will die a slow death. Gradually we will cease to see disturbed people as suffering from some kind of disease akin to cancer or diabetes. We will begin to see them as undergoing great difficulties as a result of having learned poor techniques for survival or as people engaged in a struggle to achieve a sense of meaning in their lives.

8. The growing emphasis will be on prevention rather than cure. As practitioners become more certain of the social, familial, and physiological conditions that produce emotional and mental distress, efforts will be made to reduce them on a national scale. In time, therefore, our nation can look forward to a distinct decrease in what we now call neuroses, psychoses, and behavior disorders. That time, however, is still many years ahead of us.

9. All in all, we can look forward to an expansion and improvement of the entire field for the next few generations at least. Psychology in the 1970s has not yet grown to full maturity, but it is more an adolescent than a child. Those of you who have read this book may participate in its coming of age. Some of you may prove to be the very ones to help it achieve its finest hour. We sincerely hope so.

Summary

In this appendix we have sketched, in very broad outlines, the development of psychology from the time of the Greek philosophers to the present. Democritus, Plato, and Aristotle, Descartes and Locke, Wundt and Ebbinghaus, Darwin,

Galton, Pavlov, and Freud, William James, B. F. Skinner, Abraham Maslow, Rollo May, and Carl Rogers are foremost among the leaders whose contributions we have mentioned. We have tried to portray the field as contentious but growing, riddled with debate but constantly moving forward. We have also tried to portray it as falling into two distinct parts: psychology as a science and psychology as a profession. We have made reference to the three leading schools of thought in the field today—psychoanalysis, behaviorism, and humanism—and have noted some of the leading viewpoints of bygone eras.

Finally, we have taken the bold and probably unwise step of predicting the directions the field will follow in the next thirty or forty years. Since most of you will still be alert enough to see if we were right, please remember to let us know. Drop us a line sometime between 2010 and 2020 A. D. If we have passed to the Great Beyond, perhaps psychology will have invented a way of communicating nevertheless.

Class Projects

1. Close your eyes and have someone touch you simultaneously at two points on your arm with two pencil points. First have them keep the points very close together, then systematically widen the space between them. See how far apart they must place the points before you can feel that you are being touched in two separate places. You will be duplicating a psychophysical experiment of the 19th century, one designed to investigate what was called the "two-point threshold" and the "just noticeable difference."

   The same sort of experiment can be carried out on other senses—detecting the difference in length between two lines, the difference in weight between two bags of sand, the difference in pitch between two tones played on a flute.

   If you wish to pursue the matter, attempt to determine how much difference there must be between lines of various lengths before you can discern the difference by eyesight alone. On a slide that can be used with a slide projector, draw two identical lines. On another slide, draw two lines identical in all respects except that one is slightly longer than the other. Project them from various distances in order to find the precise point at which most observers can reliably tell which line is longer.

2. As a project in futuristic psychology, attempt to envision a system by which we might communicate with visitors from outer space. As you learned in this chapter, psychologists are using sign language to talk to chimpanzees and other apes. Do you think this would work with aliens? If so, what kind of signs would you use? If not, what other suggestions do you have? Don't be afraid to play around with ideas. That is how progress often begins.

References

1. EUGENE LINDEN, *Apes, Men, and Language,* (New York: Saturday Review Press, 1974).
2. BARBARA BROWN, *Stress and the Art of Biofeedback* (New York: Harper and Row, 1977).
3. Ibid.

Suggested Readings

1. EBBINGHAUS, HERMANN. "A Sketch of the History of Psychology," in *Psychology for Our Times*, ed. Philip Zimbardo and Christina Maslach. Glenview, IL: Scott, Foresman, 1977, pp. 7–10.

2. KAZDIN, ALAN E. *History of Behavior Modification: Experimental Foundations of Contemporary Research*. Baltimore, MD: University Park Press, 1978.

3. LUNDIN, ROBERT W. *Theories and Systems of Psychology*. Lexington, MA: Heath, 1979.

4. MURPHY, GARDNER. *Historical Introduction to Modern Psychology*. New York: Harcourt, Brace, and World, 1949.

5. SCHULTZ, DUANE P. *A History of Modern Psychology*. New York: Academic Press, 1969.

6. WATSON, ROBERT I. *The Great Psychologists*. New York: Harper and Row, 1978.

Index